INSCRIBING SOVEREIGNTIES

CRITICAL INDIGENEITIES

J. Kēhaulani Kauanui (Kanaka Maoli) and
Jean M. O'Brien (White Earth Ojibwe), editors

Series Advisory Board
Chris Andersen
Emil' Keme
Kim TallBear
Irene Watson

Critical Indigeneities publishes pathbreaking scholarly books that center Indigeneity as a category of critical analysis, understand Indigenous sovereignty as ongoing and historically grounded, and attend to diverse forms of Indigenous cultural and political agency and expression. The series builds on the conceptual rigor, methodological innovation, and deep relevance that characterize the best work in the growing field of critical Indigenous studies.

A complete list of books published in Critical Indigeneities is available at https://uncpress.org/series/critical-indigeneities.

INSCRIBING SOVEREIGNTIES

Writing Community in Native North America

PHILLIP H. ROUND

THE UNIVERSITY OF NORTH CAROLINA PRESS

CHAPEL HILL

© 2024 Phillip H. Round
All rights reserved
Set in Minion Pro by Rebecca Evans
Manufactured in the United States of America

Cover art: Page from "Flame's History," 1877, courtesy of the Smithsonian Institution.

Library of Congress Cataloging-in-Publication Data
Names: Round, Phillip H., 1958– author.
Title: Inscribing sovereignties : writing community in Native North America / Phillip H. Round.
Other titles: Critical indigeneities.
Description: Chapel Hill : The University of North Carolina Press, [2024] | Series: Critical indigeneities | Includes bibliographical references and index.
Identifiers: LCCN 2024020870 | ISBN 9781469680682 (cloth ; alk. paper) | ISBN 9781469680699 (pbk. ; alk. paper) | ISBN 9781469680705 (epub) | ISBN 9781469680712 (pdf)
Subjects: LCSH: Indians of North America—Languages—Writing. | Indians of North America—Languages—History. | Indians of North America—Languages—Writing—Political aspects. | Indians of North America—Communication—History—19th century. | Indians of North America—Social life and customs. | Indians of North America—Social conditions. | BISAC: SOCIAL SCIENCE / Ethnic Studies / American / Native American Studies | SOCIAL SCIENCE / Media Studies
Classification: LCC E98.W86 R68 2024 | DDC 305.897—dc23/eng/20240531
LC record available at https://lccn.loc.gov/2024020870

This book will be made open access within three years of publication thanks to Path to Open, a program developed in partnership between JSTOR, the American Council of Learned Societies (ACLS), the University of Michigan Press, and the University of North Carolina Press to bring about equitable access and impact for the entire scholarly community, including authors, researchers, libraries, and university presses around the world. Learn more at https://about.jstor.org/path-to-open/.

CONTENTS

List of Illustrations / vi

Prelude / ix

Note on Orthography / xi

INTRODUCTION. Logos and the Indigenous Word / 1

CHAPTER 1. Spelling "Indian" / 38

CHAPTER 2. *Kahiatónhsera*:
  Marking the Matters of the Good Message / 83

CHAPTER 3. *Wowapi*:
  Inscribing the Oceti Sakowin / 131

CHAPTER 4. *Paw-pa-pe-po*:
  They Told Me That One Had Invented an Alphabet / 183

CODA. The Sovereign Reality of Phonemes / 219

Acknowledgments / 229

Notes / 231

Bibliography / 253

Index / 271

ILLUSTRATIONS

Figure 0.1. Page from the *Western Apache New Testament* xiv
Figure 0.2. Map of Native languages and language families 8
Figure 0.3. Bark book inscribed with Mi'kmaq characters 11
Figure 0.4. Mouth map 12
Figure 0.5. Mouth map of the Quee'esh language 13
Figure 0.6. The Cherokee syllabary 20
Figure 0.7. Silas John Edwards script, ca. 1933 32
Figure 1.1. Title page of *Dictionary of Indian Tongues*, 1865 39
Figure 1.2. Title page from John S. Pulsipher's *Phonal Depot*, 1848 44
Figure 1.3. Title page from the *Deseret Primer*, 1868 46
Figure 1.4. "And God said, Let there be light" 52
Figure 1.5. Pages from *The General Specimen Book*, 1856 53
Figure 1.6. Albert Gallatin's *Map of the Indian Tribes of North America* 55
Figure 1.7. Surrender by Chippewas of the Land at Penetanguishene and Nottawasaga Bay, 1795 64
Figure 1.8. Copybook of John Ridge (Cherokee) 67
Figure 1.9. Blank word list 68
Figure 1.10. Ration card from the Rosebud Reservation, 1890 69
Figure 1.11. Page from *Gallaudet's Picture Defining and Reading Book* 72
Figure 1.12. Frontispiece and title-page spread from *Mitchell's School Geography*, 1839 75
Figure 2.1. Replica of Hiawatha wampum belt 82
Figure 2.2. Lewis H. Morgan's *Map of Ho-De-No-Sau-Nee-Ga*, 1831 85
Figure 2.3. Wampum strings of requickening 88
Figure 2.4. Page from François Picquet's prayer book, 1750–1752 94
Figure 2.5. Title-page spread from the Church of England's *Book of Common Prayer* 95

Figure 2.6. First page of John Deserontyon's "Roghya Gonghsera," 1782 101
Figure 2.7. Page from a letter written in Mohawk, 1784 104
Figure 2.8. Treaty of Canandaigua, 1794 111
Figure 2.9. Henry Two Guns's announcement of a general council meeting, 1854 116
Figure 2.10. Seth Newhouse, "Deganawidah Epic" 118
Figure 2.11. Seth Newhouse's preface to "Cosmology," 1885 124
Figure 2.12. Title page of Eleazar Williams's *Gaiatonsera*, 1813 128
Figure 2.13. Pages from John Archiquette's journal 129
Figure 3.1. Page from "Flame's History," 1877 130
Figure 3.2. Map of Dakota Territory, 1878 133
Figure 3.3. March 1888 issue of *Iapi Oaye* 135
Figure 3.4. Standing Bear, "Flaming Rainbow" 138
Figure 3.5. Map of present-day Minnesota showing land cessions after the 1830 Treaty of Prairie du Chien 140
Figure 3.6. Cover of Riggs's *Dakota Tawoonspe / Dakota Lessons*, 1850 149
Figure 3.7. "The Constitution of Minnesota in the Dakota Language," 1858 151
Figure 3.8. Letter of Robert Hopkins to Stephen Riggs, 1863 155
Figure 3.9. Announcement of Custer's death in the *New York Herald*, 1876 160
Figure 3.10. Half Moon's drawing of a Sioux chief 162
Figure 3.11. A page from "Sitting Bull's Autobiography," 1876 164
Figure 3.12. American Horse's Winter Count in 1879 166
Figure 3.13. Post office masthead of Pine Ridge Agency, 1879 169
Figure 3.14. "Waiting for rations at commisary [sic] P.R. Agency S.D." 173
Figure 3.15. George Sword 177

Figure 3.16. Page spread from George Sword and Lucy Sword's diary, 1890 179

Figure 3.17. George Sword's ledger 181

Figure 4.1. Letter of Robert Young Bear to Edgar Harlan, 1934 182

Figure 4.2. Map of the Anishinaabewaki 184

Figure 4.3. Syllabary book cover of James Evans's *Hymns, Swampy Indians, Their Speech* 189

Figure 4.4. Dedication page spread from Black Hawk's *Life of Ma-Ka-Tai-Me-She-Kia-Kiak* 192

Figure 4.5. George Catlin, *Kenekuk*, ca. 1865 198

Figure 4.6. George Catlin, *Ah-tón-we-tuck, Cock Turkey, Repeating His Prayer*, 1830 200

Figure 4.7. Milo Custer, "A Sample of Kickapoo and Pottowatomie Text," 1906 202

Figure 4.8. The Fox (Mesquakie) syllabary (basic matrix) 205

Figure 4.9. Mr. Bill Leaf's handwriting 209

Figure 4.10. Sam Blowsnake's manuscript "Autobiography" 213

PRELUDE

Go where you will in North America, and you'll find yourself in Indian Country. Catch a flight to Los Angeles, rent a car, and somewhere, you'll look up to see an off-ramp—perhaps the one to Cahuenga Boulevard—and know that even there, in the City of the Angels, the signs, the words of an Indigenous homeland continue to declare their sovereign right to exist. On the transit platform in the freeway median, commuters waiting sleepily on the Gold Line are Indigenous people from Guatemala, Salvador, Los Angeles. Although you can't hear them, later, in their neighborhoods after work, they will speak the way they've always spoken, switching between the colonial diction of Spain and England, and the Mixtec, K'iche', Diné of their protests and their dreams. Maybe you will find yourself in the Cahuilla homeland in spring. There, in the desert hills near Banning, California, you'll hear the shuffle of condensed milk cans recycled into Bird Song shakers. Go east, and at a funeral in Southern Ontario, hymns are sung in Cree. In a Nebraska farmhouse late at night, feel the warbling gong of a water drum. In Montana, listen to honor songs for returning Iraq War veterans.

The "disappearing" Indians of the American nineteenth century are rapidly reappearing in the twenty-first—precisely because they never left. And with them, the land itself has taken on a new aspect. Oil pipelines do not simply cross some "vast and horrid wilderness, full of wild beasts and men."[1] They plow through the farms and fields, the backyards and pasture lands of Native people. And these people are not "stoic." They protest; they bring court cases; they restore, repatriate, renew.

Inscribing Sovereignties offers a history of the period in which the colonial powers of the United States and Canada worked tirelessly to stamp out Native sovereignty. The story it tells is one of perseverance and triumph. Indigenous values, languages, ceremonies, and citizens did not go away during the withering attacks on their sovereignty during the period between forced removal and American citizenship (1830–1927); they went underground, into battle, into court. Native communities husbanded their knowledge, languages, and personhood in media tuned to frequencies out of the range of European hearing. The tone-deaf colonizers clucked with self-congratulation in the 1880s, sure they had silenced Indian languages, confirmed in their belief that "nothing can be gained by teaching Indians to read and write in the vernacular, as their literature is limited."[2] But they were dead wrong.

For all the battles and massacres (and battles wrongly called massacres and massacres euphemistically labeled battles), the Indigenous peoples of North America participated in a communications revolution of enormous scope as part of their tactical engagement with colonialism. They were heard by the few colonizers who deigned to help them. They were heard by their fellow community members against the ravages of colonialism that often deafened close relations to the suffering of their own families and the commonality of their struggles.

NOTE ON ORTHOGRAPHY

Because this book offers a history of Native vernacular orthographies in a variety of historical and social settings, I have chosen to not modernize the spellings of contemporary observers and tribal members when I cite their work. In the older forms of the Lakota/Dakota orthography, for example, the word now most often written as "wašté" (good) was spelled in various ways over the second half of the nineteenth century—waxte/wašte/was·te. Thus when I refer to works written in the nineteenth century, the word will often appear as "waxte," but in modern Lakota usage, it would be spelled most often as "wašté." Similar circumstances applied to the orthographies of the languages of the Haudenosaunee Confederacy and those used by Central Algonquian speakers, and I similarly employ the spelling that the early tribal adopters used.

INSCRIBING SOVEREIGNTIES

THE GOSPEL ACCORDING TO
JOHN

1 Dantsé godeyaadá' Yati' golį́į́ lę́k'e, Yati' Bik'ehgo'ihi'nań yił nlį́į, Yati'íí Bik'ehgo'ihi'nań nlį́į. ² Yati'íí dantsé godeyaadá' Bik'ehgo'ihi'nań yił nlį́į. ³ Áń dawahá áyíílaa; áń doo hak'i dayúgo dawahá álzaahíí doo álzaa le'at'éé da. ⁴ Ihi'naahíí biyi' golį́į́; áí ihi'naahíí nnee yee daago'į́į. ⁵ Got'iinı́í godiłhiłyú idindláád; godiłhiłíí got'iinı́í doo yitis nlį́į da.
⁶ Bik'ehgo'ihi'nań nnee John holzéhi yides'a'. ⁷ Áń Begot'ínihíí nnee yił nagolni'go nyáá, bíí bee nnee dawa da'odlą́ą doleełgo. ⁸ John doo Begot'iinı́í nlį́į da, áídá' Begot'iinı́í yaa nagolni'go nyáá. ⁹ Da'anii Begot'ínihíí nnee ni'gosdzáń biká' daagolíínı́í dawa bee daayo'į́į. ¹⁰ Áń ni'gosdzáń nneehíí yitah silį́į, áń ni'gosdzáń áyíílaa, ndi ni'gosdzáń biká' nneehíí doo bídaagołsį da lę́k'e. ¹¹ Dabíí áyíílaahíí yaa nyáá, áídá' dabíí hat'i'ihíí doo hádaabit'į́į da. ¹² Áídá' hadíí hádaabit'iinı́í, daabosdlą́ądíí, Bik'ehgo'ihi'nań bichąghashé daaleehgo yaa goden'ą́ą́; ¹³ Áí nádaagosdliinı́í doo nnee hadaazt'íí bee da, doo kots'íhíí bee da, doo nnee bits'ą́'dı́'go da, áídá' Bik'ehgo'ihi'nań bits'ą́'dı́' nádaagosdlį́į. ¹⁴ Yati'íí nnee silį́įgo nohwitahyú golį́į́ lę́k'e, dawahá ye'at'éhihi biłgoch'oba'íí ła'íí da'anii ágot'éhi nlį́į, (Bik'ehgo'ihi'nań biYe' dała'áhi nlį́įhíí bighą́ ízisgo at'éégo bits'ą́'idindláád, áí bits'ą́'idindláádíí daahihiiltsąą ni'.)
¹⁵ John baa nagolni'go nádidilghaazh lę́k'e gánı́ı́go, Dı́ń áłdishnii ni', ágádénii d n'dá', Shiké'dı́' híghahíí dashı́ntsé golį́į́híí bighą shitisgo at'éé. ¹⁶ Dawahá yegoyiłíínı́í nohwaa hi'né', biłgoch'oba'íí dałiké'go nohwaa hi'niił. ¹⁷ Bik'ehgo'ihi'nań yegos'aanı́í Moses biláhyú ngot'ą́ą lę́k'e, áídá' biłgoch'oba'íí hik'e da'anii ágot'éhi Jesus Christ yił nyáá. ¹⁸ Doo hadíń Bik'ehgo'ihi'nań yo'į́į da; biYe' dała'áhi Bik'ehgo'ihi'nań ádíbółtą'ihi, áń zhą́ ch'í'nah áyíílaa.
¹⁹ Jerúsalem golzeedı́' okąąh yedaabik'ehi hik'e Lévites daanlínihi Jews daanlíni odaabis'a', Hadíń łą́ą́ áńt'ee? daabiłniigo nabídaadiłkidá' John gánı́ı́ lę́k'e, ²⁰ Shı́í doo **Christ** ánsht'ee da, doo nayił'į'go da da'aniigo ádaa nagolni'. ²¹ Áídı́' nayínádaadiłkid, Hadíń áńt'éé gá? **Elías** ńlį́į́ née? Dah, doo áń nshłį́į da, nii lę́k'e. Bik'ehgo'ihi'nań binkááyú na'iziidihíí, ya' áí ńlį́į́ née? Dah, niigo hadzii. ²² Gánádaayiłdo'niid, Áídá' hadíń áńt'éé gá? Nohwił nagolnı́'go hadíń daanohwides'a'íí bił nadaagohiilni'. Hant'é nniigo ádaa nagolni'? ²³ Áídı́' gánı́ı́, NohweBik'ehń bádįhyú iłch'ígodezdǫhgo ádaahłe', dishniigo shíí da'igolį́į́yú dilwoshi nshtłį́į, **Esáias**, Bik'ehgo'ihi'nań binkááyú nada'iziidi ánı́ı́ n'íí k'ehgo. ²⁴ Nnee na'ídaadiłkidihíí Phárisees daanlíni daabinł'a'. ²⁵ Nabídaadiłkidgo, Doo **Christ** ńlį́į́ dadá', ła'íí doo **Elías** dagohíí Bik'ehgo'ihi'nań binkááyú na'iziidihíí ńlį́į́ dadá', nt'é bighą baptize áń'į́į? daanii. ²⁶ John bich'į' hadzii, Shihíí tú bee baptize ash'į́į: áídá' ła' nohwitahyú sizį́į, doo bídaagonołsį dahi; ²⁷ Da'áń shikédı́' híghahíí shitisgo at'éhi, biketł'óól k'e'ish'adgo ndi doo bík'eh sítį́į́ da. ²⁸ Áí Bethábara golzeeyú Jórdan túníłíínı́í hanaayú ágodzaa, John baptize ágole'gee.
²⁹ Iskąą hik'e John Jesus bich'į' higaałgo yo'į́įgo gánı́ı́, Daadeh'įį, dibełį́į́ **biZhaazhé** Bik'ehgo'ihi'nań biyéhi áídı́' higaał! Áń ni'gosdzáń biká' nnee binchǫ'íí da'íłį́į́ yiłchiih. ³⁰ Dı́ń áłdishnii ni' gádéniid n'dá', Nnee ła'

Figure 0.1. First page of "The Gospel according to John." In *Western Apache New Testament*. Courtesy of Wycliffe Bible Translators, 2012.

Introduction

LOGOS AND THE INDIGENOUS WORD

> Do you see? Far, far away in the nothingness something happened. There was a voice, a sound, a word—and everything began. The story of the coming of Tai-me has existed for hundreds of years by word of mouth. It represents the oldest and best idea that man has of himself. It represents a very rich literature, which, because it was never written down, was always but one generation from extinction. But for the same reason it was cherished and revered. I could see that reverence in my grandmother's eyes, and I could hear it in her voice. It was that, I think, that old Saint John had in mind when he said, "In the beginning was the Word . . ." But he went on. He went on to lay a scheme about the Word. He could find no satisfaction in the simple fact that the Word was; he had to account for it, not in terms of the sudden and profound insight, which must have devastated him at once, but in terms of the moment afterward, which was irrelevant and remote; not in terms of his imagination, but only in terms of his prejudice.
> —N. Scott Momaday, *House Made of Dawn*, 1968

The above excerpt from N. Scott Momaday's Pulitzer Prize–winning *House Made of Dawn* might serve as a shorthand summary of Native Americans' relationship to the alphabetic scripts that settler colonists served up to them as part of the "civilizing process." Momaday retells his grandmother's story of Tai-me, the sacred being empowered by the Kiowa sun dance, through the character Tosamah, a Kiowa Road Man preaching out of a postwar Los Angeles storefront.[1] The legend explains how the Kiowas were delivered from "bad times" and hunger by a Voice that told them, "Take me with you, . . . [and] I will give you whatever you want."[2] This disembodied voice (or alternatively, a voice so embodied in every *thing* that it was impossible to "place") becomes the crux of Momaday's meditation on the *logos*, λόγος in the original Greek text of the Gospels, most often translated as "word":

Say this, "In the beginning was the Word . . ." There was nothing. Darkness! There was darkness and there was no end to it . . . a single star, flickering out in the universe, is enough to fill the mind, but it is nothing in the night sky. The darkness looms around it. The darkness flows among the stars and beyond them forever. In the beginning, that is how it was, but there were no stars. There was only the dark infinity in which nothing was. And something happened. At the distance of a star something happened, and everything began. The Word did not come into being, but *it was*. It did not break upon the silence, but it was older than the silence and the silence was made of it.[3]

In Momaday's account, the visual gives way to the aural, even if the aural is represented as a deeper form of silence. From stars to no stars to silence to the Word that gives rise to the silence itself. For Tosamah, the key distinction between the *logos* of the Christian hermeneutic tradition and the Kiowa one imparted to him by his grandmother is this: "Old John caught *sight* of something terrible. The thing standing before him said, 'Why are you following me? What do you want?' And to that day, the Word has belonged to us who have *heard* it for what it is, who have lived in fear and awe of it."[4]

The *logos* at the center of Momaday's depiction of "bringing Indians to the Word," was a complex concept that drew out many different reactions from those who tried to translate it into an Indian language. First, the *logos* represented "a term worthy to express the absolute nature of Christ, in whom the eternal, self-revealing God was incarnate."[5] Indeed, most Christian theologies consider the "Word" in the Book of John to "shadow forth" (as Reformed Protestants of old would have said) the figure of the Body of Christ. In the context of missionizing non-Western peoples, the logos embodied the evangelical goal of returning the world to a time when, as the Book of Genesis says, "the whole earth was of one lip."[6]

Thomas Smith Williamson, a missionary to the Dakotas in the 1830s and 1840s, felt that even though his grasp of the language was not very good, the use of the vernacular in his tract and Bible translations was critical to the Indigenous community's conversion: "Whatever imperfections it may have they may acquire from it some more correct ideas of God and the way of salvation through Jesus than they have at present." Only in the Dakotas' own language could the "correct ideas" replace those of a traditional religion that the missionaries viewed as profoundly flawed: "[The Dakotas], who worship everything they see, cannot be expected to have very consistent ideas of the works of 'that God in whom we move and live and have our being.' The *Great*

Spirit of the Sioux is not the God of the Bible. They possess scarcely any properties in common." For Stephen Riggs, Williamson's colleague at the Lac qui Parle Mission in Minnesota Territory, the translation of the Gospel into the Indigenous vernacular was also to be valued as a step toward English-language literacy: "Our object was to preach the Gospel to the Dakotas in their own language, and to teach them to read and write the same, until their circumstances should be changed as to enable them to learn English."[7]

It was a tricky task, translating the logos into a language that might also have "scarcely any properties in common" with the Gospel texts. The logos had to be rendered in the Native vernacular in such a way that "the sincere cannot mistake the voice of Christ, and the reckless cannot impose upon the true disciple."[8] Yet it had to be powerful enough to break through the Indians' own systems of beliefs. The evangelical writer Richard Storrs felt that the Bible, being "like a sharp sword" to the heathen, is "mighty," and thus literacy "education must be diffused," despite what he calls "the inertness of the heathen mind." Thus, colonialist language ideologies were embedded in the theological discourse of the missionaries' translation endeavors from the very beginning, creating the ethical imperative that missionization should seek to erase the Native vernacular along the way to Christian salvation. The Indians were both pagan *and* illiterate—people without letters or literature—and North American missionaries treated as a truism the belief that if you could control a nation's literature, you might "fashion its religious creed."[9] In this way, the Word in Indian Country was conceptualized as a material object and a technology by which settlers sought to replace the Indian vernacular. Writing Indigenous languages, many settlers believed, tamped down the "noise" of Indian utterance, replacing it with the sighted word that "reduced" the spoken language's dangerous dynamism into a two-dimensional image.

Where the missionaries "saw" the Word, however, the Kiowa people "heard" it. For Momaday, this profound recognition of the aural nature of the Word, his insistence that *not seeing* is believing, leads Tosamah to the wonderful chiasmus that concludes his sermon: "In the Word was the beginning, 'In the beginning was the Word.'" Tosamah suggests that the language ideology of the settler missionaries left Native peoples in a paradoxical position. The spoken Word, the heard utterance, was not to be trusted. Only as inscription could their Indigenous vernaculars make any claims to the demands of the logos. Within the imaginary space of the novel, however, Tosamah and his parishioners are able to escape, for a moment, the inertia of this conundrum.[10] The Peyote ceremony ends wordlessly in sound: "four blasts of the eagle bone whistle" pierce the "agony of stasis."

GRAPHOGENESIS

In the lived history of Native peoples, however, it was far more difficult to escape the "stasis" of the Word made flesh. That is because to render the oral traditions of the Kiowa (or any community "without letters") into a written script is to effect a *translation* on many levels and in many directions. In some instances, Christian missionaries worked day and night in remote frontier posts, trying to sound out alphabets, letters, and then whole Gospels in their efforts to translate the Word of God into a "heathen language." In others, Native community members would learn from a missionary's translations of their language into written format how to write on their own, and they would then use the written vernacular language to sustain kinship connections, communicate with the settler state, and sustain the life of the spoken word through its archiving in written texts.

Peter Daniels and William Bright's *The World's Writing Systems*, the standard reference volume for the study of the graphic marks used to record the languages of humankind, offers a simple set of questions that suggest a starting place for our study of the creation of Indigenous writing systems in North America: "Why does someone invent a script? What is the purpose of Writing?"[11] The search for answers to these questions in nineteenth-century Indian Country falls under the heading of *graphogenesis*—the study of the generation of graphic systems for languages whose speakers had never before felt a need for them. Critical to understanding this process in Native communities—from the Wabanaki homelands of the eastern woodlands to the maritime societies of Chinook villagers in the Pacific Northwest—is accepting that all these peoples enjoyed what Euro-Americans call "civilization," a word usually unfairly reserved for societies with written records. Writing did not *bring* civilization to these communities—they were quite civil before Europeans arrived in the Western Hemisphere—but, as Daniels and Bright note, "Something happens to 'civilization' when it takes up writing." And indeed, something happened to each of the Indigenous civilizations who adopted graphic schemes for notating their spoken languages.

It is not that literature is suddenly invented with the development of script, for literature exists avant la lettre across the globe. It is not that science arises to displace myth simply because a written system of notation allows for the formulaic recitation of the "rules of nature." Script, according to Daniels and Bright, often emerges from the social sphere of "religion," in whatever way a society understands that concept: "The religions of the West and some of those of the East, rely on Scripture. The dissemination of writing often serves the dissemination of scriptures. From the earliest times, adherents have been called to both study and proselytize. The former activity produces new writing; the latter produces new scripts.... But a motif found over and over again in the stories of script inventors—grammatogenists—is divine inspiration, often in a dream, sometimes in retreat from the world."[12]

There are too many oversimplifications in this general description of the origins of writing to apply it directly to Native America. If, however, we make some necessary changes to this formulation, a useful model emerges for understanding why some Native peoples invented scripts of their own for writing their languages, and why some adopted the orthographies of others to begin to employ writing in their home communities.

The first correction we must make to this model lies in its erasure of power and domination. Daniels and Bright, the authors of *The World's Writing Systems*, discuss only the "material benefits" of speaking through writing over distances; they never mention the important political valences that accompany almost every example we will study in this book. In every case, when Europeans spoke to each other about finding ways to write formerly unwritten languages, they referred to the process as a way of "reducing unwritten languages."[13] Thus, the historical development of Indigenous alphabetic orthographies in North America must be understood as functioning within colonial systems whose cross-cultural linguistic practices are at the center of the field of contact linguistics, which "covers all the linguistic consequences of contact, including phenomena such as simplification and various other kinds of restructuring that characterize the outcomes of contact." The key word here—and for this study as a whole—is "structure," for linguistic change is never just the product of ad hoc decisions or singular events. Thus, students of contact linguistics "need to distinguish among the various social contexts of language contact," because the "goal of contact linguistics is to uncover the various factors, both linguistic and sociocultural, that contribute to the linguistic consequences of contact between different language varieties." In the case of North American linguistic contact between Europeans and Indigenous peoples, the first social context to consider is the "asymmetry of power and prestige of the languages involved."[14] Europeans' pursuit of "power" over Native languages is especially apparent in their efforts to write out formerly unwritten languages. In seeking a solution to what missionaries liked to call "the alphabet problem," most agreed with the German philologist Friedrich Max Müller (1823–1900), who argued, "We shall take for granted... the Latin alphabet, which, though of Semitic origin,... has really the greatest and most natural claims on our consideration."[15] Reduction and "conquest" were as much a part of making written forms of Native language as was the virtue of communicating at a distance.[16]

Moreover, Native peoples already had many graphic systems by which to communicate with each other "out of earshot" and over great distances. For the Haudenosaunees ("Iroquois" of European historiography), communication was famously grounded in beaded shell belts and strings called *wampum*. These media were themselves founded on an origin story about the establishment of the Haudenosaunees' political economy, and their use was structured by a built environment of sacred structures called a Longhouse as well as by forest clearings sanctified by ceremonies. Where early ethnographers and settlers thought of wampum as simple mnemonic devices, contemporary Haudenosaunee intellectuals celebrate them as "intrinsically linked to Haudenosaunee visual code . . . their aesthetic engagements serve as extensions of the ideas recorded in purple and white shell."[17] A similar set of media informed the creation and maintenance of the Anishinaabewaki, the Ojibwe homeland centered in the Great Lakes. There, bark carefully stripped from birch trees in wide rolls served as a medium for the graphic inscription of symbols that guided liturgical practices in a sacred structure called the *Mide* lodge. Farther west, on the northern Plains, the medium was hide and the method was paint. Lakota tipi covers, buffalo robes, and their *waniyetu iyawapi* (Winter Counts) all formed part of a visual code and a set of material practices that grounded story and song to the materiality of Lakota life. In fact, for each of these Indigenous communities, the medium (hide, bark, shell) signifies as an organic element of a homeland, constantly anchoring the communications they fostered to the land from whence they came.

In addition to graphic inscription practices that predate alphabeticism, Indigenous peoples' vernacular-language choices for describing written scripts are revealing in how they sought to link the new alphabetic practices to traditional modes of inscription. In Lakota, for example, the word *wowapi* is used to describe writing in general, a book, a piece of epistolary correspondence, or even a flag. Its etymology lies in the noun *owa*—to paint. Writing an orthography thus entailed integrating linguistic sound systems with other, nonalphabetic graphic systems. In the case of the Lakotas, there were at least two major modes of *owa* in play before Europeans arrived: first, the *waniyetu iyawapi* (Winter Counts) mentioned above, painted calendars that recorded the history of band groups as well as the hide blankets and tipi covers that recounted the individual deeds of warriors; and second, the ceremonial protocols of medicine societies housed in the lodges that bore their iconography.

For the Ojibwes of the Great Lakes, the word for writing and print is *mazina'igan*—combining the verb *maazinaa*, to make an image, and a nominalizer, *igan*. As with so many concepts in Anishinaabemowin (the language of the Ojibwes), it is an active, verb-centered approach to writing, far removed from the "reduction" envisioned by Europeans. In this Indigenous etymological relation, alphabetic scripts became part and parcel of inscriptions on *Midewiwin* medicine society birch bark scrolls, which in turn point to *actions*, social practices that accompany ceremony and generate community cohesion. By thus harnessing the social and cultural power of traditional inscription practices to the "new" modes of alphabetic and syllabary writing, Indigenous intellectuals forged potent hybrid communications discourses that both embodied respect for tradition and made way for cosmopolitan innovation.

SOUND TRANSCRIPTIONS

Europeans would soon discover that the translation of Indian languages into alphabetic forms was rendered extremely difficult by the linguistic complexity of North American Native languages.

Before European contact, more than 300 separate languages were spoken in the North American portion of the Western Hemisphere. As ethnolinguist Marianne Mithun explains in her authoritative study of the Indigenous languages of the region, they were "mutually unintelligible ... and differ[ed] in fascinating ways not only from the better-known languages of Europe and Asia, but also among themselves."[18] Whereas European languages can be categorized into only three distinct "families" (Indo-European, Finno-Ugric, and Basque), there are about fifty Indian language families in North America, none originally written in alphabetic form.

Amid such linguistic diversity, several factors stand out as influencing the way Native vernacular alphabetic and syllabary writing emerged in Native communities. First, there was significant phonological variation among the Indigenous idioms of the region. North American languages such as Mohawk contain only nine consonants, while Tlingit, an Athabaskan language, contains forty-five. Then there are the different approaches to words found in the largely synthetic languages of North America. A word, as Mithun reminds us, is best defined from within the language system itself, and "the best criterion is usually the judgment of Native speakers." Native speakers of any language tend to pause between words; words "have no more than one primary stress, and in some languages it regularly occurs on a specific syllable." In Yupik, a language spoken in western Alaska, the word *kaipiallrulliniuk* is translated into the English phrase "the two of them were apparently really hungry."[19]

Yet settlers who encountered such polysynthetic words found them difficult to comprehend and awkward to parse into lexical segments. The trader Joseph Howse noted that "ideas are often differently grouped—in those groups the ideas are often differently disposed, and the terms expressing them differently arranged." In 1850, the settler missionary to the Mi'kmaqs, Silas Rand, was still struggling with "the terrible long words of the Indians." The problem persisted

Figure 0.2. *Native Languages and Language Families of North America.* Compiled for inclusion in Goddard and Sturtevant, *Languages*.

throughout the nineteenth century and across huge linguistic and geographic divides. In 1879, the missionary educator John Manual lamented his difficulty in writing the Laguna language and traced the problem to word formation: "We have no means of analysing the words or of finding out how they are formed."[20] Even among bilingual Native writers fluent both in their own language and in English, there appears to be a real resistance to word-for-word translation because of the way their Native language conceptualizes lexical units. In the Okanagan language, for example, as the bilingual poet Jeanette Armstrong explains, "When you say the Okanagan word for dog (*kekwep*), you don't 'see' a dog image, you summon an experience of little furred life." This is because the two syllables in the word suggest a combination of "a happening and a sprouting profusely (fur)." Armstrong thus observes that "speaking the Okanagan word for dog is an *experience*." In Okanagan, the word is more verb than noun, and when Armstrong employs this understanding to her English-language works, she "attempt[s] to construct a similar sense of movement and rhythm through sound patterns."²¹

Beyond diction and phonological differences, however, Native languages also exhibit (as perhaps do all languages) a complex relationship to their physical environment. In observing the map that is included in volume 17 (*Languages*) of the *Handbook of North American Indians* (fig. 0.2) and locating the landscape in which Yupik is spoken, it makes sense that this language employs terms like *caginraq* ("skin or pelt of caribou taken just after the long winter hair has been shed in the spring"), a word whose specificity derives from generations of experience in Alaskan ecosystems. Modern-day linguists, in fact, catalog place-names and species-specific terminology to locate a linguistic homeland. In the case of Central Algonquian—the language of the Ojibwes, Potawatomis, Odawas, and others—linguists have used lists of terms for those species that have the most "sharply defined ranges" within a given geography and set of ecosystems to narrow down when and where Central Algonquian might have emerged.²²

But Indigenous language theorists and practitioners go further than simple diction-level analysis. For some, there is a much deeper connection between land and language. For every homeland that grounds Indigenous writing, there is a language or languages that, quite literally, shape the orthography. Jeanette Armstrong argues, for example, that there is a direct correlation between her Native Okanagan and the land of the Columbia Plateau where it flourished. Armstrong asserts, "Okanagan, my original language, constitutes the most significant influence on my writing in English." She also strongly believes that "the language spoken by the land which is interpreted by the Okanagan into words, carries parts of its ongoing reality." For Armstrong, "All indigenous peoples' languages are generated by a precise geography and arise from it."²³ Although this restatement of the "Sapir-Whorf hypothesis that language determines thought" might seem outdated in a post-Chomsky linguistic world, the Ojibwe/Dakota scholar Scott Lyons notes that it remains "common in language circles on reservations." Such statements, Lyons observes, "are always intended to produce a desired result—the survival of the language itself—but they also impart a lesson or (dare we say it?) a worldview: namely, the speaker's understanding of language as a carrier of culture."²⁴ Similarly, Keith Basso's work on the interrelationship of land and language in Western Apache communities beautifully recounts how Apache place-names have sedimented within them historical events and detail in such an integrated way that the language becomes "interanimated" with the land. "In this discursive fashion," Basso writes, "even in societies where writing ... [is] absent or devalued, historical knowledge is produced and reproduced."²⁵

Finally, many of the diverse languages of North America have been accompanied by "symbolic systems ... in such forms as pictographs on hides or bark, petroglyphs on rock, strings of wampum beads, and notched sticks." Mithun argues that such symbols systems "have served as records of events and covenants, as trail and territory markers, as invitations, as mnemonic devices, and more.... These symbolic systems have sometimes served as a foundation for the development of writing."[26] The Mi'kmaqs of present-day Maine developed a writing system from early ideograms inscribed on bark through conventionalized hieroglyphic signs on paper. Missionary Silas Rand described the literacy practices of the community in 1850:

> They have a book which they read. Some of them can write both English and Micmac in a very fair hand.... They are in the constant habit of corresponding among themselves by letter.... The method of writing and spelling is curious.... Their book is written in peculiar characters. They have nothing in Roman print. Most of them are acquainted with the contents of this book.... Copies of it are multiplied indefinitely, by transcribing. And it embraces important matter. It enters into some of the most elevated regions of knowledge and thought. It is their Prayer Book. It contains condensed extracts from the historical portions of the Bible; a Catechism of Religion; Psalms and Hymns, and Prayers.[27]

In Alaska, around 1900, an Indigenous man named Uyakow developed a syllabary for Yu'pik speakers "by writing ideographically, using pictures to represent words and sometimes ideas"; and he later developed a symbol system "adopted from English but given different values, and others evolved from his earlier ideographic system."[28] It remained in use until the 1970s. Some tribal communities, like the Taos Pueblo, have no script to represent their language and are rightfully proud of that fact as a sign of their resistance to European assimilation. Other groups use more than one script.[29] In Southern New England, a Roman orthography was introduced by the missionary John Eliot in collaboration with a Nipmuck convert, the English renamed James Printer. Among Aleut speakers near the Bering Sea, contact with Russian sailors and missionaries led to the adoption of Cyrillic alphabetic translations of devotional tracts and Bible verses.

Of course, the settler colonists of North America did not usually recognize what Native people were doing as "writing."[30] More than one missionary observer scoffed at Indigenous efforts to claim literacy through nonalphabetic inscription practices. When a Jesuit missionary first saw the Kickapoo congregation of a spiritual leader named Kenekuk at worship in 1832, he was skeptical of its claim to authenticity: "The proof of his mission was a chip of

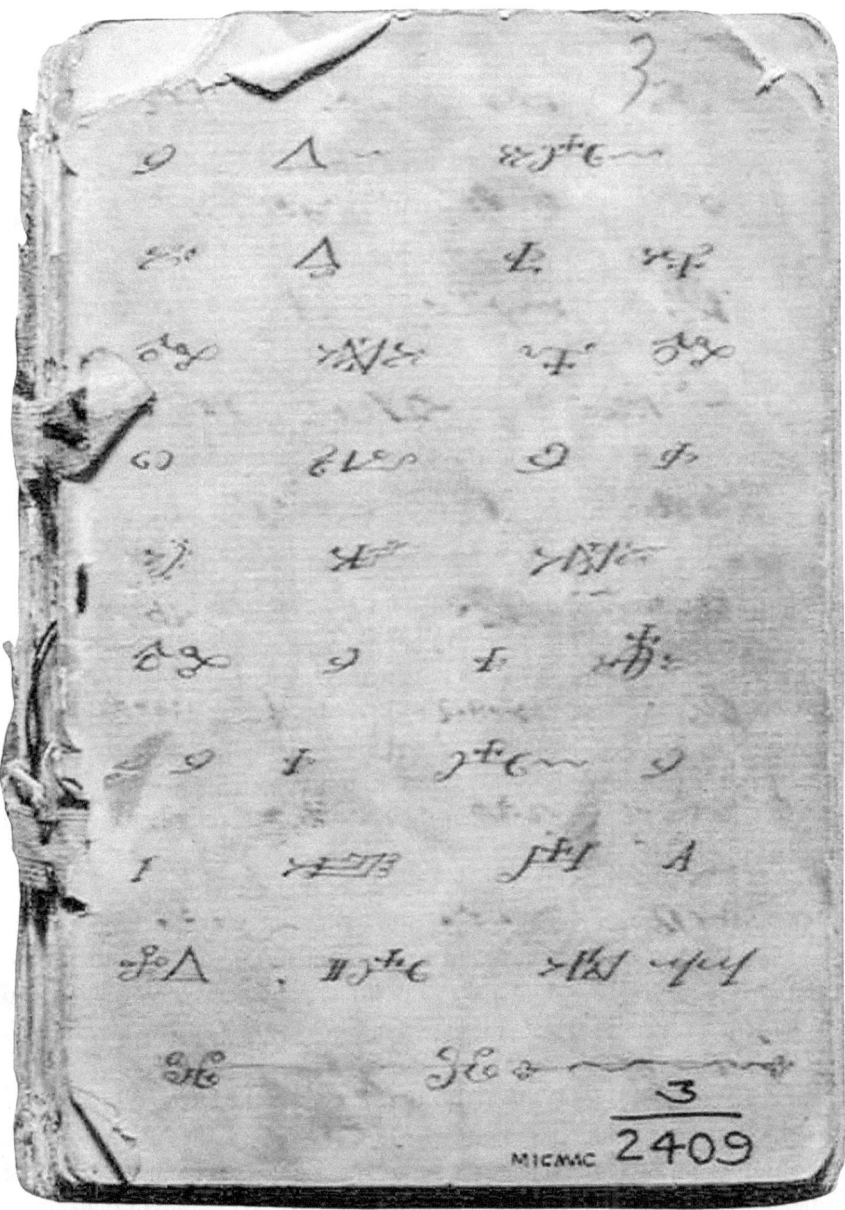

Figure 0.3. Bark book inscribed with Mi'kmaq characters. Indigenous Knowledge and Records, catalog no. 3-2409, National Museum of the American Indian, Smithsonian Institution, Washington, DC. Photo courtesy of NMAI Services.

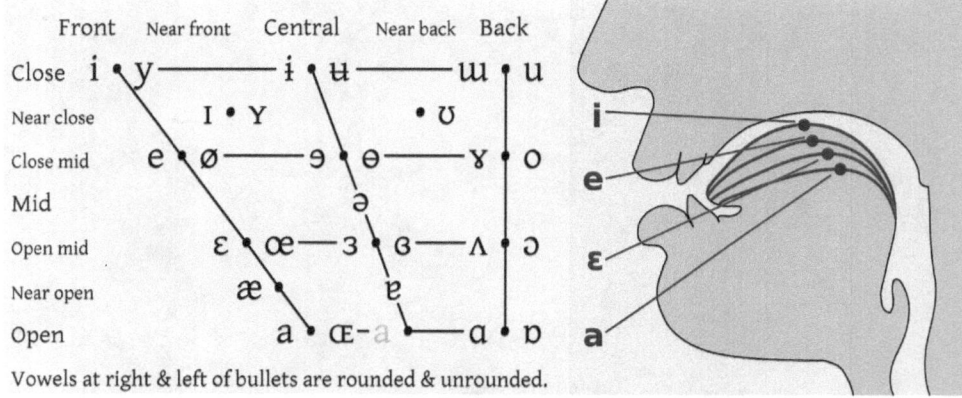

Figure 0.4. Mouth map. From Taylor Jones, "Why the International Phonetic Alphabet (IPA) Is the Best Ever," *Language Jones* (blog), December 24, 2016, www.languagejones.com/blog-1/2016/12/24/why-the-international-phonetic-alphabet-ipa-is-the-best-thing-ever.

wood two inches wide and eight long, which was inscribed with outlandish characters symbolizing the doctrines he under took to teach."[31] In 1816, the military leader of Spain's Pensacola colony was bemused by a letter purportedly written by the Muskogee rebel leader Hillis Harjo. Harjo sought help from the Spaniards in fighting the Americans, explaining to Spanish negotiators that the letter detailed the arms and munitions the Muskogee required. For his part, the Spaniard looked at the letter and saw only "a paper full of crooked marks," not "writing."[32]

Improvisational scripts like these would not do for the many settlers who wanted to "carry on sufficient conversation with our Indian nieghbors [*sic*] to make a bargain without the aid of an interpreter."[33] Thus, the settlers who sought to "reduce" these languages to a written script were primarily focused on phonetic issues, as had been the case since the very first attempts by English speakers in America to record Indigenous speech. In *A Key into the Language of America* (1634), Roger Williams argued: "Because the Life of all Language is in the Pronunciation, I have been at paines . . . to cause the Accents, Tones, or Sounds to be affixed."[34] He borrowed diacritical marks from the Greek to indicate those aspects of the Southern New England Algonquian dialects he encountered in New England that exceeded the explanatory power of the Roman alphabet.

In the nineteenth century, the phonetic transcription of sounds from "new" languages was largely viewed as an issue of mechanics. Writers of the day spoke of the "organs of speech" as a mechanical complex, and the pho-

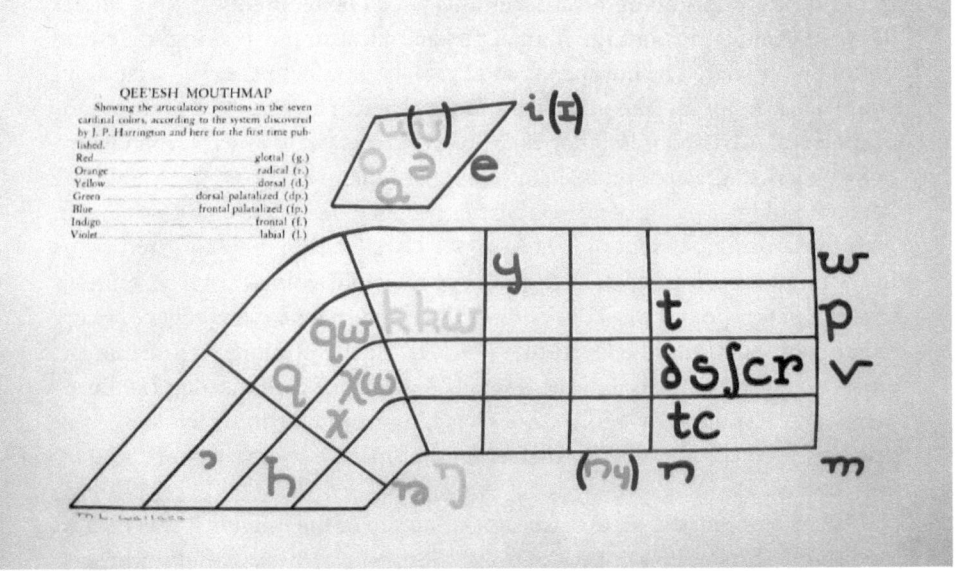

Figure 0.5. "Qee'esh Mouthmap," by J. P. Harrington. In Boscana, *Chinigchinich (Chi-nich-nich)*. Courtesy of the Huntington Library, San Marino, California.

netic alphabets they developed mapped the sounds of the recorded language onto a grid representing the human mouth and throat. Thus, the word "cat" in English would be written phonetically like this: [ˈkæt]. Where these sounds are generated within the vocal apparatus can be mapped onto a grid showing which symbols should be used to represent the word. Such mapping described what one philologist called the "physiological value" of the sounds being represented. Using this system, it was believed that all languages could be written and pronounced by any educated person anywhere in the world. By the beginning of the twentieth century, the mapping process had become abstracted or rationalized to the point that when ethnographer J. P. Harrington sought to alphabetize the K'iché Maya language, his phonetic map stood in for the whole bodily process of making verbal sounds in that society. Here, the human body becomes a universal mechanism by which the sounds of all languages are made.

Yet even European linguists who had never set foot in the Americas recognized that there were probably sounds in Indigenous languages that European ears had never encountered. In 1864, Prussian linguist Karl Richard Lepsius (1810–84) lamented, "Few of the American languages have been carefully analyzed with respect to their sound system, and we are not able to trace rightly the alphabets of the Kri, Odžibwa, and Mikmak, and others, after the imperfect descriptions and transcriptions which lie before us."³⁵ Max Müller likewise wondered about the human physiological sound-making structures undoubtedly shared by Europeans and Indians (mouth, lips, etc.). What script could account for all "the principal sounds that can be formed by our organs of speech?" Advising missionaries to "be guided entirely by ear" when working with languages not "yet fixed in writing," Müller was especially troubled by "the physiological scale of vowels" in Native languages. "How," he wondered, "can these principal sounds, after proper classification, be expressed by us in writing and printing, so as to preserve their physiological value, without creating new typographical difficulties?" In the vernacular languages of many tribal peoples, Müller believed there lurked "new and more formidable enemies . . . in the palatals and the linguals" capable of confounding the European ear.³⁶ Typography and sound, physiology and classification—an entire linguistic project haunted by the settler colonial discourses of "encounter" and "enemies."

Müller's militaristic diction was not some slip of the tongue; it was instead a central discursive component of translation, especially cross-cultural translation. Translating a spoken language into a codified system of inscriptions can have distorting effects on both language and society. The transformation of aural into graphic signs, one form of translation, often entails elements of what has become a hallmark principle of contemporary translation studies: the concept of "assimilative violence." This occurs, translation studies scholar Laurence Venuti argues, during the translation of an Indigenous language into the settler target language. Alphabeticism, in this formulation, is "ultimately ethnocentric in its privileging of the receiving situation." That is, moving from an unwritten language into a written form of the settler language privileges all the norms of the settler language: syntax, word breaks, and so forth. "Ethnocentric violence," Venuti reasons, "far from arbitrary, coincides with an interpretive act."³⁷

Although Venuti is specifically referring to the interpretive acts involved in the semantic translation of words, the same holds true for the material transformation of sounds into graphic markings. In the case of our initial scene from Momaday's *House Made of Dawn*, this violence appears in the way that the Gospel ideal privileges both the linguistic and social codes of the settler target language (in Tosamah's case, English over Kiowa, written over spoken). As it does, a false correspondence is created "between the source and translated texts, . . . [based on the assumption] that a textual effect is an invariant, an assumption that is put into question not only by the variability of reception but by the replacement of source-language contexts with those constructed in the translating language."³⁸

Moreover, to write in an alphabetic script often involves dealing head on with the disciplinary protocols of Euro-Western colonialism. In English, the word *script* embodies several social practices—to enter, to enroll, to record, to register, to plot—many of which were implicated in the oppression of Native people. That is because, as Mark Sebba reminds us, "Orthographies and the conventions which they embody, as well as the means by which they are imposed, may come to symbolise colonial power relationships which currently or formerly subject peoples are determined to reject."[39] Thus, an orthography is much more than an alphabet. Sedimented in its graphic signs and diacritical marks are a history of the negotiations between Native speakers of a language and the impositions of outsiders.

Finally, scripts enable *entextualization*, the "process of rendering a given instance of discourse . . . detachable from its local context" as a material object. In this formulation, discourse is "the unremarked and unrepeated flow of utterances in which most human activities are bathed." That is, it is language as lived experience. Text, by contrast, is created when instances of discourse, now isolated from their immediate social milieu, "are made available for repetition or recreation in other contexts." Texts are thus "stretches of discourse which can be reproduced and thus transmitted over time and space."[40] In the context of Indigenous discourse, however, texts can be terribly confining, almost a linguistic diorama. Though portable and reproduceable, written Indigenous vernacular speech acts lack the lived dimensions of their original utterance. Entextualization thus must be factored into our understanding of Indigenous writing practices so as to provide us with conceptual resources for thinking about texts cross-culturally and, especially, for bringing oral and manuscript traditions into relationship with print and media.

INDIGENOUS SCRIPT AND THE CONCEPT OF MEDIA

Countering colonialist discourse and making way for Native agency in literacy practices (the goal of this book) is especially difficult because so much of the historiography of contact was generated from within a conceptual framework anchored to a dichotomous communications paradigm based in false epistemological hierarchies that pit orality against literacy, and Indigenous "myth" against European rationality. In the following pages, I utilize a media-based methodology similar to that employed in the essays collected in Matt Cohen and Jeffrey Glover's *Colonial Mediascapes*, which offers constructive ways "to resist the magnetism of teleological stories of cultural development that follow from the valorization of writing and print."[41] By employing the concept of media to help interpret Indigenous representational practices and to reframe discussions about the movement of spoken languages into written form, we can circumvent the liability of the oral/literate polarities present in general textual analysis.

Media, in the sense used in this book, may be defined as "socially realized structures of communication comprised of technologies and protocols that make meaning."[42] It differs from a purely text-centered approach in that it expands the field of available "works" to include things like hide painting, ceramics, and beadwork. It also forces us to consider the material medium of the text as meaningful in and of itself. Finally, media theory opens to view the material practices that generate communication. This allows us to experience texts as material culture and, as archaeologist Timothy Pauketat observes, "Material culture, as a dimension of practice, is itself causal. Its production—while contingent on histories of actions and representations—is an enactment or an embodiment of people's dispositions—a social negotiation—that brings about changes in meanings, dispositions, identities, and traditions."[43]

Media theory is an especially useful methodology for parsing out the three distinct layers of material practice most often embedded in inscribing: the physical act of making a mark, the tools involved, and the social and cultural protocols necessary to render that mark "legible" (as well as for someone else to register its legibility). Taken together, these methodological recalibrations allow us better access to the Native actors of North American history with a fuller sense of their historical agency and the geographic and chronological scope of their representational practices.

Archaeologists Katherine Piquette and Ruth Whitehouse observed of this new approach to writing as material practice that the "physicality" of the medium, in particular, admits of material study. Writing is done in the context of bodily practice: "viewing, touching, carving, incising, applying ink." In addition, scripting practices demand some sort of technological component. A stylus, pen, or paintbrush mediate the bodily practice of inscribing. Finally, scripts are both produced and consumed in ways that demand certain protocols of their writers, readers, and listeners. Piquette and Whitehouse explain, "[Scripts] are mediated to varying extents by cultural knowledge (e.g., tacit, explicit) for a given mark-making system—conventions of script production and meaning to both creator and intended/unintended audiences. When viewed on all three levels, the process of inscribing writing can be treated as 'both a process and an outcome.' This is useful because it allows us to experience a form of social and cultural practice that partakes of both the individual and the collective."[44]

This ability to view the social practices involved in vernacular literacy from the perspective of both the individual and the community makes this approach especially fitting for the present study. That is because script is a medium in which the oral/aural protocols of a society and the material practices involved in the human inscribing processes allow its readers/viewers/listeners to reproduce words as they would be heard in native speakers' speech, not simply as "sound," but within a codified "protocol" of social and cultural "practice." Caroline Wigginton's important study, *Indigenuity* has uncovered the significant relationships between Indigenous craft practices and alphabetic literacy activities that—combined with Kelly Wisecup's work, in *Assembled for Use*, on the material practices of assemblage that went into many nineteenth-century Native textual productions—confirm that social and material practices flowed both ways within Euro-American and Indigenous communities navigating alphabetic literacy during this period.

In an effort to produce a more complete history of the information technologies known as "writing" among Native North Americans during the nineteenth century, *Inscribing Sovereignties* works to illuminate these material and social practices and the many settler/Indigenous structures of power that informed them. At the same time, it seeks to acknowledge how Native communities adopted or invented written scripts in ways that integrated new technologies into their larger continuum of precontact graphic representational modes. If to Christian missionaries scripted signs on a page of the Bible were "the Word made flesh," then we must first explore how words became "incarnate," how a scripted spoken language might be transformed into media.

The first step in this process is to place script-making into a cultural continuum that includes the visual culture of a society. Thus, I treat the Native scripts I examine as part of the broader "domain of images" within Native communities, as does James Elkins in his revelatory work of the same name. For Elkins, the graphic marks that make up alphabets and scientific notations have too often been considered "incapable of the expressive eloquence that is associated with painting and drawing, making them properly the subject of discipline such as visual communication, typography, mathematics, linguistics, printing, and graphic design."[45] Central to Elkin's thesis, and integral to the work I do in this book, is an underlying desire "to call all images *writing*," even when that is not totally accurate or applicable to a specific historic moment. For this reason, Elkins uses the Greek words *gramma* and *graphien* to denote the commonality shared by written scripts and other forms of design and inscription. Elkins writes, "*Gramma* [is] a word that means picture, written letter, and piece of writing. The verb *graphien* is even more open-ended. It means to write, draw or scratch." In this formulation, "gramma and graphien preserve a memory of a time when the divisions we are so used to did not exist, and they help us to remember, when we need to, that picturing and writing are both kinds of 'scratching'—that is, marking on and in surfaces."[46]

Yet even Ekins's helpful reimagining of writing as image partially reinscribes a teleology of orality and literacy in which there has been a movement from "a time when the divisions [between image and script] we are so used to did not exist." In most Native North American communities, however, the process of *graphogenesis* continues to embrace the conjoining of gramma and graphien in its efforts at Native language maintenance and social cohesion. Thus, understanding writing in Indian Country demands that we pay close attention to the instrumentality of the making, the painting, the marking process. This is because orthographic inscription (like other accompanying graphic marks) is produced through social activity, which in turn folds into other image practices and takes on cultural resonances consonant with those precontact modes of inscribing.

Consider, for example, the Cherokee syllabary, devised by tribal member Sequoyah as a scribal practice and eventually commissioned in print form by the Cherokee Nation in 1828.[47] The material practice of making the shapes that would characterize Cherokee language syllables originated in part in Sequoyah's previous artisanal experience. He adapted his skills as a metalworker to form the syllabic characters. But he may also have drawn upon older Cherokee traditions of inscription that had fallen into disfavor among Cherokees by the early nineteenth century.[48]

If Sequoia initially fashioned the syllabary to simply demonstrate that settler alphabeticism was "nothing . . . so very wonderful or difficult," and that he could create a writing system just as effective for the Cherokees, it quickly evolved into something much more socially and culturally significant. Sedimented within its shapes and the traditional material practices that Sequoyah employed to form them, the syllabary also encoded a language ideology that figured both the spoken word and graphic signs as "powerful" things whose production exceeded their simple communicative value. Its inventor, Sequoyah, came to occupy a special social position in a Cherokee society that would fracture into civil war over the period 1829–33. Margaret Bender calls the inventor of the Cherokee syllabary "a progress-oriented separatist pagan." In their remembrances of him, Cherokee leaders note that Sequoyah was a cultural revitalizationist and that during the early period of invention, while addressing groups of Cherokees assembled around kegs of rum he provided, Sequoyah would "good naturedly enter into huge discourses with his friends; and urge upon them that they should love one another, and treat one another as brother; and then he would sit himself down and sing songs for their amusement."[49]

The earliest use of the Cherokee syllabary suggests it was intended primarily as a writing system for the maintenance of scribal communities. As Ellen

Cushman explains in her foundational work on the Cherokee syllabary, the Sequoyan writing system flourished first "in manuscript form seven years before print arrived on the scene." For nearly a decade, then, a handwritten system encoded the Cherokee vernacular as visual image and bodily marking, which differed in important ways from how movable type communicates meaning. "In order to show [ordinary Cherokees] the power of his invention," a Cherokee leader recalled in 1835, Sequoyah returned from a trip to the western country carrying "letters from Arkansas, written by Cherokee[s] whom he had taught in the native character; and when he emigrated to Arkansas, he took back answers of the same description." Sequoyah's invention had the practical effect of holding together a nation experiencing piecemeal removal. It provided a way, as the narrative recounts, for the Cherokees both "to talk from a distance" and to knit back together the removed and dispersed communities of Cherokees spread across Georgia and Arkansas.[50]

Missionaries and some community members, however, sought to increase the Cherokee syllabary's effectiveness by rendering it in printed form. New England clergyman Samuel Worcester lobbied the American Tract Society to commission a foundry to produce syllabary type and printed this schema of the syllabary as he understood it. In Cushman's view, outsiders have given this standardized arrangement of the print syllabary (see fig. 0.6) "too much attention ... diverting attention from the ways in which the syllabary actually represents much more than sound." In her view, this has led literacy scholars incorrectly to see "the Cherokee syllabary through an alphabetic lens, a perspective that privileges alphabetic writing systems and contributes to the 'great divide' theories that posit intellectual differences between oral and literate cultures."[51]

In fact, Cushman argues, "The glyphs for each syllable can potentially indicate sound as well as semantic and grammatical information and thus impart elements of the Cherokee worldview" in addition to basic phonetic information. Cushman's study demonstrates that the "syllabary codifies eighty-six meaningful units, grammatical markers, not just sounds." One of the great contributions of Cushman's study to my broader explorations of graphogenesis in this book is her effort to explain how "the use and impact of meaning-making technologies must be incorporated into the understandings of knowledge, cultural tradition, and identity" within the communities where they flourished. Cushman's work clearly establishes "how reading and writing in a script other than the Roman alphabet became a vehicle for and symbol of tribal sovereignty" for the Cherokees.[52] In *Inscribing Sovereignties*, I extend that reasoning to both alphabetic and nonalphabetic scripts in nineteenth-century Indian Country and explore the less well-known systems at work in

Figure 0.6. The Cherokee syllabary developed by Sequoyah. In James Mooney, *Myths of the Cherokee* (Washington, DC: Government Printing Office, 1902).

Haudenosaunee, Oceti Sakowin, and Great Lakes Algonquian communities during the period.

SCRIPTS AND SOVEREIGNTY

The important question remains, how can graphesis extend tribal sovereignty? Several theoretical models put forward by Native researchers help us connect vernacular-language literacy practices to a shared political discourse that asserts a community's legal sovereignty. The first, "rhetorical sovereignty," was devised by Ojibwe/Dakota scholar Scott Lyons, who proposed that "rhetorical sovereignty is the inherent right and ability of peoples to determine their own communicative needs and desires in this pursuit, to decide for themselves the goals, modes, styles, and languages."[53] By linking rhetoric to sovereignty—a European legal term initially intended to describe the unitary (and unilateral) power invested in the person of the monarch, but which eventually came to be associated with the power of states in general—Lyons connects the precontact persuasive practices of Native North Americans to their forceful engagement with settler colonial discourses of power and usurpation in such a way as to deny the settler state hegemony over discourse and to free his own Indigenous intellectual tradition from the disenfranchisement involved in calling Indian persuasion "the other."[54] For Lyons, rhetorical sovereignty is a term that offers Native interlocutors the ability "to assert [themselves] renewed, but only insofar as this renewal is collective rather than individual." Sovereign rhetoric releases "a peoples' right to rebuild." In the process, it foregrounds "an adamant refusal to dissociate culture, identity and power from the land." It is, Lyons believes, "precisely this commitment to place that makes the concept of rhetorical sovereignty an empowering device for all forms of community."[55]

In Osage scholar Robert Warrior's interpretation of how sovereignty works in the context of Indigenous intellectuals' going about the business of being intellectuals, he focuses especially on the role of writing in sovereignty's deployment. While analyzing the literary work of Osage writer John Joseph Matthews, Warrior realized that Matthews's literary practice opened to view "how the act of writing functions in the struggle for self-determination and is continuous with both tradition and survival." Warrior called this coupling of writing and self-determination "intellectual sovereignty." Key to his concept is the idea that "tradition is able to live in new written forms." Significantly, in subsequent work, Warrior expanded the definition of intellectual sovereignty to include the "intellectual trade routes" through which Indigenous ideas flowed, thus adding the landed element so necessary to Indigenous languages into the equation. Finally, like Lyons, Warrior folds his sense of sovereignty back into the collective: "The process of sovereignty, whether in the political or intellectual sphere, is not a matter of removing ourselves and our communities from the influences of the world in which we live."[56]

Recent work on Kanaka Maoli (Native Hawaiian) print culture builds on these concepts, allowing us to visualize the relationship between the cultural protocols encoded in the oral tradition and those that emerge in written forms. Learning to read and write in Hawaiian involves first grasping the hermeneutic traditions of the unwritten language. This is because as the writers and readers of these texts produce and consume them, they archive the storytelling *traditions* of their ancestors. At the same time, they document the listening/auditory *protocols* of the "unlettered" tradition. Take, for example, the *kaona*, a popular rhetorical trope that is "a Hawaiian poetic device implying hidden meanings," providing a vehicle through which Kanaka Maoli can make rhetorical appeals. Both in the early days of missionization and in contemporary battles between Native islanders and settlers who would destroy or alienate the traditional land base, Kanaka Maoli orators, writers, and artists employ kaona to "further decolonization" and provide "a means of ancestral reconnection." Thus, "historical kaona is an expression of rhetorical survivance and sovereignty." It is but a short step to a collective goal: "Native Hawaiians are enacting cultural citizenship as a starting point for an imagined national citizenship."[57] Audible through the kaona puns and allusions is a long-standing reference to this tradition that allows its Indigenous auditors and writers/speakers an opportunity to invoke the power of this storytelling tradition against the settler colonial narratives of disappearance and its concomitant legal machinations of land theft and community displacement.

Over the past twenty years, Indigenous scholars and their non-Native allies have developed a highly sophisticated set of methodological practices by which we may more clearly view what early Native writers were doing, including those who wrote in their vernacular language. One set of practices, what the literacy historian Hilary Wyss has called the "tactical appropriation of language," came about as young Native boys and girls were sent to mission-sponsored institutions like Moor's Charity School, where Samson Occom and Joseph Brant learned to write. There was also Connecticut's Cornwall Mission School, where important Cherokee leaders like Elias Boundinot and John Ridge were educated, as were the progenitors of Cherokee literary culture in Cherokee and English, David Brown and Catharine Brown.

Once literate and invested in alphabeticism only to the extent that it served a tactical advantage, Native writers confronted the debilitating effects of the entextualization of the spoken word into written texts by providing critical paratext and careful contextualizations to their transcriptions of Indigenous language discourse. This is a process that Gros Ventre scholar Joe Gone has termed "judicious entextualization." In his study of his great-grandfather Fred Gone's work collecting Gros Ventre's vernacular stories on the Fort Belknap Reservation for the Works Progress Administration (WPA) in 1940, Joe Gone argues that his ancestor's transcription and formatting techniques of the oral narratives outline a kind of "best practice" for the kinds of entextualization that predominate in Indian Country. First, a transcription must be "written just as the storyteller told it." It should also include "orienting commentary regarding ritual performance[s] described in the story" and provide "any relevant information gleaned from subsequent questioning of [the storyteller] in commentaries and asides." Finally, ethical transcription of Indigenous texts must always recognize the limitations of the exchange, including "potential constraints of lost knowledge, limited experience, or faded memory."[58]

Ultimately, translation itself has come under revision, and Kanaka Maoli poet and scholar Jamaica Osario has begun to apply what she calls the concept of "rigorous paraphrase" to the vernacular-language materials contained in the archive. In Osorio's definition, rigorous paraphrase involves several things: giving "visible priority" to the Hawaiian language texts that make up the archive and providing outsiders with a reading of the texts that denies "the alluring distraction of a full translation," which obscures the real differences between the two conceptual systems. Such revision, in turn, reflects on the kinds of identity politics that flow from a new vision of self-government. Like sovereignty, the concept of "identity" as it plays out in the "identity politics" of peoples whose community membership has been distorted by its association with individualism rather than collectivism, demands a reconnection to the Indigenous concept *pilina*. For, as Osorio points out, "pilina are not 'identities,' but complex relationships. Pilina breathe, move, and shape-shift."[59] Pilina are thus "relationships," not a static category of being. Identities in such reimagined communities are a "way," a method.

Finally, contemporary Native authors have devised ingenious ways to circumvent the oral/literature divide encoded in most settler language ideologies. Cherokee scholar Christopher Teuton has noted a "preoccupation with juxtaposing oral and graphic forms of expression" in Native writing from its earliest forms to the present.[60] Within each tribal community, Teuton argues, there exists a textual field that encompasses both the oral and inscribed, the individual and collective forms of expression. Although often theorized as the obverse of written words, Native oral tradition, as anthropologist Julie Cruikshank observes, is "better understood as a social activity than as a reified text."[61] In this understanding, traditional Native textual practice—the performative orature of so many tribal communities—has, over time, expanded to include a role for alphabetic writing, syllabary, and other graphic practices. Native textual cultures can thus best be understood as sites of interchange between two kinds of *social* activity—speaking and inscribing. In many cases, Native writers manipulate older tribal material practices to suit the needs of the new book media they are exploiting. Thus, Indigenous orthographies clearly encode not just information but also the aural and performative regimes that obtained for spoken language and graphic images in their home communities. In this way, Native peoples worked to protect their vernacular languages from the reification imposed by inscription and print.

They did so by reinvesting translation and transcription with what one anthropologist has called the "neglected sonic dimensions of social experience." Increasingly, more ethnographers, and even some literary historians, have begun to explore "the subject-creating dimensions of listening: an active and socialized process—one in which 'literacies of listening' are inculcated."[62] Because, at least in US history, the period during which many tribal communities began to experiment with alphabetic and syllabary transcriptions of oral practices coincides with Euro-American "interest in the ear, listening, deafness, and acoustics in fields such as medicine, psychoacoustics, and physiology," it makes sense to explore early Native texts as "legible representations of aural experience." Writing and print are two "technologies of the legible [that] made and continue to make sound circulation possible"; they thus embody "the dialogic relationship between sound and sight" that constituted early Native textuality. Thus, it is necessary to consider written texts as physical objects that circulate culturally legible sounds in specific social settings.[63]

If we return to Scott Momaday's depiction of the colonial communications paradigm that obtained for Tosamah's grandmother in the Kiowa Nation, we can better appreciate the value of the media/material methods outlined above for recovering the voices and scripts emitted by the Tai-me story. What the Road Man calls a Tai-me "doll" is actually a media object of great spiritual power to the Kiowa people. The ethnographer James Mooney, who developed a close relationship with significant Kiowas in the 1890s, described the Tai-me's role this way: "The great, central figure of the *k'adó*, or sun dance, ceremony is the *taíme*. This is a small image, less than 2 feet in length, representing a human figure dressed in a robe of white feathers, with a headdress consisting of a single upright feather and pendants of ermine skin, with numerous strands of blue beads around its neck, and painted upon the face, breast, and back with designs symbolic of the sun and moon."[64]

The care with which the Tai-me was treated and its rare public appearances (Mooney reported that, "it is . . . never under any circumstances exposed to view except at the annual sun dance"), signals that it is understood to be much more than an image.[65] But Tosamah's Tai-me story, as Momaday portrays its telling during a Peyote ceremony, is also about the present, about how stories work in an Indigenous community uprooted by the federal government's program of relocation in the novel's 1950s setting. The story is not just about Tai-me and the Book of John but also about how such a story might gather together a community out of a disparate body of listeners. As Gus Palmer, the Kiowa scholar of his community's storytelling practices, puts it, "Kiowas tell stories within stories. They construct a kind of metanarration. They make commentaries about the story."[66] In Scott Momaday's retelling of the Tai-me story, the powerful protector of the Kiowas is "a Voice." When that Voice tells the community, "Take me with you, . . . [and] I will give you whatever you want," they receive visions instructing them how to embody the Voice for the journey. Thus, the Tai-me is both speaker and listener, containing the interlocutive protocols of prayer and power that guide the Kiowas' sense of community and place in the cosmos.

In the novel, the Native men gathered to hear Tosamah preach represent a diverse set of tribal backgrounds—Jemez Pueblo, Navajo, Kiowa. They are there to practice a Peyote ceremony similar to that of the Native American Church, seeking refuge from their alienated lives in Los Angeles where they have been sent as part of the Indian Relocation Act (1956). Again, Mooney describes the overlap of Kiowa and Peyote practices as having become common in the Kiowa Nation during the late nineteenth century: "Their most sacred objects of religious veneration are the *Âdalbeáhya*, the *Taíme*, the *Gadómbitsoñhi*, and the *señi* or peyote. Their great tribal religious ceremony is the *k'ado* or sun dance. Their tribal religion is that which centers around the *a'dalbeáhya* and the *taíme*. The worship of the peyote, although now general, excepting among the oldest men, is comparatively modern with the Kiowa, having been adopted from the more southern tribes. These two systems are compatible and auxiliary to each other."[67]

The eagle bone whistle that Tosamah blows at the end of the ceremony is yet another medium for transmitting the story of Tai-me and a material manifestation of the oral tradition. The Road Man's breath is transformed into a shrill, wordless call to the four directions.

Part Peyote rite and part allusion to the eagle whistles blown by dancers at the Sun Dance, it is a petitionary plea to the supernatural powers—a form of words made flesh and bone. The word here is pure sound, letterless, but never disembodied. It animates the eagle bone, turning its whistle into a plaint. It eddies and flows through the buckskin of the Tai-me effigy and buoys the spirits of the wordless men, gathered in resistance to the forces of US government relocation in an unused storefront in Los Angeles.

"MEDICINE MAN TALK" AND VERNACULAR SCRIPT IN THE APACHE HOMELAND

The interplay between Native vernacular orthographies, tribal sovereignty, and colonialism that is the focus of this book may be previewed in a brief case study of Western Apache communities in present-day Arizona during the twentieth century. At the San Carlos and Fort Apache Reservations, Western Apaches of various backgrounds and beliefs sought to reestablish Apache society within the severely confined social and cultural spaces that settlers had grudgingly allowed them. The San Carlos Reservation emerged, like so many settler colonial institutions in Indigenous homelands, through the aegis of what ethnographer David Samuels has described as a "suite of military, governmental, educational, and commercial institutions" established by the US government in 1880.[68]

The year 1880 marked the end of an extended period of military conflict between the Apaches and Anglo-American settler-colonists who flooded the region when gold was discovered there in 1871. Although Geronimo would not surrender until 1886, the Western Apaches had sought peace with the Americans several years before, and by 1880 were settled on reservations and subject to the US government. Even before the reservation was established, questions about alphabetic literacy and Apache language and cultural identity emerged as integral to both the Apaches and US understanding of what the San Carlos Reservation would mean for those living there and for the settlers now permanently squatting on Apache homelands. As Samuels notes, during his treaty negotiations with the Americans, Apache leader Santa "brought a stone ... meant as a metaphor of his desire for a lasting and permanent peace." Passing the stone to his American counterpart, General Howard, Santa emphasized literacy as a barrier between the two nations: "I don't know how to read and write, ... that stone is my paper. I want to make a peace that will last as long as that stone ... to make a peace as lasting as a rock."[69]

Fast-forward to the twenty-first century, and the politics of Apache sovereignty still focuses on vernacular usage, orthographic integrity, and translation. Eleanor Evans, a linguistic anthropologist hired as a language revitalization consultant by the Fort Apache tribal government (near San Carlos), discovered firsthand that "language projects, and persons—including tribal members—associated with them, were often received ambivalently and often became the target of controversy, despite the fact that nearly everyone voices concern about keeping Apache language [*Ndee Bik'ehgo Biyatí'*] going in the face of apparent loss in fluency among young people." The Apache community had to contend not only with differences of opinion inside the community but also with the constant meddling of the settler state in the politics of language usage. During the first decades of the twenty-first century, Arizona promoted an English-only political movement known as the "Unz initiative," which withdrew state funding for bilingual education and mandated exclusive instruction in English for state-funded schools. An exemption from the federal government was necessary to protect Apache language instruction.[70]

The ongoing role of language usage, orthography, and revitalization in the Apaches' struggle for sovereignty suggests that vernacular literacy practices provide one through line connecting Apache society at San Carlos in 2010 to its predecessors from the previous two centuries. It indicates that vernacular literacy practices are salient "cultural expressions" that in part index Apache culture writ large and that cultural expression (and indeed language itself) is constantly changing to meet the needs of a community.[71] That is, writing and reading in Apache engenders new social practices with roles analogous to cognate activities that Apaches in pre-reservation times employed in their various communications strategies. To return to 1880 and Santa's metaphoric stone, we can think of the material object he chose as a proxy for script as "land," an enduring piece of his homeland that was "lasting." It represented his community's desire to forge some kind of new communications technology that maintained their links to their homeland, as spoken *Ndee Bik'ehgo Biyatí'* had been in previous generations.

Because San Carlos Reservation (like all US reservations) was founded as an artificial social and cultural construct, neither General Howard nor Santa knew what future Apache society would look like, encircled as it was by settlers and pushed toward "civilization." Of course, government representatives like Howard knew the formula most often prescribed for the transformation of Native societies into assimilated communities—Richard Pratt, founder of the Carlisle Industrial School for Indians, often said that "individualizing" the Indian demanded a special mixture of industrial labor for boys and domestic chores for girls with alphabetic literacy at the forefront of formal schooling. This model of educating Western Apache children was put in place in 1881. Initially, it was a makeshift affair, with classes held in the Indian agent's quarters. By 1887, however, a two-story stone-structure boarding school opened for reservation children. The government tasked Apache police officers with rounding up children and forcibly enrolling them in the new school. Called "Children Catchers" by the Apaches, they "went all over looking for kids, and if [they] found one that's not in school, . . . [they] captured them and marched them over there." The school worked the children very hard, and many former students complained, "They didn't give us enough to eat. We were always hungry."[72] As in the boarding school system across Indian Country, families were displaced, children died at much higher rates than in traditional communities, and many ran away to seek wage-paying jobs in the rapidly developing territory.

Christian missionizing of the Apaches was an integral component of this literacy education. Methodist missionaries from nearby Globe, Arizona, were only marginally successful in establishing schools and churches at San Carlos, but in 1893, the Lutheran missionary Johannes Plocher arrived to establish a firm Lutheran base for Apache conversion. From then on, the ethnic identity of community members in San Carlos, Fort Apache, and surrounding areas featured elements of Christianity. The Influenza Pandemic of 1917–18 marked another major turning point in the Western Apaches' social organization, as hundreds of Native people died and nearly everyone fled to remote, kin-centered encampments out of communication range of fellow tribal members. A Lutheran missionary recalled in his journal, "The Indians were scattered so widely in all directions that hardly anyone knew whether his neighbors had gone. Part of every day was spent in looking for families we had not yet found." From the perspective of the Western Apaches themselves, it is remembered as a time when "we were always moving."[73] Meanwhile, federal water projects and their attendant roads and infrastructure demanded back-breaking work of Apache men and women. The Roosevelt Dam project, begun in 1911, employed hundreds of Apache men in manual labor. Other dams followed in 1920 and 1930, with similar demands for Apache work and further diminution of Apache homelands.

Throughout this period, alphabetic literacy—both in Apache and English—was promoted as the social glue that would hold a modernizing, civilized Apache society together. In their effort to create this bond, many missionaries simultaneously encouraged social divisions between Christian converts and traditionalists. It thus came to pass that first-generation men and women on the reservation encountered not only doctrinal debates but also what we might call a "script war" between different factions of San Carlos society that sought to define how written discourse could be mapped onto already existing Apache communications protocols. Despite their best efforts, missionaries failed to establish an either/or social or cultural division in the Apache communities they missionized. And this story was repeated in broad outlines across many Native communities during the nineteenth century. Indigenous peoples who embraced some form of alphabetic or syllabary literacy did not fall into predictable political "camps." Time and again, those in favor of "traditional religion" used scripts to archive their ceremonies and cosmologies right alongside Christian tribal members who were looking for new ways to worship. At Pine Ridge Lakota Reservation in 1888, for example, the leader Red Cloud advised his community that they should adopt literacy but did not need to adhere to the Christian faith.[74]

If we examine the Western Apaches' "script wars" from the vantage point of the very human agencies and cultural stakes at play, we can reimagine what might be dismissed as a simple doctrinal dispute as essential exercises in Apache sovereignty. Two Apache men stand out as paradigmatic: Britton Goode (1911–81) and Silas John Edwards (1883–1953). They represent a demographic cohort in the emerging Western Apache reservation community who came of age in a time when new social roles demanded creative adaptation of traditional Apache practices. This cohort includes individuals who lived during the first generation of Western Apache confinement to a reservation (1880–1930). Each of these men occupied an Apache social space that had only recently been created, and each also had a distinctly different historical horizon from the Apache leaders most commonly discussed in the historiography: Geronimo (1829–1909) and Cochise (1805–74).

Silas John Edwards and Britton Goode were generationally poised to enter traditional social positions just as the reservation system forever precluded them. Although almost thirty years apart in age, they shared many social experiences during the first decades of the twentieth century that resulted in them being members of an Apache social cohort for whom writing and literacy centered several debates within a rapidly changing tribal community. Britton Goode was born in Cibecue in 1911, moved to San Carlos when he married, and lived there until his death in 1981. He maintained deep roots in traditional Apache ceremonialism, and "in his younger days . . . [was] a dream interpreter in a traditional Apache manner." As was traditional in his community before the reservation, Goode experienced conversion through a vision that led him to his own new kind of religion: "One morning while sitting in his house, he had literally seen the light—a soft glow in the corner of his kitchen that convinced him of the presence of the Lord and Savior." Late in life, Britton would carry on lengthy conversations with his youngest son, Phillip, about scriptural interpretation and the implications of translation. "I didn't really understand English until I really understood Apache," he told his son. Phillip credited these conversations with teaching him the insides of both languages—the semantic intricacies of English and Apache—and for giving him an approach to language and interpretation. Britton Goode always insisted on calling his work "interpretation," not "translation."[75] Through his efforts with the missionaries and the new script, he came to occupy the new social roles of "language expert" and "Christian."

In a fascinating article detailing his work with Western Apache language preservation, anthropologist David W. Samuels explains how Goode's Lutheran-sponsored word-for-word literal transcription of the Christian Bible transformed both the language and the community missionized by the Wycliff Bible Society. In exploring how Goode worked on a Bible translation in his community, Samuels encountered an ontology of language very similar to that of Momaday's Old Saint John: "Bible translation and interpretation," he concludes, "contributed to a 'reification of the word.'" That is because, while trying to produce Apache language Bible texts, missionaries sought out individuals like Goode who were willing to create "transparent" translations. In other words, according to Samuels, translations that "effectively reduce[d] socially contextualized vocal practices to [mere] lexicon and syntax." As a result, missionaries in Native communities tended to be invested in the semantic purification of a living language, in the stripping bare of its socially embedded practices. In the particular case of Phillip Goode, Britton's son who inherited his father's social role, great care had to be taken when translating the Bible to avoid "medicine man talk," the term Apache Christians use to mark speech considered "dangerous" or traditionally "powerful," and therefore not suitable for Christian practice.

Britton Goode remembered that "when people first heard the New Testament in Western Apache," they blanched at phrases like *yaa dilit*, because they said, "that's medicine man talk." Even when he explained that the phrase had a completely secular meaning ("the sky at night"), it was hard for these listeners to shake their knowledge of a social context in which these words had special and specific power and signification. Slowly but surely, among the Christian Apaches, a form of their language began to emerge that was scrubbed of such usages. By employing this version, translators from the community came to think only of semantics and denotative definitions when they rendered English texts into Apache. Thanks to the Wycliffe Bible group and others, Samuels argues, "official" written Western Apache now exhibits "a semanticist approach to language." It embraces a linguistic epistemology of "words and referents."[76]

Meanwhile, Apaches like Silas John Edwards were engaging with the new religion and associated language ideologies quite differently. Silas John was born in 1883. Like many young Apache men of the time, he had few choices of employment and was constantly under threat of being taken away to a government school. When his family moved to East Fork, Arizona, he attended the Fort Apache boarding school. By 1911, Silas had learned to speak the English language reasonably well and showed a deep interest in serving as an interpreter for the Lutheran missionaries working with the Apaches. It was the experience of a book, a "liberally illustrated Bible history book," that inspired him to employ literacy and Christianity to forge a social role for himself in the community. The coercive nature of government schooling soon outweighed its benefits, however, and he ran away to work at the Roosevelt Dam construction site, digging ditches with mules and draglines, toiling in the Arizona desert on a federal water project. While working at the dam site one day, Silas John had a vision of an owl that was so powerful that it caused his nose to bleed profusely. The vision told him to leave the worksite and seek refuge at Superstition Mountain, where he could contemplate the meaning of his vision. At that point, he recalled later in life, "My father came for me [and] I go back to Ft. Apache. The same day we came back[,] . . . I became a medicine man."[77]

Significantly, Silas John Edwards chose to employ written script to follow through on the calling bestowed upon him by this vision. He sought to write out all of the sixty-two prayers he received, which offered his community a new kind of religion. The ethnolinguist Keith Basso has recounted Silas John's vision:

> There were 62 prayers. They came to me in rays from above. At the same time I was instructed. He [God] was advising me and telling me what to do, at the same time teaching me chants. . . . All of these *and the writing* were given to me at one time in one dream. God made it [the writing], but it came down to our earth I liken this to what has happened in the religions we have now. In the center of the earth, when it first began, when the earth was first made there was absolutely nothing on this world. There was no written language. So it was in 1904 that I became aware of the writing; it was then that I heard about it from God.[78]

Silas John Edwards painted the symbols he saw in his vision onto pieces of "tanned buckskin." Twenty years later, his followers began circulating the prayer texts "written in ink on squares of cardboard." Only trained assistants in the religion "were taught to read and write and, after demonstrating these skills, went through an initiation ritual in which they were presented with painted buckskins of their own." From the very beginning, access to the system was tightly controlled by Silas John himself, and competence in it was intentionally restricted to a small band of elite ritual specialists.[79]

Silas John called his movement *sailiš jaan bi' at' eehi*—which means "Silas John, His Sayings." In doing so, he positioned himself and his script in direct opposition to individuals and the script of evangelical Lutherans like the Goodes. Samuels explains: "The sectarian disagreements of the Lutherans with the 'misguided' religious practices of Apache theology on the one hand and the 'Romish' religious practices of the Catholics on the other, came to a head in a sort of running battle with the Holy Ground theology of Silas John Edwards and his followers . . . Silas John's syncretic ceremonial practice competed with the Lutherans as well as other churches moving onto the reservation."[80]

A closer examination of Silas John Edwards's writing system shows it to be a quite different approach to translating oral practice into writing than the one the Goodes had taken. In Silas John's system, performance, social context, and "medicine man talk" remain in place. Perhaps the most interesting thing about this script is that it contains symbols that articulate not only semantic features but also ceremonial gestures. Basso calls this a "phonetic-semantic sign [system]" and argues that Silas John's "kinesic symbols" open

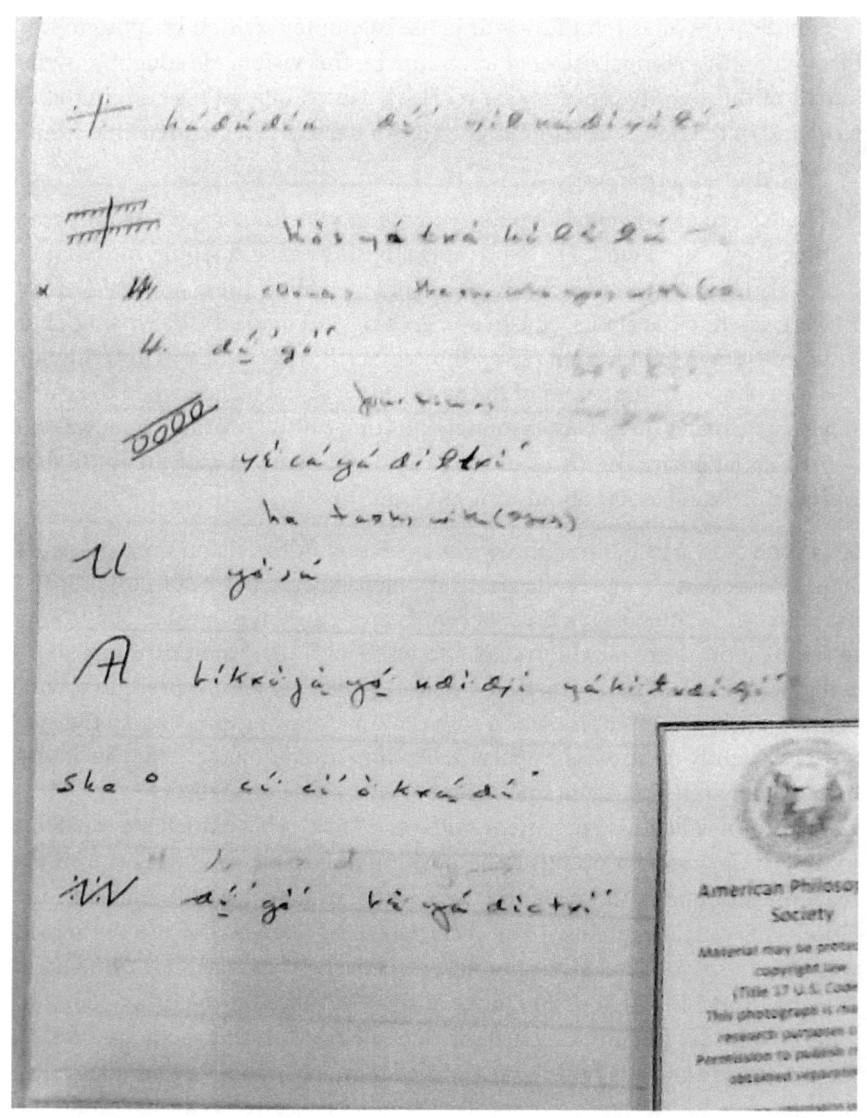

Figure 0.7. Silas John Edwards script, ca. 1933. In David Mandelbaum Papers, San Carlos Apache Texts, series 3, box 7, MSS 497.3.H68, Harry Hoijer Collection, American Philosophical Society Library and Museum, Philadelphia, Pennsylvania.

to view most ethnographers' fundamental misunderstanding of non-Western sign systems and, thus, of translation and meaning themselves. He remarks, "This oversight may be a product of Western ethnocentrism; after all, it is we who use alphabets who most frequently associate writing with language. On the other hand, it may simply stem from the fact that systems incorporating symbols with kinesic referents are exceedingly rare and have not yet been reported." For Basso, writing in 1973, however, Silas John Edwards's system clearly showed "that fundamental emic distinctions remain to be discovered and that existing etic frameworks are less than adequately equipped to describe them."[81] In layman's terms, Basso suggested that Silas John's writing system included performative gestures and material practices whose meanings exceeded the expectation of an alphabet for Europeans, who consider alphabetic writing to be primarily "forming words by arranging their proper letters in due order."[82] When set alongside Phillip Goode's biblical translations, however, Silas John's script also suggests that the Western Apaches could find voice in a writing system whose epistemological underpinnings were their own and that the social circulation of that writing system as material practice countered the semanticist and colonialist assumptions of the Christian missionaries.

This comparative approach guides my analysis throughout this book. The way graphogenesis played out among the Western Apaches at the dawn of the twentieth century is in many ways a template for understanding the process as it developed in Haudenosaunee, Oceti Sakowin, and Anishinaabe communities in the nineteenth century, and as such, it provides a model for the other, more extended case studies I present. The comparative approach offers several advantages. First, it will lead us to methods that enable a crossing of the "Great Divide" between orality and literacy that has hampered so many earlier studies of Indigenous writing.[83] Second, it can help us focus on the local origin of script usage and thereby downplay interpretive strategies that tend to treat vernacular orthographies as entirely other-directed and colonialist. Because the research of Eleanor Nevins and David Samuels is so detailed and derived from lived experience in the Apache communities, they offer us a template for working on materials far less studied in other Indigenous settings. It also, importantly, reminds us that these issues and practices, like the Indigenous communities themselves, are still present and active across the United States, and integral to the ongoing struggle for political sovereignty within the settler state that every Indigenous community pursues to this day.

VERNACULAR SIGNS, VERNACULAR SOVEREIGNTY

Along with the battles and massacres of the American nineteenth century, the colonial history of Indigenous communities always featured a struggle to reassemble the communal whole. Native peoples fought this fight through innovative media improvisations designed to reestablish what I call "interlocative communities," groups of people separated by geographic space and power imbalances but knit together by hybrid systems of communication that partly compensated for these holes in the social fabric. Although the majority of Native American communities could perhaps have been labeled "oral societies" at the beginning of the nineteenth century, none of the 500 now federally recognized tribes relied on sound alone to carry forward information into the future or across their homelands. Each also mobilized a complex set of social protocols designed to guarantee the preservation of a message. These protocols can properly be conceived of as media.[84] They are social technologies. Moreover, the rules of engagement in the aural sphere were supported by a wide array of graphic and material culture objects and systems. By the middle of the century, many Native Americans used pen and pencil, paper and canvas, telegraph and railroad, to extend their communication influence in wider and wider circles of community. Along with these innovations, they continued to employ older, traditional media.

Looking back over this period of Native American history, Lakota scholar Vine Deloria Jr. has argued that media was central to the colonization of Indian Country and would in turn be at the center of Native peoples' resurgence. "Trying to communicate is an insurmountable task," Deloria observes, "since one cannot skip readily from a tribal way of life to the conceptual world of the non-tribal person. The non-tribal person thinks in a linear sequence, in which A is the foundation for B and C always follows. The view and meaning of the total event is rarely understood by the non-tribal person, although he may receive more objective information." So it was that in the period from 1830 to 1927, the communications circuits of America were at cross purposes, with "tribal society [oriented] toward a center[,] and non-Indian society . . . toward linear development, the process might be compared to describing a circle surrounded with tangent lines."[85]

Throughout the nineteenth century, Native peoples fought fiercely and righteously in defense of their homes over and against settler occupation. Yet martial struggles with invading armies and militias aside, Native communities sought first and foremost to reassert their ties to the land. Anthropologist James Clifford has put forward a way of theorizing this process in what he calls "articulation"—"a non-reductive way to think about cultural transformation and the apparent coming and going of 'traditional forms.'"[86]

In articulation theory, "the whole question of authenticity is secondary, and the process of social and cultural persistence is political all the way back. It is assumed that cultural forms will always be made, unmade, and remade." All such transformations are closely linked to the inherent landedness of Indigenous life and identity: "When thinking of differently articulated sites of indigeneity . . . one of the enduring constraints in the changing mix will always be the power of place."[87] As Keith Basso has so memorably recounted, for Native peoples in America, communication and media are essentially "'situated talk,' a discursive mode in which history is place as well as time."[88]

In some ways, then, *Inscribing Sovereignties* is an extended meditation on Vine Deloria Jr.'s prescient reading of the relationship between Native and non-Native peoples in America via the then emerging electronic media of postmodernity. In *We Talk, You Listen*, Deloria comments,

> Indian people are just as subject to the deluge of information as other people. In the past decade most reservations have come within reach of television and computers. In many ways Indian people are just as directed by the electric nature of our universe as any other group. But the tribal viewpoint simply absorbs what is reported and immediately integrates it into the experience of the group. In many areas whites are regarded as a temporary aspect of tribal life and there is unshakable belief that the tribe will survive the domination of the white man and once again rule the continent. Indians soak up the world like a blotter and continue almost untouched by events. The more that happens, the better the tribe seems to function and the stronger it appears to get. Of all the groups in the modern world Indians are best able to cope with the modern situation. To the non-Indian world, it does not appear that Indians are capable of anything. The flexibility of the tribal viewpoint enables Indians to meet devastating situations and survive. But this flexibility is seen as incompetency, so that as the non-Indian struggles in solitude and despair, he curses the Indian for not coveting the same disaster.[89]

In Deloria's application of Marshall McLuhan's analysis of Native American history, we can see that the nineteenth-century American communications revolution (mass printing, telegraphy, etc.) was the nexus of what would become two divergent paths in humanity's grappling with postindustrial modernity. As non–Indian Americans yielded their humanity, their oral and aural regimes, and face-to-face experiences to greater abstractions and the media that enabled them, they eviscerated the symbolic power of their own languages and mythologies, thus unwittingly removing one critical set of cultural techniques by which humankind had managed change—ecological, historical, and so forth—for thousands of years. If Native peoples in 1880 were "submerge[ed] with concepts for which nothing [had] prepared them," by the 1960s, they were more than prepared for postmodernity, for innovations made in the media formations of their traditional ways of life that had shepherded them into the twentieth century and that remained viable cultural practices for the preservation of their communities. *Inscribing Sovereignties* celebrates these achievements by tracing the development of such resiliency to its nineteenth-century roots.

This book is divided into four chapters. The first, "Spelling 'Indian,'" charts the development of a settler language ideology directed toward Indigenous peoples that fostered a discourse of *people without letters* that effectively mirrored other settler discursive constructs aimed at "disappearing" the Indian and rationalizing robbing them of their land. The remaining three chapters present extended case studies of different linguistic and culture groups. Chapter 2 focuses on the Haudenosaunees (Iroquois) and their adoption of alphabetic script to supplement other media such as wampum, woodcarvings, and the built environment in their efforts to sustain the all-important Condolence Ceremony into the nineteenth century. It is followed by a chapter that examines the Dakotas of present-day Minnesota and the six-year imprisonment of more than 250 tribal members that led to their adoption of a missionary alphabet for their language. This section then moves to consider how that alphabet migrated west to the Lakotas of the northern Plains, again not replacing older media but supplementing it to compensate for the social disorder created by the reservation system. The final chapter of *Inscribing Sovereignties* surveys the wide variety of nonalphabetic scripts that Native communities employed during their removal from the Great Lakes. At the center of this discussion is the script called *pa-pe-pi-po* by the Meskwakis of Iowa and Kansas. This script, which was also adopted by many Ho-Chunks (Winnebagos) even though their language is not part of the Algonquian family, is known to linguists as the Great Lakes syllabics, and is in use to this day.

Although this study is centered on vernacular literacy, it does not argue that such literacy or fluency is a necessary component of an Indigenous community's sovereignty. Rather, it maintains that studying alphabetic and syllabary practices will greatly enhance our historiographies of Indigenous community-formation in the nineteenth century. Ultimately, the goals of this book are fairly modest: to introduce readers to the variety and scope of scripts in languages from Indigenous North America; to survey the many different ways that Native communities adopted, adapted, and invented writing systems to meet their various needs (political, social, cultural); and to offer some possible routes for pursuing comparative studies of Indigenous language orthographies across the Western Hemisphere and around the globe. By these same methods, our search for understanding of the written Native past becomes a decolonizing gesture. With the help of Native speakers, of "rigorous paraphrase" and the awareness of the centrality of land, kinship, and the collective, we may better encounter Indigenous writing on its own terms and, within it, many varied histories of usage.

In the end, I hope the reader will come away with a greater appreciation for the innovative communication strategies that have ensured the survival of Native American peoples and their communities and that will continue to do so. This study reveals how Native Americans have been among the most adaptive and inventive of the many peoples who call the present-day United States home, especially when it comes to engaging with modernity to resist the homogenization and erasure of their societies.

1 : Spelling "Indian"

> The want of a standard system of orthography has been experienced by all persons engaged in the study of languages, written or unwritten. The philologist, the historian, the geographer, and . . . the missionary,—he whose message of good tidings is to all nations,—are harassed in their labors by the diversity of alphabets; and the difficulties hence arising may be judged second only to those caused by the diversity of language:—that main barrier, we may confess with Humboldt and St. Augustine, against the establishment of the Civitas Dei, and the realization of the idea of Humanity.
> —Max Müller, *Proposals for a Missionary Alphabet*, 1854

> As *speech* is the noblest gift that God has bestowed upon man, so *writing* is the most useful acquisition that has been produced by the exertion of human intellect. The former endowment distinguishes man from the inferior part of animal creation; while the latter gives the members of civilized society a vast superiority over the uncultivated tribes of the savage nations.
> —F. B. Ribbans, *Essay on the Utility, Origin, and Progress of Writing* (1840)

To understand how Indigenous languages in North America became scripted, we need first to examine the language ideologies that underwrote orthography practices in the early republic's settler state. In nineteenth-century America, spelling anchored important debates over citizenship, national identity, and assimilation. Although the arrangement of the alphabet's arbitrary symbols into sounds might seem to us something of little importance, to earlier generations of Euro-Americans it was a subject of great interest. Samuel Worcester, missionary to the Cherokees and author of a spelling book for settler schoolchildren, asserted that spelling was simply the art of "forming words by arranging their proper letters in due order."[1] Few of his countrymen would have agreed. For sedimented in the silent "h" and strange rules like "sometimes y" that shadowed the American English vernacular, there was a great deal of social and political angst. That is because, as the linguist Mark Sebba has noted, orthography is "the place where phonology meets ideology,

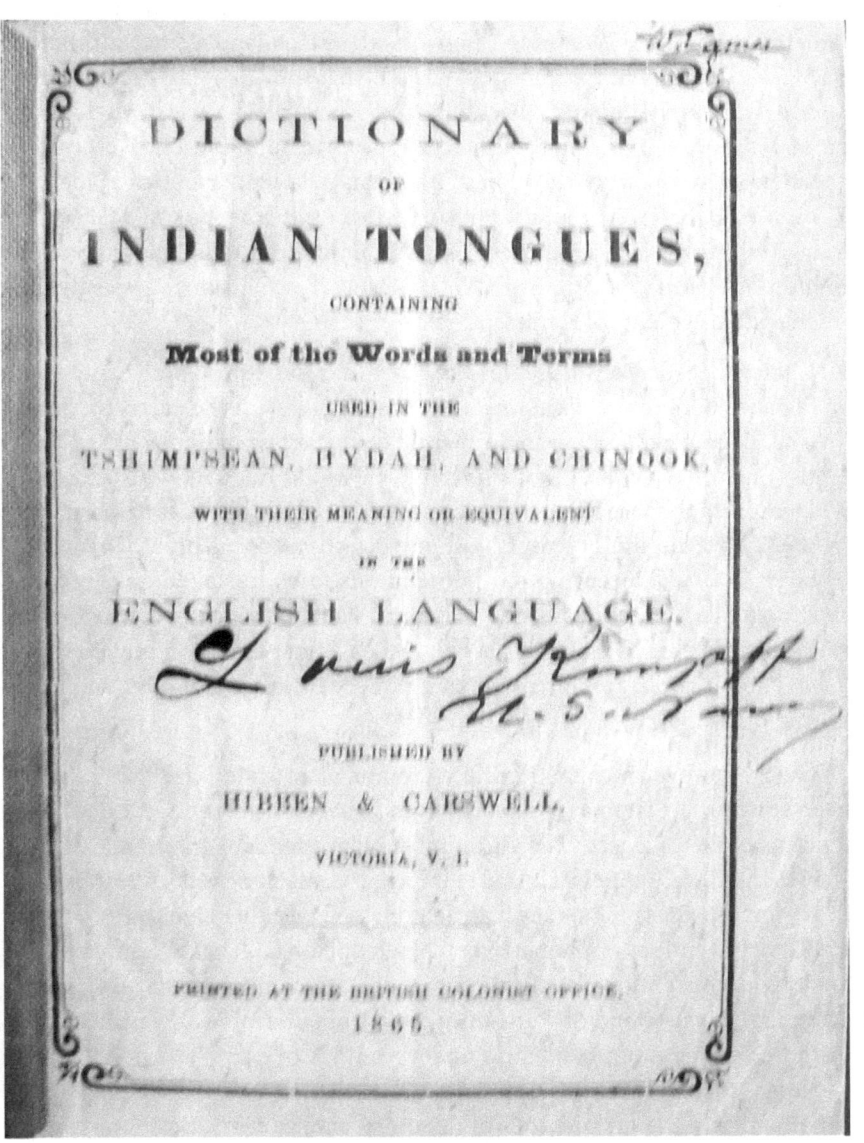

Figure 1.1. Title page of *Dictionary of Indian Tongues* (Victoria, BC: Hibben & Carswell, 1865). Courtesy of the Huntington Library, San Marino, California.

where sound and politics collide."[2] For US citizens of the era, the sounds that inspired the most angst were those they felt were uniquely "American"—those which Walt Whitman celebrated in *Leaves of Grass* (1855) as the "barbaric yawp" of fellow citizens.

The literary scholar Tim Cassedy has characterized this time in Euro-American history as "a cultural moment when language seemed a plausible basis for a stable identity category."[3] Yet, as he has shown, spelling was far from codified across the Atlantic World. Within the North American anglophone cultural sphere explored in this book, it appears to be an especially precarious social practice upon which to base national, political, or personal identity. Take, for example, the following passage from the notebook of Meriwether Lewis. Viewing this as an index of Lewis's identity could lead one to conclude that this individual, so important to US westward expansion, represented the uneducated elements of settler society:

> I had proceeded on this course about two miles with Goodrich at some distance behind me whin my ears were saluted with the agreeable sound of a fall of water and advancing a little further I saw the spray arrise above the plain like a collumn of smoke which would frequently dispear again in an instant caused I presume by the wind which blew pretty hard from the S. W. I did not however loose my direction to this point which soon began to make a roaring too tremendious to be mistaken for any cause short of the great falls of the Missouri. Here I arrived about 12 Oclock having traveled by estimate about 15 Miles. I hurryed down the hill which was about 200 feet high and difficult of access, to gaze on this sublimely grand specticle.[4]

Lewis, however, was neither illiterate nor ill-educated. He had, after all, been secretary to Thomas Jefferson. Linguistic analysis of the Lewis and Clark journals, in fact, suggests that "the number of nonstandard grammatical forms [Lewis] used was quite small," and that what seems to a modern reader to be orthographic signs of illiteracy "can be explained by either eighteenth-century spelling conventions or phonetic or analogic spellings." That is, Lewis was following the conventional societal script, and at the same time he was spelling according to the sound of words in spoken discourse. It is only by attending to these "phonetic or phonemic underpinnings of many . . . nonstandard spellings" that we can truly appreciate how spelling was performed as a social practice in the first decades of the nineteenth century. Both Meriwether Lewis (1774–1809) and William Clark (1770–1838) were educated before the introduction of Noah Webster's *American Spelling Book* in 1788 and thus represented a social cohort of Euro-Americans for whom spelling was not yet standardized, and whose written texts reflected the close relationship between the oral and inscribed.[5] Moreover, Lewis's hastily penned descriptions (of the "tremendious" "specticle" he has observed) also reveal the extent to which orthographic marks represent much more than the shadow of the oral in the written. They demonstrate, as well, the power of the aural—and the social-cultural regimes of hearing employed by fluent listeners—that guided the way that words were inscribed on the page. Meriwether Lewis did not write so much as he spoke but rather as he heard.

Writing as one heard was at the center of early nineteenth-century arguments about the need to reform American spelling systems. Spelling's problematic place in a very oral society that was becoming more and more invested in the written and printed word would become a concern of educators during the rise of the common school in the 1830s.[6] In these new educational institutions, both oral communication and proper spelling were deemed essential, so that an educational publication of the day might include both in its title, as in Benjamin Dudley Emerson's *The National Spelling-Book, and Pronouncing Tutor [. . .]* (1828). Recitation and spelling were taught side by side, demanding attention to the relationship of writing to speaking among teachers and pupils alike. While the scientific virtuoso Joseph Priestly could, at the end of the eighteenth century, confidently say that script is "but a substitute for the art of speaking; and, where both can be used, vastly inferior to it," by the 1840s, handwritten and printed scripts had become so important to a rising middle class in America that Albert Wright, writing from Rome, New York, had to accept that script and voice were now forever intertwined and that "characters or letters [originally] invented to represent the elementary sounds of spoken language," now often introduced "the perplexity of what are called irregular sounds." "The truth is," he reasoned, "there are no irregular *sounds* in the English language. Letters may be irregular in representing sounds, but the sounds themselves cannot be irregular."[7] In this climate, the recitation of written works, particularly poetry, served as a way for teachers and students to transit between the two forms of language while also serving as an "occasion for social exchange, staging texts as 'theatrical' performance pieces." As students read, memorized, and then repeated the verse they had read to their assembled classmates and instructor, they in a sense began to complete and standardize the oral/aural/orthographic circle that appears in earlier American writers like Meriweather Lewis. Public, oral interpretation of the alphabetic markings on a page through recitations thus enabled learners to "perform . . . their roles as middle-class" citizens of the United States.[8] After the Civil War, settler colonial educators formalized this role of literacy in the formation of an American middle class that might include immigrants, or even Indigenous peoples, if they were correctly vetted through the orthographic system of inscription, recitation, and listening. By 1865, Americans of good social standing were expected to hew much closer to the societal norms of rote spelling and to eschew writing the American vernacular simply as they heard it. There was no place for Meriweather Lewis's haphazard style in an industrializing United States.

The story of how spelling became an index of citizenship and middle-class civility is essential to understanding how alphabetic literacy came to Indian Country inflected with settler conceptions of citizenship and class that were alien to Native communities. Richard Henry Pratt, the architect of the US government's Indian "industrial" education program, described his plan as embodying "a citizenizing influence upon the Indians." For Pratt, to "citizenize" the Indian required adherence to the ideal of the new common schools sprouting up across the country:

> Under our principles we have established the public school system, where people of all races may become unified in every way, and loyal to the government; but we do not gather the people of one nation into schools by themselves, and the people of another nation into schools by themselves, but we invite the youth of all peoples into all schools. We shall not succeed in Americanizing the Indian unless we take him in exactly the same way . . . purely Indian schools say to the Indians: "You are Indians, and must remain Indians. You are not of the nation, and cannot become of the nation. We do not want you to become of the nation."[9]

THE ALPHABETIZATION OF CITIZENSHIP

Book historian Patricia Crain has called this growth of interest in spelling a part of the "alphabetization" of America, a process she defines as based in "the array of individual, social, and institutional practices surrounding the internalization of the alphabet, the first step in literacy training." Over time, these alphabetic practices accrued "'narrative and tropic devices' that increased [the] range and power [of the Roman alphabet] as an essential component of acculturation and socialization in early America."[10]

It was by no means a simple procedure. Not even the ABCs were a done deal in nineteenth-century America. Writing scripts had been swept up in the simultaneous communications and industrial revolutions, serving as a central medium for prosecuting land deals and filling out balance sheets. In this commercialization of writing and scripts, effort, speed, and accuracy were of the essence. Pamphlets touting shorthand systems "a hundred times quicker" than any other, "brief and rapid writing" methods, and "the laws governing mental, physical and mathematical action in rapid writing" proliferated.[11] Writing to "men of business" in 1835, Benjamin Franklin Foster remarked, "quackery has got to be so universal now, and so profitable, that he who proposes anything new, can hardly hope to escape the imputation." Nonetheless, Foster proceeded to flog his own scheme of a modernized system of writing, geared to the communications revolution's new class of scriveners "who get their living one way or another by Penmanship."[12]

For others, spelling took on a curiously moral cast in the pamphlet wars that accompanied the national discussion about the virtues of improving spelling in the new nation. Abner Kneeland voiced the opinion of many when he said, "To attempt to point out the origin of the irregularity of English orthography would be like attempting to point out the origin of moral evil."[13] Daniel Smalley echoed Kneeland's concern, proclaiming "our present orthography a moral failure."[14] Others saw phonetic writing as a part of the "sacred cause" of disseminating the Christian Bible "to unevangelized nations in their own languages," arguing that "a phonetic orthography will render the Bible—that infinite repository of truth for the healing of nations—. . . a phonetically-spelt bible is, in reality, a people's edition, which the poorest and the most illiterate may read in a few weeks."[15]

Some even went so far as to propose giving up on the old alphabet altogether, casting their fortunes with new symbols systems that they believed could more accurately represent the sound of English as really spoken. John S. Pulsipher's *Phonal Depot* (1848), for example, proffered "a new specimen of the English language clothed in a new dress for your generous consideration." The "new dress" took the form of an orthography "using a new set of characters; each character to have one invariable sound, and to adapt the orthography of all words to the sound as they are pronounced in good common parlance."[16] Pulsipher's choice to call his collection a depot and "a depository of phonal stores" also signals his interest in relating his work to larger progressive communication and unification projects ongoing in the early republic.

He was not alone. When its sovereignty was threatened by the State of Georgia in the 1820s, the Cherokee Nation sought every means available to assert its cultural and social independence. Part of that larger project involved the Cherokee government sponsoring efforts to establish a vernacular-language orthography.[17] In 1825, missionaries from New England had begun the process of rendering the Cherokee language into Roman alphabetic form, an effort not embraced by many Cherokees. By 1826, the missionaries were forced to relent under pressure from Cherokee leaders, who pointed out the superiority of Sequoyah's syllabary over the Roman type forms the missionaries were advocating.[18] In 1828, the newly established Cherokee Constitution

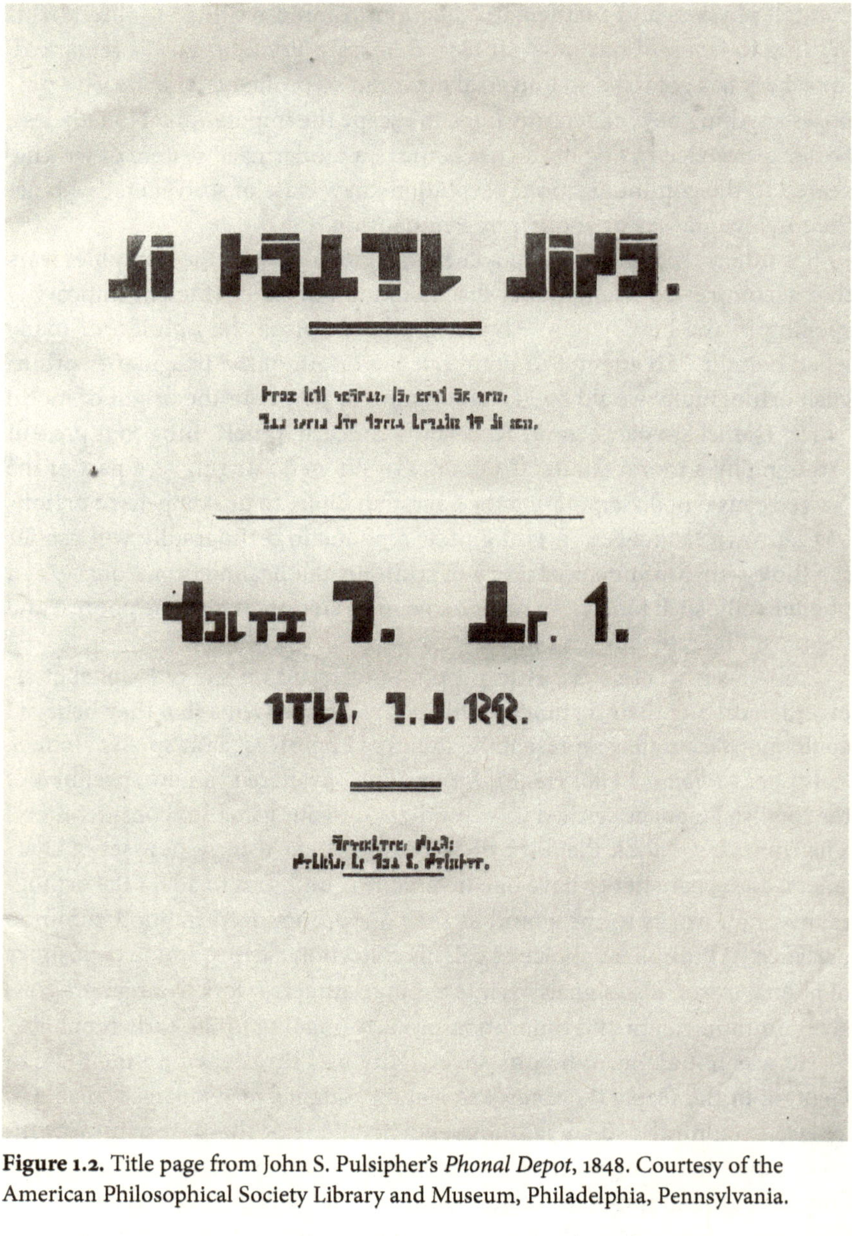

Figure 1.2. Title page from John S. Pulsipher's *Phonal Depot*, 1848. Courtesy of the American Philosophical Society Library and Museum, Philadelphia, Pennsylvania.

mandated the syllabary's use in government publications. To most Cherokees, Sequoyah's updating of the old graphic system embodied a new, literate Cherokee nationalism. To white missionaries, the syllabary initially also smacked of "witchcraft," and they forbade its use precisely because it was native and associated with traditional medicine practices that threatened their evangelization projects. Cherokee medicine people were the most fervent users of the syllabary in the 1820s. Many kept personal manuscript notebooks filled with formulas and ceremonial practices frowned upon by white Christians.[19]

The Sequoyah syllabary became a print culture medium in 1828, when the Cherokee Nation and the American Board of Commissioners for Foreign Missions (ABCFM) joined forces to raise money to have special types cast at a foundry in New England. In this print manifestation, the Sequoyah syllabary took on a distinctly nationalist tenor. The Cherokee tribal council "made the move to obtain a printing press and types in the Sequoyah syllabary and to establish a national academy" before its Constitution was even ratified.[20] Despite its unique roots in a Native-produced syllabary and nationalist movement, however, the actual running of the Cherokee Nation press, like missionary counterparts throughout Indian Country, required the bicultural cooperation of American missionaries and Native converts. David Brown, a Cherokee convert, had completed a manuscript translation of the New Testament into the Cherokee syllabary in 1825. In 1828, transplanted New England minister Samuel A. Worcester became one of the founders of the *Cherokee Phoenix*, the first *national* Indian newspaper. Yet the syllabary, even in this missionary-sponsored print form, never lost its semiotic value to everyday Cherokees as a sign of national identity.

This success did not go unnoticed in the settler public sphere. The Mormons, upon their arrival in Utah in 1847, worked quickly to establish a settler state distinct from that of the United States, which they called Deseret. The logic of the Mormon social experiment employed concepts of popular sovereignty and cultural nationalism that were then circulating in the United States, albeit to achieve distinctly nonfederal goals. Deseret would be a state in no union, but rather an independent republic of believers. Like the Americans of the early republic, the Mormons sought a new alphabet to express their new kind of society. Known as the Deseret Alphabet, it was actually a form of syllabary mandated by Brigham Young in 1853. Young assigned the task of its creation to English-born convert George D. Watt. Watt, who had studied with Isaac Pitman in England, proposed an orthography based in simple phonetics and formed of nonalphabetic characters. Between 1853 and 1854, he devised a thirty-two-character syllabary whose implementation briefly created a uniquely Mormon print culture, with type punches being made in Salt Lake in

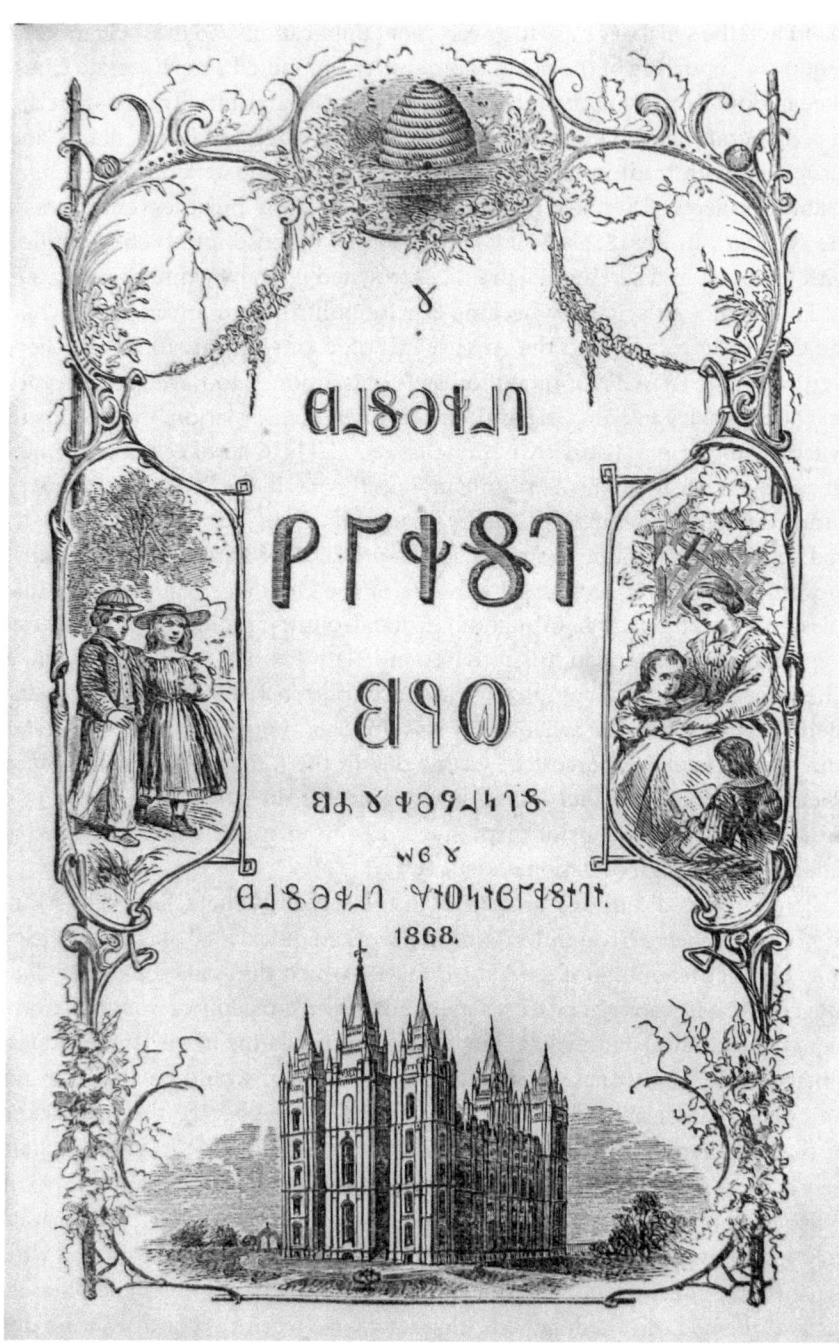

Figure 1.3. Title page from the *Deseret Primer*, 1868. Courtesy of the Huntington Library, San Marino, California.

1855. Watt drew some of his inspiration from the Cherokee Nation's syllabary, which he had read about in the *American Annals of Education* in 1832. There, he had learned of a people who had discovered that "so few syllabic characters are sufficient to write a language, and that, in a manner vastly more perfect than the English language is written by the Roman Alphabet of letters."[21]

For the Mormon settlers, this new alphabet would serve several functions. First, it would establish a culturally distinct form of Mormon media. Second, it would facilitate community formation by offering a simplified spelling system that immigrants and non-native English speakers, who were expected to fill out the ranks of the faithful through extensive missionizing, could quickly learn and easily share. In 1859, the Gospel of Matthew appeared in syllabary form in the *Deseret News*. Books in the syllabary, including an all-important primer for Mormon children, were also printed directly from relief types or from stereotyped plates. When Brigham Young died in 1877, the Deseret Alphabet fell out of use.[22] Eventually, the republic of Latter-day Saints acquiesced to becoming Utah, the forty-fifth of the United States. A special spelling system was no longer needed. The Cherokee syllabary, on the other hand, is used to this day—and the Cherokee Nation remains a sovereign entity, dealt with on nation-to-nation terms by the federal government within the United States of America.

ORTHOGRAPHIES OF EMPIRE

Apart from these two famous examples of syllabary writing put to nationalist purposes by distinct counterpublics within the American state, writing in the Roman alphabet remained the norm for the expression of citizenship in the United States. Thus, alphabeticism became integral to the "civilizing process" that the settler state attempted to impose upon the Indigenous peoples of America. Across the country in the 1830s, intellectuals were hard at work devising alphabets for the more than 100 Native languages still being spoken, before, as one ethnographer put it, "they were gone."

From Columbus's first letter describing the New World, in which he blithely translated the Native people's greeting ("Come, come and see the celestial people") without much possibility of having understood them, Europeans had been collecting and transcribing the vernacular languages of the Americas.[23] At first, these efforts amounted to little more than vocabulary lists that served as "vade mecums for the trader and traveler," or autobiographical accounts of missionaries in the earliest stages of learning a Native tongue. By the seventeenth century, vocabularies had become a conventional feature of printed travel and missionary narratives, functioning as "authenticating and decorative devices." Works like William Wood's *New England's Prospect* (1630) and Roger Williams's *A Key into the Language of America* (1647) featured glossaries of Southern New England Algonquian words along with short dialogs. Because, as Laura Murray has explained, a "vocabulary is a more idiosyncratic and culturally evocative linguistic genre than the dictionary or grammar," they enacted "dramas of encounters with strangeness," while simultaneously serving as spaces for "preservation of loose ends of live talk" that constituted colonial relations in the Western Hemisphere.[24] In the European colonization of the New World, then, Indigenous vernacular inscription found itself at the nexus of trade and missionization, and thus mediated the complex (and seemingly oxymoronic) formula of Christian empire articulated in 1622 by Plymouth governor Edward Winslow: "Religion and Profit jump together."[25]

When North America came under the purview of a new settler political entity called the United States, European colonial expansion took the form of settler colonialism, a distinctive and different kind of imperial activity than the extractive colonialism of the English in India or the Belgians and Germans in Africa. For the purposes of this study, settler colonialism may be defined as a form of European expansion focused on establishing permanent settlements of peoples of European descent in the Western Hemisphere. These settlers then asserted political dominance over Indigenous peoples by developing elaborate political and economic infrastructures to directly ensure their subjugation. Their efforts were aided by an inherent centrifugal force endemic to settler colonialism that encouraged colonies to declare independence from the metropolis based on claims of the autochthonous roots of their new "vernacular" societies. These societies, in turn, managed the social heterogeneity endemic to squatting in Indigenous spaces through complex hierarchical discourses of class, ethnicity, and race.

There are several ways that recognizing settler colonialism as a "structure, not an event"—the now-famous formulation that Patrick Wolfe once coined to accentuate its difference from other "colonial" theory methodologies—is critical to any interpretation of Native American historiography.[26] First and foremost, settler colonialism was preoccupied with the appropriation of Indigenous land. Unlike extractive colonialism, which sought to wrest resources from the colony that the metropolis could then "refine," settler colonialism was based on the accumulation of real property. The second element of settler colonialism, the construction of a discourse of elimination, follows closely from the first. Land would be taken only from those who had not improved it, or who had "disappeared" from it. Hence, the infamous trope of the vanishing Indian that has animated US literature and history since at least the time of James Fenimore Cooper. Taking land from the "last" of the Mohicans was not really taking land at all. When Alexis de Tocqueville recounted the achievements of the US settler society in 1832, he could do so only after inscribing and then erasing a "savage" Indigenous presence: "Although the vast country which we have been describing was inhabited by many indigenous tribes, it may justly be said at the time of its discovery by Europeans to have formed one great desert. The Indians occupied without possessing it. It is by agricultural labor that man appropriates the soil, and the early inhabitants of North America lived by the produce of the chase. Their implacable prejudices, their uncontrolled passions, their vices, and still more perhaps their savage virtues, consigned them to inevitable destruction."[27]

Finally, settler colonialism is a historic formation that remains in place to this day, thus rendering a history of its unfolding as relevant now as it was in the nineteenth century, especially to the many Native nations that still live colonized lives within the borders of the United States and Canada. With this conceptualization of US colonial rule in mind, it becomes obvious why "even after the Indian wars had ended, . . . the government still acted upon the logic of elimination in its unceasing attempt to gain more Indian land, . . . [and that] a wide variety of Americans supported [and continue to support] this policy, from idealistic reformers . . . to land-hungry squatters."[28]

By locating "conflicts between American Indians and incoming settlers [at] the *very center* of American history,"[29] the settler colonial model, like the media concept I described in the introduction, presents a unique point of entry for its reinterpretation. Settler colonialism offers us not only a clearer understanding of Native people's colonial worlds (and thus, of their agency in historical events) but also a clearer understanding of the social practices that settlers employed to shape the terms of their invasion. Settler colonists, for example, proposed and promulgated a story in which non-Indian "Mound Builders" had fashioned the amazing earthworks they encountered in the Ohio and Mississippi River valleys, only to die off mysteriously, leaving the ruins of their civilization and the remnant cast-off peoples they now called "Indians." Euro-Americans also elaborated what has come to be known as Manifest Destiny and other subnarratives that structured a discourse of elimination that enabled the dispossession of Native peoples. Ojibwe scholar Jeanie O'Brien has explored how the establishment of a specialized genre of settler local history contributed to the erasure of the Native presence in nineteenth-century New England by mobilizing narratives that commemorated the settler past and diminished the continued presence of Indigenous peoples in the region.[30] Robert Gunn has similarly employed the settler colonial model to tease out how "speech acts organize and distinguish parallel projects of racial classification" in nineteenth-century US ethnographic and exploration texts that sought to describe the borderlands to settler readers unfamiliar with the nation's new acquisition in the Southwest. In these texts, Gunn shows clearly that by the 1850s "American romantic personhood was already mapped onto the emotional cartography of manifest destiny."[31] In all of Gunn's examples, "race" as a conceptual category figured prominently in the discursive mix.

However, as Wolfe himself acknowledged in "Land, Labor, and Difference," racial discourse is not the only discourse that helped settlers structure the "various regimes of difference" that they employed in their efforts to "disappear" the Indians.[32] Educational discourses surrounding literacy and citizenship also inflected both settlers' framing of Native expressions/utterances and Indigenous writers' own understanding of how literacy might enable community cohesion in a time of violent displacement and dispossession. Over the course of the nineteenth century, Native peoples, alphabetic literacy, manuscript texts and print came to occupy an important nexus in the symbolic economy of this discourse of erasure. For our study of vernacular scripts and the role they played in nineteenth-century Indigenous nation formation, it is important to unpack the specific set of tropes and techniques that enabled a subdiscourse within the broader settler colonial regimes of "disappearance" and "erasure." I will call that discourse the discourse of *people without letters*. In the concurring opinion written by Supreme Court justice McLean as part of *Worcester v. Georgia* (1830), the jurist presents its archetypal expression:

> The language used in treaties with the Indians should never be construed to their prejudice. If words be made use of which are susceptible of a more extended meaning than their plain import, as connected with the tenor of the treaty, they should be considered as used only in the latter sense. To contend that the word "allotted," in reference to the land guaranteed to the Indians in certain treaties, indicates a favour conferred, rather than a right acknowledged, would, it would seem to me, do injustice to the understanding of the parties. How the words of the treaty were understood by this unlettered people, rather than their critical meaning, should form the rule of construction.

It was also an essential part of the discourse of missionization. When Christian philanthropists imagined the audience for their tracts and Bibles, they often succumbed to reveries about "the instruction, comfort, and encouragement which these writings are so well calculated to afford," and how they might "find their way into the log-hut of the backwoodsman, to the negro in his bondage, to the Indian in his expatriation."[33]

Quite often, the question whether Native people had literature provoked musings on their letterlessness. When, for example, Silas Rand, missionary to the Mi'kmaqs, attempted to explain the role of literacy in his project of missionization, he found himself discussing things like "literature" and the "imagination":

> What can be meant, it may be asked, by the Literature of the Micmacs. We have been in the habit of looking upon them as miserable, ignorant, stupid looking beings. We have been aware that there have never been, to any extent, schools established among them, and that no effort, except on the smallest scale, has been made by the whites, to teach them. We have treated them almost as though they had no rights, and as if it were somewhat doubtful whether they even have souls. And have they a Literature? By what effort of imagination can it be made out? And truly the term must be taken with some restriction in its meaning. They possess, however, some knowledge of the Arts and Sciences.[34]

Educators and policy makers also participated in the discourse of peoples without letters. Caleb Atwater, US congressman, amateur archaeologist, and historian of Ohio, mused on the ruins of Mississippian cities in his state and immediately thought of the people's "letterless" existence: "Their authors were rude, and unacquainted with the use of letters, yet they raised monuments calculated almost for endless duration, and speaking a language as expressive as the most studied inscriptions of later times upon brass and marble. These monuments, their stated anniversaries and traditionary accounts, were their means of perpetuating the recollection of important transactions. Their authors are gone; their monuments remain: But the events which they were intended to keep in the memory, are lost in oblivion."[35]

US print culture incorporated this discourse of letterless peoples into its own justification for being. Consider the lithograph from the 1871 publication, *American Encyclopaedia of Print* (fig. 1.4). Along with the enslaved African kneeling in the left foreground, a generic "Indian" surrenders her arrows before the power and light of the printing press. As both subjects *of* the sensational visual culture of illustrated weeklies and subject *to* the "civilizing" and missionary efforts of printers, Indigenous Americans found themselves crowded into the margins in such print versions of settler erasure fantasies.

Throughout the period, Euro-American media thrived on images of imagined Native peoples who could be easily "removed" as obstacles from the progress of the settler state. Printer's catalogs routinely included variously sized and detailed images of generic "Indians" alongside their manicules and rules. As Shari Huhndorf has observed, this was because "racial ideologies rely on the legibility of the body," and in nineteenth-century America, the

Figure 1.4. "And God said, Let there be light." Frontispiece from Ringwalt, *American Encyclopaedia of Printing*.

bodies most important to colonization were those of American Indians. The logic of elimination here is embodied in the domestication of the "savage" body, its reproducibility and off-hand usage suggesting the disappearance of real Indigenous peoples and their powerlessness against the colonizers.[36]

US settler expansion in North America coincided with a revolution in communications technologies in which the discourse of letterless peoples played its part. This overlap was not coincidental. The republican discourse of the new nation would demand, Thomas Jefferson said, a "more General Diffusion of Knowledge." From 1800 onward, the United States pursued a project of "internal improvements," the enhanced transport of goods and information being linked to the ideal of a "more perfect union." In 1808, Secretary of the Treasury Albert Gallatin submitted a report to Congress that outlined the centrality of infrastructure to the free circulation of peace and liberty:

> The inconveniencies, complaints, and perhaps dangers, which may result from a vast extent of territory, can no otherwise be radically removed, or prevented, than by opening speedy and easy communications through all its parts. Good roads and canals, will shorten distances, facilitate commercial and personal intercourse, and unite by a still more intimate community of interests, the most remote quarters of the United States. No other

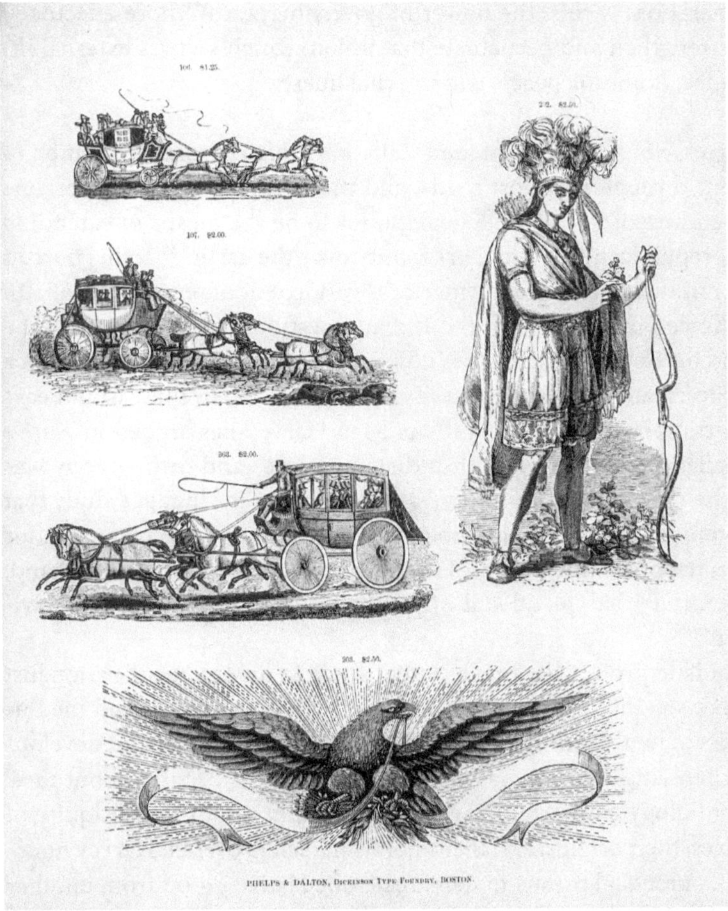

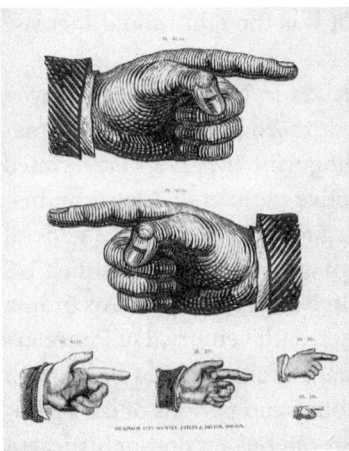

Figure 1.5. Pages from *The General Specimen Book of the Dickinson Type Foundry: Comprising types for letter-press printing of every variety [. . .]* (Boston: Phelps and Dalton, 1856). Courtesy of the Huntington Library, San Marino, California.

single operation, within the power of government, can more effectually tend to strengthen and perpetuate that union, which secures external independence, domestic peace, and internal liberty.[37]

Many "progressive" Americans shared Gallatin's dream of total unification of the continent through rail, post roads, and the telegraph. Of the latter, one nationalist enthused: "This noble invention is to be the means of extending civilization, republicanism, and Christianity over the earth."[38] In his pursuit of better communication across America's "vast extent of territory," Gallatin had little choice but to confront the Indian question. In his retirement, he would spend his time cataloging the Indigenous languages of North America in an effort to create a system of classifying Native peoples that "would ease the administration of colonialism."[39] As Sean Harvey has argued in *Native Tongues*, Gallatin's fascination with Indian languages and orthography was integral to the rise of "New Philology," a methodology in language study that moved beyond word lists and etymologies to examine Native languages for evidence, on the one hand, of Indo-European ancestry, or on the other hand, of "a 'savage mind' [that] justified the hypothetically temporary rule of a 'civilized empire.'"[40]

This linguistic project became a potent force in an emergent nationalist discourse that sought to forge a link between Native Americans and the European settler state though recourse to histories of the origins and development of Indian languages. It was at the center of most debates about race. Although philology supported contradictory claims about the antiquity of Native peoples, their origins, and their moral characters overall, Harvey notes, it "provided a practical means to demarcate one Native group from another and establish which had the authority to cede land." It also served as the framework for "an education program, that, it was thought, would increase the assimilation of Native peoples."[41]

Pierre Du Ponceau, a critical mover and shaker in New Philology, played a pivotal role in securing its participation in the discourses of nation formation and westward expansion by employing linguistic theories that elevated Indian eloquence to "nobility." During disruptive periods of American history like the War of 1812, however, Harvey argues that there was a general turning away from etymology in favor of language theories that justified US expansion as civilizing the savagery inherent in Native languages. According to Harvey, throughout the first half of the nineteenth century, Du Ponceau's celebration of the complexity of Native language grammars did battle with such opposing views during shifts in Indian policy and periods of land grabbing. If Du Ponceau's grammar-based philology offered a more sophisticated

Figure 1.6. Albert Gallatin, *Map of the Indian Tribes of North America about 1600 A.D. along the Atlantic; & about 1800 A.D. Westwardly*, 1836. Courtesy of Rare Books Division, New York Public Library, New York.

and nuanced view of Native peoples than did the etymological studies of the past, it did so in a polarized cultural field where would-be philologists seized on it as proof of the Indians' civilizing potential, while apologists for Indian Removal embraced it as evidence of the Indigenous communities' fundamental and alien "difference."

Yet even as the settlers struggled with Indigenous sounds and communication, they were enjoying a transformation in communications technologies that would have global reach. Daniel Walker Howe, in his Pulitzer Prize–winning history of the period, *What Hath God Wrought*, argues that it was information exchange, "rather than the continued growth of the market economy," that proved to be the most salient feature of the period. "During the thirty-three years that began in 1815," Howe observes, "there would be greater strides in the improvement of communication than had taken place in all the previous centuries."[42] Beginning with the invention of the telegraph, the country witnessed the deployment of a transatlantic transmission cable and coast-to-coast railroads and postal networks as well as, by century's end, the gradual implementation of the telephone. Itinerant hawkers gave way to organized battalions of colporteurs, whose solicitation and circulation of books in the hinterlands was managed by major print centers in Cincinnati, Ohio, and Lexington, Kentucky. Electrotype printing of images and stereotype plates (reusable and cheap) and steam printing presses soon completely transformed the circulation of print in America.

The same was true of Christian missionization in the period. Like Gallatin's philology, Christianization projects and settler colonialism were united by similar long-term goals; the one aided and abetted the other. For most Euro-Americans, extending civilization and Christianity entailed removing an "impediment" in the form of the Native peoples of the continent. This raw doctrine of removal was, however, supported by a curious ideological foundation that, as Vine Deloria Jr. noted in *God Is Red*, would exacerbate the stark "contrast between Christianity and its interpretation of history—the temporal dimension—and the American Indian tribal religions—basically spatially located." Where Indigenous peoples looked out on a landscape of "sacred mountains, sacred hills, sacred rivers, and other geographical features sacred to Indian tribes," Europeans saw "millions of free acres . . . at 6 per ct. interest and low prices."[43]

Communication was essential to the process of unifying the colonial occupation of Indian lands, and settler Americans understood it to be primarily a function of speed and distance. Efficiency, rather than clarity or tradition, were the hallmarks of this ideology. As one British visitor to America commented in 1852, "Fast, seems the talismanic word. They eat, drink, work, speak, walk, and think, fast. Their visits are short, so are their sermons."[44] Beyond mere speed, however, Americans sought to dominate both space and time. The settler colonial project, so closely linked to Christian millenarianism, was itself an ongoing space-time experiment. Its goal was to reduce the two into a single, manageable continuum. This idea lies at the heart of the phrase John L. O'Sullivan coined in 1839 to describe the colonization of the west, "Manifest Destiny." Destiny is teleological. It is "manifest" in the land itself, broken into 160-acre parcels for the use of the invaders. Within this undertaking, settlers were deeply invested in reducing the time it took to do everything. The railroad and telegram served as forms of spatial "shorthand." Through them, settlers elided the reality of place with all its quotidian features in favor of a universalizing abstraction called time. With railroads and the establishment of a national postal system, settlers began to realize what Bernhard Siegert calls "the homogenization of space."[45]

Over time, settler colonists began to argue that the study of Indigenous languages was also necessary because the colonial conquest of the West required the accurate and uniform reproduction of the myriad Indian tongues American adventurers encountered. Without an understanding of these idioms, negotiation and treaty writing, integral to colonial expansion, could not go forward. Traders studied Native languages simply "to carry on sufficient conversation with our Indian neighbors to make a bargain without the aid of an interpreter." With Lewis and Clark's foray west in 1804–6, the governmental and scientific communities involved in western exploration began to formulate uniform guidelines for the collection of data—geological, topographical, demographic, and linguistic. In fact, both explorers carried with them printed word lists that they used to elicit Native equivalents from people they met along the way. These were lost, but the practice continued over the century, with greater and greater refinements of the kinds of words and orthographies used. By the time the word lists were officially written into the westward expansion of the United States through the auspices of Thomas Jefferson, they had assumed an Enlightenment rationalistic hubris, suggesting "that language is a code that can be broken," and that the strange, Indigenous encryptions such vocabularies cataloged could be rendered impotent once "the list of equivalences ha[d] been established."[46] Yet, as Sarah Rivett has shown, even Jefferson's empiricism ultimately failed to metaphorically remove the Indian from the land by removing the land from Indigenous languages: "The intrinsic link between indigenous land and the land could not be severed." Ultimately, Rivett argues, "Indigenous speakers thwarted Jefferson's desire for uniformity" and New Philologists' efforts to locate Native utterance forever in a "primitive past."[47]

Still, the rationalist ideal persisted well into the nineteenth century. In 1836, Pierre Du Ponceau, in his capacity as the American Philosophical Society's language collection expert, wrote a letter to the secretary of the navy, urging the Wilkes Expedition to the South Sea to elicit a version of the Lord's Prayer in every Native language they encountered. Not only was this text, in Du Ponceau's estimation, the "best in a grammatical point of view," it was also one "which philologists have chosen since time immemorial . . . [and] because it is easiest obtained from missionaries."[48] Here, indeed, "religion and profit jump together." Du Ponceau's vision, however, would be much harder to realize than it first seemed.

INDIAN ALPHABETS

The major difficulty with Du Ponceau's scheme, of course, was that few if any of these South Sea languages had writing systems European explorers could recognize or be able to use to record them. Therefore, many nineteenth-century missionaries and most adventurers relied on a phonetic orthographic system developed by philologist John Pickering in 1820. Pickering's *Essay on a Uniform Orthography* mingles nationalism with orthographic simplification to serve "the more practical purpose of possessing the means of communicating with the various tribes of our borders, either with a view to the common concerns of life or the diffusion of the principles of our religion." This service "is peculiarly within the province of American scholars, and will richly reward us in the honour we shall acquire in Europe." Accompanying this pride in nation is a lament for the "devoted race of men, ... who have been stripped of almost every fragment of their paternal inheritance except their language."[49]

As an act of salvage anthropology and a useful tool in rationalizing the reproduction and transcription of languages more generally, Pickering's book attempts to remedy a situation in which the "capricious and ever varying orthography of the Indian languages" had rendered many early word lists useless for real linguistic study. In Pickering's frustrated view, "Every man, however little qualified, think[s] himself adequate to the task of inventing new characters." His solution was to "ascertain, in the first place, every elementary sound, and then arrange the letters, by which we may choose to represent those sounds, in the order of our own alphabet." Thus, Native languages could be "reduced" to written form. The one caveat Pickering offers is that this alphabet should assume the vowel sounds of "foreign" European languages because they are "more consistent and match the Roman alphabet better than English."[50]

After the Civil War, J. Hammond Trumbull, an expert on the Southern New England Algonquian dialect, published *On the Best Method of Studying the American Languages* (1871) as an update to Pickering. Trumbull based his recommendations for change on a survey of his predecessors' methods of language collection, lamenting, "Collectors and editors have impaired the value of their materials by endeavoring to fashion them into an English pattern." Signaling the end of an ethnographic era dominated by vocabularies and word lists, Trumbull exclaims, "The real work of the linguistic scholar begins where the provisional labors of the word-collector end." There was little point in making word lists, he argues, and even less utility in trying to equate Indian languages with Indo-European cognates. "The American languages," Trumbull reasoned, "differ from the Indo-European both in grammatical structure and their plan of thought," and it was "nearly impossible to translate *any* Indian name or verb by an English name or verb, and the converse."⁵¹ While English was an "analytical" language, North American Indigenous idioms were "synthetic"; that is, they required the cobbling together of a whole host of Native nouns, verbs, and modes to signify expressions that were culturally distinct to Europeans.

Using John Eliot's attempt to translate the English word "kneeling" into Southern New England Algonquian for his Indian Bible as an example, Trumbull showed that because "the Algonquian word needs to have the verb for folding legs down and for supplication in it," it took Eliot "eleven syllables . . . for [an] accurate interpretation of eight or ten English words." That is, when printed, the Bible in Algonquian presented its reader with a formidable wall of type with few word breaks, and the long chains of multisyllabic "words" taxed missionaries with the daunting task of pronunciation without any real sense of the syllables' accents and rhythms.⁵² Instead of this syllabic literalism, Trumbull called for something "more than mere translation." Indian languages would have to be "taken to pieces" and "studied [at the] root." In a significant departure from past linguists in America, Trumbull's proposed methodology recognized language change as part of the nature of language itself. It would be "thoroughly 'self-defining,'" drawing on "tradition, society and literature, to maintain words which can no longer be analyzed at once."⁵³

In 1877, John Wesley Powell, leader of the famed US expedition that explored the Colorado River, took charge of the newly formed Bureau of Ethnology and promptly released a circular publication designed to centralize and standardize the transcription of Native languages along the lines that Pickering and Trumbull described. However, Powell remained wedded to the ethnocentric notion that the Roman alphabet (especially as used to transcribe the English language) would be best for this task. "By frequently and carefully comparing the sounds of an Indian tongue with the known sounds of his own language," Powell reasoned, "the alphabet of his language will become the basis of the one used in writing the Indian language."⁵⁴ To Powell the logic of this was obvious: "First, it is the alphabet with which the greater part of the civilized people of the world are acquainted . . . it is used in all printing rooms where the English tongue is spoken, and in very many others; and if a new tongue is written in these characters it can be reproduced without difficulty in almost any printing office of the civilized world."⁵⁵

By not requiring a new type (as with the Cherokee syllabary), and by avoiding the use of "diacritical marks as are not usually found in printing offices," Powell could produce alphabetic transcriptions that were cheap, practical, and uniform. While admitting that "the English language itself is burdened with a barbaric orthography," Powell believed that employing the Roman alphabet so "each sound . . . [had] a letter of its own, each character . . . represent[ing] only one sound," all variations in Indigenous languages could be recorded.[56]

Powell's alphabet was essentially phonetic, based on the widely held belief in the 1870s that transcriptions were intended to record sounds in such a way as to indicate how "they are made by the organs of speech in positions and with movements." By contrast, Trumbull had called for transcribing Indigenous languages "at their root, . . . drawing on tradition, society and literature." In a gesture toward this, Powell cautioned, "Care should be taken to obtain words from the Indians themselves. Indians speaking English can be found in almost every tribe within the U.S." Vocabulary "cannot be obtained accurately from white men who are supposed to speak the Indian tongue," Powell continued, "because . . . the general method of communication between white men and Indians is by conventional jargon, composed of corrupted Indian and English words, with many words from other European tongues."[57] Powell thus wisely sought the assistance of bilingual collaborators drawn from local Indigenous communities. Euro-American translators were notoriously suspect, and even missionaries with "scholarly knowledge" had to be screened for the effectiveness of their language skills. Powell's plan revealingly calls all these linguistic informants "collectors," thus marking their activities as contiguous with the larger colonial project of the appropriation of resources and land at the center of the settler colonial project.

COMMUNICATIONS CIRCUITS

The process by which the United States attempted the alphabetization of Indian Country was two-fold. First came the development of a special sector of the English (and eventually, American) book trade dedicated to missionizing Indian peoples. This was supplemented by an extensive print culture devoted to the production of treaties and land tenure documents. By 1824, with the establishment of the Bureau of Indian Affairs (BIA), there was an equally substantial body of printed blanks available to facilitate the bureaucratization of Indian Country. Finally, with the emergence of the common school movement, which swept across urban and rural Euro-American communities in the 1830s, a large body of English-language (and some Native vernacular) textbooks became a systematic element of the "civilizing process" (what Richard Pratt called education's "citizenizing influence upon the Indians") for American Indian pupils.

The alphabetization of citizenship would not have been possible without the sophisticated US communications circuit that was already well established by 1830. The standard history of the English book trade in America, the five-volume *History of the Book in America* has provided scholars with a sound foundation for the exploration of dominant-culture communications circuits and their role in colonial cultural development. Its editors define the "colonial book" as "what the colonists bought and read, as well as what they printed or reprinted," maintaining that these activities were "structurally interrelated with the book trades of western Europe." While avowing a structural and Eurocentric focus, the volumes argue for improved histories "of reading and writing, and of efforts to regulate readers and writers."[58]

But the broad outlines of the print circuits it describes must be overlaid with another set of transmission pathways, ones forged by Africans and Native American peoples, colonial and US diplomats, and Christian missionary societies. American demography, skewed toward a high number of semi-illiterate and unconverted Africans and Native Americans, drove the expansion of a submarket for evangelical and missionary print much faster than in England. This, coupled with the uneasy relationship of the thirteen American states with the colonial dominions of France, Spain, and England that hemmed them in on all sides, also drove a peculiar manuscript and print distribution system centered on diplomacy. Like the missionary system, this one relied on Native Americans as mediators and as producers and consumers of texts across the backcountry and borderlands.

The missionary print trade involved books specially targeted at Africans and Indians, and it developed a unique hybrid system of patronage and market capitalism to deliver these productions into the hands of prospective readers in America. When he was baptized in London in February 1759, the enslaved African Olaudah Equiano received a gift book that was typical of the genre: Bishop Thomas Wilson's *An Essay Towards an Instruction of the Indians*. Its preface proclaimed the tract suitable for both "the Indians . . . a tractable People" and the "Hottentots, who are supposed to be the dullest of Mankind."[59] The Society for the Propagation of the Gospel (SPG) had perfected a system for "the dispersing of [books]," signing up "Corresponding Members," who were "intitled [sic] to have a Supply of [books], to be disposed of among such of the Neighbouring Clergy or Laity as desire them." They offered these to members "at the prime Cost in *Quires*, . . . [and] Stich'd Books, at one *Half* of the Price there set down, as the prime Cost of each."[60] Wilson's language here reflects the mercantile side of book publishing and distribution so well documented in *A History of the Book in America*. But it is especially interesting in the way that it imagines a kind of evangelical instrumentality for this otherwise neutral business apparatus.

Mohegan missionary Samson Occom viewed his peripheral location within the British mercantile system to be an integral part of the trouble he was having in crafting an intertribal Christian Indian community woven together using tracts such as Bishop Wilson describes. Writing to Benjamin Forfitt in England, Occom explains, "I live near a Center of five Towns of Indians and they come to me for books—We used to be supplyd in Some measure with Books from Dr. Wheelock's Indian School, but he is now removed with his school far up into the County to the distance of 150 miles; and Boston and New York are a great distance from us."[61] Occom's journals (1743–90) are punctuated with commentary related to themes of time and distance, itinerancy and marginality, that jeopardize his relation to the dominant communications circuits. Clearly, the print centers that served the rural Anglo-American public were not sufficient for the needs of Native Americans.

In response, missionaries and Native and Black congregants developed ways to extend the English book trade proper, relying on what Robert Warrior (Osage) has called "intellectual trade routes" of intercultural exchange through Native space. Media of all kinds flowed along woodland information networks that had existed long before contact. From Montauk villages on Long Island to Mohegan towns in Connecticut, Narragansett settlements in Rhode Island, and on up the Connecticut River valley to Deerfield and Stockbridge, prayer books, treaties, and hymnals made their way from print centers to the seaboard interior before turning west to the upper Ohio River, where Mohawk and Oneida communities staked claim to the western "door" of the Iroquois Confederacy.[62]

Books were exchanged and writing was debated in geographical and political hubs that emerged at critical nodes in the interface between British (later, American) colonial administration, Native space, and the Black Atlantic. Much like the coffee houses, bookshops and taverns that supported the Anglo-American public sphere along the Eastern Seaboard, places like Buffalo Creek in New York, Detroit, the Ohio River valley, and (by the 1830s) New Echota, Georgia, and the Shawanoe Mission in Kansas, became communication hubs that intertwined print and colonial policy. Yet importantly, they remained (as Richard White has reminded us) profoundly "non-state world[s]," where the traditional council ground in the woods, or a kitchen table in a Native cabin or slave quarters, might serve just as well as the center of written sociability as the salon of the colonies' urban centers.[63]

Diplomacy also drove the circulation of books in the colonies and the new republic, but the logic of its circulation networks differed considerably. While print and manuscript texts had served governance since the founding of the Massachusetts Bay Colony, during the eighteenth century, relations between Native peoples and non-Indian allies were increasingly mediated by alphabetic texts. Historian Colin Calloway explains how treaties "functioned as steppingstones of empire. They allowed colonists to establish a foothold ..., colonies to expand their domains, and the United States to march westward." Between 1776 and 1871 (when the US Congress abrogated all treaties), some 400 agreements had been drawn up between Europeans and Native in America.[64] These took their respective places in print culture, occupying a small niche in an eighteenth-century American book market in which government publications accounted for 6 percent of local printing.[65]

Calloway describes how Indian negotiators soon grasped the power of the written version of their diplomacy and began to demand their own clerks for recording the transactions they engaged in. As early as 1756, the Cherokees employed the colonial British diplomat Henry Timberlake as a scribe for many of their policy-making assemblies. In his journal, Timberlake recalls, "[The] Indian senate, indeed, would sometimes employ me in reading and writing letters for them; of which I generally acquitted myself to their satisfaction."[66] When treaties and agreements were put to paper, hybrid forms of inscription indicated the many levels of acquiescence implied by the document. Take, for example, the agreement between the Canadian government and the Nishinaabe on a cession of land at North Bay in 1795 (fig. 1.7). Notice the several layers of signification involved here, especially the visual qualities of these signs. Like many Indian treaties, this one reads in several registers: alphabetic script, pictographic signs, and even (deep within the paper fibers) a reminder of the imperial enterprise in the form of a watermark featuring the crown of England. As Scott Lyons has observed of scribal acts such as this: "While one text might be called 'the oral tradition' and the other text denigrated as 'the white man's way,' the fact of the matter is: both are texts. As texts, they must be inscribed, signed, given an x-mark signifying consent to some way of life."[67]

By 1783, print and manuscript circulation served as a form of virtual *representation* as the United States sought to forge an "extensive republic" across the vast continent. Manuscripts written and dictated by Native diplomats in the interior were sent by messenger or post to printers in the east and "refined" into codices and broadsides. Their distribution soon functioned to lead Americans "to believe that humanitarian concerns about Indians had been resolved, especially by disseminating the literary portrayal of the vanishing Indian."[68] Once formed into an official manuscript and signed, these scribal publications made their way back from Indian Country to the print centers of the Eastern Seaboard. There, the manuscripts were set into type and printed to government specifications. Over time, they took on genre conventions that signaled their special place in colonial American book markets. Lisa Brooks, quoting Carl Van Doren, has suggested that they were a popular form of on the part of his Majesty Ratify and confirm all the articles subscribed the last April not excepted therein, and promises that the same shall be strictly observed, as well with regard to the punishment of Offenders as concerning the enjoyment of all their Rights, Privileges and Possess[ions]

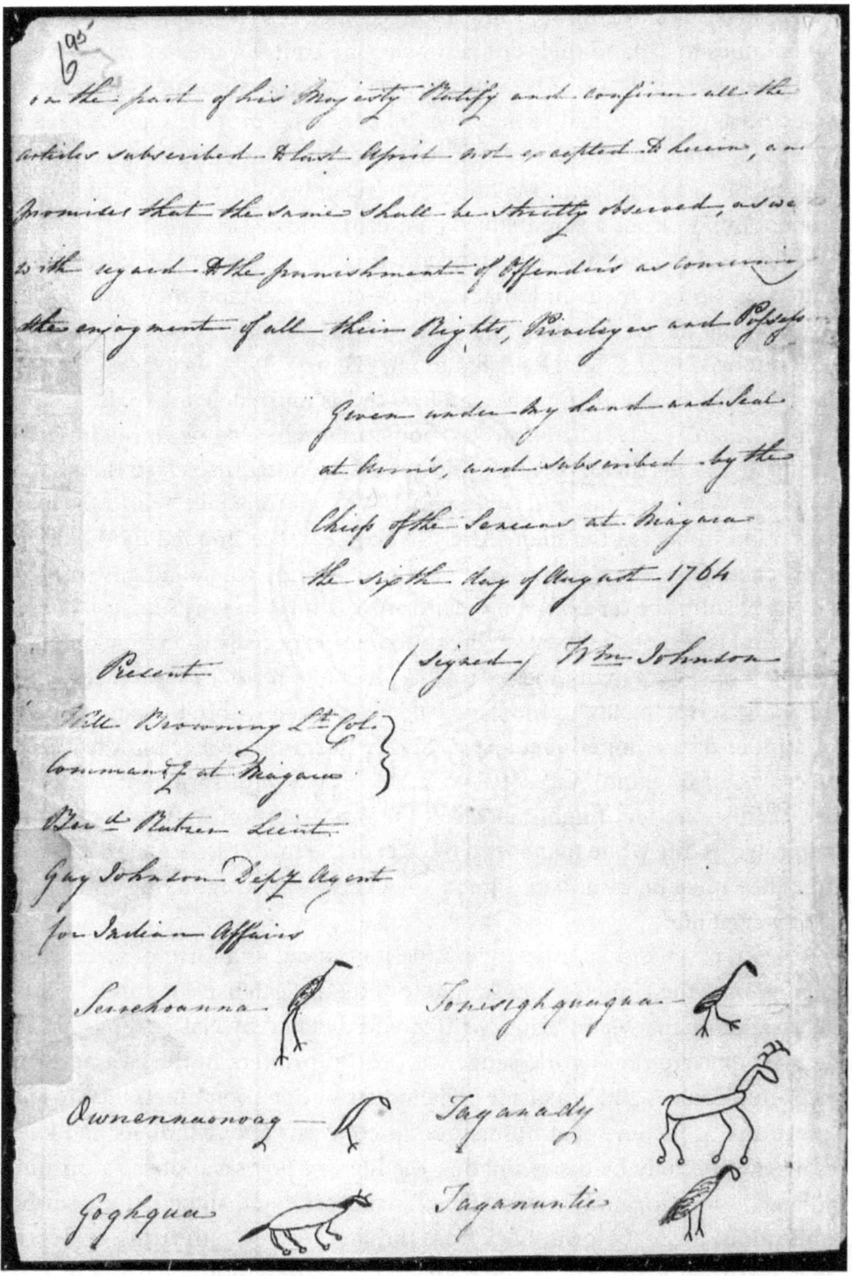

        Given under my hand and Seal at Ninvis, and subscribed by the Chief of the Senecas at Niagara the sixth day of August 1764

        (Signed) Wm Johnson

Present
Will Browning Lt Col.
Command'g at Niagara
Ben'd Ratzer Lieut
Guy Johnson Depy Agent
for Indian Affairs

Senechoanna
Ownennaonoag
Goghqua

Tonieghquagua
Taganady
Taganuntie

Figure 1.7. Surrender by Chippewas of the Land at Penetanguishene and Nottawasaga Bay, York, May 19, 1795. Claus Family Papers, Manuscript Division, Public Archives of Canada, Ottawa, Ontario.

entertainment, formatted and presented much like a play, and thus deserving to be called "diplomatic dramas."[69]

Likewise, because European diplomacy "took shape in and through the innovative rhetorical culture of Renaissance humanism," it tended to stereotype the rhetorical practices of Native orators and negotiators as "noble," or "Roman."[70] Once again, Thomas Jefferson supplies the most salient example of this when in his *Notes on the State of Virginia* he lauds the speech of Logan, a Lenni-Lenape leader whose family was massacred by white people: "I may challenge the whole orations of Demosthenes and Cicero, and of any more eminent orator, if Europe has furnished more eminent, to produce a single passage, superior to the speech of Logan, a Mingo chief, to Lord Dunmore, when governor of this state." Versions of Logan's speech were included in elementary school readers.[71] Thus excerpts from Indian treaties made their way into colonial American textbooks, serving as examples of "native eloquence" that young Anglo-Americans could draw upon for the establishment of a national oratorical style. Samuel Willard's *Secondary Lessons; Or, The Improved Reader* (1827), for example, included snippets of Indian oratory for young scholars to peruse. Finally, Indian speeches redacted from treaty publications were sometimes published in the national media as freestanding works of literature. Publications like the *Monthly Anthology* and the *North American Review* "certified the literary importance of the speeches" and, by doing so, "called forth an American public"—urban and rural editors and readers—who constituted themselves as a public through their shared appreciation and recitation of Native oratory.[72]

By the first decades of the nineteenth century, new historical forces—political, demographic, and technological—had radically altered the means by which books were produced, distributed, and consumed in America. The evangelical print consortium of local printers and metropolitan missionary societies had matured into a full-fledged national distribution network as missionary printing concerns like the American Bible Society (1816) and the American Tract Society (1825) took shape in major Eastern Seaboard cities. Satellite publishing hubs in Lexington, Kentucky, and Cincinnati, Ohio, facilitated expansion into the American West. The missionary print system embraced cutting-edge technologies like stereotype printing, steam presses, and paper making, reducing costs to realize the missionaries' visions of Christian books "always at hand."

In 1810, the ABCFM was formed to extend these networks worldwide. Fundraising publications featured maps that located their missions in a world system of Christian print circulation. These and other elements of their activities promoted the settler colonial discourse of erasure. In addition to "books, maps, [and] manuscripts" promoting assimilation and portraying conversion as a geographical appropriation of the homelands of "unevangelized nations," the Board maintained a museum of "curiosities" composed of "idol gods and other objects of superstition, together with specimens in natural history, etc. interesting on account of their being brought from countries which are fields for missionary exertion."[73]

Meanwhile, the federal bureaucratic goal of managing the "Indian question" in the nineteenth century was being strengthened by a print culture matrix whose foundation was the blank book, "bound sheets of unprinted writing paper in which records are kept, . . . day-books, or ledgers"—namely, books whose very character is defined by their lack of pictorial features.[74] Across the century, settlers used large numbers of blanks in various ways. Merchants tallied their accounts in the double-entry ledgers. Soldiers took daily diaries into battle throughout the Civil War. After the war, a burgeoning middle class gobbled up autograph books, gift books, and scrapbooks with relish. The same period that saw these innovations in blanks witnessed the establishment of the common school system across America, which in turn spurred the consumption of another permutation of the blank—the copybook.

Cultural historians have described the role of blank books, especially those that encouraged handwriting, as critical to the formation of bourgeois individualism in Anglo-American Victorian society. Tamara Plakins Thornton observes, "If handwriting worked to create authorized versions of the Victorian self, it also held out the enticing possibility that alternate versions were possible." The blank book was especially liberatory: "Open the book to find a copy text and a ruled page, and there is no choice but to copy the standardized model and obey the rules . . . open the book to find a blank page, and there is no script to follow."[75] The copybooks' simultaneous (and contradictory) invitation to emulation and improvisation was especially provocative when placed in Native hands. When Cherokee student John Ridge was given a blank book, he used it to perfect his spelling and penmanship (and thus his "civility"), but also for something Hilary Wyss has described as "his tactical appropriation of language."[76] Wyss, who studied the generation of Indigenous children educated at the Cornwall Missionary School in Connecticut, observed of these blanks "to read the words and actions of Native participants in conjunction with these documents is to uncover a very different set of practices and outcomes attached to these schools." John Ridge and his classmates, Wyss observes, "lived in a critical political moment through which their ability to convey the concept of Cherokee Nationhood was contingent on their ability to deploy the rhetorics through which they were understood by the dominant white culture."[77]

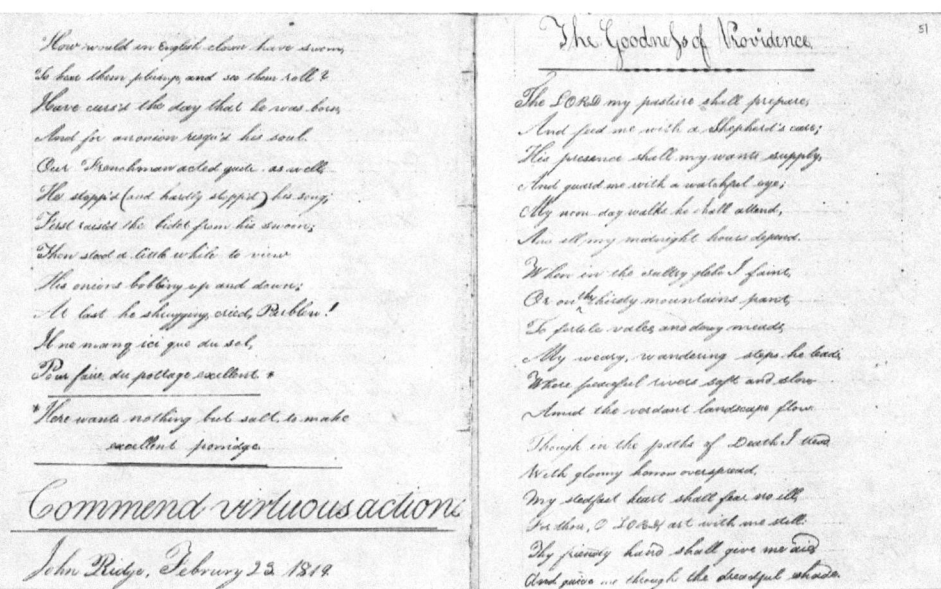

Figure 1.8. Copybook of John Ridge (Cherokee). In John Howard Payne Papers, Newberry Library, Chicago.

Kelly Wisecup has examined the way Ridge applied the techniques honed in the blank books of the Cornwall School later in life, when seeking to defend the Cherokee Nation against the encroachments of the State of Georgia. First, she remarks, Ridge employed "literary strategies of compilation to collect textual excerpts from multiple sources, to re-assemble them in his articles, and to reinterpret their meanings." This represents the classic use of the blank as a commonplace book by writers from all backgrounds in nineteenth-century America. Ridge's methodology creates a space in which past, present, and future practices of Cherokee political relations can exist against federal and state expectations of vanishing tribal sovereignty and peoples. Second, Wisecup notes Ridge's "assimilationist" efforts "to facilitate the Cherokees' adoption of practices that centralized governance and allowed the United States to recognize them as a political state imagined in western terms." Clearly his use of certain rhetorical strategies (like "compiling" sources) reflects "a critical methodology," and this practice was multiplied hundreds of times in different Indigenous communities across the century.[78]

By the 1840s, the blank book served as the cornerstone of a full-blown government print bureaucracy that historian Oz Frankel has characterized as "print statism."[79] It was especially active in Indian Country. John Wesley Powell, at the beginning of his tenure as head of the Bureau of Ethnology in

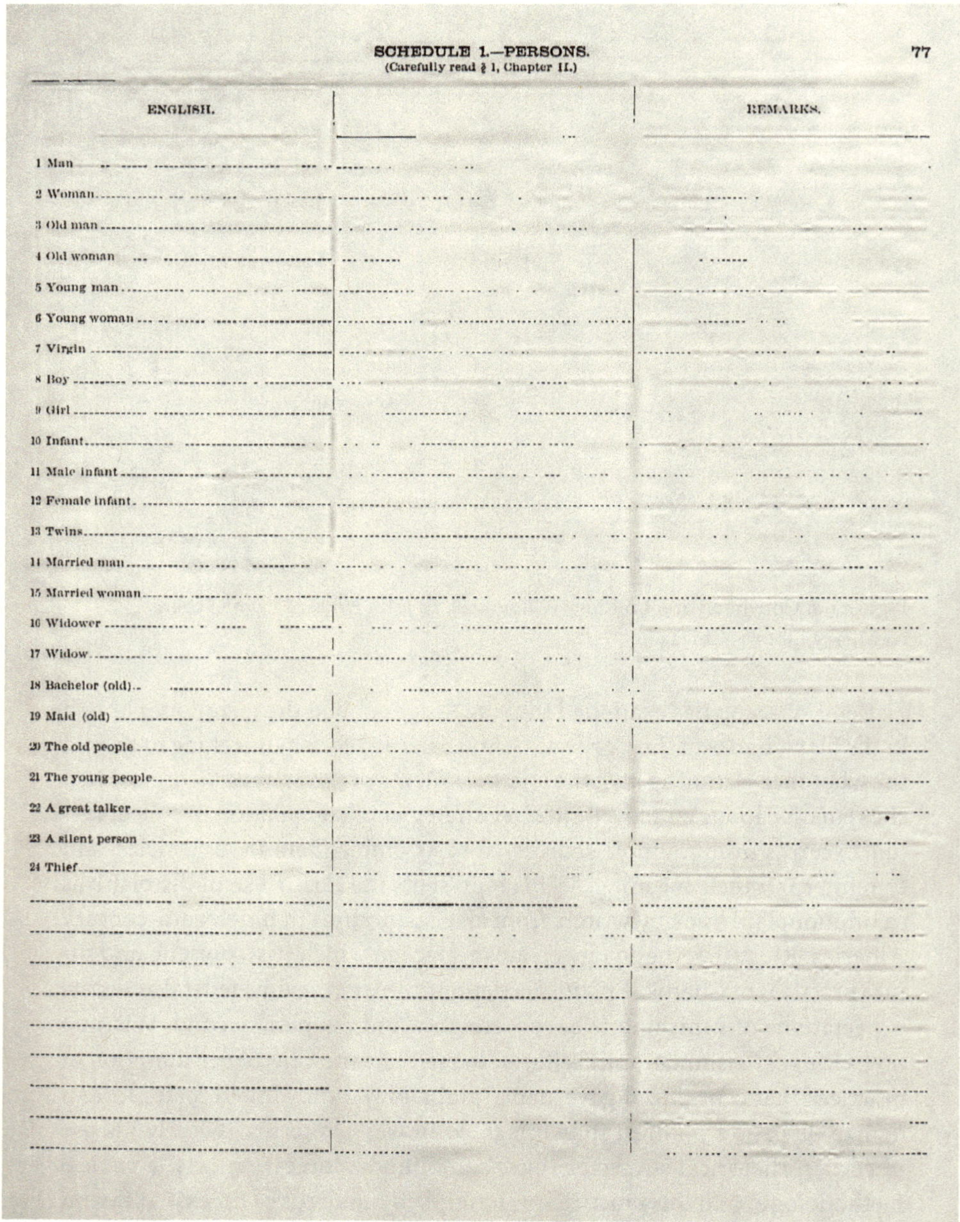

SCHEDULE 1.—PERSONS.
(Carefully read § 1, Chapter II.)

ENGLISH.		REMARKS.
1 Man		
2 Woman		
3 Old man		
4 Old woman		
5 Young man		
6 Young woman		
7 Virgin		
8 Boy		
9 Girl		
10 Infant		
11 Male infant		
12 Female infant		
13 Twins		
14 Married man		
15 Married woman		
16 Widower		
17 Widow		
18 Bachelor (old)		
19 Maid (old)		
20 The old people		
21 The young people		
22 A great talker		
23 A silent person		
24 Thief		

Figure 1.9. Blank word list. From Powell, *Introduction to the Study of Indian Languages*.

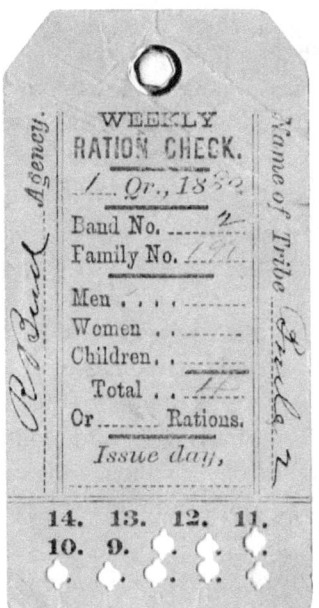

Figure 1.10. Ration card from the Rosebud Reservation, 1890. Pine Ridge Agency, series 119: Ration Punch Strips, 1877–77, Records of the Bureau of Indian Affairs, RG 75, National Archives and Records Administration, Kansas City, Missouri.

1877, ordered that linguistic information collected from tribal communities be standardized through a series of printed forms that could be filled in by the collector in the field. In *Paper Knowledge*, Lisa Gitelman spells out the several ways that blank books functioned in nineteenth-century America. For one, they "incited" manuscript production. Faced with the space on the page, their users inevitably filled it with words. In the case of Bureau of Ethnology blanks, they forced or prompted the inscribing of Indigenous sounds in alphabetic form. They also sought to lay claim to both Indigenous peoples and their languages, disciplining them through forcing them to participate in "the institutions their creators hoped to engender with [blanks]." "Blank books," Gitelman observes, "had the potential to give their users 'techniques of entry' to use to gain entrance to settler society," even though they most often relegated them to "reduced" and secondary status.[80]

Actual blank books produced by print statism and used by Native people demonstrate the myriad of Native-centered uses such blanks enabled. A Kiowa soldier named Silver Horn decided to use his army target practice book as a storyboard for trickster tales. A Lakota family head whose people were on the verge of starvation had little recourse but to use the government's preprinted ration tickets to supply his family's needs.

THE COMMON SCHOOL

Most Native Americans learned to speak English, and perhaps to read and write alphabetic writing, in missionary classrooms. Harvard and Dartmouth were established in the seventeenth and eighteenth centuries, respectively, as "Indian Schools." Failing to deliver much in the way of an Indigenous "harvest," they soon transformed into schools for New England's Anglo-American elites. In 1806, the establishment of the New York public school system ushered in a new era of reaching out to a broader student population, employing the pedagogical theories of Englishman Joseph Lancaster.[81] As Ronald Rayman explains, "The fundamental premise of Lancaster's system revolved around mass public education utilizing older or more advanced students, or 'monitors,' as instructors. . . . [It] was hailed as a milestone in public education." The method demanded "strict discipline," and the curriculum "consisted exclusively of reading, writing, arithmetic, morals or religion, and development of the memory. Talking was prohibited, and infractions of the rules met punishment of the most severe proportions."[82]

In 1817, Cherokee students at the Brainerd Mission School near Lookout Mountain in Tennessee were subjected to this system. Hilary Wyss points out that students tended to have a difficult time adjusting to the system's strict requirement for "complete obedience within a mechanized, impersonal structure." She observes that the model sought primarily to indoctrinate Cherokees into "docility and obedience," rendering those students deemed "'successful' anonymous and void of personhood."[83] By the 1840s, however, the system was falling out of favor in both Indian and public schools, and by 1853, even "New York City, originally the bastion of Lancasterian education, discarded it . . . signaling the system's end as a viable educational model."[84] The common school system, with its "centralized supervision, tax support, teacher training, and consolidated school districts," as well as fresh classroom pedagogies, slowly took its place.[85] These schools took advantage of mass-produced, amply illustrated readers and spellers, and delivery systems like slate chalkboards. Edward Goodbird recalled that he was first attracted to the Christian religion and its mission school by the minister and schoolmaster's implementation of the new common school approaches. When his teacher "preached," Goodbird remembered, "he often drew pictures on the blackboard."[86]

During this period, Native American mission schooling and the schooling of non-Native students converged as part of a nationwide response to "accelerating urbanization, industrialization, and immigration."[87] For Anglo-Americans, emerging technologies and the colporteur system of marketing books were tied to larger economic and social trends that simultaneously spurred public discussion of personal morality and social order. Before the

Civil War, this resulted in a "shift of educational responsibility from the family to the schools." According to educational historian Carl Kaestle, the push for a government-sponsored, centralized public school system was focused on teaching "children a common English language and a common Protestant morality." In the *Baptist Missionary Magazine* of July 1842, a minister among the Ojibwes declared "a system of common school education in which the bible will have precedence" as was being put in place for Euro-American students.[88] From Kaestle's analysis, we could reasonably reenvision the whole common school movement as a nationwide effort to "civilize" all non-elite students—Anglo-American, immigrant, and Indigenous—who had so far escaped the private school system. An examination of several readers from the period suggests that there was indeed significant crossover between Indian missionary school practices and mainstream Anglo-American common school pedagogical innovations.

One fascinating example of this interchange in the period 1830–60 is the work of Thomas Hopkins Gallaudet (1787–1851), a Protestant reformer who championed the education of deaf children. In his *Sermon, on the Duty and Advantages of Affording Instruction to the Deaf and Dumb [. . .]*, Gallaudet pleads for the support of deaf children's education by explicitly linking them to America's Native population: "these children of misfortune, who look to you for the means of being delivered from a bondage more galling than that of the slave; from an ignorance more dreadful than that of the wild and untutored savage!! One tear of gratitude, I only crave a cup of consolation, for the Deaf and Dumb, from the same fountain at which the Hindoo, the African, and the Savage, is beginning to draw the water of eternal life."[89]

Gallaudet was not alone in drawing such comparisons. Writers across the century consistently discuss common school literacy practices within the framework of the "savage" other.[90] Some missionaries to the Ojibwes put his theories into practice with *Gallaudet's Picture Defining and Reading Book . . . in the Ojibwe Language* (1835). Both the book's layout and its woodcuts are borrowed directly from readers designed for Anglo-American students. Although the language is *Anishinaabe-mowin* (that of the Anishinaabe peoples), it is rendered in a highly regularized orthography that is in turn "civilized" by being framed with illustrations and lessons taken from dominant-culture schoolbooks. As poet and linguist Meg Noodin observes, "Despite [Gallaudet's reader] being mentioned by McNally in *Hymn Singers* as part of the varied orthography, dialect-rich tradition of missionary writing," the book actually employs "standard orthography and textbook use of the language," suggesting that "the person writing the book wanted to teach the nuances of the language efficiently and with an eye to comparison between English and

ABINOJI

MUZINIBIIGUN GAIE UINDUMAGOUIN

MUZINAIIGUN.

Abidi Uindvmi.

Mishiminatĭk.
Unibishvn.
Pebamitakuĭsiĭn.
Uvtvbi-mvkvk.
Usĭni-Mĭjikvnakobĭjigvn.

Uvdĭkuvnvn.
Kuândauâgvn.
Nanvn Kuiuizeñsvg.
Mishimĭnvg.

Ogo Kuiuizeñsvg omamoshvginauân mishimnvn.
Bezhĭk mĭtigo odonjimvmauân.
Bezhĭk Kuiuizeñs omoshkĭnaton omvshkimutekuâjigvnvn.
Bezhĭk omoshkĭnaton uvtvbi-mvkvk.
Nizh Kuiuizeñsvg mishiminvn odvmuâuân.

Figure 1.11. Page from Thomas Gallaudet's *Gallaudet's Picture Defining and Reading Book*. Courtesy of the Newberry Library, Chicago.

Ojibwe."⁹¹ Efficiency and English-language models make the reader a "common school" technology whose main purpose is to standardize and assimilate.

Gallaudet's text for Ojibwe children was just one of several Native language literacy projects across Indian Country that directly adapted "model" Euro-American readers to the teaching of Indigenous languages. Another example is the Dakota reader *Wayawa Tokaheya* (1873), produced by missionary educator Stephen R. Riggs, which uses as a template a schoolbook published by a mainstream Chicago firm: J. Russell Webb's *Model First Reader* (1873). Riggs's "translation" method was quite simple. He merely placed "Dakota words into the space between English lines," suggesting, according to some literacy historians, that such models had the capacity for cross-cultural manipulation and assimilative power precisely because they "offer little overt regional identity, no direct references to historical events, public figures or places, or to specific religious or political groups."⁹²

In fact, as Jean Carr, Stephen Carr, and Lucille Schultz, the authors of *Archives of Instruction*, have determined from their exhaustive examination of hundreds of reading instruction books, such texts "frame an instructional project in terms of the body—and often of particular bodies, by focusing on the organs of pronunciation, gesture and stance, the regulation of the eye, and the modulation of the voice, and by developing distinctions about gender, class, educational level, and authority." In nineteenth-century America, reading was a fundamentally oral practice, and its embodied performance was seen as enabling "the transactions and intercourse of civilized life."⁹³ Texts like the *McGuffey Readers* were filled with poetry samples that students were expected to read aloud, with clear enunciation and performative declamation. Its readings were thus designed, in part, "to allow less privileged students to taste some riches previously restricted to an elite[,] . . . compress[ing] some of the values of a classical or clerical education into a secularized volume."⁹⁴ Much more than just books of words to be learned, these readers dramatized the "power of the upper class . . . as a 'manner' or 'grace' of speaking."⁹⁵

Both subjects of and subject to the revolution in the production and consumption of printed matter, Native peoples in the United States were uniquely situated at the center of this cultural transformation. Their very visceral responses to the experience provide some of the most vivid and detailed auto-ethnographic accounts available of the communications revolution. As perceived literacy needs changed across the United States, educational reform movements blossomed, and pedagogical theories were often first tested on Native students. From the introduction of the Lancastrian movement to the rise of the Sunday school movement in 1824, Native children were on the front lines of the reading revolution. These children and their teachers were, in turn, the focus of an expanding print trade in didactic and pedagogical books. In the 1830s, works like Rev. Legh Richmond's *The Dairy [Man's Daughter]* could be found in Sunday school classrooms around the United States. By 1847, the book had been published in a Cherokee syllabary translation at the Park Hill Mission Press in the Indian Territory. The same print marketplace also encouraged literary productions by Native Christian converts, and books like William Apess's *A Son of the Forest* (1831) and the *Memoir of Catharine Brown* (1831) were published by the American Sunday School Union Press to bring the message of Native literacy-as-conversion to non-Indian school readers as models of inspiration.

In fact, Native students experienced explicit "civilizing" rhetoric throughout the common school curriculum. It was often far from benign. The title page of a geography commonly used in nineteenth-century American schools, for example, explicitly depicted Indigenous life as a "place" in the past, collapsing time and space into a progressive history of America in which Indians had no choice but to assimilate. Francis La Flesche's autobiographical account of his elementary school years, *The Middle Five* (1900), describes the actual experiences of Indian children with the common school literacy curriculum at the same time that it deftly thematizes its author's canny negotiation of these so-called civilizing practices to the purpose of establishing a new kind of Omaha ethnicity, one that included English-language literacy as part of its own arsenal of cultural sovereignty.

The Middle Five is dedicated, significantly, "To Universal Boy," and a close reading of the preface offers a clear indication of what this means. Despite having their hair cut and being forced to wear uniforms, La Flesche and other Omaha students resisted wholesale assimilation, putting a positive spin on these "civilizing" techniques: "While the school uniform did not change those who wore it, in this instance, it may help these little Indians to be judged, as are other boys, by what they say and do." La Flesche informs his readers that he will rarely use the students' Omaha names, precisely "for the reason that Indian words are not only difficult to pronounce, but are apt to sound all alike to one not familiar with the language, and the boys who figure in these pages might lose their identity and fail to stand out clearly in the mind of the reader were he obliged to continually struggle with their Omaha names."[96]

While many Euro-American autobiographies from this period emphasize school learning as central to the birth of the bourgeois individual, La Flesche's memoir resists this. He introduces his book not as "a continued story with a hero" but rather as "a series of sketches." Indeed, the book's title points to the group dynamic of the Omaha boys' identities in the school. The "middle five," like the Omaha clan and kinship systems the ministers and school-

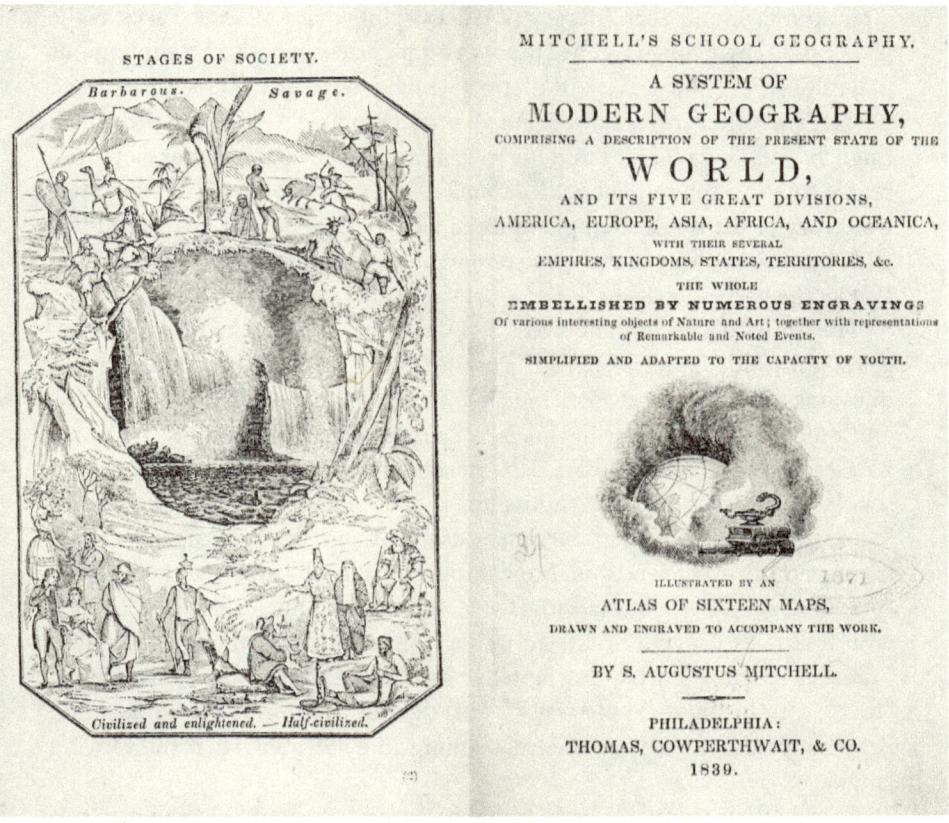

Figure 1.12. Frontispiece and title-page spread from *Mitchell's School Geography [. . .]* (Philadelphia: Thomas, Cowperthwait, 1839).

masters encouraged Native students to abandon, is a schoolyard clique that soon becomes a powerful guardian of both individual and group identity for La Flesche and his friends.

That is not to say that La Flesche sugarcoats the oppressiveness of his schooling. In the preface he acknowledges, "When we entered the Mission School, we experienced a greater hardship, for there we encountered a rule that prohibited the use of our own language, which rule was rigidly enforced by the hickory rod, so that the newcomer, no matter how socially inclined, was obliged to go about like a little dummy until he had learned to express himself in English." Still, La Flesche seems to prefer this system (with its potential for covert bilingualism within the gang of "middle five") to a romanticized "translation" of Native language experiences produced by "the average interpreter [who] has generally picked up his knowledge of English in a random fashion." Such literacy practices spoil what La Flesche sees as the power of his own language, its "beauty and picturesqueness, and euphonious playfulness, . . . the gravity of diction which I have heard among my own people, and other tribes as well, are all but impossible to be given literally in English." While La Flesche and his friends are teased by tribal members who refuse to go to school, and called "make-believe white men," the narrative trajectory of the book attempts to forge a balance between Omaha and English literacy in a way that is quite remarkable, given the coercive pedagogies La Flesche had to navigate.[97]

The leader of the "middle five," the Omaha boy La Flesche most admires, is a slightly older student named Brush, who was orphaned as a child and so does not return home at weekends like the others. Brush is "a bright fellow and quite a student," and in the early part of the autobiography, he tutors La Flesche in his lessons from *McGuffey's Second Reader*. Yet Brush has no scholastic or assimilationist motive for this. He simply wants La Flesche to "catch up" so "we can be in the same classes." Again, the impetus to learning is community and friendship. Most importantly, in the evening after classes, Brush becomes a traditional storyteller, entertaining his "middle five" clique with folk tales. Having first tried to read Bible stories to the boys at night, Brush gives up when La Flesche tells him that he prefers the stories Brush "told . . . in his own simple way."[98] Throughout the rest of the book, when Brush appears, he is associated with nighttime storytelling in the Omaha language.

Brush's other significant role in the narrative is to represent the unraveling of traditional Omaha social structures in the face of American colonialism. Brush is alone, without mother or father (who mysteriously disappeared). Even his grandfather died soon after having taken charge of the boy. La Flesche underscores this aspect of Brush's character by recounting how he brought Brush home for a weekend, despite the older boy's protests and fear of being unwanted in the La Flesche home. In this chapter, La Flesche's father virtually adopts Brush, after having the boy recite his lineage: "Who are you, little brother?" asked father. For a moment Brush looked embarrassed, then lifting his eyes to father's face answered, "I am Tae-son's grandson and Sas-su [La Flesche's] friend." When the father hears the name of the old chief, he immediately embraces the boy, saying, "I am glad you like the company of my boy. You must always come with him on his visits home from the House of Teaching."[99]

Yet, as promised in the preface, La Flesche resists making Brush the hero of the autobiography by employing an episodic, almost picaresque narrative style in which various Native children take a central role within each "sketch."

Thus, when he recounts the book's archetypal scene of literary education, he does so through an exchange between the schoolmaster (called "Gray-beard") and an Omaha boy named Bob:

> "Third reader," called Gray-beard, and some ten or twelve boys and girls marched to the place of recitation, and put their toes on a crack in the floor. The reading lesson had some verses on "Summer," prettily illustrated with a picture of a boy and a dog, the lad racing over a meadow, and the dog frisking at his side.
>
> "Now, Robert, begin!" said Gray-beard to little Bob, who in some unaccountable way had reached the head of the class.
>
> The boy put his index finger on the first word, and slid it along as he read, in a low, sing-song tone, "Come, come, come, the Summer is now here."

In response, Gray-beard slams his hickory rod down on the student's desk, exclaiming to the stricken boy, "Read it loud, as though you were out of doors at play." With this admonition to be himself, to be the Omaha boy he is outside the schoolroom doors, Bob declaims heartily, "Come, come, come, the Summer is now here." Rather than being silenced by English-language literacy education, the boy shouts, releasing his fellows into the summertime world of recess.[100]

In a continued reversal of assimilative tropes, when the book ends with Brush's death, unlike traditional missionary representations of the repentant dying Indian, La Flesche's version gives voice and agency to a specifically Omaha identity. As he enters his friend's room, he sees a deathbed scene familiar to all nineteenth-century American readers: "A candle stood burning in the midst of a number of bottles on the little table near the head of the bed. I knelt by the bedside, and Brush put his arm around my neck. We were silent for a while, finally he whispered in the Omaha tongue: 'I'm glad you came' I've been wanting to talk to you. They tell me I am better; but I know I am dying." Not only is the fact of the boy's switch into the Omaha language significant, but so too is the way that La Flesche translates the conversation, eschewing any "romantic" diction or "othering" epithets. While the scene includes the requisite attestation of the dying boy's faith in God ("You mustn't be troubled; I'm all right; I know God will take care of me"), La Flesche does not end it there. Instead, he extends it to include Brush's repatriation to Omaha culture: "A breath of wind came and moved the flickering flame of the candle. . . . The boy stared fixedly through the vacant doorway. There was something strange and unnatural in his look as, with one arm still around me, he stretched the other toward the door, and, in a loud whisper, said, 'My grandfather! He calls me. I'm coming, I'm coming!'"[101]

After the Civil War, reading education in the United States took yet another turn in the direction of increasing standardization and centralization. And again, Native American pupils were often at the center of the changes. With stereotype printing well established by 1865, the reconstructed union of the states demanded new "model" readers that could figuratively bridge the sectional divides that had split the country in two. Publishers and educators pushed for "national standards, [as] mass markets made school readers of the last third of the century more uniform, more conservative about new methods."[102] Along with greater emphasis on "modern efficiency" and "practical education," the 1870s and 1880s witnessed the proliferation of cheap printed reading matter like dime novels and illustrated weeklies.

In Indian Country, this standardization and centralization of educational practice was brought into even sharper focus with the recommendations of the Peace Commission of 1868: "Under the plan which we have suggested the chief duties of the bureau will be to educate and instruct in the peaceful arts—in other words, to civilize the Indians."[103] Between 1868 and 1900, the federal government did, indeed, increasingly oversee the literacy education of America's Native peoples. Focusing on English-only curricula and an "industrial" school model in which Indian children were often literally worked to death in fields and shops, the BIA system rapidly became anathema to Native parents and children everywhere.[104]

Nez Perce writer James Ruben protested against this sort of education when he placed the following note into a time capsule set into the cornerstone of the new school being erected on his reservation in 1880:

> For the last two years Joseph's people[,] though in strange land, yet
> have made some progress in civilization. But take it in the right light—
> Nez Perce have been wrongly treated by the Government and it cannot
> be denied, not Nez Perce only but all other Indian Nations in America.
> I wrote this about my own people. I am a member of Nez Perce tribe and
> Nephew of Chief Joseph at present I am employed by the Government
> Interpreter and Teacher for my People. As before stated there are 1650
> Nez Perce living now in Idaho Territory of which I belong that's where
> I got my education. When this is opened and read may be understood
> how the Indians have been treated by the Whiteman.
> Writer
> James Reuben
> Nez Perce Indian[105]

Woven into Reuben's withering critique of settler colonialism is a recognition of the centrality of reading to making the plight of Native peoples in the nineteenth century visible. "When [it] is opened and read," Reuben believed, the Indian school's cornerstone would reveal the role its "civilizing practices" had in the dispossession of the Indigenous homelands.

The Paiute lecturer and educator Sarah Winnemucca devoted much of her life to overturning these pedagogical methods that threatened the intellectual sovereignty of Native communities. In "Sarah Winnemucca's Practical Solution of the Indian Problem" (1886), Elizabeth Palmer Peabody outlines how one Native intellectual sought to divert the alphabetics of assimilation into scripts of sovereignty by "founding a school based on 'Indian' principles, not those of outsiders."[106] Peabody describes Winnemucca's "new departure" in a method of school that rejected "a passive reception of civilizing influences proffered by white men who look down upon the Indian as a spiritual, moral, and intellectual inferior, it is a spontaneous movement, made by the Indian himself, *from himself*, in full consciousness of free agency, for the education that is to civilize him." Winnemucca's plans, in fact, might serve as an outline for the several methods of adopting alphabetic scripts to Native utterances in a way that preserves "Indian principles"—much like those we examine in the rest of this book. Genealogy and lineage are the foundation of Winnemucca's pedagogy, and she grounds her lessons in her father's desire for literacy as a form of empowerment, and within an ironic reversal of the government's blood quantum logic that had done so much damage to Indian people. "You know me," Winnemucca intones at the outset of her educational pamphlet, "many of you are my aunts or cousins, We are of one race,—your blood is my blood—so I speak to you for your good." Similarly, following a technique that was at least as old as Samson Occom's teaching practices at Mohegan in the eighteenth century, Winnemucca used Paiute language in the classroom to level up the settler and Indigenous language practices with each other. Peabody described to her settler readers what such a class session looked like: "Speaking her native tongue, [Winnemucca] requested the children to name all the visible objects, repeat the days of the week and months of the year, and calculate to thousands, which they did in a most exemplary manner. Then she asked them to give a manifestation of their knowledge on the blackboard, each in turn printing his name and spelling aloud." Visitors to the schoolroom saw that Winnemucca deftly wove together common school practices (spelling aloud, using a blackboard) with cross-cultural modes of communication. "Pupils in the Second Reader," Winnemucca's observers noted, "said every lesson in English and Piute [sic], and in Sarah's reading them (from the Bible, for instance) there was the same use made of both languages, and the conversation upon the subject matter that accompanied it was extremely lively."[107]

Between the time when Francis La Flesche recited the poems of Felicia

Hemans from the pages of the *McGuffey Reader* and the 1880s, when James Reuben penned his polemic, literacy education in the common school movement had lost its innocence. The federal government had taken over the education of Indian children, virtually forbidding education in their Native languages. But here and there, in protected Indigenous spaces like in Sarah Winnemucca's classroom, Indigenous learners found ways to keep their languages alive and, with them, the various forms of sovereignty—intellectual, cultural, and linguistic that would preserve their communities into the twentieth century.

CONCLUSION

In the following pages, I offer case studies of three different Indigenous language families—Iroquoian, Siouan, and Central Algonquian—to demonstrate the myriad of possibilities vernacular alphabetic literacy offered to Native communities suffering from diaspora, disenfranchisement, and dispossession. Although each group developed distinctive literacy practices gauged to meet their specific historic circumstances, some general patterns emerge. Alphabetic and syllabary literacy offered all these groups an opportunity to maintain kinship and governance relations over the great distances imposed on them by the Indian Removal Act of 1830. Thus, alphabetic epistolary discourse is especially pervasive.

Writing also presented Native communities with a way of archiving certain social and religious practices that were constantly being upended by war and removal. Iroquois writers wrote out "scripts," much like a prompt book at a playhouse, that listed the order of the all-important Condolence Ceremony performed at critical diplomatic events. When buffalo hides became scarce, Plains communities turned to new media to record important dates and events—sometimes using muslin instead of hide, sometimes using the pages of an accountant's ledger book—often supplementing traditional graphics with alphabetic signs. For a mixed Kickapoo/Potawatomi community removed from the lower Great Lakes to Kansas, wooden staffs marked with a visionary's secret symbols provided a liturgical script/plan for the regrouped parishioners.

Perhaps inspired by a settler audience hungry for stories about "real Indians," some Indigenous writers plied their trade by producing autobiographies that could simultaneously record important historical details for their society to refer to later and archive those elements of their language that were falling into disuse because of the social fissures brought on by colonialism. Writing in a vernacular script, or reciting their life stories to alphabetically literate kinsmen, these visionary community members understood that a written record might serve as a welcome supplement to the graphic and oral communications networks that had sustained their communities in the times before colonization. Writing could thus at once be seen as a progressive act of embracing new technologies and information systems and a conservative gesture toward preserving essential social and religious practices. Most importantly, however, these Indigenous writers sought visibility in the settler public sphere and a voice in the way their communities' histories were to be written and their futures realized.

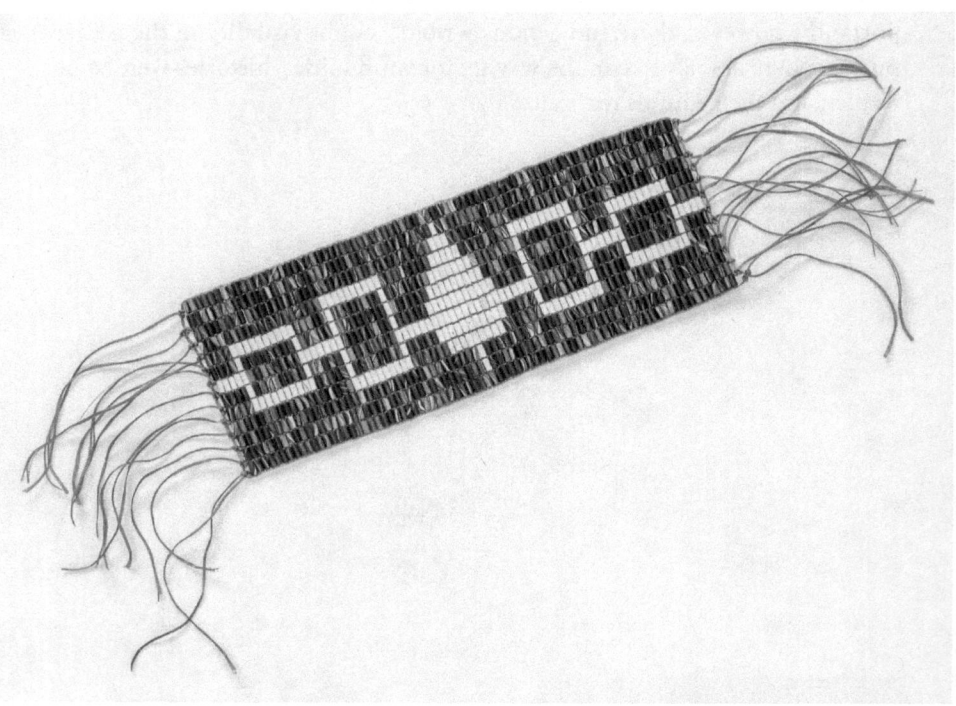

Figure 2.1. Replica of Hiawatha wampum belt. The original belt, housed at the Onondaga Nation, "was created at the beginning of the Haudenosaunee confederacy of peace." No. 26/9056, National Museum of the American Indian, Smithsonian Institution, Washington, DC. Photo by NMAI Photo Services.

2 : *Kahiatónhsera*
MARKING THE MATTERS OF THE GOOD MESSAGE

> This is what happened when it originated, the Great Law. This is what happened in ancient times: There was warfare, and they habitually killed each other, the Indians of the several nations. . . . This is when Haweniyo decided to send Tekanawita here, and his mission [was] to end their killing one another. . . . That, then, is how it was and in a short time a boy was born. Thereupon the old woman said, "Now, indeed, Tekanawita has arrived." . . . And very soon he began to walk around, and when, quite soon, he began to talk, this is what he began to speak about: It is not good for people to be unkind to one another.
> —John Arthur Gibson (Seneca), 1912 (English translation in *Concerning the League*, 1992)

Before the Haudenosaunee peoples—known as "Iroquois" in European writing—decided to live together in one confederacy of five nations, they were at war all the time. To end the constant fighting, Haweniyo, the Breathmaker, the Giver of Life, sent a boy to be born among them with a lesson of peace and a vision of proper social order. The boy was raised among the Mohawks along the northern shore of Lake Ontario. When he grew up, Tekanawita—sometimes spelled Deganawidah and also called Peacemaker—bade his mother and grandmother farewell, fashioned a canoe out of white stone, and journeyed east with his message of harmony, called *Kaianere'kó:wa* in the language of the people. Seneca ceremonial leader John Arthur Gibson told this story many years later, in 1900, as part of an interconnected set of ceremonials known as the Condolence Ceremony.

Tekanawita spread his message of peace among the warring Haudenosaunees, collecting a following of those who saw the wisdom of his teaching. The most famous of them was Hiawatha, who was mourning the deaths of his daughters. Theretofore inconsolable, meeting Tekanawita gave Hiawatha a mission. As the Peacemaker's emissary, he traveled from village to village preparing the way for the prophet. At one camp, just outside a small settlement, "he saw a cornfield and beside the field a lean-to; and when he got there he lit a fire. Thereupon he cut off a sumac branch, cored it, cut it into short lengths, and then strung up the sticks making several short strings."[1] This was the birth of wampum, the material culture mode of communication that would become a hallmark of Six Nations' life. As he and Tekanawita proceeded to bring together the disparate bands of Haudenosaunee into an alliance, these strings, or necklaces, became the perfect medium for carrying their message.

It was not until later, after the Haudenosaunee bands had come to accept Tekanawita's peace plan, that Hiawatha received another vision solidifying wampum's role in preserving Haudenosaunee sovereignty. While walking near a small lake, he saw that it was covered by a flock of waterfowl, and as he approached them, they "flew up, all of the ducks, and in doing so they lifted up the water." Hiawatha then "saw that there was no water anymore where there used to be a lake. He saw that the place where the water used to be was white, and . . . [on] the bottom . . . [the] thickness of white objects was similar to what he himself possessed, the strung up feathers, the single strands [of wampum]." The shells uncovered by the ducks' sudden flight seemed to be the perfect new medium for Tekanawita's message. According to Gibson, who told the story in 1900, Hiawatha thought, "I'll collect as many as I am able to. . . . This, indeed, is what will get made and used, this will become a model, serving them as a reminder that symbolizes the Good Message and the Power and the Peace and the Great Law; also as to their several nations, this is what everyone will use to remind them of the matters that were used to form the league."[2]

From that moment on, the Haudenosaunee Confederacy was sustained by a media network based in oral ceremony and song, material culture objects, and periodic gatherings in a special lodge called the Longhouse. A communications web of beaded belts and a built environment featuring confederacy council houses became a synecdoche for the confederation itself. The descendants of Hiawatha would thereafter be known as "the people of the Longhouse," and this story and these ceremonies mark the birth of the Iroquois Confederacy. It brought together five independent nations—Mohawk, Cayuga, Onondaga, Seneca, and Oneida (the Tuscarora, adopted in 1722, made six total)—into a geographic and political organization that continues to this day. Each member occupies a place in the Longhouse that reflects their role in the diplomatic and military maintenance of the confederacy. In turn, each represents a cardinal direction in the Haudenosaunee homelands, essentially mapping out an enormous symbolic Longhouse across the region.

As the first to have received Tekanawita's vision, the Mohawks occupy the place of "older brothers," keeping watch over the eastern door; the Senecas, as guardians of the confederacy, take their place at the western door. The Cayugas and Oneidas sit opposite in the role of Younger Brothers. As the last

Kahiatónhsera 85

Figure 2.2. Lewis Henry Morgan, *Map of Ho-De-No-Sau-Nee-Ga: Or the Territories of the People of the Long House in 1720* [. . .] (Albany, NY, 1831). No. 2019585091, Geography and Map Division, Library of Congress, Washington, DC.

to accept Tekanawita's confederacy, the Onondagas are the keepers of the fire, and to this day the main meeting place of the confederacy is in Onondaga's country. The confederacy is governed by a Grand Council, comprising fifty sachems from each of the clans of the various nations. The title Tadodaho is still used for the chair of the Haudenosaunee Confederacy, the fiftieth chief who sits with the Onondagas in council. For contemporary Haudenosaunee peoples, citizenship and sovereignty still take shape "within a political corpus of the larger Longhouse which spreads metaphorically across Iroquoia."[3]

The wampum "symbolized" the Good Law that connected the nations; Gibson called it the Onondaga term *ekayaná?tahé.k* (a model), a phrase whose root verb refers to marking, measuring, and comparing.[4] The term also implied that the connections would need to be periodically repaired, just like the beaded strings. The Haudenosaunees thus developed a formal procedure to periodically reaffirm their social and political bonds. In English, this is known as the Condolence Ceremony. When a Six Nations leader died, all the nations would gather to help the community mourn its loss and select a new leader. The Condolence Ceremony thus reenacts Tekanawita's story, retelling how he soothed Hiawatha after the deaths of his daughters. Historian Daniel Richer relates one version of the story: "Offering strings of the shell beads called wampum, . . . [Tekanawita] spoke several Words of Condolence: the first dried Hiawatha's weeping eyes, the second opened his ears, the third unstopped his throat . . . until his sorrow was relieved and his reason restored."[5] Embodying what the Iroquois call "the Good News of Peace and Power," the ritual had the curative clout to put an end to warfare for good.

The Condolence Ceremony begins with the fallen council member's nation notifying the others of an event at "a time and place at which he would be lamented and his successor installed." The announcement is delivered by "official messengers . . . [whose] credentials [are] certain strings of wampum, appropriate to the occasion." When the day arrives, the chiefs of the other nations approach the meeting place together with "a multitude of their people, men and women." Reaching the edge of the "opening" or cleared space surrounding the town, the two groups perform the "preliminary ceremony," the *Deyughnyonkwarakda* ("at the edge of the woods"). A fire is kindled, a sacred pipe lit, and an address given by the hosts mingling "congratulation and consolation." The guests are then formally conducted to the Longhouse while a chanter recites the names of the fifty leaders of the confederacy. These ritual names are adopted by new members as they are installed in the place of those who have passed away.[6]

Inside the Longhouse, two more ceremonies are conducted in sequence. The Condoling Song mourns the lost leader, and the Requickening Address heralds the installation of the new one. Sometimes called "a great hymn of farewell," the Condoling Song (*kerenna*) is a sort of "National Hymn of the Iroquois." Punctuated by the vocables "Hai, haih," the song sets up a call and response that is evocative of the wailing of the departed spirits. The Requickening Address is a formal recitation of fourteen "matters," or topics, relevant to repairing the damage caused by the leader's death. It involves formulaic utterances intended to cleanse the Haudenosaunee world, ranging from wiping away tears and "clearing the ears" of the mourners, to replacing the sun in the sky, leveling the earth over the grave, and rekindling the council fires. At its conclusion, the speaker asks the identity of the new leader and "raises up" the new chief in symbolic rebirth of the old.[7]

When the new leader has been formally installed, another set of wampum, this time woven into wide multicolored belts, is read to the assembly.

Nineteenth-century settler ethnographer Horatio Hale stated that this was called "reading the archives," thus underscoring how the shell beads functioned as media for the assembled Haudenosaunee nations. From time immemorial to the present day, this ritual—which significantly involves a reinvestment in the hermeneutic protocols of the ceremony through the purification of the listener so that he or she is open to peace—has guided Six Nations cooperation and assisted in its dealings with outsiders. It is both a spiritual practice that embodies the central tenets of Iroquois belief and a diplomatic decorum that structures military and political negotiations. As Richter explains, "The diplomacy of peace proceeded according to strict rule" in which "contacts between two peoples began with a formal invitation to a council." Upon acceptance of the invitation and selection of a location, "the council began with the parties sitting on opposite sides of the fire." Next, "a speaker for the party that called the council delivered several distinct propositions, each accompanied by a gift. An orator from the other side repeated each proposition after hearing it, to fix the message in the minds of all and ensure that it was fully understood." The ceremony concluded with a "feast in which all parties ate from a single pot[, reaffirming] the climate of peace."[8]

The Condolence Ceremony also became a widespread vehicle for intertribal negotiations. When Mahican sachem Hendrick Aupaumut went west in 1792 to relay messages from the US government to the Shawnee and other Native nations gathered in the Ohio River valley, he encountered opposition that was voiced in the protocols of the Condolence Ceremony. His meetings with the Western Nations took place in preestablished, ceremonially prepared forest clearings or creek-side villages. Aupaumut's handwritten English-language journal relates how negotiators ritually cleansed each other so that all might "hear plain." One Native diplomat embraced Aupaumut, saying, "I put my hand to take away the dust from your ears." These rituals, the sachem Tautpuhqtheet explained to Aupaumut, are those "our good ancestors did hand down to us [as] a rule or path where we may walk."[9]

Wampum is exchanged at several points during the Condolence Ceremony. Hale witnessed the use of beads at the singing of each line of the *kerenna*, as phrase after phrase was "brought to mind by its own special wampum."[10] Gibson again used the term *etwayaná?tákwa* to describe Hiawatha's understanding of the role that shell wampum would play in this Haudenosaunee social practice: "We shall use it to mark matters [of] the Good Message."[11] This "marking" property of wampum has often, in the settler histories, been characterized as a sign of the medium's "mnemonic" character.[12] And, indeed, the Mohegan missionary Samson Occom employed wampum gifted to him by the Oneida Nation in his effort to publicize his plans to gather up a commu-

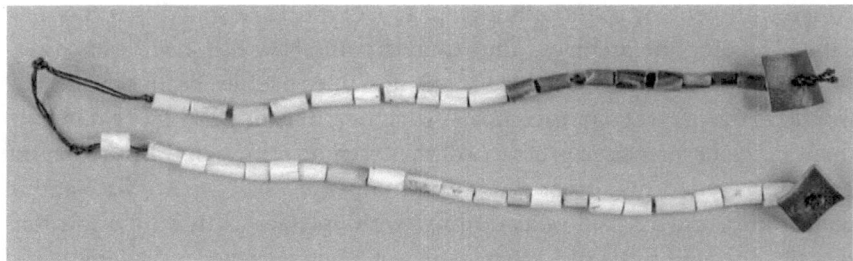

Figure 2.3. Wampum strings of requickening. No. E391950-0, courtesy of the National Museum of Natural History, Washington, DC.

nity of Christian Indians and move them away from the negative influences of the settlers in New England, sending the belts he received to Scotland in 1761. Throughout his life, Occom recorded several "readings" of wampum warning of Native distrust and antipathy toward the Americans, demonstrating the way that the beaded belts were integrated into an alphabetically literate Indigenous intellectual's literacy practice.[13]

But wampum is also part of the Haudenosaunee visual culture that extends beyond its immediately obvious script-like qualities, and work by Indigenous scholars like Penelope Kelsey suggests it embodies a richer hermeneutic than simple memorization: "Wampum composes a significant portion of what we understand as Iroquois visual code, a set of mutually understood symbols and images that communicate culturally-embedded ideas to the viewer." Wampum designs draw on "traditional forms such as pottery, beadwork, wampum, and sculpture and are contemporarily applied in media as varied as painting, film, metalsmithing, and digital displays."[14] Thus, the colors, materials, and texture of the wampum belts, in addition to their methods of construction, had touchstones in every aspect of Haudenosaunee life. Crafted from the fabric of their homeland and historically grounded in the events related in the origin story of the Haudenosaunee Confederacy, wampum is interanimated with many modes of Haudenosaunee communications and governance. In addition, as an item to be given and received, the exchange of wampum embodies critical aspects of Haudenosaunee political philosophy, particularly those elements of the Great Law that emphasize reciprocity, "co-existence, non-interference, and mutual responsibility."[15]

When seventeenth-century French Jesuit missionaries asked a group of Mohawks what the wampum belts signified, they responded, "*rivière fabriquée*." Anthropologist Margret Bruchac (Wabinaki) points out that the French-language notation in the Jesuit's journals (*fabriquée*) "might typically be translated as 'man-made' or 'manufactured,' but a better rendering would be constructed. One form of construction is 'woven.' Consider that: a wampum belt is a woven river. I believe that is what the Mohawk[s] were telling the Sulpician missionary."[16] As late as 1882, the French missionary J. A. Cuoq would associate the Mohawk noun stems of *rivière* and wampum (he calls them *racines*, or roots) in his *Lexique de la langue iroquoise*, signaling the continued understanding of the abstract concept of the "writing" and the "written" as centered in the verbs that underpin them and as flowing between the various natural materials and material practices by which the homeland was held together in its natural state. Here, the explicit merging of natural phenomena, the networks of rivers and waterways connecting the Haudenosaunees and facilitating their communications system and the technological intervention of the human community ("man-made") provokes a complex metaphor that the settler priests codified in their lexicons but that nonetheless resisted easy Euro-centered interpretation. As a "woven river," wampum is media. In terms of the present study, wampum is an integral part of the Haudenosaunees' "socially realized structures of communication." Wampum is a technology of exchange whose use embodies the very protocols it seeks to sustain.

CONDOLENCE AS CULTURE VS. CONDOLENCE AS HISTORY

The Condolence Ceremony, in the words of Mohawk (Rotinohshonni) scholar Taiaiake Alfred, "pacifies the minds and emboldens the hearts of mourners by transforming grief into strength."[17] It achieves this transformation by bringing together all aspects of Haudenosaunee governance into a harmonious interweaving of community, land, and language. In so doing, it establishes a discourse of "relatedness" that has over the years helped Haudenosaunee people defy settler erasure and affirm their sovereignty. What was forged so many years before the arrival of Europeans continues to anchor Haudenosaunee communities to this day. As Mohawk scholar Audra Simpson has observed, Native people at her home reserve of Kahnawake resist assimilation through "their relatedness to their place, to others, to a particular history, to their ongoing experiences because of this relatedness."[18] The Haudenosaunee Confederacy forged spatial relationships that in turn fostered intercommunity connections between geographically dispersed peoples. These connections were maintained by everything from the sending of wampum to the marking out of the "edge of woods" for formal negotiations.

As the first case study in this book, the story of how alphabetic writing interacted with the Condolence Ceremony is especially instructive because it illuminates those questions that define any study of graphogenesis: "Why does someone invent a script? What is the purpose of Writing?" In the case of the Haudenosaunees, alphabetic writing in the vernacular was "invented" by settlers but perfected by Haudenosaunee writers for two centuries after its introduction. More importantly, shining a light on these questions helps unveil the political dimensions of the practices involved in the Condolence Ceremony. Maori scholar Linda Tuhiwai Smith quotes Edward Said as framing similar questions that serve us well here: "Who writes? For whom is the writing being done? In what circumstances? These it seems to me are the questions whose answers provide us with the ingredients for making a politics of interpretation."[19] And it is precisely the politics of Iroquois governance, relatedness, and continued struggle that has eluded many outsiders who wished to understand how the Condolence Ceremony survived the onslaught of dispossession and alphabetic treaty-making to remain at the center of Haudenosaunee political life to this day.

In order to reorient our study of alphabetic literacy in Iroquoia away from reified concepts of "culture" and toward the historically grounded material practices that animate Haudenosaunee community coherence, we must examine the pragmatic employment of alphabetic texts by Haudenosaunees in the eighteenth and nineteenth centuries so that we may begin to re-experience those "sovereign articulations" that Audra Simpson has described as underwriting the "feeling citizenships" that the confederacy was built to sustain.[20] The settler anthropology's emphasis on the refined and fetishized "culture" of the Condolence Ceremony and other aspects of Iroquois life has become the only lens through which practically everyone (Haudenosaunees included) has "read" the Iroquois; but understanding the real issues of "membership, sovereignty, and autonomy within communities requires a historical sensibility."[21]

In the case of the present study of vernacular scripts in Indian Country, a historical sensibility requires surfacing both the long-standing graphic and verbal practices that preceded the settler introduction of an orthography and the factual, social uses to which Iroquois put these orthographies in specific historical situations. Alphabetic script entered Haudenosaunee society and sporadically found acceptance as a supplemental mode of "marking" the important matters of the confederacy while never replacing other forms of graphesis like the fabrication and exchange of wampum or the formal gathering in the Longhouse. It is also clear that the marking function of wampum is grounded in history, in the real lives of real people. Wampum marks both time past and time present, effectively connecting the two in a continuum that is Haudenosaunee sovereignty. In diplomatic negotiations, for example, the exchange of wampum punctuates each party's recitation of their historical understanding of how they came to meet for the current negotiations—What was said and agreed to before? How would this new conversation, and the agreements it inspired, dovetail with the historical trend of the negotiation between the two parties over a long period of time?

With this historicist approach in mind, it also makes good sense to open this larger exploration of graphogenesis in nineteenth-century Indian Country with the Iroquois Condolence Ceremony because the Wabanki historian Lisa Brooks has done such a comprehensive job of mapping the Native northeast where the confederacy was centered as "Native space," or that "network of villages connected by rivers and relations" within which Indigenous community and communication overlapped in a natural world most commonly imaged as a "kettle" or "pot" that fed all who lived within its borders. This is not a simple metaphor. Native space, or the "common pot," has been and continues to be shaped by historical forces, both inclusive and exclusive. For our purposes, the most important historical force in the region has been the use of alphabetic literacy for treaties, land cessions, schooling, and religious studies. Here, too, Brooks has shown that Native space is a conceptualization of the confederacy that serves us well as a framework for contextualizing the use of vernacular-language scripts in Haudenosaunee history, as they are related to place.

In *The Common Pot*, Lisa Brooks maps the seventeenth- and eighteenth-century information flow within her own homelands, the Alnobawogan, Wlogan, Awikhigan—located just east and south of the Iroquois Confederacy. There, she finds a close connection between the new European technologies of alphabetic writing and the codex and the landforms and social relationships within which they began to circulate when they reached Native communities. Brooks describes how the *awikhiganak*, "writings on birchbark," noted frequently in *The Jesuit Relations*, "traveled rapidly over rivers through the network" of preexisting Indigenous social and diplomatic channels as communities adapted older technologies "within an extant system of communication to pass new knowledge through Native space." The flow of these precontact communication technologies/systems such as birch bark and wampum exemplified an Indigenous mode of reconstructing the "Native body politic" through something she calls "a spatialized writing tradition."[22] This kind of "text," comprising graphic practices, oral recitations, and critically landed venues and routes, demonstrates for Brooks "that writing was operating as a tool of communication and delineation in Native space, independent of colonial institutions and even in direct opposition to the colonial project."[23]

The Haudenosaunee Condolence Ceremony represents a similar "spatialized writing tradition" whose practices interanimated both alphabeticism and wampum exchanges, the circulation of "texts" though Native space, and the protection of Haudenosaunee political structures through the onslaught of settler dispossession. Significantly, as Aupaumut recorded these protocols in his journal, he used its pages as a performative space. With rules and lines and indentations, he made visible the paratextual elements of his negotiations. Aupaumut's transcription of the ceremony and its attendant performances of diplomacy was somewhat unusual for Native peoples of the Northeast. He wrote in English and used a notebook instead of strings of wampum to record what he heard and saw. In doing so, he followed not only Haudenosaunee practice but also British and American diplomatic written practice, which had long since adopted textual conventions that were intended to mimic the Condolence activities in alphabetic script on a page.[24]

For most Haudenosaunee peoples, adhering to the Good Message was never about the *letter* of the law, nor was it about writing at all. It was much richer than that. But during the colonial period, the Haudenosaunees and their neighbors, Indigenous peoples like the Mahican leader Hendrick Aupaumut, were increasingly driven to add alphabetic media into their well-established protocols of communication because the nature of settler colonialism demanded new forms of record keeping and transportable media. Hale believed that "by the middle of the [eighteenth] century there were many members who could write in the well-devised orthography of the missionaries." Thus, the "Chiefs of the Great Council, at once conservative and quick to learn, saw the advantages which would accrue from preserving, by this novel method[,] their most important public duty—that of creating new chiefs—and the traditions connected with their own body."[25] But there have been times in Haudenosaunee history when an alphabetic transcription of all or part of the Condolence Ceremony has had to stand temporarily in place for the ceremony's actual performance due to epidemic, warfare, and dispossession of the very lands that once sheltered it in "the clearing at the edge of the woods."

ALPHABETIZATION AND THE CONFEDERACY

An alphabetic system for the languages of the Six Nations had been available to tribal members since the sixteenth century, although such writing was never at the forefront of Haudenosaunee media.[26] Part of the reason is that the Iroquoian dialects of its member bands are, as Akwesasne Mohawk scholar Scott Manning Stevens has pointed out, very difficult:

> Consider for a moment the challenges of writing in one of the Iroquoian languages, for our purposes, Mohawk. First we must acknowledge that Mohawk is not the name of my people in their own language; in the same

way that we use German to refer to Deutsch. Mohawk, a word derived from the Narragansett term for cannibal, is an exonym for Kanienkehaka, or People of the Flint, while Iroquois is a Franco-Algonkian denomination used for the Haudenosaunee, or People of the Long House. The structural differences are profound and as stark as those between English and Ainu might be. It is not a simple case of finding the verb and its subject, but rather a case of reinventing one's concept of how language functions. Added to this daunting conceptual difference is the fact that Mohawk, like so many indigenous languages of the Americas, was not a written language and, therefore, lacked any codified orthography. Reading early European renderings of Iroquoian words is a bit of an exercise in cryptography. Missionaries and fur traders might record lexicons that would help in everyday interactions and trade but could not be said to be sophisticated linguists.[27]

Most Christian missionaries who hoped to foster alphabetic writing among the Haudenosaunees shared the view of Asher Wright, minister to the Buffalo Creek Seneca Nation, whose sense of the necessity for written literacy among Indigenous peoples was based on the "earnest hope, that all who have anything to do with Indians . . . will strenuously exert themselves, to hasten forward the time when every Indian shall be fully able to express his own thoughts on paper, and derive his full measure of advantage from the written thoughts of others, and especially from the written Word of God."[28] But for Haudenosaunee peoples over the years, wampum has never lost its significance and its metaphoric power to depict historical change, the passing of time, all while engaging in acts of reciprocity central to Haudenosaunee governance.

Aggressively missionized by Roman Catholics, the Mohawks led the way in the use of alphabets, driven partly by their role in the Haudenosaunee Confederacy, which was that of older brothers and descendants of Tekanawita. Theirs is the official language of the confederacy. Throughout the seventeenth and eighteenth centuries, two main rival orthographies reigned—a French-language spelling system favored by Catholics, and a Protestant version derived from English and Dutch alphabets. The French system, recognizable for its use of the character 8 (a shorthand form of the omicron and upsilon ligature used in medieval manuscripts, where a lowercase upsilon letter sits atop an omicron letter) to signify the sound /w/, was crafted by Jesuits in the fifteenth century and reflects their reliance on classical philology and grammar. It was also based in their use of manuscript books rather than printed works. For missionaries in the field, using Greek letters to mark aspirated consonants that did not appear in their own language or alphabet was a quick, almost

Figure 2.4. Page from François Picquet's prayer book, 1750–1752. Courtesy of the Newberry Library, Chicago.

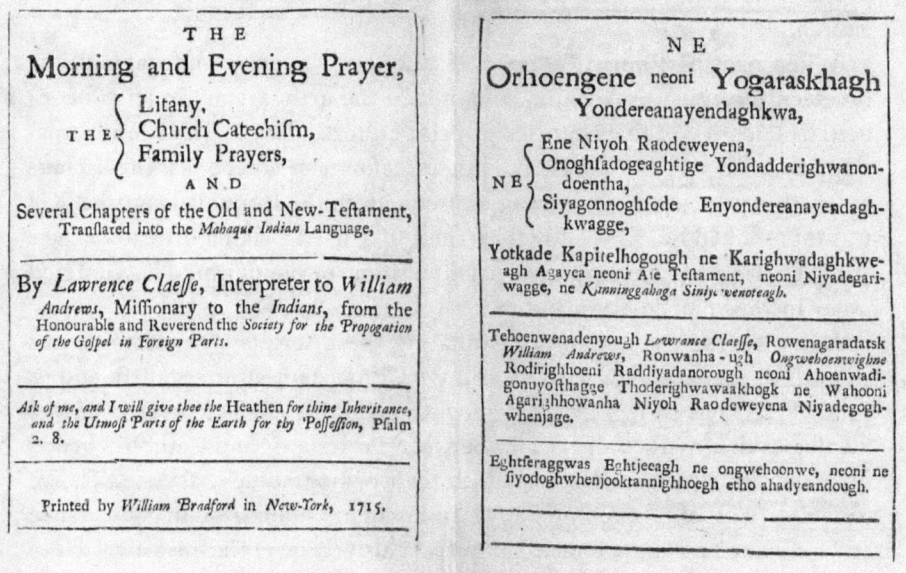

Figure 2.5. Title-page spread of Lawrence Claesse's English-Haudenosaunee edition of the Church of England's *Book of Common Prayer* / *Orhoengene*. Courtesy of the John Carter Brown Library, Providence, Rhode Island.

shorthand, method of producing usable prayers and hymns. They also had the precedent of the translation of Hebrew texts for liturgical uses. To these early missionary transcribers, Haudenosaunee languages sounded like the language of the Israelites, especially in its use of what they called *onomatopeiques*, or syllables that vary in vowel length according to their consonantal pairings.

The Protestant system was developed later, in the eighteenth century, and was much more indebted to printing than the early Jesuit manuscript works. The first important book in Mohawk to arise from the Anglican tradition, Lawrence Claesse's *Orhoengene* (1715), a translation of the Anglican *Book of Common Prayer* rolled off the press of William Bradford in New York City; and it is typographically and structurally representative of Protestant alphabetic practices among the Six Nations. Bradford used /w/ for the same or similar sounds in English and Haudenosaunee and double vowels and consonants to show length. He also rarely but occasionally employed syllable breaks. There are few if any diacritical marks, save intermittent accented syllables employed for clarity. The title page of his *Orhoengene* also engages in the Protestant tradition of scripture exegesis, using a Gospel passage for its epigraph: "Ask of me, and I will give thee the heathen for thine inheritance, and the utmost parts of the earth for thy possession" (Psalm 2:8). It is a neat précis of the baldly dominionist theology of the British Empire's established church.

When revising Roman Catholic texts for Six Nations congregants in the nineteenth century, J. A. Cuoq streamlined the orthography in an effort to better match it to the exigencies of print culture: "The ancient Jesuit missionaries used very appropriately, in their manuscript notebooks, Greek characters to represent the aspirations so frequent in the Iroquois language. KH was represented by chi, TH by theta, and they used a sigma instead of the s after SH. But what was advantageous for writing, by hand, would have offered many inconveniences for printing."[29]

Likewise, the process of disseminating these scripts was by no means smooth or regular. Between 1715 and 1787, Protestant efforts stalled, and as Sarah Rivett has shown in *Unscripted America*, the struggle over language ideologies that marked the rivalry between Protestants and Catholics belied the ease with which each side claimed their orthographies harvested Native converts. Because most comparative studies of missionization in New France and New England "have focused almost exclusively on ethno-historical genealogies, charting the various ways that French and British attitudes towards American Indians differed," we have, Rivett argues, largely missed the broader stakes in such vernacular transcriptions.

Rather than race or ethnicity, the crucial ideological categories undergirding all vernacular-language written and printed texts in both colonial worlds, Rivett argues, were drawn from "a theological contest between two competing colonial powers and against the secularizing currents of the Enlightenment." Therefore, Rivett suggests, "Jesuit and Protestant missionary linguistics contributed two distinct modes of Enlightenment thought." One, emanating from the French Jesuits, "ushered in an era of colonial anthropology, reflected in the works of Joseph-François Lafitau and Bernard Picart." The Protestants, Rivett writes, "sought to absorb indigenous words into a millennial vision of their own divine right to North America." Long after the culmination of Protestant colonial missionary efforts, "indigenous words remained repositories of an ancient sacred essence that underwrote a new national era of literary and scientific progress."[30]

But as Scott Manning Stevens rightly observes, the Haudenosaunees saw neither the Christian religious texts they translated nor the imperial desires encoded in their missionization practices as the precise means by which the Longhouse would be preserved in the face of European encroachment. As is true in all the case histories of the introduction of alphabetic script to Indigenous communities in North America, the Haudenosaunee communities had little desire for literacy or Christianity in and of themselves. War, disease, and dislocations had broken so many of the "chains" that had once linked members of the confederacy that new media were needed to forge new ties and relations against the implacable force of the colonizing institutions, military forts, townships, and range.[31]

The Mohawks who followed the Anglican Church and its orthography, for example, quickly formed "a circle of literate Mohawks who could address the problems of translation from within the language rather than from without." One such circle grew up around the famed Mohawk leader, Thayendanegea (Joseph Brant), who translated the Gospel of Mark and advised on revisions of the Mohawk *Book of Common Prayer* (based on Henry Barclay's and others' abbreviated version of 1769). Between 1769 and 1880, several editions of the Gospels were produced in the vernacular by Mohawks themselves. In 1804, the adopted Cherokee Scot John Norton, published his translation of the Gospel of John. In 1836, Henry Aaron Hill translated the Gospel of Luke and the Epistles of Paul; and in 1880, Joseph Onasakenrat offered his translation of the Gospels as a whole.

INSCRIBING CONDOLENCE

For the Haudenosaunees, the conduct of diplomacy proved to be the most lasting and efficacious venue in which to use their alphabetic literacy. The Delaware leader Teedyuscung was just one of many midcentury Native negotiators in the Northeast who demanded the right to select a clerk to record the minutes of the nation's treaty sessions. In 1756, he appointed the Quaker schoolteacher Charles Thomson to be his amanuensis over the protestations of land barons like George Croghan, who believed the Society of Friends was behind Teedyuscung's sudden turn toward alphabetic literacy. As more and more land cessions in Indian Country became clouded with rhetorical double-dealing, others also sought the protection of written contracts. Although he knew English, Teedyuscung hired fellow Lenape John Pumpshire to be his interpreter. There were, however, important social innovations beyond the utilitarian aspects of Teedyuscung's and other Native negotiators' turn toward alphabeticism. Native people like Pumpshire took on the role of "clerks" in an emerging bureaucracy that melded Haudenosaunee communication practices with those of European nation-states. As the historian James Merrell has observed, from the European point of view, the "second scribe thrust an illegitimate voice and pen into official business." Significantly, "in a larger sense, the secretary was indeed 'the thing,' because he was a teacher that could guide illiterate Indians through the forbidden recesses of the written world, a world colonial leaders wanted to keep to themselves."[32]

Some members of the Haudenosaunee Confederacy took alphabeticism a step further and began to transcribe ceremonial activities and wampum signifiers into vernacular-language written texts. In 1757, for example, a Mohawk leader named David from the village of Schoharie along the Mohawk River wrote out a version of the Condolence Ceremony in alphabetic script. While we do not know the exact circumstances that spurred him to create this hybrid media form, the text's later history suggests that some kind of social upheaval (perhaps the war itself) prompted his action. The text comes down to us through an 1832 copy made by Chief J. S. Johnson in "a small unbound book, resembling a schoolboy's copy-book." Johnson copied the text at the request of its owner, whose tribal community was experiencing an outbreak of "Asiatic cholera" that threatened to wipe out the village and its collective memory.[33] Johnson's copy of the original is one of the text sources for Horatio Hale's *Iroquois Book of Rites* (1883).

David—probably David Orighuryghsto or Otkoghraro—was most likely the son of the Mohawk Aquianer, who is recorded as having married a Mohawk woman called Sara at Schoharie on July 25, 1747. Sara, or "Old Seth," was Tehodoghwenziagegh's niece, and thus part of the important kinship relations that guided the Condolence Ceremony, as Seth was the head of the Mohawk village at Schoharie in the 1750s. A closer examination of life at Schoharie in the eighteenth century reveals the social upheaval that may have inspired David to produce an alphabetic form of the Condolence Ceremony. In the first decades of the century, as the historian David Preston has noted, "Schoharie was rich in emotional and spiritual significance for the Natives who lived there." The village was nestled in a fertile, well-watered valley, and enjoyed access to the Mohawk River. It was surrounded by mountains, one of which was called "Onistagrawa or Corn Mountain," a name suggesting its embodiment of spiritual power.[34]

The original settlement of Schoharie was buffeted by the forces of European colonialism. It was only after the 1688 French invasion that Mohawks settled there permanently in substantial numbers. By the first decade of the eighteenth century, however, Schoharie was a multiethnic village, offering shelter to Haudenosaunees forced out of their original homelands to the north. Although it was a "new" community, Schoharie quickly took on the attributes of a Mohawk political "hub," and a potent localism emerged that defined its members in the colonial record as "Schoharie Mohawks."[35] Soon, it also became home to an emigrant Palatine community. Conrad Weiser, who later became an important interpreter of the Mohawk language, was the son of Palatine immigrants and remembered that period fondly: "Here the people lived for a few years without preacher, and without government, generally in peace. Each one did what he thought was right."[36] Preston believes that for at least a brief period, the larger community of Schoharie and its surroundings were fortified by "peaceful exchanges between the Mohawks and the Palatines, and the creation of kinship ties."[37] When Weiser arrived in 1712 to study Mohawk, there was also an emerging English evangelical presence.

David probably studied at Schoharie, given the fact of his alphabetic literacy in Mohawk and the missionaries' desire to teach and use the language in schools and churches. The career of Daniel Claus, who would become a key player in Mohawk life as the Indian agent for the region, also began in Schoharie, and the settlement's multiethnic nature nurtured his facility with the Indigenous dialect and his knowledge of the people. Transcribing his memoir later in life, Claus recalled that he learned how to speak and write Mohawk "by getting his Indian tutor to dictate him speeches, messages, and other forms and customs used by the Indians in councils[,] ceremonies of Condolences, &c &c." Thus, form and content, protocol and phonetics went hand in hand.[38]

By the mid-eighteenth century, however, the Mohawk River valley was in turmoil. In 1753, negotiations between the Mohawks and New Yorkers broke down when the powers at Albany treated Mohawk leader Hendrick's (Theyanoguin's) land claims with insulting disdain. He responded in no uncertain terms. "The covenant chain is broken," he declared. Concerned merchants and colonial officials hastily arranged a meeting the following year. Known as the Albany Congress, it attempted to reset relations between the Mohawks and the British. Global forces intervened, however, in the form of Europe's Seven Years' War, in which the French and English empires faced off against each other. In America, French forces had begun to occupy the Ohio River valley, building forts along the Allegany. In July 1754, they delivered a major defeat to the British at Fort Necessity. Mohawks were once again forced to move, this time from Khanawake to the Ohio valley.

At Schoharie, factionalism developed as the community, "beset with 'jealousy and disagreement' split into two parties over . . . whether to allow the British to build a Fort at their village."[39] Outright warfare and forced emigration unleashed disease, which also took its toll on Schoharie social cohesion. In 1757, "malignant fever" swept through the Mohawk communities, with Old Seth among its victims. The social fabric of the Native community was so frayed by this point that Old Seth was not replaced (and perhaps not "requickened") until the war ended in 1764.[40] Contemporaneous diplomatic journals report that the Schoharie Mohawks were literally in a "starving condition."[41] Under such pressures, the kinship and political ties binding Palatines and Mohawks quickly unraveled, and many Europeans exploited the social disorder to scoop up Indian land under suspicious circumstances.

David of Schoharie figured prominently in the Mohawk community's pushback. In 1758, he represented the village as a go-between for Sir William Johnson, British superintendent of Indian Affairs (1756–74), who intervened in the controversy on the side of the Native people. Johnson's plan was to employ the Condolence Ceremony to reconcile the Mohawks and Europeans. David and Johnson's emissary, Captain Fonda, met with the local non-Indian representative to exchange wampum and explain how a further Condolence Ceremony would take place to settle an inter-Indian murder case to the satisfaction of both sides. At the end of his report, Fonda mentions "a string of two rows [of wampum]."[42] Later, when Johnson needed Native scouts, David came to his aid and served throughout the campaign on the British side.

By May 1756, a leadership struggle was underway among the Schoharie Mohawks, between those following Seth Tehodoghwenziagegh and those under David's stewardship. On December 26, 1758, Sir William Johnson gave David twenty pounds to start a settlement at Avigo on the Susquehanna River, perhaps in an attempt to ease the leadership crisis at Schoharie. Seth appears to have died in the summer of 1756, but political division at Schoharie delayed his formal condolence (and replacement) until the following January. David, now "Chief of the Schoharie Indians," came to Fort Johnson for the Condolence Ceremony. Dissent probably continued, however, for that spring two rival groups offered candidates to replace Old Seth—David in May and Seth Jr. (Turtle Clan) in early June.[43]

Given these circumstances, it makes sense that David would put his alphabetic skills to use in service to his community. His manuscript likely represents his effort to preserve history and tradition in the face of the overwhelming loss of life and geographic separation of communities during wartime. Internal evidence within the manuscript copy suggests other reasons why this gesture might have seemed appropriate to him. The manuscript reads today as a composite hybrid text, and (in the view of at least one linguist) it "functions like a prompter's book," because it is not in the right order and can be fitted to various speaker's roles: "Handwritten copies of [this] version are owned by ritualists or their descendants at Six Nations Reserve, [and] the versions dating since the turn of the century show signs of influence by Hale's Mohawk text."[44]

What we do not know about the "shape" of the original manuscript from Schoharie may be partly surmised by evidence drawn from the earliest extant original manuscript version of the Condolence Ceremony, written by Capt. John Deserontyon, a Mohawk war leader who joined Joseph Brant in fighting the Americans during the Revolution. The manuscript, "Roghya Gonghsera," is dated 1782 and was written in the village of Lachine, near Montréal. Like the

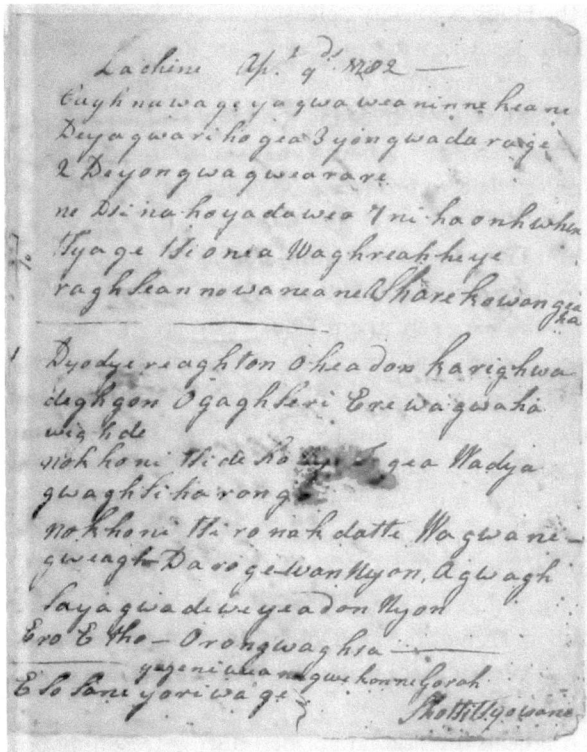

Figure 2.6. First page of John Deserontyon's "Roghya Gonghsera," 1782. Deserontyon, *Mohawk Form of Ritual of Condolence*.

Schoharie manuscript, this text is sedimented with the communication protocols of the Haudenosaunees' new political order meant to address European colonialism. The manuscript was published in facsimile in 1928 as *A Mohawk Form of Ritual of Condolence, 1782*.

John Deserontyon was alphabetically literate in both Mohawk and English, and his original home community of Fort Hunter along the Mohawk River was an early adopter of Anglicanism. In 1712, the Society for the Propagation of the Gospel (SPG) had sent missionary William Andrews to the newly constructed fort in an effort both to make inroads against previous Catholic missionizing and to drive a wedge into the Dutch influence over the fur trade in the area. Writing home to the SPG the following spring, Andrews noted that while some members of the Mohawk community viewed him with skepticism, a great many welcomed the opportunity for literacy: "I have proposed to the Mohawks the Teaching of their Children to read and write, and they are very well approved." Andrews was not sure, however, if the Mohawks' demand for instruction in their own language would pass muster at the SPG. "Whether they should be taught English or their own Language," he noted in his report,

"I would willingly know the Honble. Society's pleasure, but in Submission to give my Opinion that ... the best way will be to keep them to their own Language, for it has been observed That those who speak English are the worst, because it gives them Opportunity of conversing the more with the English ... and so to learn their vices."[45] By 1715, Andrews had collaborated with the military interpreter Lawrence Claus to produce a *Book of Common Prayer* in the Mohawk language.

Andrews's students soon grew bored of his mission as its novelty wore off, and the Fort Hunter Native community did not have a regular missionary again until 1735, when the SPG sent them Henry Barclay. Barclay was American-born and spoke English and Dutch. By 1741, he had supervised the construction of a chapel at Fort Hunter and hired two Christian Mohawk leaders to serve as schoolmasters there. John Deserontyon was born during this period; he was baptized in the Anglican faith and taught to write alphabetic Mohawk. In 1779, Anglican minister John Doty preached to the Fort Hunter Mohawks at Lachine, observing, "It gives me great pleasure to assure the Society that as far as I have been able to hear and observe, the Mohawks of Fort Hunter are more civilized in their manners than any other Indians."[46] Yet many details of life at Fort Hunter during Deserontyon's formative years belie historians' oft-repeated verdict that he, like many Mohawks of his generation, was "assimilated."

As we have seen, the Anglican mission languished during Deserontyon's teenage years, as one military conflict after another ravaged the Mohawk homeland in the 1750s and 1760s. On the eve of the Revolutionary War, Anglican missionary Rev. John Stuart collaborated with Mohawk leader Joseph Brant (an alumnus of Wheelock's Indian School) on Mohawk language religious texts that finally reestablished a lasting presence for the Church of England among the Fort Hunter Mohawks. Soon after the war started, the Reverend Stuart was jailed, and his parishioners fled to Canada. It was this unique combination of alphabeticism, Christianity, and staunch Mohawk nationalism and traditionalism that actually marked Deserontyon's place in the British American colonial world.

In 1777, Deserontyon had participated in the British siege on Fort Stanwix, serving under Col. Barry St. Leger, who found him an amiable, if brash companion. Many years later, fellow Haudenosaunee leader John Norton produced a somewhat unflattering portrait of Deserontyon after his first major battle. According to Norton, the Native fighters and their British allies had won the first round of combat, but St. Leger misunderstood why the Haudenosaunees left the field and took their wounded to safety in villages "of two or three day's travel." Thinking they had completely retreated, St. Leger "raised the siege and beat a retreat, leaving his tents and stuff." Deserontyon was not in such a hurry. "Not being willing to leave in haste such good fare as was on Col. St. Leger's Table," Norton tells us, Capt. John Deserontyon "remained with his comrades, regaling themselves, until they were surprised by a Party of the Americans who had sallied from the Fort." In the ensuing skirmish, "a discharge of musketry brought Deserontyon to the ground—his comrade made his escape through them,—and after the enemy had retired, returned in search of his friend whom he found weltering in his own blood,—his shoulder was broken, but the vital parts were untouched,—he carried him off,—& he was perfectly cured."[47]

Between the 1777 battle at Stanwix and the 1779 Sullivan Campaign that laid waste to Fort Hunter and its surrounding communities, Deserontyon (known now as "Captain John") appears sporadically in the European historical record as both an eager and valued scout for the Crown and as the young, impetuous, bellicose man Norton describes. In one letter, dated just before the exile of the Mohawks to Canada, one Robert Langan complains that John has been "trouble," primarily because Colonel Butler has "spoi'd" him.[48] Deserontyon seems to have been a favorite of the officers, an emerging cosmopolitan of sorts, equally at ease at European tables and Haudenosaunee council grounds. Although he has been eclipsed in histories of the period by Joseph Brant, he was in many ways very similar to the more famous Mohawk leader he supported in so many diplomatic and military dispatches of the war. He was also very much his own man and did not consider Brant his superior. He had his own community to lead, and when the war ended, he led them to a settlement on the Bay of Quinté on Lake Ontario instead of joining Brant's Grand River community.

By the 1780s when he penned the Condolence Ceremony manuscript, Deserontyon had matured a great deal. He had assumed leadership of a destitute, starving community exiled to Canada. In addition, he remained a determined warrior. On May 13, 1781, he posted a letter to Daniel Claus stating that he had taken prisoners at Carajoharce. Throughout the period, he wrote alphabetic Mohawk letters to his superiors, outlining his actions and proposing strategies to defeat the Americans. He also seems to have been part of the establishment of a new Mohawk Confederacy north of the American border, a coalition calling itself the Seven Nations. In a 1780 letter, Deserontyon says that the Seven Nations have decided to "be of one mind," apparently having formed a sort of rump confederacy in Canada.[49]

Deserontyon's Condolence manuscript thus emerged from within a community in exile that was completely ignored by the Treaty of Paris that officially ended hostilities later that year. The Americans were not fond of these

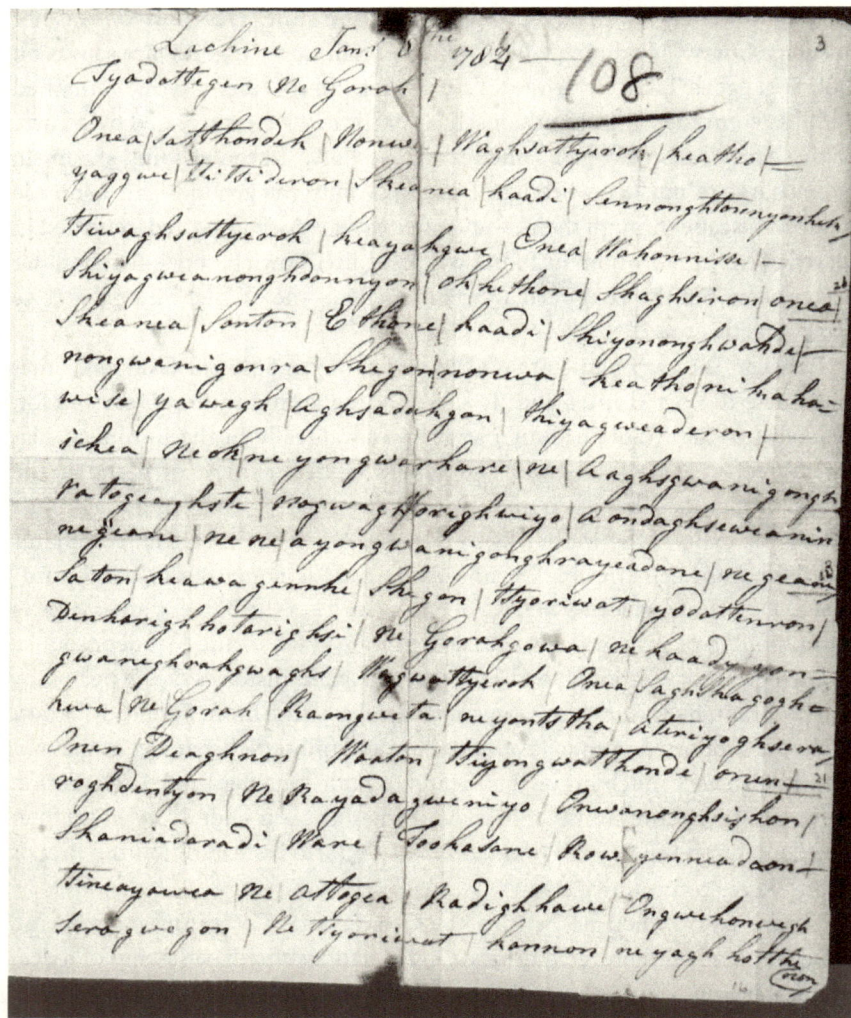

Figure 2.7. Letter written in Mohawk, "John Deserontyon to Daniel Claus, January 8, 1784." The vertical lines demonstrate how translators of written Mohawk parsed out "words" from the strings of particles employed in the spoken language. Claus Family Papers, C-1478, Manuscript Division, Public Archives of Canada, Ottawa, Ontario.

Mohawks who had emigrated to Canada when the fighting broke out, and the community now needed to find a permanent safe haven. The local British governor, Frederick Haldimand, was eager to resettle the Mohawks into "reserves" well removed from Canadian British villages and under the supervision of Indian agents of the Crown. Haldimand carved out a place for them at Grand River, and Joseph Brant's community settled there. Deserontyon refused. His mind was set on the Bay of Quinté.⁵⁰ As Daniel Claus observed, the Mohawks considered this land to be part of their material culture of communication and tradition:

> A disagreeable proposal this to people who lived at their Ease upon a rich tract of Country left them and possessed by their ancestors from time immemorial and they chiefly by the natural monuments of that native Land of their, such as Rivers, woods, Mountains, Rocks, and its environs preserved the Thread of recollection of their General History handed down from Father to Son, besides to leave the Graves of their deceased Friends and Relations to be demolished and abused by their Enemies. Notwithstanding these severe Trials and Reflections, I prevailed upon them last Spring to go and look out for a future Abode in the Neighborhood aforesaid. Al [sic] the objections they had against it was that the Country was inhabited by a people they did not understand and having been conquered as they pretend & believe by their ancestors they have a contemptible opinion off [sic].⁵¹

In 1784, Deserontyon's Lachine community wrote to the Commander of Indian Affairs to express their extreme disappointment at their treatment following the British surrender:

> It is a long time ago since you told us it was peace, which troubled our mind very much, since which we have been kept in the dark, expecting from time to time that news to be confirmed to us with certainty and truth for you told us then which was last spring that it wanted only one thing . . . the Definitive Treaty to be signed by the King and the respective powers. Now we were not a little surprised when we first heard that the kings people were reduced and disarmed, next that Sir John Johnson, alia x, was gone for England . . . for which reason we say that our minds are troubled besides we are ashamed to death for we don't consider ourselves conquered, and our warriors spirits are still strong and firm.⁵²

In his prefatory remarks to the modern edition of the work, Tuscarora linguist and ethnographer J. N. B. Hewitt touches on these contexts in passing: "This manuscript briefly records a naïve specimen of the class of traditional literature relating to the ceremonial side of the League of the Iroquois which arose when the disintegrating pressure of European culture on the integrity of the institutions of the League became increasingly evident to the intelligent leaders of the Iroquois people."⁵³ Under these circumstances, the Six Nations experienced what Hewitt calls "a pronounced striving for the preservation of the usual, customary forms and content of the several sacred rituals and chants employed in League ceremonials."⁵⁴ While acknowledging the colonial context within which Deserontyon produced his manuscript, Hewitt rebukes him for what he considers its "inauthenticity," noting disapprovingly that the text's "odd innovations," such as the distribution of wampum in a ceremony that traditionally did not feature it, or the use of "brothers" as a form of address rather than the more appropriate "fathers" and "mothers."[55]

Yet even if these changes do reflect what Hewitt terms "a lack of knowledge of the ritual which the recorder was seeking to write out," that is clearly not the manuscript's main point. Deserontyon's written Condolence Ceremony partakes of much traditional Mohawk practice. Like all traditional oral recitations of the Condolence Ceremony, this one was occasioned by the death of leader Peter Asharekowa (Great Knife), who passed in March 1782, after having had held the ancestral role of Asharekowa in the original Longhouse. This left the exiled Mohawk community at Lachine in an even more tenuous position. Deserontyon, as Captain John, likely held a role similar to that of a council leader in older times. Claus recalled, "He is allowed the best speaker according to the old Stile the Six Nations now have and has an excellent memory."[56]

The Six Nations were widely dispersed by the time Deserontyon set pen to paper, and gathering for a real Condolence Ceremony was thus out of the question. In addition, many Mohawks suspected some Oneidas of conspiring with the Americans to undermine their communities. In this social milieu, Deserontyon's supposed lack of knowledge about the old ways is less important than the way the manuscript functioned socially in its time. In Detroit in 1793, for example, Deserontyon exchanged tense words with Captain McKee over his party's desire to do a League ritual, fearing that the British commander would not allow it to be performed in a woodside clearing, a prohibition that would have rendered the ceremony unacceptable. "We are determined," Deserontyon wrote his superiors, "to have our law proceeded with."[57] Given this wartime state of affairs, the Condolence manuscript seems to suggest itself as a hedge against outside forces that were threatening to co-opt the Lachine Mohawks under Deserontyon's command into a wholly assimilationist posture toward warfare and diplomacy. If we set aside Hewitt's skepticism regarding Deserontyon's knowledge of the ceremony and his commitment to its forms, we are left with a fundamental question of social practice and communication: Why, in the middle of all this chaos, in a community touted for its Anglican zeal, did Deserontyon organize a modified Condolence Ceremony, and most importantly, why did he write it down?

The manuscript's provenance offers one possible clue, for it comes down to us through the papers of Daniel Claus. Presumably, the ceremony (even a "degraded" form) could have taken place in a more traditional way, with oral

Kahiatónhsera 107

recitations in the combination church and council house Reverend Doty described. Although it appears that Deserontyon recited the text for his small community as a gesture of tradition, there is good reason to believe that it was also written with a British imperial audience in mind. Why? Perhaps it would not have been appropriate or practical for Claus to have attended the actual ceremony and performance, and perhaps Deserontyon decided to provide the manuscript as a record of his community's stability. After all, there are hundreds of comparable reports of treaties and councils of a very similar form. Or it may have simply been that it was not convenient for Claus to attend, but he (or Deserontyon) nonetheless desired to have a record of it. Because it was written in Mohawk, which Claus's superior Haldimand could not read, it would appear that the manuscript's influence was intended to be local, with Claus alone woven into a communal relation with the Mohawks at Lachine as the imagined auditor whose ears were "cleared" by Captain John's recitation. All of this, however, hardly justifies Hewitt's claim that Claus "dominated the affairs" of the Lachine community.

Internal evidence in the manuscript suggests, instead, that Deserontyon sought to reaffirm Claus's kinship relation to the diasporic Lachine Mohawks. At one point in the manuscript, Deserontyon deviates from tradition to comment: "I have smoothed over the rough earth whereupon, indeed, landed the flesh of him that is our business, the later Asharekowa, that is, we as one, had him as the embodiment of our affairs, so that when we speak words over the corpse, that is it, he and I, and the Gorah [Indian Agent] are unanimous." Condolence Ceremonies were often about alliances, and it seems this one was no different in that regard. By adding Claus into the list of condoling parties (he and I, and the *Gorah*) Deserontyon expands the meaning of the Condolence Ceremony to include the diplomatic relationship his community enjoys with the Haldimand regime.

This gesture may also explain other elements of the manuscript that Hewitt singles out as evidence of Captain John's ignorance of tradition. At the end of each of his "matters" (*wake'*), Deserontyon offers a string of wampum: "The first thing is 'The Forepart of the Ceremony.' The tears, we have born them elsewhere. And also from his open throat we have dislodged the several lodgements. And also from his outspread mat [his dwelling place], we have wiped away the several bloodspots. Thoroughly again, we have readjusted the things (there). Indeed, there[,] a wampum string (is required)."[58]

Hewitt characterizes the manuscript's use of the phrase *E'ro, E'tho,' oron'kwā' sâ* as "an odd innovation," explaining that "the reference to the use of wampum at the close of the paragraphs shows that the manuscript was intended to record [that] which [I have] called the Requickening Address . . . no other ritual employs wampum in any form." What Hewitt must have known, but chose not to acknowledge, was that Deserontyon's manuscript was an intentionally truncated form of the Condolence Ceremony with elements carefully selected to fit his specific historical situation. The same holds true for Hewitt's complaint that "outside of the phrase ['The Forepart of the Ceremony'] . . . there is nothing in the manuscript" from the "preliminary rites at the edge of the forest, consisting of the Chant of Welcome by the mourning side and the first three unit paragraphs of the Requickening Address." Hewitt misses the point entirely. There are no neighboring nations with which to condole. There is no "edge of the woods." The community is outside the city of Montréal; the men are often away on military raids; the land around them is a battlefield.[59]

Deserontyon's Condolence Ceremony manuscript also offers clues to its hybrid generic place in eighteenth-century Haudenosaunee orature through its physical properties, the way it appears to have been inscribed, and its gestures toward its broader relationship to the well-established practice of Mohawk language epistolary discourse that appears in the archives of Daniel Claus and Frederick Haldimand. The opening page of Deserontyon's manuscript includes, curiously, a calendrical date that echoes the opening of all letters exchanged between literate Mohawks in the Mohawk language and others within their social sphere. In the traditional rite, there would be no need to date the performance in this way or as it unfolded. The traditional form of the Condolence Ceremony would have woven the present experience of the Mohawks in the battlefield into the whole history of the confederacy since the Condolence Ceremony had begun in time immemorial. Other marks on the page suggest that the manuscript balances this timely, epistolary gesture with performative elements that are not completely codified in the alphabetic tradition. What are we to make of the long rules or dashes that Deserontyon employs halfway down the page, and again to set off the traditional recitation, "*Ero & tho—Orohgaghia—*"? Like the manuscript at Schoharie, there seems to be an element of the prompt book here. The manuscript both performs and archives the liturgical shape of the Condolence Ceremony. In this way, it echoes the techniques that Hendrick Aupaumut used in his manuscript journal of his embassy to the Western Indian nations in 1792. There appears to be an effort in both sets of scribal practices to make the two-dimensional page do the work of an in-person performance. It seems clear that for postwar Haudenosaunee refugees like John Deserontyon, vernacular-language script, pen, and paper had begun to take their place among more traditional communication practices, especially in the face of settler colonial scribal and print practices that effectively excluded the Indigenous nations that participated in the war from any meaningful engagement with the inscription of peace that came in the form of the Treaty of Paris in 1783.

INSCRIBING "A THING OF THE HEART"

At the conclusion of the Revolutionary War, the Iroquois Confederacy was scattered across a now-partitioned traditional homeland further severed by an international border. Four of the six nations of the confederacy—the Mohawk, Seneca, Onondaga, and Cayuga Nations—had sided with the British, and many Mohawks migrated to locations in Canada. Thayendanegea (Joseph Brant) accepted Sir Frederick Hallimand's offer of Grand River and moved his community there in 1792. John Deserontyon, as we have seen, chose another location in Canada, the Bay of Quinté, for his exiled Mohawk community. The Senecas, who also fought with the British against the Americans, regrouped at Buffalo Creek and Cold Springs, and the confederacy as a whole, for a time, considered the Seneca town at Buffalo Creek to be the new home of the confederacy's council fire. Because the Senecas had been allies of the defeated British, the United States forced them to cede most of their territory. When the Treaty of Big Tree was signed in 1797, the Senecas relinquished all of Western New York except for twelve reservations, including Buffalo Creek.

It was during this period of reorganization and decolonial struggle that another set of Haudenosaunee vernacular-language texts emerged among the Six Nations to guide new social practices in the face of the further social dislocation and unrest that characterized the postwar period. These texts comprised the prophetic Code of Handsome Lake, called the *Gai'wiio'* (pronounced guy-we-you), a set of religious teachings that offered an alternative to Christianity on the one hand and a revitalization of the "old way" of the Condolence Ceremony on the other. As Arthur C. Parker explains, "Gai'wiio' is the record of the teachings of the Seneca prophet Handsome Lake, and purports to be an exact exposition of the precepts that he taught during a term of sixteen years, ending with his death in 1815. It is the basis of the so-called 'new religion' of the Six Nations and is preached or recited at all the annual midwinter festivals on the various Iroquois reservations in New York and Ontario that have adherents."[60] In 1913, Parker published an English-language translation of the Code, explaining its social context in an imaginary conversation with fellow Senecas who followed Handsome Lake's teachings. "The social and economic and moral order all about them is the white man's, not theirs. How long can they oppose their way to the overwhelming forces of the modern world and exist? How long will they seek to meet these overwhelming forces with those their ancestors devised not with a knowledge of what the future would require?" Parker asks. His respondents answer, "Of these things we know nothing; we know only that the Great Ruler will care for us as long as we are faithful." Asked about the clothes they wear, the houses they live in, the Longhouse they worship in, they reply, "All these things may be made of the white man's material but they are outside things. Our religion is not one of paint and feathers; it is a thing of the heart."[61]

Handsome Lake, whose 1799 prophetic visions gave rise to the Good Message, was born around 1735. Although Parker claims that "nothing of any consequence [is] known of his life up to the time of his 'vision,'" when recounted a century later, Handsome Lake's life story resembles a myth that completes the Tekanawita story.[62] It is true, however, that at his birth, no one expected much of him. Handsome Lake was considered such "a tiny unpromising babe" that his own Wolf Clan rejected him, and he had to be adopted by the Turtle Clan. By early adulthood, however, Handsome Lake had become a renowned hunter with a prestigious marriage, and he had so distinguished himself as a member of the Seneca community that upon the death of its foremost Council chief, the women of the Wolf Clan elected him to undergo the Condolence Ceremony and take the place of the deceased leader. His election was somewhat problematic because he had been adopted by the Turtle Clan, but he soon was given the "name-title" Ga-nio-dai'yu (Skannadario, or Handsome Lake) and took his seat in Longhouse as a leader. Parker reports that "the people hailed him as their wisest councilor."[63]

Yet Handsome Lake had a troubled mind, which Parker describes as "moodiness." After the war, he appears to have grown increasingly disconsolate in the face of the unceasing advance of Europeans into the Seneca homeland. In 1794, Handsome Lake affixed his signature alongside those of Hendrick Aupaumut and Henry Young Brant—Joseph Brant's nephew—to the Treaty of Canandaigua, an agreement that was to "recognize and affirm the rights of the people of the Longhouse to their lands and way of life." But as the historian Michael Oberg has observed, "The legacy of the treaty for the Six Nations [was] far more ambivalent."[64] Despite the hopes of its signatories, the Treaty of Canandaigua did little to stem the tide of the settler onslaught; and in 1795, Handsome Lake was driven out of his native Genesee country as it was slowly sold to the usurpers. It may have been Handsome Lake's role in treaty-making and its failure to save the land that caused him to utter in 1799, at the onset of his prophecies, "I have been distressed since four years ago."

In Parker's telling of the Handsome Lake story, the prophet's melancholy deepened when his wife died, followed soon by one of his daughters, thus ushering in a part of his life that eerily mirrors Hiawatha's. Like the ancient leader, Handsome Lake's mourning and inconsolable sadness made him neglect his

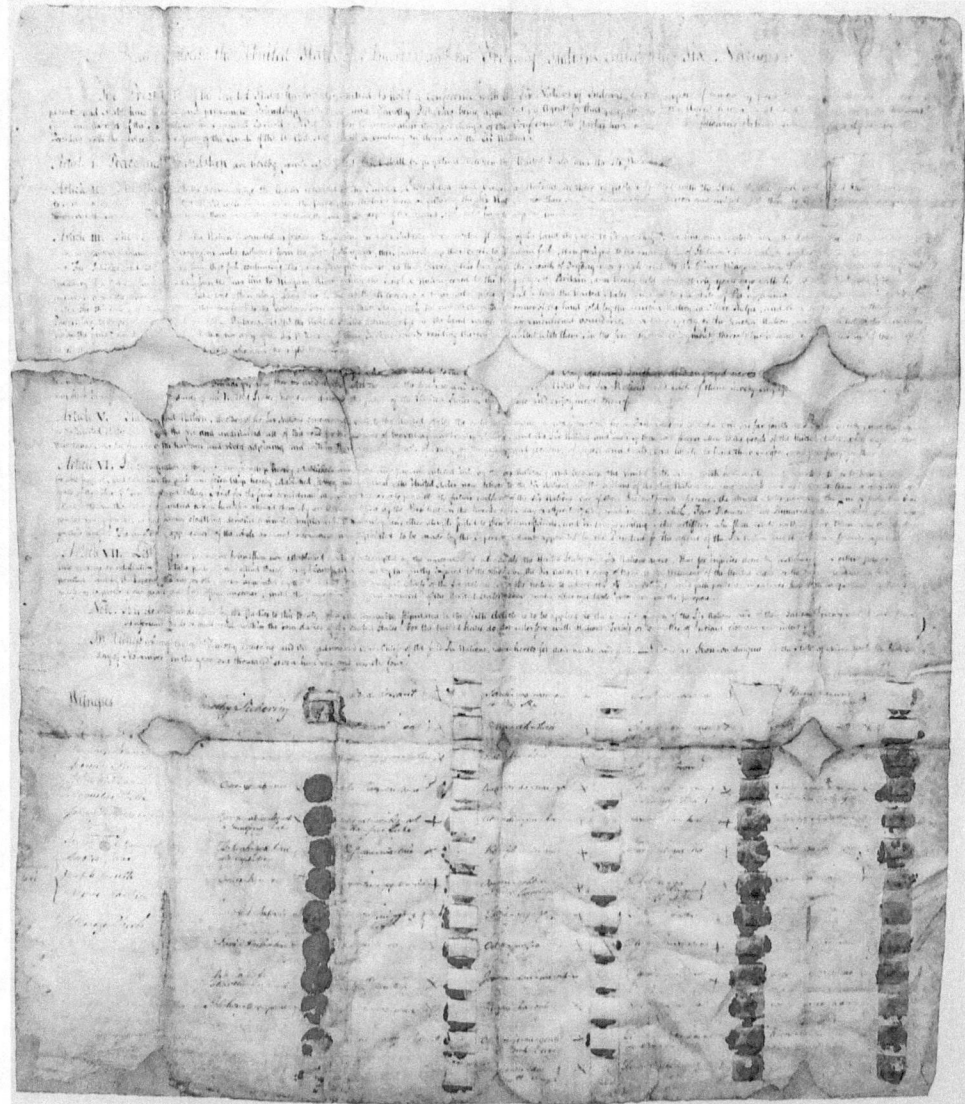

Figure 2.8. Treaty of Canandaigua, 1794. Handsome Lake's signature is in the second column from the left, third down. Courtesy of the Ontario County Historical Society, Canandaigua, New York.

leadership responsibilities, and he drifted aimlessly. He soon took to drink, moving to a plot of land owned by his relative Cornplanter on the Allegany River in Pennsylvania. Accompanied by his remaining daughter, who nursed him in his alcoholic suffering, he lived apart from the community he was chosen to serve, in a "solitary cabin of bark." By 1799, bedridden and virtually alone, he fell into a coma from which his daughter was unable to wake him.

Cornplanter witnessed this event and later corroborated that four people had appeared at Handsome Lake's door, but only briefly, for "in a moment they were gone." When Cornplanter reached Handsome Lake, he "took examination and discovered his breath [was] gone." He rushed to the nearest neighbor and got him to help him take the body back into the house and lay it on his bed. As they stood vigil, the village council met and decided that Handsome Lake would be interred at seven o'clock the following morning. Once again, the community checked to see whether Handsome Lake was dead, feeling his chest for a heartbeat. People were shocked to find his chest "still warm" and determined to put off the burial for a time. On the fourth day, Handsome Lake revived, suddenly blurting out, "I am called to death and now I came to life again, and I have been with the happy company for the angel of the lord hath descended from Heaven—and came to us to teach the disobedient children." Handsome Lake went on to teach, in a series of "matters" much like those of the Condolence Ceremony, a set of moral protocols involving temperance, sexual probity, and the confession of sins.

For all its surprising revelations, however, Handsome Lake's prophecy did not signal a major deviation from the Great Law of the Longhouse for members of the confederacy. In fact, as Annemarie Shimony observes,

> When Handsome Lake awoke from his trance in 1799 to utter the first of his prophetic revelations—now incorporated into the body of dicta, anecdotes, and laws which comprise the Good Message—he did not introduce a radically new ethic. Rather, he propounded a doctrine taken largely from the existing body of Iroquois religion, which he had reinterpreted and syncretized with the Christian, and particularly Quaker, teaching familiar to his community. . . . These observances are the Six Nations convention and the chiefs' convention. Both are primarily meetings for the purpose of reciting the Good Message of Handsome Lake, which today involves the revelation as described by the Prophet himself and memorized and transmitted through several lines of preachers, an explanation of the necessity of the revelation, and certain biographical details about the life of the Prophet and the circumstances of the revelation to him.[65]

Handsome Lake's visions and teaching have provided the basis for an oral text that is recited yearly in the longhouses of his followers in Canada and New York. The text is extensive, taking three or four days to recite.

What interests me here are not the specific rules of the Code but rather the textualities and social practices that embody them; for by the 1840s, the Code had expanded beyond oral recitation to include aural transcription in fascinating ways. Parker summarizes this transitional period:

> The present form of the Gai'wiio' was determined by a council of its preachers some fifty years ago. They met at Cold Spring, the old home of Handsome Lake, and compared their versions. Several differences were found and each preacher thought his version the correct one. At length Chief John Jacket, a Cattaraugus Seneca, and a man well versed in the lore of his people, was chosen to settle forever the words and the form of the Gai'wiio'. This he did by writing it out in the Seneca language by the method taught by Rev. Asher Wright, the presbyterian missionary. The preachers assembled again, this time, according to Cornplanter, at Cattaraugus where they memorized the parts in which they were faulty. The original text was written on letter paper and now is entirely destroyed.[66]

Parker's description of the manuscripts that made up the Code parallels the earlier history of alphabetic transcriptions of Condolence Ceremonies outlined above. Like David of Schoharie and John Deserontyon, the preachers of the Code appear to have employed alphabetic Seneca script to buttress their spiritual arguments against social disorder among their parishioners, using a recently established orthography to create a material text that paired well with the sacramental power of the wampum distributions in traditional ceremonies. In fact, during the yearly recitations of the Code, "the preacher stands at the fireplace which serves as the altar. Sitting beside him is an assistant or some officer of the rites who holds a white wampum strand."[67] The original Handsome Lake belt is still displayed at the religious council at Tonowanda.

The alphabetic script that enabled the scribal circulation of the *Gai'wiio'* had its origins in the confluence of social and historical forces that emerged after the Revolution. As we have seen, the historical events of the war between the two settler powers in the region had transformed Buffalo Creek from a long-hallowed Haudenosaunee space—whose natural setting evoked the two-row wampum and its protocols of political consensus—into an important "political hub" in the geopolitical world of the eighteenth-century American backcountry that featured a heterogeneous Native population, active Christian missionizing, and aggressive land appropriation.

As Alyssa Mt. Pleasant demonstrates in her study of the community, "After the Whirlwind," the pan-tribal villages constellated around Buffalo Creek and its American mission developed a political culture that gradually advocated for limited alphabetic productions and that grew out of its melding of traditional "two stream" consensus-building and a pragmatic response to American encroachment. "With a growing American settlement only a few miles from their villages," Mt. Pleasant explains, "the people of Buffalo Creek were forced to acknowledge that increased familiarity with American customs and practices was necessary for their continued survival and prosperity."[68]

In 1818, an unexpected revival of spiritual fervor swept through Buffalo Creek and its surrounding Seneca communities. The 1815 death of Handsome Lake and increasing pressure from land speculators appears to have reawakened the Senecas to their sense of prophetic mission, and a small group of supporters of the Christian mission began to emerge among the Senecas as well. This revival combined with the surfacing of a local Christian movement was the Native context out of which the first substantial vernacular-language publication emerged—Jabez Hyde's hymnal. It was followed, in the "gradualist" two-row Haudenosaunee tradition, by the establishment in 1823 of the Seneca Mission Church. That was followed in 1825 by a Mission School for Native children; but again, in Mt. Pleasant's view, the "construction of the missionary-run school reflected the goals of the Haudenosaunee people at Buffalo Creek. Their interest in Euro-American-style education sprang from the desire to maintain their land and life ways."[69] Even once the schoolhouse was in place, Haudenosaunee history in the region did not become a tale of assimilation or even widespread alphabetic literacy. For the period 1780–1825, Mt. Pleasant has not found "any records created by a Haudenosaunee person in Seneca or another Haudenosaunee language bearing on Buffalo Creek."[70]

The Treaty of Buffalo Creek (1840) marked the end of that gradualism, and through its draconian efforts to move the Senecas to Indian Territory in present-day Oklahoma, the treaty inadvertently made literacy fairly commonplace among the ruling elites in the Seneca Nation. When in 1841 the missionary Asher Wright purchased a "hand printing press, . . . equipped with fonts of specially prepared type for printing books and papers in the Seneca language," a virtual flood of Seneca language texts followed. Just as printers and print houses were becoming part of the settled infrastructure of the expanding missionary enterprise across Indian Country, printed books could now be produced in the New York backcountry where prospective converts actually lived. With the help of printer Benjammin Duzee, Wright's press was "set up in a 'lean-to' attached to the house." During his tenure at the Buffalo Creek Mission, Wright produced *A Spelling Book in the Seneca Language with*

English Definitions (1842) and *The Mental Elevator* (1841–50), a Seneca language newsletter.

At the height of this alphabetic onslaught, the social forces within the Indigenous community at Buffalo Creek were arrayed broadly between two political parties—treaty and nontreaty—but, as Thomas Abler has cautioned, "It is important to note that this period in Seneca factionalism was unrelated to religious affiliation. Indeed, since the chiefs under the traditional system were more likely to be Christian than the warriors who supported the new republican government, Wright, in the limited support he lent the supporters of the new government, turned his back on a large portion of his own congregation and allied himself with practitioners of the traditional."[71] The difference between the settler conception of the civilizing power of alphabeticism and the actual scribal practices of the Senecas on both sides of this divide are illuminating. For his part, Wright worked hard to produce a vernacular-language version of the legislature's proposed constitution for the republican faction, because he believed that alphabeticism possessed "the tendency to elevate the mass of the people, and expedite their civilization." Wright had no affection for the Code of Handsome Lake and its followers, once calling Handsome Lake "a masterly device contrived" by Satan "to forestall the influence of the Gospel."[72]

It was in this milieu in 1848 that "a majority of the people resolved to change entirely their old form of Government, threw off the authority of their Chiefs, and adopted a constitution, modelled essentially, on the republican system. This constitution was approved and sustained by the Government of the State."[73] The Wright script served the "republican" Senecas well in the years ahead, giving them the "power of the press" to back up their constitutional authority. For their part, the "traditionalists" actually harnessed the power of the Seneca script to their own purposes, despite the fact that Handsome Lake had called things like the alphabetic writing of the settlers a "corruption" and had advised his fellow Haudenosaunees to avoid participating in such things at the cost of their mortal souls. Soon, everyday correspondence was conducted in both English and Seneca, and by the late 1840s, even the rituals of medicine societies were sometimes written out to supplement yearly oral ceremonial recitation.[74] Like Schoharie in 1756 and Lachine in 1783, Cold Springs Reservation in the 1840s was experiencing a social upheaval that historians have since labeled the "Seneca Revolution." As a result of the "frauds the Six Nations suffered" at the hands of Americans, terrible civil hostilities broke out in many Seneca communities. It was a time when "there was not much energy in a despairing nation who see themselves hopeless and alone, the greedy eyes of their conquerors fastened on the few

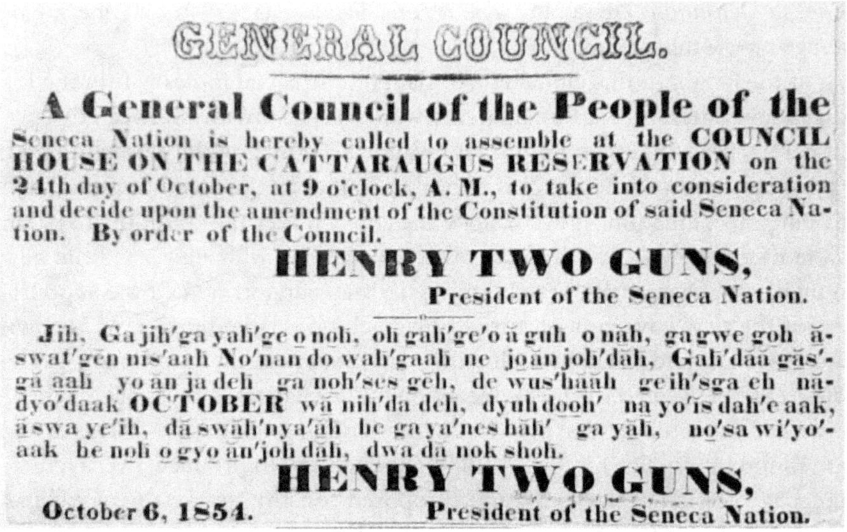

GENERAL COUNCIL.

A General Council of the People of the Seneca Nation is hereby called to assemble at the **COUNCIL HOUSE ON THE CATTARAUGUS RESERVATION** on the 24th day of October, at 9 o'clock, A. M., to take into consideration and decide upon the amendment of the Constitution of said Seneca Nation. By order of the Council.

HENRY TWO GUNS,
President of the Seneca Nation.

Jih. Ga jih'ga yah'ge o noh, oh gah'ge'o ă guh o năh, ga gwe goh ă-swat'gen nis'aah No'nan do wah'gaah ne jo ăn joh'dăh, Gah'dăă găs'-gă aah yo ăn ja deh ga noh'ses geh, de wus'haah ge ih'sga eh nă-dyo'daak **OCTOBER** wă nih'da deh, dyuh dooh' na yo'is dah'e aak, ă swa ye'ih, dă swăh'nya'ăh he ga ya'nes hăh' ga yăh, no'sa wi'yo'-aak he noh o gyo ăn'joh dăh, dwa dă nok shoh.

HENRY TWO GUNS,
October 6, 1854. President of the Seneca Nation.

Figure 2.9. Henry Two Guns's announcement of a general council meeting, October 24, 1854. Ely Samuel Parker Papers, MSS 497.3.P223, series 1: Correspondence, box 4, American Philosophical Society Library and Museum, Philadelphia, Pennsylvania.

acres of land that remain to them."[75] From Parker's perspective, the Code was especially useful in helping to heal this social rupture: "Handsome Lake's teachings did much to crystallize the Iroquois as a distinct social group. The encroachments of civilization had demoralized the old order of things. The old beliefs, though still held, had no coherence. The ancient system had no longer definite organization and thus no specific hold."[76]

Like the Condolence Ceremony manuscripts, the Code of Handsome Lake circulated as sheaves of paper, passing among practitioners of the Code from the 1850s until 1903, when Edward Cornplanter (a descendant of the Cornplanter who aided the Prophet in his illness) "began to rewrite the Gai'wiio' in an old minute book of the Seneca Lacrosse Club." Parker explains that he "implored [Cornplanter] to finish it and give it to the State of New York for preservation. He was at first reluctant, fearing criticism, but after a council with the leading men he consented to do so. He became greatly interested in the progress of the translation and is eager for the time to arrive when all white men may have the privilege of reading the 'wonderful message' of the great prophet."[77]

The manuscript culture born of this upheaval clearly served to further knit the diasporic community of followers around the circulation of the sacred texts and its yearly recitation. As Parker explains, those who held the manuscripts and performed the Code formed

> a social unit . . . that holds itself at variance with the social and accepted economic systems of the white communities about them. They assert that they have a perfect right to use their own system. They argue that the white man's teachings are not consistent with his practice and thus only one of their schemes for deceiving them. . . . They are largely instrumental in conserving the systems peculiarly Indian and though they are a minority they control a majority of the offices in the nations to which they belong.[78]

Anthony F. C. Wallace recounts the genesis of a manuscript culture around the Code as originating with a Seneca language version produced by Chief Cornplanter (Sosondowa) in 1903, that was in turn "translated by William Bluesky, the Native lay preacher of the local Baptist church. Sosondowa's version is embedded in the Cattaraugus tradition and is supposed to have descended from Chief John Jacket's version of about 1863."[79]

Like the Condolence Ceremony, the Code of Handsome Lake was a social practice, performed at special times and places in oral recitation. In both cases, alphabetic textuality mirrors the social practice and takes advantage of its material properties in much the same way that belts of wampum functioned in the original ceremonies. Parker provided a version of this Code of Handsome Lake in English, but since then efforts of scholars to record the entire code have not met with much success. Parker's text is of sufficient quality, however, that it is used as a reference by contemporary ritualists. What is more important is that by 1900, both the Condolence Ceremony and the Code of Handsome Lake had existed in many manuscript forms for 100 years (since 1800). This evidentiary trail also suggests that the manuscript form (rather than a print version) was especially instrumental in forging these social units in often diasporic Haudenosaunee communities. When, for example, the Anglo-American antiquarian William Beauchamp saw one of the Condolence manuscripts, he was very surprised that it contained verbal material that print versions like Horatio Hale's routinely omitted: "Those who have attended a condolence will remember the continual repetition of 'Ha-i-i-i,' much prolonged, and this hardly appears in his book. In the great [manuscript] song with names before me it is written nearly a thousand times."[80] This observation suggests that the manuscript versions of the Condolence Ceremony and the Code of Handsome Lake were directed toward preserving what Dell Hymes calls the "patterns" of the texts' performance, signaling the significance of the genre within Haudenosaunee society, despite being in an alphabetic form.[81]

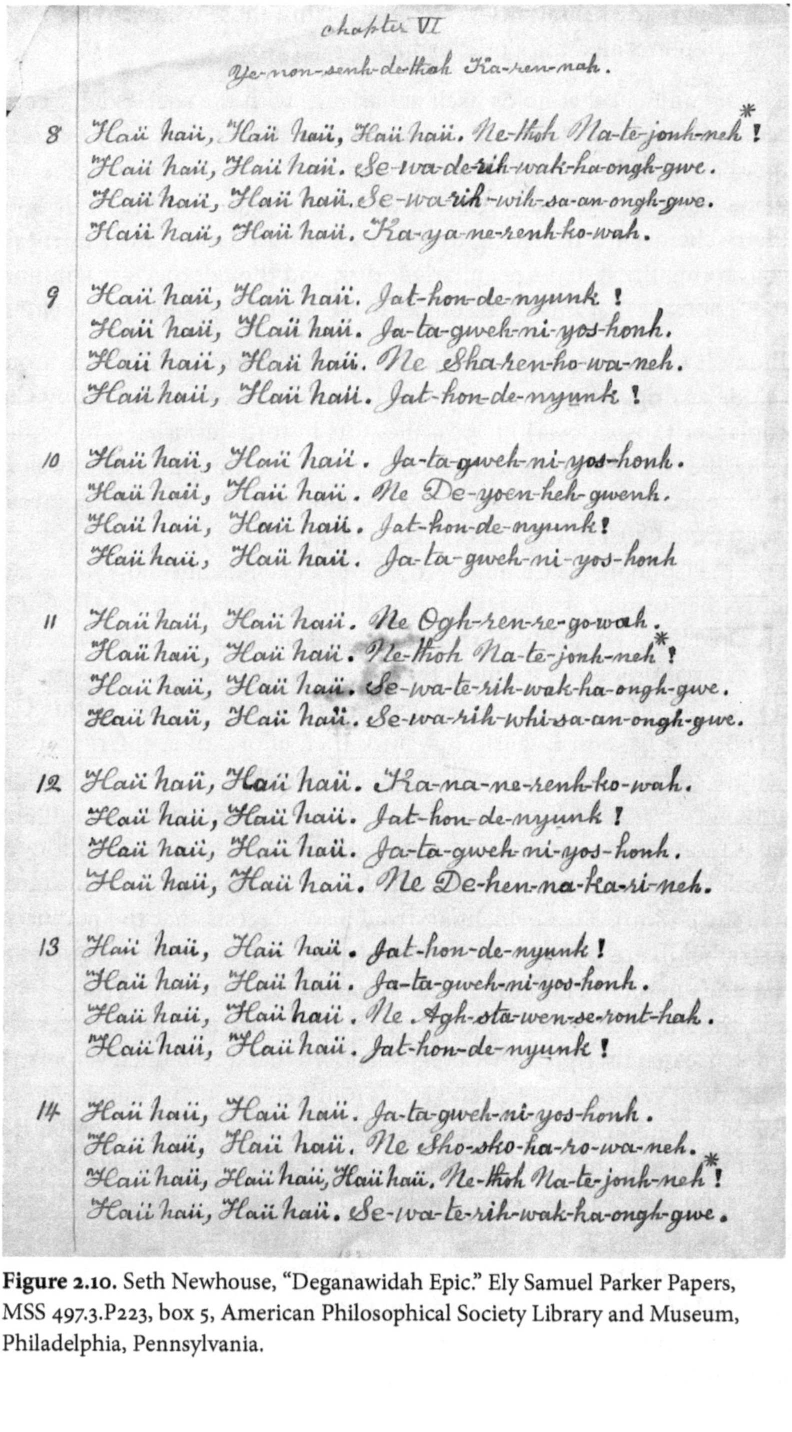

chapter VI

Ye-non-senh-der-thah Ka-ren-nah.

8 Haü haü, Haü haü, Haü haü. Ne-thoh Na-te-jonh-neh!*
   Haü haü, Haü haü. Se-wa-de-rih-wak-ha-ongh-gwe.
   Haü haü, Haü haü. Se-wa-rih-wih-sa-an-ongh-gwe.
   Haü haü, Haü haü. Ka-ya-ne-renh-ko-wah.

9 Haü haü, Haü haü. Jat-hon-de-nyunk!
   Haü haü, Haü haü. Ja-ta-gweh-ni-yos-honh.
   Haü haü, Haü haü. Ne Sha-ren-ho-wa-neh.
   Haü haü, Haü haü. Jat-hon-de-nyunk!

10 Haü haü, Haü haü. Ja-ta-gweh-ni-yos-honh.
   Haü haü, Haü haü. Ne De-yoen-heh-gwenh.
   Haü haü, Haü haü. Jat-hon-de-nyunk!
   Haü haü, Haü haü. Ja-ta-gweh-ni-yos-honh

11 Haü haü, Haü haü. Ne Ogh-ren-re-go-wah.
   Haü haü, Haü haü. Ne-thoh Na-te-jonh-neh!*
   Haü haü, Haü haü. Se-wa-te-rih-wak-ha-ongh-gwe.
   Haü haü, Haü haü. Se-wa-rih-whi-sa-an-ongh-gwe.

12 Haü haü, Haü haü. Ka-na-ne-renh-ko-wah.
   Haü haü, Haü haü. Jat-hon-de-nyunk!
   Haü haü, Haü haü. Ja-ta-gweh-ni-yos-honh.
   Haü haü, Haü haü. Ne De-hen-na-ka-ri-neh.

13 Haü haü, Haü haü. Jat-hon-de-nyunk!
   Haü haü, Haü haü. Ja-ta-gweh-ni-yos-honh.
   Haü haü, Haü haü. Ne Agh-sta-wen-se-ront-hak.
   Haü haü, Haü haü. Jat-hon-de-nyunk!

14 Haü haü, Haü haü. Ja-ta-gweh-ni-yos-honh.
   Haü haü, Haü haü. Ne Sho-sho-ha-ro-wa-neh.
   Haü haü, Haü haü, Haü haü. Ne-thoh Na-te-jonh-neh!*
   Haü haü, Haü haü. Se-wa-te-rih-wak-ha-ongh-gwe.

Figure 2.10. Seth Newhouse, "Deganawidah Epic." Ely Samuel Parker Papers, MSS 497.3.P223, box 5, American Philosophical Society Library and Museum, Philadelphia, Pennsylvania.

THE BLACKSNAKE NARRATIVE

It was in this context that another alphabetic manuscript emerged from Seneca country—this time in English—when a Seneca leader who fought with the United States against the British was sought out by a fellow Seneca living at Cold Spring on the Allegany Reservation and asked to narrate his life story. Like Hendrick Aupaumut and John Deserontyon, the leader—known to the Senecas as "Governor Blacksnake" and "Chainbreaker"—spoke of how he and his warriors would gather in council to "talk on the subject . . . for to see clear with the Naked eyes and open . . . ears," not wishing to "hold their heads down and see nothing." The transcription by Seneca writer Benjamin Williams also bears evidence that its author struggled to make the two-dimensional page perform a social practice more akin to the Condolence Ceremony than to the silent reading characteristic of the European codex. At the urging of Chainbreaker's son, Williams attempted to sell the manuscript for publication to Wisconsin antiquarian Lyman C. Draper, in whose voluminous collection of manuscripts it remains today.[82]

There are two drafts of the manuscript, and as the modern editor of this work, Thomas Abler, explains, "Neither variant is clearly superior to the other in completeness, or seeming closeness to what Blacksnake must have dictated. Nor does it appear that one is an initial or early draft and the second a more polished version."[83] The process begins almost immediately in the text with Benjamin Williams's ritual recitation of Chainbreaker's name and ancestry, a paragraph directed at both non-Seneca audiences unfamiliar with the linguistic complexities of the old man's formal title and the Seneca oral tradition's customary way of locating a speaking subject within family and clan lineages. Interestingly, it was this very cross-cultural performance that Williams's contemporary editor, Thomas Abler, an accomplished ethnologist with close ties to the Senecas, relegated to an appendix, calling it "a lengthy, confused introduction, not closely related to the story that follows and possibly more difficult to read than any other section of the text."[84] Yet it is precisely its impenetrability to the modern reader that suggests its relevance to another, alternative set of scribal practices.

A close examination of both manuscripts, however, *does* suggest a discursive source for this introduction and, thus, a uniquely Seneca social position for the narrative that has come down to us as an "autobiography." Several elements of both manuscripts suggest that Benjamin Williams and Chainbreaker self-consciously modeled their manuscripts on the Condolence Ceremony and the Code of Handsome Lake, perhaps even drawing on the written corpus of these rites to put Chainbreaker's narrative into a recognizable shape for both its authors and its prospective settler audience. Like the Condolence Ceremony, the Williams manuscript opens with a recitation of Chainbreaker's name and lineage that appear in a set of short lines justified to the left of the page:

> The Birth of Governor Blacksnake
>
> Or more correctly of Ten, wr, nyrs—for such was
> his Real name—interpretation is Chainbreaker
> his last name given to him at the time he
> became chief warrior
> . . .
> But when Boyhood
> Was then called—Dahgr, yan, Doh—until he
> Became young man than, Tan, wr, nyrs, as
> Chainbreaker—following to according to the
> Custom of their Rules and traditions—concern-
> Ing changing their nams when became
> Man—
> . . .
> This can be asurtained fect of the Said Life of Goverer
> Blacksnake, and others connected with it and
> Traditions of their ancient history—account of
> Creation of the world and late prophets, and
> Sanctuary of three times in a year.

This opening passage suggests that the manuscript was intended to channel many ingredients of the Condolence Ceremony into the life story of the Seneca leader. It contains a recitation of genealogy and is contextualized in both place ("the river Avone") and cosmology ("ceremony of the Seneca Nation").

Williams goes on to list something like chapter headings that he apparently planned to place after the autobiographical material:

> A Sketch of Blacksnake—
> Which Idea being handed down from
> Generation to generations—we cannot tell the
> Number of years ago for we have no written
> Account, . . . and it may be some sketch of
> Iroquois onondagas, when the omission is
> Supplied by a head from an ancient pipe
> Hereafter described under the class of all above

Described and Ruler under their confederacy, named
Tar, to-tar, ho, he is the first Rule of the Iroquois—[85]

These headings allude to the installation ceremony of the Longhouse ("sanctuary of three times a year"), where the "head" of the Longhouse, "from an ancient pipe" explicates the ruling leaders of generations past, locating the power with the Onondaga. "Tar, to-tar" refers to Atotarho, the first leader of the Longhouse. In this way, Chainbreaker is situated within the Longhouse and the archival history of the Six Nations. Finally, both manuscripts shift abruptly from the third person to the first person once the "historical" life of Chainbreaker begins:

> Life of Governor Blacksnake
> In During the America Revolutionary I
>
> Governer Blacksnake
> When I was about fourteen years of my age

These are admittedly scant pieces of evidence, but when combined with one of the more puzzling aspects of the manuscript—a recitation of the important role Chainbreaker played in the life of the Seneca prophet Handsome Lake—the Williams/Chainbreaker collaboration begins to look more and more like a social practice tied to the Condolence Ceremony and the confederacy than a random act of self-expression or an abstract gesture of cultural identity.

Like David of Schoharie and John Deserontyon, Chainbreaker and Williams appear to be responding to a specific historical situation in the Seneca Nation with an alphabetic text based in oral performance and aimed at sustaining the Condolence Ceremony and requickening rites central to the continuation of the confederacy. The 1840s were a period of virtual civil war in the Seneca communities. It is important to remember that this was a time during which the "frauds the Six Nations suffered" at the hands of Americans, culminating in the terrible civil hostilities of 1838–48. Seneca anthropologist Arthur C. Parker describes it as a time when "there was not much energy in a despairing nation who see themselves hopeless and alone, the greedy eyes of their conquerors fastened on the few acres of land that remain to them."[86] Perhaps the two men saw this collaborative text as a necessary act of "requickening" in a community riven with political divisions.[87]

In much the same way that the Williams-Chainbreaker manuscript reinscribed the Condolence Ceremony in its introduction and chapter heads, a fragment of the manuscript that is not filed in sequence with the autobiography among the Draper Papers suggests that the story of Handsome Lake was also being woven into the fabric of the old warrior's story. In this fragment, Blacksnake recounts what happened to his Seneca relation (Handsome Lake) after he fell into a coma: "That year he was sick confined on his bed and was not able to Rise from bed and it happened one morning. He was called to the door, and the moment he felt so that he was able to rise and go to the door. He did so he saw three or four persons standing by the door and taken hands with him all and commenced that he felt faint and fall down on the ground by their feets and lost his senses."[88]

Chainbreaker's uncle, Cornplanter, witnessed this event, and this kinship tie seems to have been an important aspect of the fragment's inclusion in some versions of the Chainbreaker memoir that Benjamin William wrote. Thomas Abler speculates that the emergence of other Native-authored works during the time Williams and Chainbreaker collaborated on this text (most significantly, *David Cusick's Sketches of Ancient History of the Six Nations* [1827]) and increasing non-Indian interest in Indian stories might have spurred the Williams-Chainbreaker collaboration.[89] But when read within the context of a century of Haudenosaunee alphabetic vernacular writing, it can also be seen as an example of an emergent genre, one that took elements from Haudenosaunee performance and alphabetic epistolary practice to establish a new place from which to communicate sovereignty both to outsiders, who thought of the Iroquois as "frozen in time," and to their fellow confederacy members, who sought to affirm their continued presence and continuity with the Haudenosaunee homelands.

ALPHABETICISM AND THE INDIAN ACT

I will close with the story of Dayodekane (known in English as Seth Newhouse), who wrote a draft of the Longhouse rites in alphabetic Mohawk in 1885. Titled "Cosmology of De-ka-na-wi-da's Government of the Iroquois Confederacy" (or Traditional History and Constitution of the Iroquois Confederacy), it is composed of a large ledger of some 300 numbered pages, replete with paratextual materials (a preface, affidavits of authenticity, and appendixes) that locate the work in a complex set of social practices intended to supplement the Condolence Ceremony in a written form that could help sustain Haudenosaunee sovereignty over and against the alphabetic legalism of the Canadian settler state.

The immediate social upheaval that spurred Newhouse's writing was Canada's Indian Act of 1867. As Canadian First Nations historian Rick Monture explains, "In spite of the Crown's desire to subjugate the Haudenosaunees in their new lands, the Confederacy Council remained in place until 1924, albeit under the ever-watchful eye of the local Indian Agent on the reserve. Up to that time, the traditional leadership had endured Canadian Confederation in 1867, the Introduction of the Indian Act in 1876, and an ever-increasing population of Canadian citizens in the most heavily populated region of the country."[90] Faced with the Canadian government's plan to force the nations into an electoral method of choosing leaders—thus doing away with the condolence traditions—Dayodekene rewrote the traditional Condolence Ceremony to affirm its existence, adding paratext to supply arguments against the government's intervention in Native affairs. Although the ethnographer who first dealt with the manuscript, William Fenton, dismissed the cultural authenticity of much of this text ("the myth is at all times warped by the author's projecting into the dim reaches of history forms of Mohawk ritualism that were current in the late nineteenth century," Fenton says), it is precisely this present-making effort on Newhouse's part that exemplifies my view that texts like it represent active social practice, not static cultural remembrance.[91]

Seth Newhouse (1842–1921) lived at Grand River Reserve, went to the Mohawk Institute Residential School in Brantford, Ontario, and was a member of a Christian family. He spoke and wrote Onondaga and Mohawk as well as English. He was also "raised up as an Onondaga Pine Tree Chief in 1875." As a Christian member of the Council at Grand River, Newhouse was, as Monture notes, "positioned socially between two camps"—those who wanted to continue the tradition of Council governance of the community, and those who sought to "dehorn" traditional leaders and form an elective tribal government. Newhouse was also of the opinion that the community ought to pay attention to the federal government's warnings about enforcing the Indian Act of 1876 with draconian measures, and that the Council ought to be proactive in demonstrating its "civil" and "civilized" authority.

Monture, who has analyzed Newhouse's literary efforts in this regard, has commented that Newhouse's version of the Condolence Ceremony was either "commissioned by the Council to embark upon his translation work or [he] was acting on his own accord, but all sources agree that he did so as a response to the mounting pressure felt at Grand River to comply with the Indian Act." Monture speculates that "some members of the Council, including Newhouse, felt that if the federal government required documented proof that the Haudenosaunees had an established political structure, they merely needed to put their traditions down on paper."[92]

From the title page of the manuscript, it is apparent that Newhouse wished to stress the cosmological origins of the Haudenosaunee Confederacy, along with its "heaven-sent" status. He also penned an English-language preface to his compilation, underscoring the intellectual property rights inherent in his work (emphasizing the "originality" of this "first edition"), and his personal

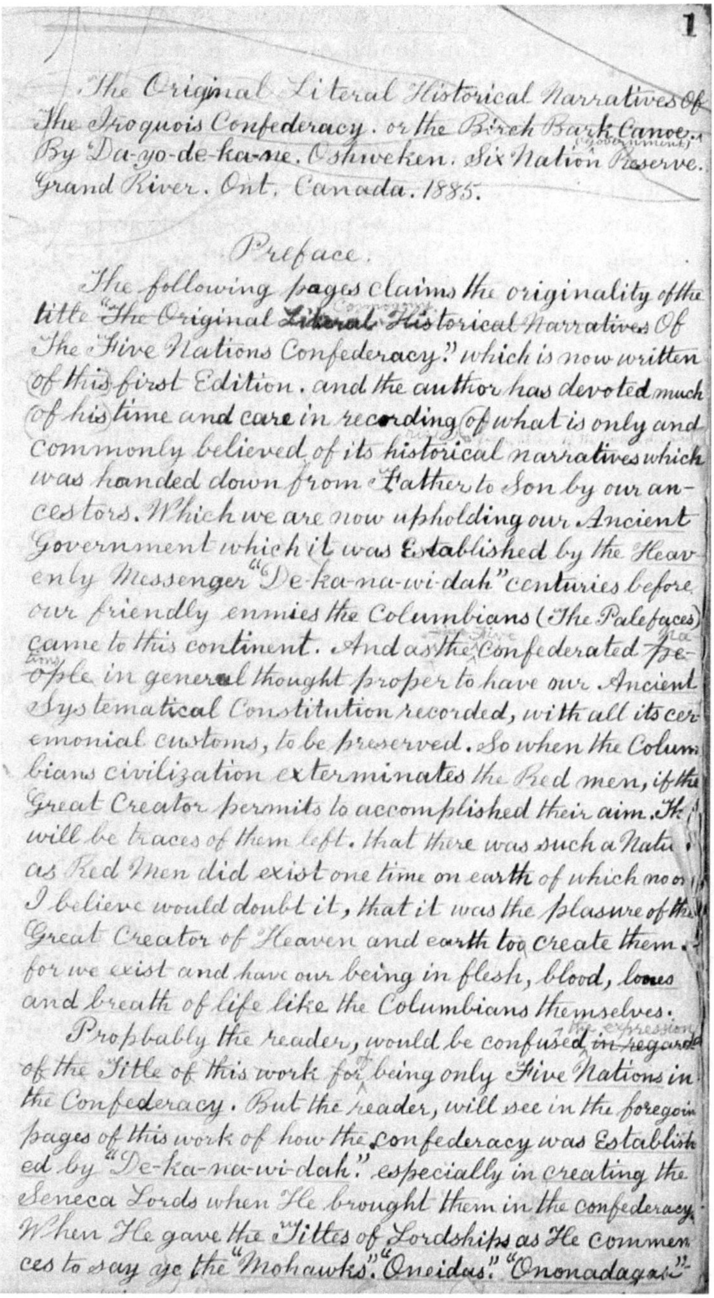

The Original Literal Historical Narratives Of
The Iroquois Confederacy. or the Birch Bark Canoe.
By Da-yo-de-ka-ne. Ohsweken. Six Nation Reserve.
Grand River. Ont. Canada. 1885.

Preface.

The following pages claims the originality of the title "The Original Literal Historical Narratives Of The Five Nations Confederacy." which is now written of this first Edition. and the author has devoted much of his time and care in recording of what is only and commonly believed of its historical narratives which was handed down from Father to Son by our ancestors. Which we are now upholding our Ancient Government which it was Established by the Heavenly Messenger "De-ka-na-wi-dah" centuries before our friendly ennies the Columbians (The Palefaces) came to this continent. And as the Confederated people in general thought proper to have our Ancient Systematical Constitution recorded, with all its ceremonial customs, to be preserved. So when the Columbians civilization exterminates the Red men, if the Great Creator permits to accomplish their aim. It will be traces of them left. that there was such a Nation as Red Men did exist one time on earth of which no one I believe would doubt it, that it was the plasure of the Great Creator of Heaven and earth too create them. for we exist and have our being in flesh, blood, bones and breath of life like the Columbians themselves.

Propbably the reader, would be confused in regard of the Title of this work for being only Five Nations in the Confederacy. But the reader, will see in the foregoing pages of this work of how the Confederacy was Established by "De-ka-na-wi-dah." especially in creating the Seneca Lords when He brought them in the Confederacy. When He gave the "Tittes of Lordships as He commences to say ye the "Mohawks" "Oneidas" "Onondagas"

Figure 2.11. Seth Newhouse's preface to "Cosmology of De-ka-na-wi-da's Government of the Iroquois Confederacy," 1885. MSS 970.3.IR6, American Philosophical Society Library and Museum, Philadelphia, Pennsylvania.

authorship role in the "time and care in recording" the Condolence Ceremony. Like Williams-Chainbreaker and David Cusick, Newhouse directed his readers' attention toward the historicity of the text as well as, "its historical narrative which was handed down from Father to Son by our ancestors." In restating its meaning, Newhouse calls the history of the Haudenosaunee Confederacy an "Ancient Systematical Constitution."

There is also a real sense of foreboding that hangs over the opening pages of the manuscript, as the threat of the Indian Act looms large in the writer's imagination. In his preface, Newhouse foresees a time "when the Columbian civilization exterminates the Red men, if the Great Creator permits to [be] accomplished their aim, there will be [no] traces of them left." In this scenario, Newhouse reasons, a written document that attests "there was such a Nation as Red Men did exist one time on earth of which no one I believe would doubt it, that it was the pleasure of the Great Creator of Heaven and earth to create them. For we exist and have our being in flesh, blood, bones and breath of life just like the Columbians themselves."[93] Flesh, blood and bone, historicity, genealogies, and authorship—these were the stuff of the text of Iroquois governance Newhouse wished to project over and against the Columbians' genocidal practices and strange romanticization of Iroquois "culture." Newhouse also improvised formatting methods by which to translate the oral and metaphorical practices of the Condolence Ceremony into an alphabetic document. First, he split the Ceremony into three parts, labeled "The Tree of the Long Leaves," "The Emblematic Union Contract," and "Skanawatih's Law of Peace and War." Then he "reduced" the narrative sections of the Great Law in favor of roman numeral and arabic number subdivisions, perhaps as Monture suggests, "as a way to better represent lawmaking procedures."[94]

Newhouse had reached page 176 of his manuscript when his tribal council took on the Canadian government and asked to see his text, thinking that it might aid their cause. Even though they eventually rejected his initial draft and asked for the revision suggested by other elders, Newhouse comments in the paratextual apparatus that "it stands like this, the Chiefs of our Council has asked me, to hold this work for them, & I have promised to do so & I have done so, so far." Was this a case of the Council engaging in a kind of "ethnographic refusal," denying the settlers an opportunity to co-opt an alphabetic and English-language version of the Condolence Ceremony? Was Newhouse's manuscript too literal, or did it threaten to rob the exchanging of wampum, the gatherings in the Longhouse, and even the critical social role of the Council itself of their necessary and efficacious role in Haudenosaunee governance? Perhaps alphabeticism was too much a part of the settler colonial project of dispossession and disenfranchisement to be trusted with such a critical task. For Monture, Newhouse's alphabetic and formatting improvisations were "quite foreign in structure and therefore unacceptable for a variety of reasons," not least, as Monture points out, was the way Newhouse had "elevated" the Mohawk chiefs in the confederacy to a far higher position of authority than most interpretations of the Great Law allowed.[95]

The Council instead chose to pen a collaborative version of their own and in 1900 produced the "Chief's Version" in which John Arthur Gibson, whose story of Tekanawita appears as the epigraph to this chapter, played a significant role as translator and transcriber. Despite their best efforts, the Confederacy Council was unable to stem the tide of Canadian aggression, and in 1924, the Royal Canadian Mounted Police physically removed the council and seized the wampum belts that the council displayed as an affirmation of their authority.[96]

CONCLUSION: "CAN'T YOU HEAR THAT 'H' IN THERE?"

The longevity of the early scripts and the varied uses they served for the Haudenosaunee peoples are brought into focus by an incident that occurred in the Wisconsin Oneida community in the 1930s. The Oneidas of Wisconsin trace their beginnings to post–Revolutionary War encroachment of settlers into their original homelands in New York. In the 1820s and 1830s, many Oneidas began to relocate from New York to Wisconsin, where they had been offered land. By 1838, with the Treaty of Buffalo Creek, the Oneidas accepted a reservation in the Wisconsin territory, and Chief Patrick James Brault negotiated to ensure that the land was to be held communally by the tribe. The community arrived in Wisconsin with the story of Tekanawita and the Great Law intact and often remembered, along with the same alphabetic script tradition that had supported John Deserontyon and Seth Newhouse.

In 1938, the Columbia-trained ethnographer Floyd Lounsbury set up shop with the Oneidas and set about putting together a grammar of the language as part of a larger Roosevelt Works Progress Administration (WPA) project. Lounsbury selected a group of two dozen Oneida citizens, many of whom were "amenable to the idea, in part because most were transferred from outdoor WPA projects during the cold winter." After a two-week training session, he worked with them for nineteenth months to develop a "better" writing system than the one they already had. One participant who was interviewed by the local press at the time pointed out the irony of the situation: "It's quite funny, having a white man come here and teach us how to write our own language. But it's interesting. And I think it will be a good thing for the tribe."[97] In their history of the Oneida writing project, Jack Campesi and

Laurence Hauptman cast Lounsbury's efforts as a welcome revelation to this community: "When Lounsbury insisted that their language contained voiceless vowels, the Oneidas responded by maintaining that 'we've been speaking this language all our lives and we've never realized we did this.' Out of these sessions, Lounsbury developed a 19-character orthography which the Oneidas practiced writing."[98]

Writing in his memoir of this venture, however, Lounsbury recalled that the Oneidas were already happy using their "traditional" orthography:

> [Morris] Swadesh and I came to Oneida and did preliminary work trying to decide what orthography to use. It was a difficult decision based on the state of linguistic theory in the 1930s. We decided to depart from the system that had become traditional among the Mohawks and had also been employed by the Oneidas, at least in the copying of hymns and in some private writings. John Archiquette, an Oneida who had been in the American Civil War, had kept a diary from the 1870s into the 1890s and had written it in the same traditional orthography.[99]

The orthography to which Lounsbury referred was a descendant of the script employed by the Haudenosaunee Anglican minister Eleazar Williams (1787–1858). It had served the community well over the 100 years since Williams helped codify it with his vernacular-language pedagogical and liturgical print texts. But Lounsbury had youth and science on his side, and he was certain that an orthography that recognized the Oneida's voiceless vowels would improve the chances of revitalizing the language among community members as fluent speakers became increasingly hard to find. So, he asked the participants in his workshop to adopt a new way of writing.

It was a fateful decision, and one he would regret in time. Fresh out of graduate school, he pressed ahead, believing "that there was only one correct way to write any language." Soon, however, he "began to have misgivings" when at time one of the members of the project would say: "Can't you hear that 'h' sound in *there*? This comment would occur after a 't' or after an 's' and I would explain to him/her that, of course, I heard it because that we regard the 'h' sound as belonging to the same unit as the letter before it." In the end, Lounsbury had to admit, "If I had known in 1939 what I now know about the two orthographies, I would have never departed from tradition whether that older tradition is right or wrong. That's what one learns from experience."[100]

It was not until the WPA project that vowel length and other phonetic features were written into a new Oneida alphabet; but as Lounsbury learned, such "improvements" did not always suit the everyday needs of the community. While phonetically "correct," the corrections were not historically

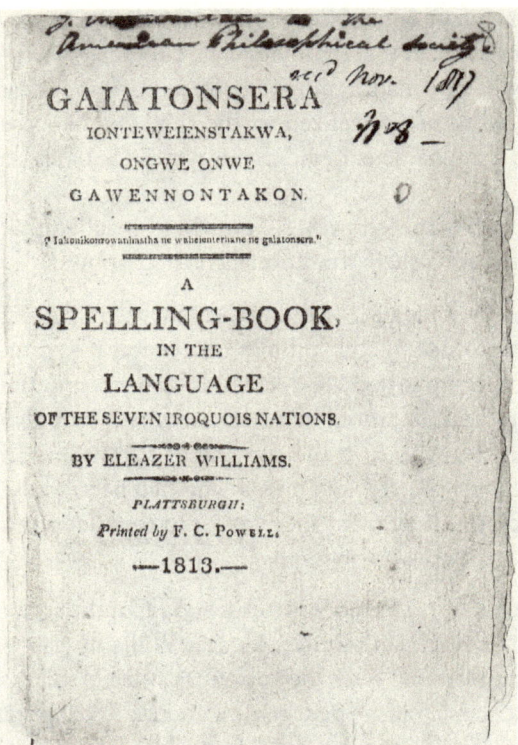

Figure 2.12. Title page of Eleazar Williams's *Gaiatonsera*, 1813. Courtesy of the American Philosophical Society Library and Museum, Philadelphia, Pennsylvania.

grounded in the lived language of the Oneidas of Wisconsin. The Oneidas had been writing for a long time, and two of their leaders, John Powess and Archiquette, had been keeping journals about the community in the old orthography since about 1868. Thus, when Lounsbury made his effort to replace the community's old, handwritten hymnals with a printed version in the new script, the community graciously accepted them. But even Lounsbury had to admit his new system had "one serious defect." It did not recognize an important phonemic rule in Oneida—when the h sound follows a t sound, the h is not written. Only Native speakers of Oneida would know this and sing a hymn accordingly. Although the older and more accomplished speakers of the language embraced the hymnal, Lounsbury and his local editors created a more phonemic system to teach new learners of the language.[101] Despite their "imperfections," the old hymns continued to circulate, and the new orthography never really caught on as a way to transcribe Oneida church singing.

Alphabetic media were thus employed by Haudenosaunee communities only when they were central to the social and political needs of the people. Missionaries and ethnographers who wielding alphabeticism in the service of

Kahiatónhsera 129

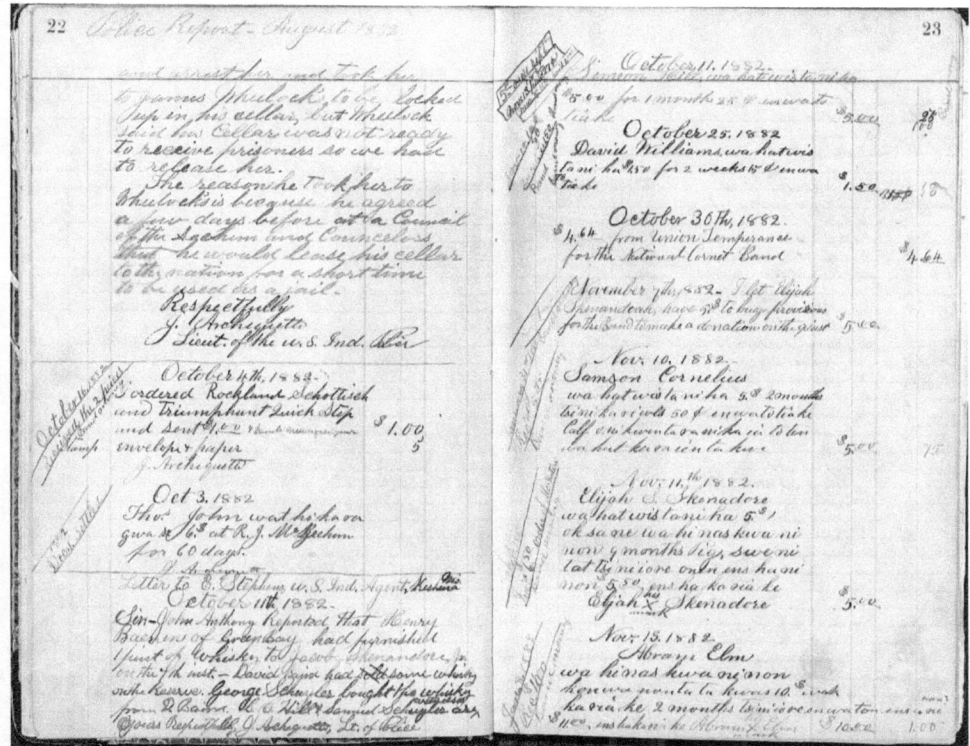

Figure 2.13. Pages from John Archiquette's journal. Yale Collection of Western Americana, Beinecke Rare Book and Manuscript Library, New Haven, Connecticut.

Christian evangelism and philological research have enjoyed, at best, moderate success in establishing a place for their uses of script in the Native communities they encountered. Like the Oneidas in Wisconsin, whose handwritten hymnals served their congregations for generations, most Six Nations communities judged that textual meaning tied to social practice and writing that did not immerse itself in the daily life of the people had no real place in their societies. Only when alphabetic media are interwoven with traditional communications practices, like the *rivière fabriquée* of the living wampum still in use today, does the written vernacular have a real place in Haudenosaunee governance and celebration, in the peoples' ongoing resistance.

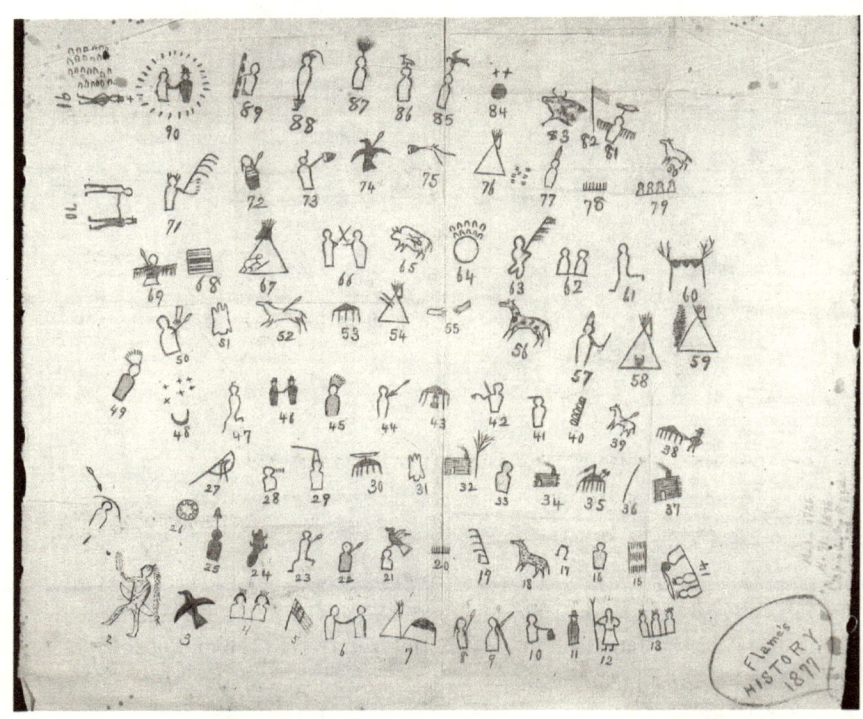

Figure 3.1. Page from "Flame's History," 1877. Winter Count covering the period 1786–1876. Black and red ink on muslin, MS 2372, National Anthropological Archives, Smithsonian Institution, Washington, DC.

3 : *Wowapi*
INSCRIBING THE OCETI SAKOWIN

Buffalo Bill's Wild West Show, Manchester, England, Feb. 15, 1888.
Wi'd West ośkate kin le el tokel waun kin lehanl owaglakin kte lo. Mitawacin on ohinniyan woope bluha na ohinniyan. Wakantakna kiksuya waun. Tka ośkate kin anpetu na hanhepi ko inyanke cante masaśkanśkan oape nonpa hehanyela owanjila unyankapi. Tka ohinnyan Wkantanka kiksuya waun kin hechel taku oyasin okihi makiye lo. Hopo, Mitakuye Lakota oyate kin, lehanl Wasicuu tawidonhan kin tanyan slolwaye. Tuwa Wakantanka awacin kin taku wicohan waste iyeyin kte lo, he wake lo. Na taku wicohan Wasicun econpi kinota tehike lo. Tuwa Makoce nica hena tiwokitahena ye lo. Na Makoce kin otankaya qeyas ohinniyan Wisicun ojulaye lo. Hehanl maka ohinni taku icante wasteya waun we lo. Miye wanna Omaka yamni leci wann welo; Yunkan Wasicun iapi wanjigji owakihi yunkan mitakola wotanin ieska wowapi wanji lecala iwacu, ua lila ibluskin ye lo Lakota. Wasicun ieska okhipi kte kin heciyantanhan.
—Nicholas Black Elk

Buffalo Bill's Wild West Show, Manchester, England, Feb. 15, 1888.
Now I will tell you how I am doing with the wild west show. Always in my mind I hold to the law and all along I live remembering God. . . . So, my relatives, the Lakota people, I know the white men's customs well. One custom is very good. Whoever believes in God will find good ways—that is what I mean. And many of the ways the white men follow are hard to endure. Whoever has no country will die in the wilderness. And although the country is large it is always full of white men. That which makes me happy is always land. Now that I have stayed here three [two] years. And I am able to speak some of the white men's language. And a little while ago my friend gave me a translated paper [the *Iapi Oaye*] and I rejoiced greatly. Thus the Lakotas will be able to translate English.[1]
—Nicholas Black Elk

Nicholas Black Elk (1863–1950) was twenty-five years old and performing in Buffalo Bill's Wild West show in England when he wrote these words in 1888 and enclosed them in an envelope bound for the missionary newspaper *Iapi Oaye* (*Word Carrier*). Although he was only a young man, he had already witnessed great turmoil in his Lakota homeland, the newly created Great Sioux Reservation that covered much of South Dakota and parts of Nebraska. Although generally lumped together as "Sioux" by Europeans, Black Elk's community was in reality a part of the Oceti Sakowin, or the Seven Council Fires—a linguistic and cultural designation for an interconnected series of Plains communities that numbered about 1,600 people in the 1880s. To the east, in present-day Minnesota, were the bands known as Mdewantankowan ("Santee"), Wahpekute ("Leaf Shooters"—sometimes also "Santee"), Wahpetonwan ("Leaf Dwellers/Wahpeton"), and the Sisitonwan ("Sisseton"). Often grouped under the name of their dialect, "Dakota," they were the first to experience the ravages of America's westward expansion in the 1830s, with all its attendant land grabbing, violence, and missionary zeal.

Farther west along the Missouri River, the Ihanktonwan ("Yankton") Ihanktonwanna ("Yanktonai," or Crow Creek Sioux Tribe) spoke a slightly different dialect, known as Nakota, and were so designated by members of the Seven Council Fires. Finally, Black Elk's people, the Titonwan (or Teton Sioux), spread across the Great Plains of South Dakota, were likewise known primarily by their dialect name, "Lakota," and had arranged themselves into seven subdivisions—Hunkpapa ("Head of Circle"), Oohenumpa ("Two Kettles"), Mniconjou ("Plants by the Water"), Oglala ("To Scatter One's Own"), Itazipco ("Sans Arc"), Sihasapa ("Blackfoot"), and Sicangu ("Brule").

Black Elk's life spanned the years during which the free Teton bands of the Great Plains became increasingly hemmed in by US colonial expansion. As a young man, Black Elk was known as Kahnigapi ("Choice"); and at the age of nine he was blessed with a powerful vision from the sacred Thunder Beings (Wakinyan) "that foreshadowed the special powers he would use later in his life to cure illness and aid [Lakotas] in war."[2] Because of his youth and the uncertain state of affairs in his homeland (his family retreated to Canada after Crazy Horse was assassinated in 1877), Black Elk kept his vision secret until 1881, when he confided to Black Road, an honored elder, what he had seen and been instructed to do. Black Road and other elders then asked Black Elk to perform a sacred horse dance before his entire kinship group. "By acknowledging the vision in this manner before his people," the ethnographer Raymond DeMallie explains, "Black Elk at last put himself in harmony with the spirit world and publicly announced his spiritual calling."[3] For the last two decades of the nineteenth century, Black Elk occupied the social position of

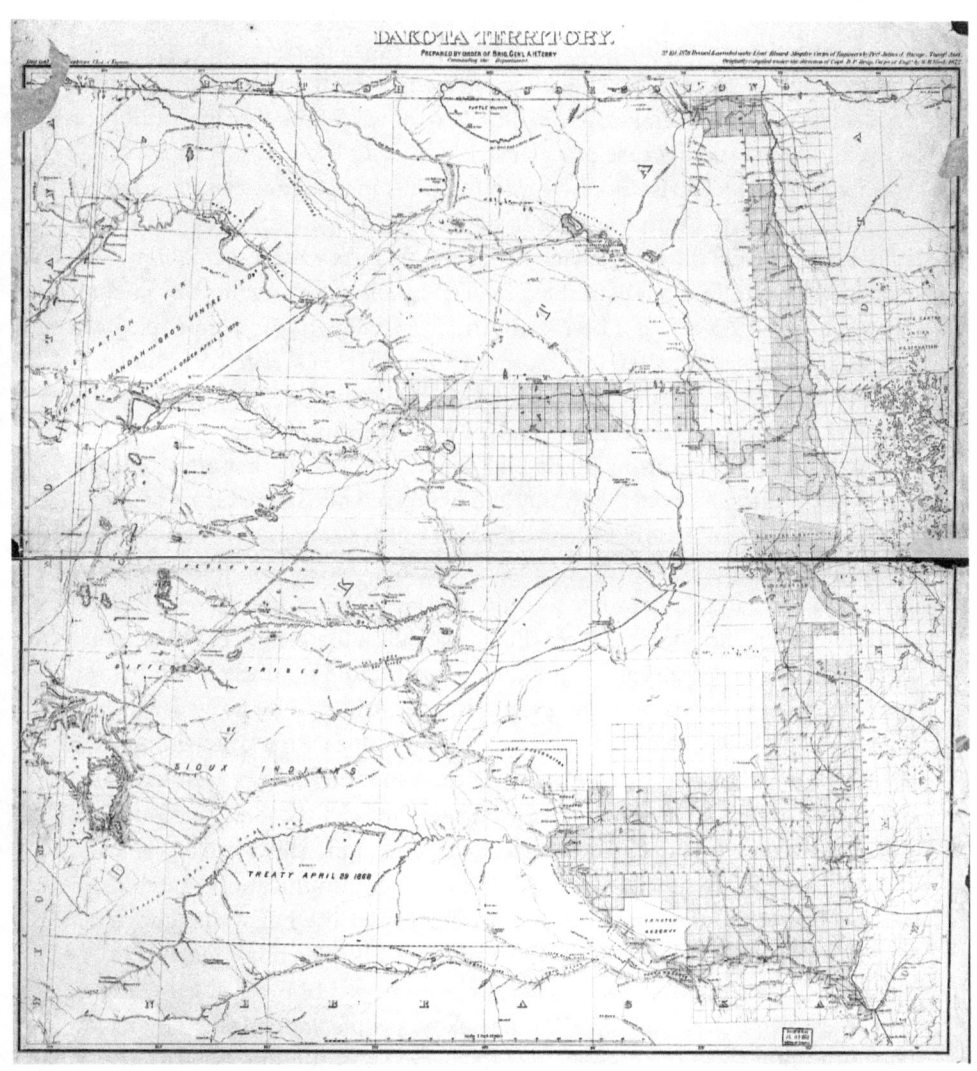

Figure 3.2. *Dakota Territory.* Map by Julius Durage, 1878. No. 2007626713, Geography and Map Division, Library of Congress, Washington, DC.

wicasa wakan (holy man), performing curing rituals and even joining a party of warriors in 1890 to protect Wounded Knee massacre survivors.

In 1886, however, "disgusted" with his community's lack of spiritual progress in the face of the challenges presented by the reservation system, he decided to join Buffalo Bill's Wild West show.[4] While touring in Europe with the show (and because of a clause in the Wild West show's contract) he was baptized as a Christian and given religious instruction from a missionary Bible translated into the Dakota dialect.[5] A fringe benefit of gaining an understanding of "the white man's belief about God's will" was that Black Elk learned to write in alphabetic Lakota. The opening passage to this chapter represents his first effort at literacy in the form of a letter to his people back home. He notes how, when he first saw a copy of *Iapi Oaye* in Manchester, it made him "rejoice greatly." His happiness derived from the fact that the paper allowed "Lakotas . . . to translate English" into their mother tongue.[6]

Two things stand out in Black Elk's letter. The first is that after 1888, he employed a missionary orthography and expressed himself in terms of Christian theology, even as he considered himself fully Lakota, never relinquishing the traditional medicine ways of a *wicasa wakan*. As his son, Ben Black Elk, recalled years later, "My father was a Christian. . . . But he still believed the Indian religion." Speaking to DeMallie in the 1980s, Black Elk's granddaughter outlined the practices that accompanied this middle ground: "Grandpa . . . used his pipe in the morning—evenings, too. And still he prayed with the rosary; so he believed in both."[7] It would thus appear that even though the missionaries published Black Elk's letter (and those of Lakota men like him) as "proof" of his conversion and commitment to "civilization," he thought of his own literacy practices and Christian prayer quite differently. Black Elk did not "convert" to literacy; he used alphabetic communication strategically.

This becomes more apparent when we consider the Lakota-language usages as employed by the missionaries and Black Elk. The missionaries clearly thought of their publication, the *Iapi Oaye*, as an act of evangelical witnessing—it carried the Word (*Logos*) to the Lakota people. *Iapi* means "language"; *oaye* is a noun form of the verb *aya*, to carry. Thus, the missionaries translated the phrase as *Word Carrier*. Yet, Black Elk's reading is different. He says, "Wasicun iapi wanjigji owakihi yunkan mitakola wotanin ieska wowapi wanji lecala iwacu, ua lila ibluskin ye lo Lakota. Wasicun ieska okhipi kte kin heciyantanhan." That is, he speaks of the white man's *language* (*Wasicun iapi*) and his own happiness (*ibluskin*) at the Lakotas' ability to receive news (*wotanin*) that they could use in their own idiom as well as translated from the English. For the written text, he uses the word *wowapi*, derived from the verb *owa*, to paint.

IAPI OAYE.

SANTEE AGENCY, NEBRASKA. TAKU WAŚTE OKIYA, TAKU ŚICA KIPAJIN. A. L. RIGGS, PUBLISHER.

VOLUME XVII. NUMBER 3. MARCH, 1888. WOKAJUJU KAŚPAPI ŚAKPE.

ANPETU OYAKAPI.

Feb. 22 Dakota Territory en Woyaco Wankanta kin woope wanji on iwangapi Otonwe kin miniwakan aniciyutapi woope kin hee. Qa wanna yukcanpi qa woope suta eyapi. Heon tona miniwakan tokayapi owasin iyuśkinpi qa miniwakan piya kuwapi.

Feb. 22. President Cleveland towicu kici qa takodakuwa wanjikśi om inaśni ozizeiye kte e on Florida makoce ekta ipi. Heciya taspanzizi ieaga ece, qa waniyetu wetu iyecece.

Feb. 27. Hemani canku tanka wanji, Chicago Burlington qa Quincy R. R. he anpetu kin en ta se wanke. Tona Hemani en awanyakapi qa aeatipi kin owasin ayustanpi. Opawinge śakpepi. Qa tona wicośan he onapepi owasin okodakiciye wan yuhapi qa okodakiciye kin etanhan tuwedan kamani okiyapi śni. Wokajuju sanpa dapi heon ayuśtanpi.

March 9. Berlin Germany, Inśica makoce ekta wicaśtayatapi tanka yuhapi kin te. Emperor William cajeyatapi. Wicaśtayatapi wicośan yuha iconhan oyate tanka kaġa. Qa dehan Europe ekta Germany he oyate tokapa ee.

March 9. Mitchell, Dak. Tev. en Methodist okodokiciye Woonape Wankantu yuhapi. Inyan tipi qa owanyag waśte. Tuka iwecinka iśe qa nunaga. Hanyetu hehantu qa owasin iśtinmpi. Wankan tipi towanye kin etanhan waonspekiyapi qa wayawa unpi lyeapi qa ota kuuwicayapi. Waonspekiye waji pa kahuga qa wayawa unpi wanji ip.

Mar. 11, 12, 13. Wiyohiyanpata, New York, Philadelphia, Washington ekta icamna tanka qa wicośan owasin anpetu wakan wanji hehanyan anapta. Hemani hiyaye śni. Mazaapi mazu kin kun ehpeyapi. Wowapi tokan wanica. Wicastapi hapi śni hduhapi. Qa nape een wicakihan yukan keyapi.

March 21. Dakota makoce kin en ake wkangapi kte. Congress ekta Tunkansidan kin eaje en eiciunake kta keyapi. Hehan ecadan owakpamini en Dakota oyate Miniśoce un owasin Pahasapa okitahedan unpi kin iwicawangapi kte.

March 28. Woyaco Wankantu ituncan kin Chief Justice Waite heehan ta. Waynco owotanna qa kaspa. Wicaśta hoccca iyayapi eca oyate coowasin wahpaniwicayapi.

March 26. Washington otonwe ekta Winohinca Owohdake Taaka yuhapi. Token winyan kaspapi kte qa yuoninhapi kta e iwohdakapi. Woope eciyataahan wiecapi iyecen unpi kta iyecenkiyapi. Hehan tohanyan wacin kupe śni kin wiyopeciye kta okihi kte śni einpi. Ituyetu wanji en Tunkansidanyapi tawicu kici iye tipi kin ekta wicakicopi.

March 27. Miniwanen akasanpa Germany ekta. Elbe wakpa muitan qa otonwe wicemna topa anmitanpi. Wicaśta kektopamnige wikcemna tankana owanin ihangupi.

Watertown, Dakota, hen Congregational Okodakiciye kin tipi wakan wanji kaġapi. Qa deren hen wanuayanpi. Makoce owanacaya Sunday School en wicakidapi qa tuwe cin kinhan makaśpan wanji kaspapi wanji un opetonkiyapi. Hena owasin akicita wicayawapi. Qa tuwe wicacaje saptan mnaye cinhan he akicita itancan, Captain, kaġapi. Qa tuwe wicacaje wikcemna zaptan yuhe cinhan he Colonel kaġapi. Qa iyotan ota wicayuhe cinhan he akicita itancan tanka General kaġapi.

WOWAPI MAQUPI.

Santee Agency, Neb., March 15. —Iśnanti oyate kin dehan wetu kin nina wojupi on nuihciciyapi kta naeceeu. Ecin dehan iye tawanaśtanpi ongetunkansidan kin en yanke cin, he etanhan ongc on wojupi sa kiepai qa wanna awicayaptapi qa wojupi sa dena wicaqupi. Aguyapi sa iyutapi, 13,000; Wayahota su iyutapi, 14,000; Wabdi su iyutapi, 110; Wamnaheza su iyutapi, 200; hemaken naka maben cbnakapi kiuhan ito cca tonakeca teiByapdka.

Isanati oyate kin wanna tunkansidan tawonmaye kin ouśpa opapi, wahpaya wokajuju (tax) he wanna wicaśta onge eeonpi, naka taku iye kamnapi qa opeton yuhapi kin hemaea eu wonmaye opapi qa hehan taku tona tunkansidan eciyatanhan wopamni yuhapi kin heca e yawapi śni. Okini wicaśta wikcemma nonpa cetupi, hena wanna tunkansidan tawomnaye opapi.

Rosebud Agency, D. T. Feb. 4 1888. Ileha nil Sintegleska oyanke kin lel owolitaton we lo. Tka Lakota wanjini el opa śni ye lo. Owakpamni cen iye waśicun unpi kin eca cece owolitaton iciengapi lo. Tka iśeka einaa wanjila el opa, Inśed he waape lo. Na Inś Sicanju Ateyapi kin npape lo. Na tunkansilayapi kin eciyntanhan waśicun hca wan lel i ma un yunkan he eea apapi. Canke mina cignli un ye ha mi tka inpemieaye lo. Ho waśicun kin Tunkanśila eciyatanhan wanspekiye itancan hca en i na la led no, yunkan hce ca apapi, canke anpetu he na inaini Tunkanśidan ckta kigla cin canke iye cen waśicun kin Illa koki.papi lo. Iho heeetu we lo. Cante waśte ya nape eiyunpi lo.

JOSEPH L. BRAVE.

WILD WEST OŚKATE KIN.

Buffalo Bill's Wild West Show, Manchester, England, Feb. 15, 1888. Wi'd West oskate kin le el tokel waun kin lehanl owaglakin kte lo. Mitawacin on ohinniyan woope bluha na ohinniyan Wakantanka kiksuya wauu. Tka oskate kin anpetu na hanhepi ko inyanke, canke mazaśkanśkan oape nonpa hehanyela owaglita wo. Tka ohinniyan Wakantanka kiksuya waua ka hecel taku oyasin okihi unkaye lo.

Hopo, Mitakuye Lakota oyate kin. yan sloiwaye lo. Wicoluan wanji lila waśte ye lo. Tuwa Wakantanka an pi kin taku wicohan waśte lyeyin kte lo, he wate lo. Na taku wicohan Waśiun ecompi kin ota tehike lo. Tuwa Makoce nica hen tiwokitahena te lo. Na makoce kin otunkaya qeyaśo ohinniyan Waśicun ojulaye lo. Hebanl naka ohini taku icantc waśte ye la ca taku owasin ktci okiiya waun qa heon koska de on un śni unkan nina cante maleen qa una waciya. Qa hecanni, elianpo wicaśa waste kicidapi wicohan unka waśte ye lo. Leci makoce kin tokees, anpetu oyasin oiyokpaze. Ohinniyan ośota canke tobinni wi kin tanyan wanuyakapi śni yelo. Tehaul leenia le wi Feb. 7, 1888 hehanl winyan wan cineaton. Winyan kin kiniimi eciyapi na atkuku kin Nacniqala eciyapi. Na le anpetu kin wanna minikanstanpi kte. Feb. 15, hehanl, mazaśkanśkan śakpe kin hehanl woope yuha kte hokśiyopa kin he. Ho, hecetu we lo. Wowte on wanaśonciyapu yo.

C. BLACK ELK, HEŚAKASAPA.

TAKODAKU KIŦE.

Iapi Oaye : nite kin akan wicaśa kaśpapi kin heon maka oraje owasin on eowinapi. Maka ska qa śi qa to qa śa hena on oniwanpi, eanken owanyan ke niwaśte qa wicayukipi hca iyeceed. Ito niś nite kin akan maka sapa wau on ociwa kte do. Nakaha Ihunktawan tipi en wiconte wan waśte waanduke, token sdonwaye cin omdake kte. Koka he decen kicipapi, Joseph Pacquett. Hayetu wanji kośka wan kici waśi iye wowapi wakan yawa qa miś woeekiye epe, qa hanhepi ataya en unqoinpi qa ake wanhanpa wowanji wakan mayanduko cin wowapi wakan yawakiye. Unkan wayazanke cin heye "ito owasin inayaukanpi cenm inanpipi, unkan kaken woeekiye eye. "Wakantanka iyotan wicakte cin hanihanna waśte kin on sdatatowan wo. Wckakije tanka komdake cin de anpetu wi kin linape ca maben iyaye cin iyecen iyaye kta. Inś tuwa kin itancanke kin he okna nde kte e miinaġi kin edekakin wo. Hehan wowapi wakan wieowoyake de nina yawa yanke qa cen inape. Psalm 23. Kośka de heye; wieonġe kin kowakipe śni, eya nawaion; unkan wicake wudake do. Tohan wana wieonte cin kiel hi ta nihniciye śni ye do. Anpetu tawa kin wicawayapi epe do. He nape tanka wicaśa kin iyeya iiduweyela we do. Wieaśa wan leimant ye kta cen katinyeya iyaye cin iyecen iyaye. Hehan Okodakiciye Wakan en ohini tanyan waokiya cin qa kośka okodokiciye en ohini wicohan tanya wawokiya qa wicohan owasin tanyan econ. Hchan iyotan tawa kin tokean tanyan on kta ohini akita secece, canken wicaśa owasin cen cante waśteya un qa ni kin cn iculnhan un śni qa iycccn un. Itinapi eciyatanhan unkan nina wawokiye qa tiwahe on canto watse wicaye. Hceen wanna wopapi kta iyehantu heceu wieaśa ota kiksuyapi kta naecce. Ohan wicasa ota wokiksuye oio iciuge wakte, qa en ciwaśa ota wamduke eca wieasa ota kiksuyapi epee do. He on kośkapi qa wicakapi pini eya tipi ekta cgmni ohiniyan epe do. Miye wanna Omaka yamini lecii wann wctu; Yunkan Waśicun iapi wanjigji owakiln yunkan mitakoln wotanln iseka wowapi wanji Iccala iwaeu, na lila ilulukin ye lo. Lakota Waśicun iseka okihipi kte kin hccyataulan.

Leei makoce kin tokees, anpetu oyasin oiyokpaze. Ohinniyan ośota canke tohinni wi kin tanyan wanuyakapi śni yelo. Tehanl leenia le wi Feb. 7, 1888 hehanl winyan wan eineaton. Winyan kin kiniimi eciyapi na atkuku kin Nacniqala eciyapi. Na le anpetu kin wanna minikanstanpi kte. Feb. 15, hehanl, mazaśkanśkan śakpe kin hehanl woope yuha kte hokśiyopa kin he. Ho, hecetu we lo. Wowte on wanaśonciyapu yo.

General Terry akicita itancan hca he ayuśtan qa Gen. Crook tohe yuhe.

PIERRE LA POINTE.

UNITED STATES EN WOICICAGE WOOPE KIN.

ÓŚPE 6.

Hunkayapi qa wawieiyewicakiyapi tawicofanpi kin on wokajuju ieupi kte, woope (law) ohnayan, qa United States, tawomnaye etanhan wicakiciciujupi kte. Ataya-waeiapi [Congress] en taku iwohdakapi chan, etanhan kupi qaiś en yapi ieunhan, en opa wanji kaskapi kte śni, tuwe kin he makoee cien cikize kahwacin, qaiś psyukśapi kta e yacopi kte, qaiś woeekiye yajupi wacin śni chantanhanś; ti pi unmatukto kaśta en taku iwohdakapi qa akinicapi kin he on tuktedan tokan iwieawanġapi kte śni.

Hunkayapi qa wawieiyewicakiyapi kin tohanyan hena kta wicakahnipi ieunhan wieofan ośiunean wan, United States woope eciyatanhan śni, qa akicita tawieolian hen śni, en opapi kin hehan kaśapi qaiś wokajuju kin yutapi kinhan tohini he wieaqupi kte śni; qa United States en tuwe otunwenicahan wanji yuhe cin, ieunhan unkan tipi unamatukte kaśta en ikan kte śni.

ÓŚPE 7.

Tuukanśidanyapi tawomnaye token occon kte cin, wawieiye tipi kin etauhan tokaheya eajeyatapi kta taku hnakayapi tipi kin en wnnge hena on woope cajeyatapi enjeyntapi qa yusuta okihipi, woope nnnna token eajeyatapi kin iyeeen. Woope eajeyatapi [bill] otoiyohi tipi napin, wawieiye, qa hunkayapi tipi kin yueeetupi ceta, chauka-hantalanyapi kin he kinapipi kte; iyeeetu dake cinhan eajo oiciwa kte, tuka iyeceetu śni dake kin he iyahna, tipi unmatukte en woope he tokaheya cajeyatapi kin en icicawin wieakieu kte; he woope cajeyatapi ko iyowinyanpi qa yanni kiyukśapi śni eye kte; ku iyececca un iwohdakapi qa yamni kiyukśapi nom han woope heea kte.

Tuka taku tona eośe ohna yuśtanpi kin hena owas lan qa biya ceedan olna yuśtanpi kte, qu tonn iyeeetu dakapi qa tona iyeeetu dakapi śni eajepi kiuhan anpetu wicocmna helianyan ieieawin hdiyo śni kiiihan woope heea kte, (anpetu wikan opo śni), qa eajo oiciwa cin yuśtca eece kte iyeeetu eye kte; Atnya wanini kin ito eajeyatapi co iciewin wieaktsu śni chantanhanś woope kte śni.

Waeeonwicaśipi, woyakean qaiś wieanjo iyolipeyapi tona Hunkayapi qa Wawieiye Tipi napin yuautapi iyececee en (omnieiye cajeyatapi kte cin he ope śni) heon owas, United States en tunkansidanyapi kipazpi kte, qa yuceetnpi śni wicayapi kta, qaiś iyeeetu śni eye kte; ita tipi napin Hunkayapi qa Wawieiye-tipi, yamni kiyuśpapi nom obnayan akta yueeetupi kte, woope eajey api [bill] cn tokanyan woope kapiapi eeonpi cece kte iyeecn.

For Black Elk the "word" is the Lakota language itself, and the "carrying" is the physical act of transporting the sonic economy of the Northern Plains to Manchester. Black Elk might say of the masthead: *Lakota Iapi Oaye*—even *here*! You can see the difference in meaning if you look at how Black Elk's Bible translated the Word/*Logos* of the Gospel of John: *Wicoie*.[8] *Iapi* simply does not signify this same meaning to Black Elk. It appears to suggest to him the materiality of spoken Lakota and its embodiment in the newspaper. The experience of seeing his language in print taught him something else—that he was fundamentally Lakota, and that his spirituality was connected directly to the homeland on the Plains. He confided to Nebraska poet laureate John Neihardt, the writer of *Black Elk Speaks* (1931), that "while he was in Europe his own spiritual power disappeared, and perhaps this led him to Christianity. As soon as he came back to Pine Ridge, his power came back to him."[9] This perhaps explains the emphasis on land in Black Elk's Lakota letter. The word *makoce* (land) appears twice in the paragraph. Another set of repetitions worth noting emphasizes kinship bonds strengthened by the arrival of a medium for written Lakota: "Hopo, Mitakuye Lakota oyate kin ... mitakola wotanin" (So, my relatives, the Lakota people, ... my friend gave me news).

Black Elk was not alone. As DeMallie points out, Lakota society experienced a literary outpouring during Black Elk's lifetime, as "literate Sioux individuals ... for a variety of personal reasons, chose to preserve records of traditional culture and history." DeMallie continues, "The impulse to use writing for this purpose appears to have been very strong, and there is little doubt that the documents of which I have knowledge are only a small representation of a vigorous—but largely private—literary tradition."[10] So it was, and when Black Elk finally returned home to Pine Ridge in 1889, it was to an already established large body of vernacular-language readers, listeners, and writers.

If in 1884 Black Elk elected to write in the vernacular orthography of the missionaries to express his Lakotaness, he later in life abandoned that medium in favor of oral performance. In 1930, he was visited by John Neihardt, who was at work on an epic project, "A Cycle of the West." Neihardt thought he needed an Indian perspective on the land, and he sought out Black Elk as someone Lakota people recommended as a holy man. On hearing some of Black Elk's stories, he became convinced he needed to devote an entire volume to the man's life. He quickly penned a letter to Black Elk, saying, "I would want to tell the story of your life beginning at the beginning and going straight through to Wounded Knee." In preparation, Neihardt enlisted his own daughters, Enid and Hilda, to act as transcribers of Ben Black Elk's translation of his father's oral performances: "Black Elk would make a statement in Lakota, which his son Ben then translated into English. Ben spoke the idiomatic 'Indian English' typical of the time—a dialect that had arisen out of the need for Indian students in off-reservation boarding schools. . . . Neihardt would repeat Ben's translation, rephrasing for clarity and standard English, Enid wrote it down in shorthand."[11]

Black Elk and Neihardt's collaboration, however, turned out to be much more than a transcription of an old man's storied life. When Neihardt arrived for the scheduled three-day interview, he was surprised to find the Black Elk place transformed into an old-time encampment: "On a knoll in front of the house a large new tipi of white duck had been erected, with the flaming rainbow of Black Elk's vision painted above the doorway and the vision power symbols painted on the sides. The material for the lodge had been provided by Roy Wooden, the trader in Manderson. . . . Around the house and the tipi a circle of fresh cut pine trees . . . had been thrust into the ground . . . [to form a/with?] a circular dance bower."[12]

The women of Black Elk's extended family were preparing a feast. Other Lakota elders (Fire Thunder, Standing Bear, Chase in the Morning, and Holy Black Tail Deer) joined Black Elk and took over the narration at key moments to which they had been eyewitnesses or more directly involved than Black Elk himself. By the time the storytelling began, more than 200 people had gathered around the arbor and tipi.

For his part, Black Elk performed a Lakota verbal genre known as *hanbloglaka*, a vision-telling story. This required not only words but also pictures. So it was that his friend Standing Bear made a large painting of his "flaming rainbow" vision and applied it to the tipi cover. The image would also appear in the first edition of *Black Elk Speaks*. Black Elk could have written down his vision in his Native language but opted not to. Instead, in old age, he returned to the mixed media of his Lakota childhood. For three days, a blending of image, spoken word, feasting, and gathering served to generate the translation and transcription practices that yielded Neihardt's book. Interestingly, the project was intergenerational on both the Lakota and Euro-American sides. The medicine healer's son translated for his father, and the Nebraska poet's daughters wrote down the text.

I will offer some possible explanations for Black Elk's mixed-media performance choices later in this chapter, but for now, I want to trace the side-by-side development of oral and graphic media among the Oceti Sakowin, exploring how an alphabetic form of Lakota in a new medium came to take its place alongside the sacred pipe, the *waniyetu wowapi* (Winter Count), ceremonial regalia, and even the Lakota homeland itself. Like other communities that appear in this study, the Lakotas of the 1880s established new

BLACK ELK BEFORE THE SIX GRANDFATHERS IN THE FLAMING RAINBOW TEPEE

Figure 3.4. Standing Bear, "Flaming Rainbow." Figure from Black Elk and Neihardt, *Black Elk Speaks*.

interlocutive communities as they became increasingly separated from each other by geographic space and power imbalances. These served to knit the people together by employing hybrid systems of communication to compensate for an unsettled social order.

When Black Elk was only a year old, a new medium for expressing the *iapi* had arisen among the easternmost Council Fires of the Oceti Sakowin. For the Dakotas of present-day Minnesota—the Mdewakanton, Wahpekute, Sisitonwan/Sisseton, and Wahpetonwan—alphabetic literacy in the vernacular took on a specifically decolonizing cast that the missionaries who helped devise it could not possibly have foreseen. Very few members of Dakota communities adopted written Dakota until war, incarceration, and removal sundered the ties of clan and *tiyospaye* (extended family) to the point that new media were needed to maintain relations against the grind of the colonizing institutions, military forts, townships, and range.

SPELLING DISPOSSESSION

On July 15, 1830, the United States framed a treaty with the Native nations of the Minnesota Territory at a council at Prairie du Chien, in present-day Wisconsin. Indigenous signatories to the treaty, which ceded great tracts of land from the Mississippi to the Missouri Rivers, included representatives from the Sauk and Fox tribes; the Medewakanton, Wahpekuta, Wahpeton, and Sisseton bands of the Oceti Sakowin; and members of the Omaha, Iowa, Oto, and Missouri Nations. A direct outcome of the Removal Act, the treaty at Prairie du Chien relinquished all Native lands from the upper fork of the Des Moines River to the Missouri River, "the Missouri state line above the Kansas; thence along said line to the NW. corner of the said state." From there the boundary of surrendered land extended to the confluence of the Missouri and Des Moines Rivers to a point opposite the source of the Boyer River, and "thence in a direct line to the upper fork of the Demoine, the place of beginning."[13]

Waves of European immigrants flooded the area after 1830. Further dispossession followed through several subsequent treaties such that by 1858, the Dakotas had largely been sequestered on "a narrow, ten-mile strip along the south shore of the Minnesota River."[14] This solitary isthmus of Indian Country was a far cry from the complex Indigenous homelands of the Great Lakes that had flourished before the Americans arrived. And the alphabetic documents such as the Treaty of Prairie du Chien that authorized the separation of Oceti Sakowin communities from their homelands and from one another led directly to the Dakotas' introduction to an orthography in their own language.

The Great Lakes and Prairie boundary lands that made up the Minnesota Territory were initially constituted from pre-Columbian Indigenous urban trade centers, small townships, farms, and hunting grounds that flourished during the first few centuries of the common era. This area of "Native space" (as Abenaki historian Lisa Brooks calls similar areas in the Northeast) was profoundly generative of social and cultural innovation, "sites within which we can investigate the emergent discourses of identity and groupness among Native American groups and their relationship with the ideological uses of Indians in American society."[15] It was, as Ojibwe historian Brenda Child points out, a "contested transition zone, a verdant region connecting the woodlands and prairies where white-tailed deer and wild rice were abundant."[16] Before the Treaty of Prairie du Chien, English and French imperial forays into the region fell short of full-blown settler colonialism in ideology and scope. The infrastructure of these European powers consisted only of fur trading posts and forts built to protect the exchange of goods in an intercultural mercantile network. It was a system sustained primarily by social rather than by military or economic relations. Susan Sleeper-Smith once characterized the glue holding this world together as a fateful interweaving of "women, kinship, and Catholicism."[17]

After the War of 1812, much of the region fell into American hands, and by 1823, the American Fur Company controlled the trade across present-day Minnesota. The company was headquartered at a post called St. Peters, at the confluence of the Minnesota and Mississippi Rivers. It was a locale known

Figure 3.5. Map of present-day Minnesota showing land cessions after the 1830 Treaty of Prairie du Chien. The body of water in the lower left is the site of the Lac qui Parle Mission, situated on the last strip of land left to the Dakotas in present-day Minnesota. Charles C. Royce and Cyrus Thomas, Indian land cessions in the United States, 1899, in *Eighteenth Annual Report of the Bureau of American Ethnology to the Secretary of the Smithsonian Institution, 1896–1897*, no. 13023487, Geography and Map Division, Library of Congress, Washington, DC.

in Dakota as *Bdote* and possessed great spiritual and diplomatic meaning for Oceti Sakowin bands in the region. The Dakotas and Ojibwes were the primary trappers of fur-bearing animals here, harvesting a wide variety in the region's woodlands and waterways. In exchange for furs, French, British, and US traders provided goods such as blankets, firearms and ammunition, cloth, metal tools, and brass kettles. The fur trade had a tremendous effect on Dakota and Ojibwe cultural practices, influencing US-Native economic and political relations in the nineteenth century, including treaty negotiations.

The Treaty of Prairie du Chien officially opened the path to a stream of American government representatives into the Minnesota Territory; soldiers, quasi-military "Indian agents," traders, and missionaries. The military presence, centered at the US Army outpost called Fort Snelling, established at the *Bdote* in 1825, was headed by Col. Josiah Snelling (1782–1828), a veteran of the War of 1812. He was joined by Lawrence Taliaferro (1794–1871), a fellow veteran and Virginia slaveholder. Taliaferro served as a go-between for the American Fur Company traders and the Ojibwes and Dakotas. Joseph Renville (1779–1846), a fur trader born of a French father and Dakota mother, was also critical to the enterprise. Like Taliaferro and Snelling, Renville had fought in the War of 1812, but on the other side—for the British. In 1827, he became an independent trader at Lac qui Parle, a village near the Missouri River.

The final piece of settler-colonial infrastructure established in the region consisted of missionaries aligned with the American Board of Commissioners for Foreign Missions (ABCFM). The organization was represented to the Dakotas by three ordained ministers—Thomas Smith Williamson (1800–79), Alexander Huggins (1808–77), and Stephen Return Riggs (1812–83). They were soon joined by two brothers from Connecticut, Gideon Pond (1810–78) and his brother Samuel Pond (1808–91). Although the Ponds were not ordained, all members of this missionary party had been inflamed by the Great Awakening and had directed their religious enthusiasm toward missionizing the Native peoples of North America.[18] Samuel Pond recalled:

> Soon after I joined the church I lost all hope that I was, or ever could be a Christian, and for many months my mental sufferings were intense. When I was brought out of that gloomy darkness into the light of the Sun of righteousness, I felt constrained by the love of Christ to go where ever my services in the cause of religion seemed most needed. My brother and I both thought we could be more useful somewhere else than in New England, where Christianity had so many friends and advocates, and we looked westward for a field of labor.[19]

When friends tried to dissuade the two men, Samuel staunchly responded, "We had the Gospel and the Dakotas were perishing for want of it."[20]

Despite protests to the contrary, the missionaries, like Snelling, Taliaferro, and Renville, were engaged in the transformation of an imperial-mercantile social field into a settler-colonial space. The ABCFM's missionary network in Minnesota, like elsewhere in the world, harnessed the latest technologies of print culture and replicated the exploration of Native homelands and the collecting of Indigenous material culture that was an integral part of the military and mercantile "conquest" of the West. Soldiers, traders, and ABCFM missionaries alike had to be vetted by the Secretary of War and, in Minnesota Territory, by Taliaferro and the current commander of Fort Snelling.[21] Like the soldiers and traders, the missionaries, too, were fixated on land and space as determinants of being and meaning. The primary ABCFM publication, *The Missionary Herald*, regularly featured maps of areas being missionized and emphasized the global "spread" of the gospels. The ABCFM also encouraged its missionaries to collect "Indian curiosities" and send them back to the offices in Boston, where they were put on display.[22]

ABCFM missionizing shared the modern infrastructure of the settler-colonial state. It was industrial, entrepreneurial, and highly bureaucratized. In fact, David Paul Nord has described this period of nineteenth-century American missionization as characterized by the "industrialization of evangelism." New printing technologies allowed groups like the ABCFM to publish and disseminate thousands of religious tracts promoting what they called their "righteous empire."[23] Cheap mass printing, stereotyping, and the emergence of western printing and distribution centers in Cincinnati, Ohio, and Lexington, Kentucky, all facilitated the rapid spread of evangelical print into Indian communities after 1830.

Like other aspects of the settler colonial expansion into the American West, the ABCFM missionary efforts took advantage of a growing discourse that rationalized the dispossession of Indigenous lands through recourse to the trope of the vanishing Indian. They also leaned on bourgeois social norms, like those idealized in middle-class American gender relations, emphasizing the role of sentiment in producing the empathy needed to evangelize, connecting by feeling—all the rhetorical techniques that other scholars have explored as central to the settler-colonial discourse of Native dispossession. In fact, missionary Stephen Riggs's 1852 description of the Dakota language for the American Bureau of Ethnography framed the purpose of the orthography he helped create in the discourse of settler colonialism and Indigenous erasure. Were Indians "disappearing?" Riggs asked rhetorically. Yes, but in the context of missionary literacy practices, in the best way possible: "by ceasing to be Indians and becoming members of civilized society." "In Minnesota," Riggs explained, "all persons of mixed blood, i.e. of white and Indian descent, are recognized as citizens of the territory. . . . The Indian tribes of our continent may become extinct as such; but if this extinction is brought about by civilization and Christianity, and merging them into our own great nation, . . . who will deplore the result?"[24]

Evangelists like Riggs also propagated settler colonial discourse in a subtler way. Unlike their brethren on international missions who were discouraged from marriage lest their wives have to survive alone in remote reaches of the globe, the ABCFM missionaries to the Dakotas modeled settler-colonial gender roles; they were asked to populate the missions as families. Because "women could only be missionaries if sponsored by a man," historian Linda Clemmons has explained how this led to women taking on an "inverted" relationship to Dakota society: "Missionary women like Mary Riggs and Cornelia Pond were disillusioned by the limited time available to devote to proselytizing. More fundamentally, however, missionary women's experience living on the frontier challenged the essence of missionary ideology: missionaries were supposed to teach and the natives were supposed to learn. In the case of the Dakota mission, the instructor student relationship was sometimes inverted, and the Dakota women became the missionary women's teachers and helpers."[25]

By 1855, the ABCFM boasted eight mission stations across the Minnesota Territory. In addition to Fort Snelling (1841–43), more permanent mission stations were founded at Traverse des Sioux (1843–53), St. Peter's (1844–47), Prairieville (1847–53), Oak Grove (1843–53), Red Wing (1848–54), Yellow Medicine/Pajutazee (1852–62), and New Hope/Hazelwood (1854–62).

The alphabetic Dakota script owed its development to these missionaries and the social and religious bonds they forged with Joseph Renville and several key Dakota leaders in the 1830s and 1840s. Thomas Smith Williamson was in the vanguard of the ABCFM-sanctioned missionaries who arrived in the Minnesota Territory in 1834, presenting his credentials to Taliaferro at Fort Snelling. It was not long before he was making his way farther west, to the Dakota villages at Lac qui Parle that were constellated around Joseph Renville's trading post. At Renville's request, Williamson had a small cabin built there, within the stockade walls and next to Renville's own house. In the first years of the mission, the missionary was clearly socially subservient to the Dakota trader.[26]

If Williamson's housing situation was totally dependent on Renville's benevolence, so too was his relationship with the surrounding Dakota community. In addition to his role as a trader, Renville maintained special power over local Dakotas through his wife's family, who hailed from a well-known Dakota lineage. In fact, Renville "kept a company of twenty or thirty men in the capacity of soldiers," as Stephen Riggs recalled, ensuring that fur shipments arrived safely. When John C. Frémont met Renville in 1839, he called him a "border chief," suggesting his hybrid social role. Riggs believed that "the company was kept quite as much for appearances as for use."[27]

The Kiyuksa, or Breakers, as these "soldiers" were called, were a band of the Mdewakanton Sioux. Their chief village in 1858 was Winona, on the site of the present-day city of that name. The members took "wives within prohibited degrees of kinship" and so were called "Breakers." Known collectively as "Tokadantee," they formed a kind of Dakota men's warrior society whose emblem was the prairie dog. They regularly kept a lodge just outside the fort and feasted, "more or less daily," thriving "especially under the guardianship of the first Mrs. Renville." Mary Renville's brother, Chatka, or Left Hand, "held a conspicuous place in the Tokadantee."[28]

From the commencement of the mission in 1835, Renville and his family were Williamson's main parishioners, meeting on the Sabbath in the Renville home. Chatka and his families came also, but because he had two wives and a number of children by each, Williamson worried that there was going to be a growing gap between doctrinal purity and community norms, church attendance and "civilization."[29] Williamson and Renville soon agreed that these meetings were insufficient to "civilize" the local Native community even though "the full benefits of civilization have never been enjoyed by any people without the gospel." Chata's situation underscored what Williamson considered to be the current state of even church-going Dakotas: "Wandering savages . . . while they continue to be such taught all the commands of the Savior of men." In addition, as Williamson confessed to his ABCFM correspondents back East, the Dakota language was a formidable challenge, creating what he and other missionaries considered the primary barrier to evangelizing the Native population. In an early letter to the ABCFM, Williamson listed "their language" as the other main impediment to missionization. The Dakota language was hard to learn and, in Williamson's opinion, full of "defects."[30]

THE LANGUAGE OF THE OCETI SAKOWIN
The dialects spoken by the various bands of the Oceti Sakowin are known in contemporary linguistic literature under the general heading "Dakota" and are spoken by some 11,000 tribal citizens. To form a written version of these dialects, as we have learned, required that European language speakers find visual ways to mark out several of the language's distinctive features. With five oral and three nasal vowels, each with a distinctive length, it is important

for an orthography to make these sounds legible in written texts. Likewise, because Dakota maintains a "clear and important distinction between aspirated and unaspirated p, t, č, and k," a useful spelling system would need to find a way to represent aspiration.[31] Dakota and its related dialects also feature "distinct gender endings for statements, questions, and commands" for male and female speakers. Closely allied to this linguistic element, Dakota employs very specific terms for male and female relatives, depending upon whether the speaker is male or female and how the speaker understands his or her relation to his or her interlocutor. Is the listener a "cousin?" A female elder? A brother-in-law? A maternal aunt? Finally, like all languages, Dakota employs a regular syntax. Idiomatic sentences in Dakota are constructed in the order: subject, object, verb. This arrangement, denoted S-O-V in linguistic studies, differs from English syntax, which is generally subject-verb-object (S-V-O).

Looking back over the history of written Dakota from the perspective of the late twentieth century, the Lakota educator Albert White Hat Sr. traced the history of orthographic development introduced by white missionaries: "Dakhota, the most eastern division [of the Oceti Sakowin], was the first Sioux tribal group encountered by missionaries and anthropologists. Consequently, Dakota was the earliest dialect to be transcribed into a written format." "This alphabet," White Hat continues, "was modified for the 'L' dialect [the Lakota dialect] by Rev. Eugene Buechel, SJ in *A Grammar of the Lakota* (1939) . . . and further adapted and extended by Franz Boas and Ella Deloria in *Dakota Grammar* (1941)."[32]

As he pursued fuller knowledge of his own language and traditions, White Hat soon realized that the spelling system he had inherited involved its own complex ideologies of colonization. At the time the missionaries arrived, the Dakota/Lakota dialects had already, according to White Hat, "built us up to a point where we were a progressive and strong people." Once the spoken language was "reduced" to writing, "the [orthographic] misuse of the language almost destroyed" the Oceti Sakowin.[33]

To teach his language in the twentieth century, White Hat realized, would require a thorough revision of its orthography, taking into account the subtle epistemological and ideological implications of some of the linguistic elements of Dakota that the Euro-American missionaries had taken for granted. First, White Hat and his community wanted an orthography that better represented the sounds of spoken Dakota, as proper pronunciation created the necessary "emotion" a language needs to remain vital and persuasive in rapidly changing circumstances. It also had to meet the needs of the many tribal citizens who could speak the language but not read or write it. Finally, the language needed to be taught in a way that highlighted the "ethical and moral" implications of its embedded worldviews.

Relative terms maintained social order, just as syntax sequenced Dakota ways of knowing. White Hat observed, "Most of the early writings were done by missionaries who attempted to translate Christian ideas into a Lakota sentence. Often such sentences followed an English sentence structure instead of reflecting the pattern of Lakota syntax." Careful study of his community's orthographic history led White Hat to conclude, "This past . . . approach to language [was] a tool for acculturation and assimilation purposes." He argued, "Our language was invaded just as our lands were. We needed to bring back our language with the strength of its spiritual values and the power of its moral force, just as we fight to reclaim the other sacred sites within our domain. Our language is *wakan*. It is our bloodline." White Hat's observations are especially relevant to this study of sovereignty because they clearly link land and language in a way that allows us to explore how the missionary spelling systems of the Dakotas and Lakotas were intimately tied to the settler colonial project of dispossessing the Oceti Sakowin peoples of their homelands.[34]

In 1835, of course, Williamson and Renville did not view their orthography efforts in such crude colonialist terms. Williamson based the spelling system on the Roman alphabet and followed the guidelines set by John Pickering. When Stephen Riggs and his wife, Mary, arrived at the Dakota mission at Lac qui Parle in 1837, he found Williamson hard at work on Bible translations with Renville. Although Riggs was interested in the Dakota language primarily for its role in converting the Dakotas to Christianity, he was also fascinated by the process through which the language was procured: "Mr. Renville . . . sat in a chair in the middle of his own reception room, and Dr. Williamson, Mr GH Pond and myself seated at a side-table with our writing materials before us. . . . Dr. Williamson read a verse from the French bible. This Renville . . . repeated in Dakota. We wrote it down from his mouth. . . . When the verse was written, someone read it over, and it was corrected."[35]

Finally, there was the alphabet itself, which was "phonetic, as nearly as possible." When Riggs and his colleagues discovered that "x and v and r and g and j and f and e, with their English powers were not needed," they suddenly realized that a phonetic transcription of Dakota was going to require some creativity in the way they used the Roman letters, for they wished, above all, "that the language . . . printed should require as few new characters as possible." The new orthography recognized five vowels (a, e, i, o, u) and twenty-five consonants. Unlike English, Riggs believed that Dakota contained "four clicks, two gutturals and a nasal that must be expressed."[36] The group decided to use n for the nasal, q for one of the clicks, and g and r for the "gutturals," employing specially marked letters to notate the other clicks and ç, j, and x to represent "ch," "zh," and "sh."

To this scene of seemingly straightforward translation, we must add a few details that both elucidate the real complexities of the enterprise and foreground the social relations upon which the Riggs-Williamson orthography was based. In the *Missionary Tribune* for 1846, the missionaries complemented Renville on his skills: "Mr. Renville was a remarkable man, and he was remarkable for the energy with which he pursued such objects as he deemed of primary importance. His power of observing and remembering facts, and also words expressive of simple ideas was extraordinary." But in private, Samuel Pond reported that "Renville could neither read nor write [a] passage of Scripture." So the missionaries "read to him, one verse at a time, and the Dakota [was] written down as he dictated it." Not only was Renville virtually illiterate in Gospel matters, but his knowledge of the Bible was drawn from a French Vulgate version he had gotten as a young man. Williamson went so far as to purchase a copy for himself so that when he needed to translate other Christian texts, he would have some sense of the "original" that Renville understood as "Gospel." When he suggested the missionaries write some hymns in Dakota, Renville had them set the words to "French airs, he had learned from the 'voyagers.'"[37] Of the 150 hymns the Dakota mission eventually published, about twelve were actually composed by Renville himself, within the French folk-music tradition of his youth.

By winter 1837, Williamson had begun using the script to teach literacy in Dakota to the young men who were members of the Tokadantee.[38] Longhand versions of this original orthography appear in all the missionaries' letters and journals from the period, as do their many complaints and confusions about the Dakota language and its efficacy in their mission. The missionaries' Dakota vocabulary, for example, was minimal, and increased only with some rather ad hoc circumstances—as when Samuel Pond went on a Buffalo hunt in 1838 to pick some "two or three hundred words from the Indians."[39] In November 1837, Alexander Huggins noted in his journal that he had "Trans scribed [sic] a little Sioux but I don't know that I learned any." Other diarists and letter writers said much the same thing.[40]

During these early days of the development of the Dakota orthography (often called the "Riggs orthography") the written word was circulated in manuscript epistles and handmade books created by the missionaries and their Dakota parishioners. As Samuel Pond recalled later, "No one person and no two or three persons could justly claim the authorship of the Dakota dictionary. It was the joint work of many men & women each contributing to it some more and some less according to his or her ability or opportunity." For his part, Pond worked hard at translation and gained Williamson's trust as a competent speaker of Dakota. The elder minister often borrowed manuscripts from Pond, "to read to the Indians, saying they understood it better than they did other translations."[41]

Archaeological evidence from the Renville homesite gives some indication of how the material culture of the written word slowly became integrated into local Dakota life at Lac qui Parle. To the long-established mercantile network of furs and kinship ties, the missionaries brought a new system of pen nibs, ink, and paper. Among the hundreds of ceramic fragments, metal belt buckles, tinklers, and glass beads recovered from the trading post in the twentieth century, there was also a curious broken tablet of catlinite "with the letters 'A, B, C, D & F' scratched on the surface." There were also graphite markers of "Rectangular ... shape ... sharpened to a rounded point."[42] Catlinite, a mineral named after the Euro-American painter, George Catlin, also know as pipestone, was a key part of Dakota material culture, providing the main material for ceremonial pipes, and a much-coveted mineral throughout Indian Country.[43] Its appearance as the material substrate of the earliest Dakota alphabetic inscriptions suggests that writing was being integrated into the broader visual and material culture of the Dakota community.

Williamson and Riggs believed that developing a scribal coterie of Dakotas literate enough in the orthography to write letters in support of the mission and to dramatize its positive effects in the eastern missionary press were of paramount importance to their goals. But the Dakota social order was not cooperating with Williamson in 1837. He saw that the role of tribal leaders was critical to the progress of his literacy project, but "some of the principal chiefs of the nation residing in this neighborhood[,] seeing that the introduction of education among their people [would] lead to the abandonment of the religion and customs of their ancestors[,] [were] opposing it with all their might."[44] Dakota gender roles also conspired against the literacy project, and many men were "reluctant to spell or read when others [were] present," leading the missionaries to break the Dakota women and men into groups.[45] Then there were the sheer physical hardships endured by the Dakota community whose traditional foodways had been severely disrupted by their removal to this small strip of land on the western edge of the territory. An early convert named Wamdiyokiye (Eagle Help) wrote to Williamson in 1837: "You told me to write and I was very desirous of doing so but could not. However I will try to do it. I wish much to do it, but we are starving and I am indisposed for doing and also I am nowhere at rest and have many things to do."[46]

Despite these setbacks, Williamson plunged ahead into the missionaries'

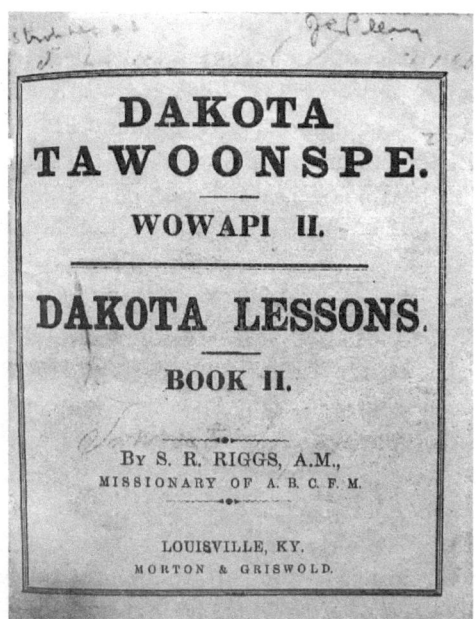

Figure 3.6. The cover of Stephen R. Riggs's, *Dakota Tawoonspe / Dakota Lessons*, 1850. Courtesy of the Newberry Library, Chicago.

dream project, a body of printed works in the Dakota orthography. Riggs made the argument for printed versions of Dakota to the ABCFM:

> In the advancement of the cause of Christ among that people required that a considerable amount of the scriptures be put into their hands in their own language. The number of Dakotas who can read intelligibly we estimated at over one hundred. This number, about half of which are adults, we hoped would be increased considerably during this year.... Another reason why I think we ought to have so much printed at present is the fact that what is printed now must in all probability be the *amount of reading* in the language for three or four years to come.[47]

For the debut volume in the Dakota language series, Williamson chose to translate from George Watt's *Second Set of Catechisms and Prayers*, employing the Dakota title *Wiconi owihanke wannin tanin kin*, whose literal translation he explained to the ABCFM: "*Wiconi* means life *owihan ke wanin* endless or eternal *tannin kin* appears or may be seen or found." Williamson was well aware of the limitations of the script: "I have spent much time and attention on it.... I am satisfied that most of it is printed correctly will be intelligible to those for whom it is made ... [and] they may acquire from it some more correct ideas of God and the way of salvation through Jesus."[48] There was also the problem of the typography, which in this first edition of a printed Dakota work, employed what Williamson called "the marked letters"—ç, p, t—sounds that were denoted by commonly available types in printing houses. Later, the missionaries would have to request special types be forged because these marked letters became confused with their common, English pronunciations.

Within a few years, the missionaries had produced a body of published Dakota-language material in this alphabet. In every case, they employed local Dakota people to help them translate and write the books. "All of our translations," Riggs reported, "are read over two or three times by our best Indian scholars." Riggs anticipated this body of printed works in Dakota would bring about a groundswell of religious enthusiasm and that Christianity would sweep through the Dakota Nation. That did not occur. Between 1838 and 1851, Riggs's letters are punctuated with statements regarding his disappointment at the failure of his literacy project to produce more converts. While early in the mission he reported that about 100 Dakotas could read this new written form of their language, his estimates did not to translate into students for his school or parishioners for his church. Of the forty-eight students listed in his classroom, only about sixteen attended church. In 1846, he could rely on only twenty Dakota people to attend church, and most Sundays might see only three or four. He also found that he still had about 100 of his Dakota books in storage and no one to use them.[49]

Samuel Pond was not as optimistic as Riggs. "I think," Pond remarked in his written recollection of his ministry, "that when missionaries cannot report that much good seems to result from their attempts to instruct the heathen, they are apt to push book making a little too fast." He supported his observation by theorizing about the role printed works played in the missionaries' own sense of self-worth:

> They wish to have something to show as the fruit of their labors and if they cannot make converts they can make books and are tempted to undertake the translation of the Scriptures before they are competent to do it well. And if one is a little ambitious of literary fame there is a tempting field lying before him, for he has little to fear from criti[ci]sm when publishing books in a language as little known as the Dakota and it does not require a man of profound erudition to do the work so that it will pass any examination it is likely to meet with in the literary world.[50]

Between Williamson's 1837 publication of *Wiconi owihanke wannin tanin kin* and the 1862 Dakota War, the ABCFM missionaries in Minnesota published several liturgical works, including the Renville collaboration, *Dakota dowanpi kin: Hymns in the Dakota or Sioux Language* (1842), and Riggs's *Wowapi mitawa: Tamakoce kaga* (1842), a primer based on Gallaudet's school books.

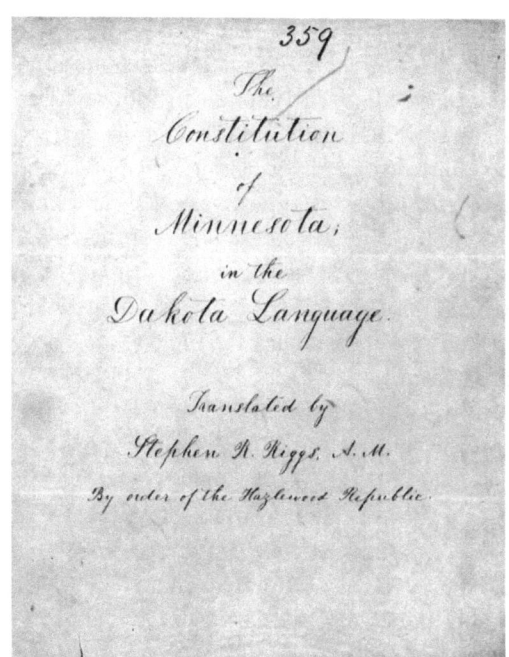

Figure 3.7. "The Constitution of Minnesota in the Dakota Language," 1858. Title page of manuscript, translated by Stephen R. Riggs. Courtesy of the Minnesota Historical Society, St. Paul.

The ABCFM also produced Gideon Pond's short-lived foray into Dakota print journalism, *Dakota tawaxitku kin*, or, *The Dakota Friend*, a serial that would lay the foundation for the much more substantial *Iapi Oaye*, in which Black Elk published his letter from England.[51]

Things began to change in the 1850s, when disputes over treaties between certain Dakota communities and the Americans caused many community members to view both literacy and Christianity in a new light. Several men proudly converted and adopted the sedentary farming practices that the missionaries advocated. In the face of a reduced land base for hunting and the procurement of traditional foodstuffs, these Dakotas separated themselves into a political unit of Riggs's devising, called the Hazelwood Republic; they had a written constitution in Dakota. Riggs wrote to the ABCFM that he viewed written Dakota as a key to the Dakota converts' "civilization" and eventual US citizenship. With that in mind, he collaborated with the Hazelwood community to "produce a copy of the MN const [sic] and to have it printed." Armed with a printed constitution, Riggs wrote that he was "anxious to have the citizenship of our people consummated, which must be done by the constitution before a district Judge. For this purpose we will have to go a hundred miles.... I am anxious to receive the Constitution before that time; as it may be needful for us to show that the *Dakota is a language of Civilization*."[52]

At the same time, it is telling that local non-Native traders put up $500 to help Riggs create a Dakota dictionary to facilitate trade and land negotiations. Christianity and literacy were becoming tied up with capitalism and westward expansion. It was this unhealthy mix of colonialism and Christianity that led Samuel Pond to leave the mission. He wrote of his decision, "If we had been located on the Reserve as Dr. W. and Mr. Riggs were perhaps we should have remained there, but we had reasons for leaving which they had not, for while they hoped the treaty of 1850 would be of great benefit to the Indians, we, taught by past experience, believed the results of the treaty would be evil and only evil."[53] By 1854, of the original ABCFM missionaries to the Dakotas, only Riggs and Williamson remained. The rest had resigned.[54]

For the next ten years, an uneasy relationship obtained between the converts, their more traditional kinsmen, and the Europeans who poured in to settle the "wasteland" left over. That ended in 1862, when war broke out between disgruntled groups of Dakotas and white settlers. In August, the Dakota leader Little Crow led a rebellion in southwest Minnesota, near the Missouri River. After having been told by the local Indian agent to "eat grass," if they were hungry, Little Crow and his warriors killed white people in the area for retribution. In the wake of these hostilities, hundreds of Dakotas were rounded up and imprisoned.[55] In 1863, several hundred Dakota men, women, and a few children were imprisoned at Fort Snelling. Thirty-eight men would be executed in the largest mass hanging in American history.

Conditions in the prison were appalling, and both Riggs and Williamson wrote impassioned descriptions of the Dakotas' suffering. In 1863, Riggs recorded the following:

> Last Sabbath I spent down at Ft. Snelling with the Indians in the camp. It is a very sad place now. The crying hardly ever stops. From five to ten die daily. There are (or were) about sixteen hundred worthy women and children. About three acres of ground is enclosed with a board fence twelve or fourteen feet high having one gate where a guard is kept. Inside of this there are more than two hundred teepees [sic] standing close together. It is a low flat place . . . [and] it has been a very bad winter. . . . The measles have swept over Minnesota. . . . The great number of deaths occurring in the Indian camp now result from these things—lung fever after measles is common.[56]

Williamson also witnessed "great silence, the Indians listening with deep, fixed attention which arrested the coughing with which their prison resounded almost incessantly at other times, owing to their confinement in a chilly atmosphere without sufficient clothes or fire to keep them warm."[57]

Aside from the terrible deprivations they suffered and the mass hanging that preceded their incarceration, these prisoners' story contains a kernel of hope and is a fascinating example of how language and translation can lead to a renewed sense of community after even such tragic events. Many of these prisoners—formerly illiterate in alphabetic writing—wrote letters in their native language asking for clemency. Lots of letters. In fact, one contemporary observer recalled seeing a bag of some 300 such letters at some point during their captivity.[58] For many years, this correspondence languished in the archives of the Minnesota Historical Society, untranslated and uncirculated—virtually erased from the history of this region and its peoples. Thankfully, two Dakota scholars—Clifford Canku and Michael Simon—rescued these works from obscurity and translated them for our better understanding of their heritage.

The letters reveal a paradigm for understanding how Siouan speakers would employ the Riggs orthography throughout the nineteenth century, as the survivors of the war increasingly turned to writing to negotiate their place in a changed political landscape. In true missionary fashion, Stephen Riggs attributed the uptick in requests for literacy education among the Dakotas imprisoned at Fort Snelling as evidence that Native prisoners had realized that, "The power of the white man had prevailed; and the religion of the Great Spirit, or the white man's God, was to be supreme. . . . They were now ready to listen to the messages of God's word; and . . . ready to avail themselves of the book-education which the great part of them had rejected with scorn."[59]

Riggs called it "a revolution in letters" and stood amazed at how reading became "'a perfect mania' among the prisoners, men and women of 60 years are trying to read." Riggs quickly exhausted his 400 copies of the little spelling book he had "improvised and printed at St. Paul." He even brought 100 copies of John Bunyan's *Cante teca* (1858; Riggs had translated the work into Dakota) to the prison.[60]

While Riggs saw a "revolution" and the triumph of the Christian God over heathenism, the Dakota prisoners and their families had distinctly different ideas. They appear to have experienced literacy as a far more nuanced, far more Dakota-centered thing. John Peacock (Spirit Lake Dakota), whose essay introduces Canku and Simon's *The Dakota Prisoner of War Letters*, gives us a glimpse into how these letters may have actually functioned as social practice for the prisoners: "Both [editors] have told me that their training at seminary in translating Biblical languages helped them translate the Dakota letters. They think of the letters not merely as historic documents but as sacred texts."[61]

Part of the letters' sacredness lies in the way the writers used formal Dakota rhetorical structures to transform them into acts of kinship. For example, throughout the letters, which are mostly addressed to Stephen Riggs, the Dakota writers call the missionary *Mitakuye Tamakoce* ("My Relative His Country"). Meanwhile, when John Peacock, a contemporary descendant of these writers tried to render them into perfect English, he discovered that he had

> deleted twelve instances of "it is so" [*do* in Dakota], the rhetorical flourish with which a Dakota man traditionally ends declarative sentences.... This repeated invocation of kinship is not just a term of address; kinship is the very topic of the letter, of every paragraph, of each sentence. The rest of every sentence, of the body of every paragraph, then addresses what is predicated on kinship—exchange between kin. In reducing those five repetitions of "my relative" down to one, I had unwittingly gutted the letter's structure as an elaborate kinship exchange.[62]

Thus, the letters functioned as a mode for redeploying the reciprocities of traditional Dakota life into this new kinship epistolary practice. The editors also decided to render the Dakota in a form of "Rez English," because it seemed to them to soften the "assimilative violence" of the colonizing aspects of intercultural textual translation that translation scholars like Lawrence Venuti have explored.

The content of these letters points to a frayed social fabric, one that the letter writers hoped to knit back together again, in part with the help of epistolary networks. Flies Twice wrote to Riggs explaining the prisoner's plight: "We are living here without a headman, we have no one to speak for us here—it is so." He continued, "I want you to tell [General] Sibley [that] Long ago, we had two chiefs, who spoke for us, now no one remembers us here, we are forgotten here, and we have no leader, and we are living terribly—it is so." The social protocols of the Dakotas demanded that they maintain a leadership system of authorized speakers who would channel diplomatic and other information through the traditional communication networks of the Oceti Sakowin. The letter writers steadfastly deploy epistolary salutations and valedictions drawn directly from vernacular spoken conventions, remapping traditional protocols onto the conventions of Euro-American epistolary practices. Many concluded in a manner similar to Flies Twice's note to Riggs: "So, my relative, that is all I have to say—It is so. I shake your hand with my heart, my relative —it is so."[63]

Other Dakota-language protocols are similarly employed in these letters to affirm Dakota epistemological forms that inhere in the vernacular language. In Dakota, for example, a male speaker ends a sentence with the word *do* when he wants to affirm firsthand knowledge of his declaration. Such sentences often appear at the end of the Dakota prisoners' letters: "I am Robert

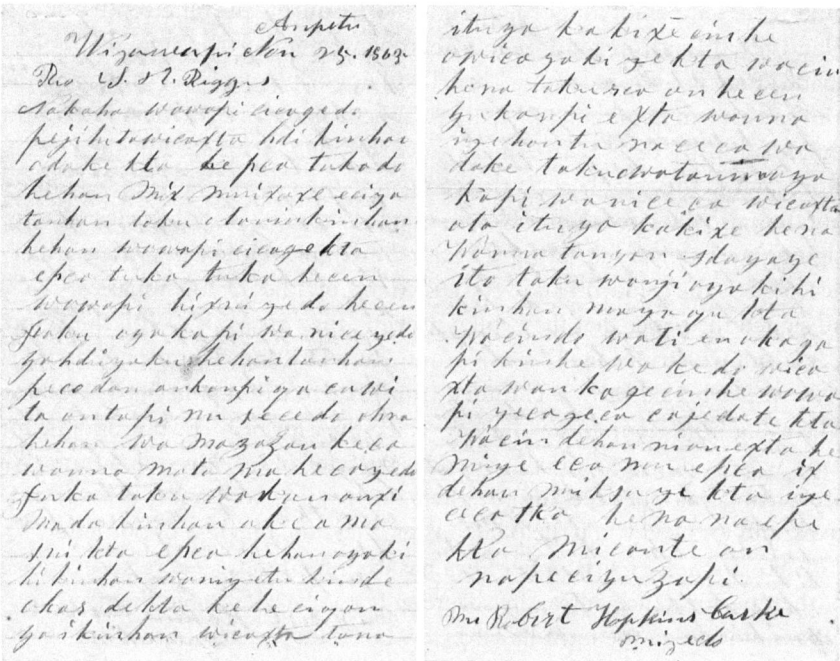

Figure 3.8. Letter of Robert Hopkins to Stephen Riggs, November 25, 1863. Hopkins opens and closes his letter with what was becoming a conventional Dakota epistolary form: his salutation, "Nakaha wowapi cicage . . ." (Today this little letter), as well as his valediction, "Robert Hopkins . . . Miyedo" (I am Robert Hopkins, it is so). Courtesy of the Minnesota Historical Society, St. Paul.

Hopkins—it is so"; "Hands That Rain, this is me—it is so." There is also a recognition of the truth-telling ideology that white people applied to written matter. Flies Twice alludes to the evidentiary nature of written testimony in several of his letters, commenting, "Although our actions have all taken place, they're all written down. There can be no lies about what we did, because it's all written down." Finally, many letters request more printed material in Dakota, especially hymnals, reflecting the prisoners' desire for communal literacy activities to strengthen their social bonds. In one of Flies Twice's letters, for example, the former Dakota leader tells Riggs, "I really want one of you to come visit, . . . to bring two black song books, and so I write this letter because I didn't see the song books. Bring as many as you can, my friend. Well, that is all I have to say. Your wife and son, I shake their hands. Also bring one of the brown Dakota alphabet books."[64]

Another communal literacy practice that appealed to the prisoners was the signing of declarations of sobriety that accompanied the print and manuscript cultures of temperance movements in America during the nineteenth century. Hands That Rain spoke for many when he wrote, "So then now the Bible is made known to me, as long as I live, I will not drink alcohol, I think, and the Holy Spirit can help those who drink." The Dakota letter writers knew how much authority their Euro-American correspondents placed in the written word, and so they emphasized this element in their accompanying signatures, but they also did it for themselves, so that they could have a shared ceremony, signing the letter of sobriety and forming themselves into a new male society accepted by the colonizing powers. Old Man Iron told the missionaries, "They all signed the paper that they will not drink, they are Walks With the Wind, Let Him Live, Brings the Cloud Around Him, Drifting, Thunder Arrow, Arrives at Daybreak, Brown Thunder, Iron Elk, Iron Pumpkin Shell, Walking Throwing Iron, Root, these I have revealed the Bible to." The bottom line for most writers, however, was simple and is reflected in Hopkin's salutation: "We are writing this letter seeking your help, my relative, we want to see our relatives, and we need you to help talk for us, that's the purpose of our letter."[65]

Dakota scholar Christopher Pexa has examined these letters for evidence of their performance of Dakota sovereignty and has described them as *translations*, finding in the term its obverse—not transparency, but willful "withholding," an opening up of Audra Simpson's concept of "ethnographic refusal." Within these letters, Pexa uncovers a rhetoric of peoplehood that is "endlessly proliferating and obscuring... the people, and thus always refusing totalizing forms of representation aimed at making the people intelligible, knowable, and thus more vulnerable to control by the settler-state."[66]

For Pexa, Dakota sovereignty between 1862 and 1868 centered on kinship—the *tiyospaye*—as the critical social network through which political action and national sovereignty have been enacted in writing. He considers the disconnect between the missionaries' expectations and Dakota prisoners' motivations to be a compelling argument for what he calls the "countertranslational moves" that would soon take shape as an emergent political discourse for a form of Dakota personhood that resisted the liberal model of individualism upon which so much of federal Indian policy was based. The discourses of kinship and reciprocity performed in those letters work well as an introduction to the whole repertoire of countertranslational moves that animate the case studies explored in the rest of this book. To read and write in Dakota within these political parameters demanded a special and emerging hermeneutics the Dakota people have used over the past century to decode the "withheld" personhood with what Pexa calls "the ear for the story."

IAPI OAYE: CARRYING THE WORD
TO THE NEW LAKOTA NATION

By the time they were released in 1868, the Dakota prisoners found themselves in a world where very little remained of their traditional homelands in Minnesota. Their surviving relations and others deemed unfit by the government to remain in Minnesota—some 1,000 people in all—were forcibly removed to the Dakota Territory near Crow Creek, not far from present-day Pierre, South Dakota. Good Star Woman remembered the awful conditions they endured: "They were put in box cars and taken over the Missouri River where they were again put on a steamboat to . . . Fort Thompson [Crow Creek] where they were kept in a stockade for three years. Many starved to death there. They were almost naked. They wound burlap around their legs to keep warm . . . and nobody had sleeves in their garments."[67]

Together with hundreds of similarly displaced Ho-Chunk (Winnebago) people, they remained in limbo until the government established a series of "agencies" to house the displaced members of the Oceti Sakowin. Eventually, the Dakotas at Crow Creek were moved to a settlement about thirteen miles below the mouth of the Niobara River, west of the Missouri River. Stephen Riggs's report on the situation in 1869 notes that the Episcopal minister S. D. Hinman had worked hard to comfort the displaced Dakotas at Crow Creek and "re-established his station at Niobara, when the prisoners and their families were reunited again." Significantly, Riggs remarks that "Mr. Hinman has translated and printed the Episcopal Prayer Book" to use at what is now the Santee Agency in Nebraska. Like Riggs before him, Hinman saw the importance of vernacular-language literacy to the missionizing endeavor as it relocated to the west.[68]

With the election of Ulysses S. Grant in 1869, the Dakotas once again found themselves pawns in shifting government strategies, this time as a result of the new administration's efforts to implement what it considered a more humane and less corrupt Indian policy. The policy was flawed from the start, primarily because Grant felt the need to appease railroad investors and land speculators who had their eyes on the Great Plains west of the Missouri River. Grant's "Peace Policy" attempted to thread the needle on these very different objectives by relocating "removed" and "hostile" Sioux communities to reservations even farther off the beaten path of the American emigrant wagon trains and far from arable land subject to the Homestead Act, land whose natural resources he deemed of no use to Indians. The Bureau of Indian Affairs (BIA) and various Christian missionary organizations would share in the job of civilizing their charges on the new reservations, fostering church attendance, literacy education, and farming.

The traditional band organization of the Lakotas served as the framework for dividing the nation into different agencies. As historian Jeffrey Ostler explains, "Although in some sense colonized by the 1868 Treaty, the agency bands retained significant practical autonomy in the early 1870s . . . [and] the government . . . established four main agencies for the western Sioux; Red Cloud agency for Oglalas, Spotted Tail for the Brules, Cheyenne River for the Minneconjous, Sans Arcs, and Two Kettles, and the Standing Rock agency for Hunkpapas, Sihaspas, and Yanktonais."[69]

In what was to prove a significant decision for literacy education on the Plains, Grant's peace policy also parceled out the agencies to the various Christian denominations that wished to convert them.[70] Yet, as with Lac qui Parle in 1838, the missionizing project initially did not make much progress. A Jesuit mission built in 1851 at Grand River Agency was abandoned within weeks of its completion. Benedictine brothers attempted to engage with Lakota people at Standing Rock, Spotted Tail, and Red Cloud Agencies but were unable to set up a permanent mission until the late 1870s. Only at Cheyenne River did Thomas L. Riggs, son of Stephen Riggs, the evangelist of the Dakotas, successfully establish a mission and school in 1872. Although the evidence is circumstantial, there is some reason to believe that the key to the missionaries' successes at Niobara and Cheyenne River had much to do with the Riggs orthography and its adoption by many Siouan speakers in trying political circumstances.

Alphabetic literacy was also central to the Peace Commission's efforts to enforce its bureaucratic structures in Indian Country. Not only were the missionaries' Bibles and religious liturgies—the scripts for ceremonies intended to supplant the Dakotas' own rites—introduced in alphabetic vernacular forms, but so too were treaties, ration cards, petitions, and land surveys. In response to an 1877 effort to move the Red Cloud and Spotted Tail Agencies closer to the Missouri River (and thus away from land coveted by speculators), the Lakotas sent a delegation in protest to Washington, DC, where they met with President Hayes. The proceedings of this meeting were circulated in print form among Red Cloud's band the next year. When the Stanley Commission arrived at the agency in the fall to yet again change the terms of the original agreement, Red Cloud publicly denounced them, producing the printed copies of the agreement as he spelled out the illegality of the Commission's continued efforts to remove his band.

Throughout his public life during the reservation period, Red Cloud employed a white amanuensis, William J. Godfrey, who wrote letters for him when the need arose.[71] Vernacular Lakota diction even expanded to include a new phrase, *mnisapa wicasa* (ink man), for those who touched the pen to paper or printed words in books. By the 1880s, some elders were reaching out to these *mnisapa wicasa* to argue not only their right to land but also to religious freedom. As Red Dog told US Army lieutenant John G. Bourke, "Our grandfathers taught us to do this [the Sun dance]. Write it straight down on the paper."[72]

WAR BOOKS AND RESERVATION LETTERS

The military confrontation between George Armstrong Custer's Seventh Cavalry and the combined forces of Cheyenne and Lakota warriors at the Little Bighorn River on June 25, 1876, would prove to be a turning point for US-Lakota relations. It also offers us a unique window into the state of Lakota literacy at this pivotal moment in their history. When the battle was over, Custer and the 210 men under his personal command lay dead. As the details reached news outlets in the east, the story of Little Big Horn erupted into a media frenzy, coinciding as it did with the nation's Fourth of July festivities. The only news reporter with Custer's detachment, Mark Kellogg, had been killed in the fighting, so his journal account of the events leading up to the battle had to be sent by telegraph a few days later when his friend Clement Lounsberry dictated a 15,000-word piece to the offices of the *New York Herald*, in a 24-hour marathon telegraphy session.[73] As Hugh Reilly explains, the coverage of what came to be called a "massacre" combined an instinctive reverence for the slain soldiers with a political battle over the Grant administration's peace policy. Democratic newspapers criticized Grant for skimping on frontier troops, while a "few republican papers criticized the Quaker 'neutrality' or kindness policy." Public opinion, judging by the newspapers, began to split over whether it was possible to still be a friend to the Indian. There was often a discrepancy between the editorial pages and the more sensational front-page materials seeking volunteers to join the fight.[74]

While this much is fairly well known, the Native peoples' medial processing of the fight is rarely, if ever, considered. After ceding the battlefield to army reinforcements who would attempt to identify and bury the dead, the Indian combatants dispersed, with many Lakotas and Cheyennes forming a camp in the Black Hills, some 300 miles away. On June 27, 1876, Phocion Howard, a reporter for the *Chicago Tribune*, accompanied a group of US Army officers in a survey of the site, and discovered a funerary tipi containing the remains of a Lakota warrior. On his chest was a ledger book filled with ink and colored pencil sketches of important events in the lives of several warriors who fought at Little Big Horn. Howard took the book as a souvenir and later had it rebound for his personal library.

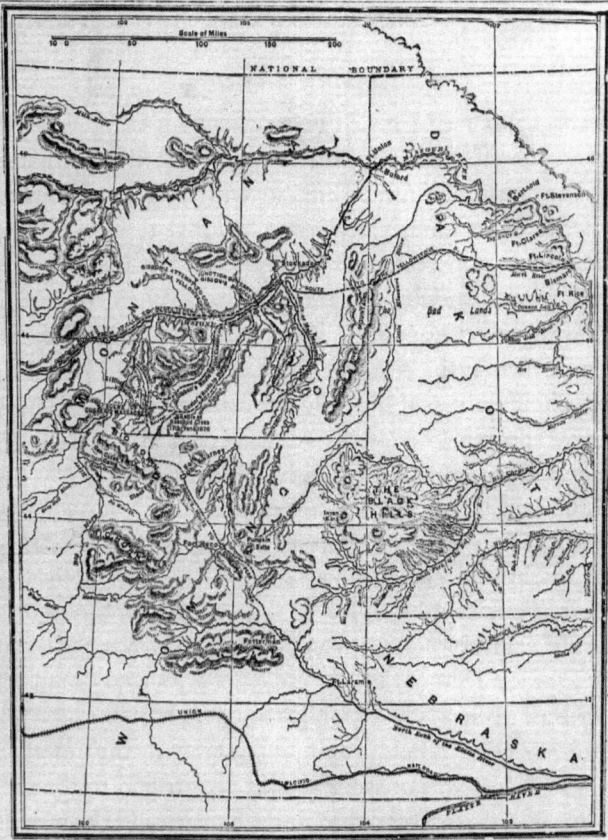

Figure 3.9. Announcement of Custer's death in the *New York Herald*, July 7, 1876.

Castle McLaughlin, the former curator of North American Ethnography at Harvard's Peabody Museum, has explained the significance of the book's "discovery" in a burial tipi, pointing out that this suggests the work was associated with the traditional burial rites of a Lakota warrior society. In *A Lakota War Book from the Little Bighorn*, McLaughlin describes her joint research effort with the late Byron Wilson, a tribal archaeologist of the Standing Rock Sioux Tribe, which determined the identities of many of the text's collaborative authors, including Thunder Hawk and Buffalo Tongue (whose name glyphs appear with their drawings), and several others for whom McLaughlin has plausibly described tribal and band affiliation through careful reading of stylistic and material culture details provided by the artists in their images.[75]

The ledger that Howard took from the burial lodge was in many ways typical of a new media form that had emerged on the Plains over the course of the 1860s. Although such books were usually categorized as "ledger art," McLaughlin explains that the book Howard acquired represented an earlier media tradition that was less about "art" and much more about autobiography and spiritual power. The ledger from Little Big Horn recounts a narrative in pictures, working against the conventions of the rectilinear ledger format, with its Native artists often telling stories from right to left, employing the book's gutter as a "ground line" (a traditional artistic practice in Plains pictorial art). It freely mingles different people's stories of significant personal and "national" events into a material object that was captured in battle and overwritten with exploits in order to dramatize their power over their American enemies.

Like most examples of its genre, this Lakota War Book is inscribed within a memorandum ledger of linen and cotton rag pages probably taken from the body of J. S. Moore, who was killed by a Lakota warrior in 1868. McLaughlin searched the historical record to provide a plausible "biography" of this codex that made its way from a bookseller's shop in a Euro-American settlement to a tipi at Little Big Horn. Using evidence drawn from the book's circuit of ownership, its paratextual materials, and Plains culture significance, McLaughlin traces the ledger's physical movements and its shifts in meaning as it passed through different hands over different historical times. She argues that this and other ledgers are "War Books" (quite different from the "ledger art" produced by Kiowa prisoners of war at Fort Marion in 1875–78, for example). This is especially significant in that it opens a window into the media economies emerging in Indian Country during the 1860s and 1870s, communications systems that reflected a growing awareness of and interest in the US communications revolution.

Archives across America contain many such War Books that have been similarly mislabeled as "ledger art" and whose "autobiographies" remain little

162 Chapter 3

Figure 3.10. Drawing from the pictorial autobiography of Half Moon, an Uncpapa Sioux chief (between 1868 and 1876). This ledger was taken from a funerary tipi at the Little Bighorn. MS Am 2337, Houghton Library, Harvard University, Cambridge, Massachusetts.

understood. Take, for example, the ledger once owned by a Cheyenne warrior named Little Fingernail. On January 22, 1879, a group of Cheyennes who had escaped imprisonment at Fort Robinson, Nebraska, were cornered in a dry creek bed along the present-day Nebraska–South Dakota border. Their leader, Little Fingernail, arranged the eighteen men and fourteen women and children in his group into protective positions against the banks of the draw. US Army captain Henry Wessells, who had been pursuing Little Fingernail's band, ordered his four companies of 150 soldiers to attack. Infantrymen raced up to the edge of the creek bank and discharged hundreds of rounds into the encampment. Amid the carnage, something caught Wessells's eye: "I saw an Indian with [a] book pressed down between his naked skin and a strap around his waist; another strap went between the middle of the back and around his shoulder. I turned to Private Leslie of H troop, who was near me and said, 'I want that book if we come out all right.'"[76]

He got the book.

When the smoke cleared, all men, women, and children in the ravine were dead. The aftermath was pro forma looting. An eyewitness described "the dead Indians being pulled out of the rifle pit." Little Fingernail was among them, "with the book, apparently dead."[77] The book was "injured to the extent of a carbine ball through it and was more or less covered with fresh blood." The microfilm images show a business ledger turned horizontally and illustrated with narrative colored pencil drawings depicting Little Fingernail in battle. The rifle ball did considerable damage to the book, passing all the way through. Many pages were nearly washed out by the warrior's blood. The backstory provided by the army officer's letter leaves many questions unanswered. Why was Little Fingernail carrying the book into battle? Was it a common practice? Where did he get the ledger in the first place? What stories does it tell? Are there any remaining relatives, Cheyenne people who might not know the details of the life story that lies in a vault in a library, blotted with blood?

Even Sitting Bull produced a War Book. Currently housed in the National Anthropological archives of the Department of Anthropology at the Smithsonian National Museum of Natural History, the Hunkpapa leader drew his War Book on the leaves of an army ledger while he was held prisoner at Fort Randall, Dakota Territory, in 1882. The pages were then acquired by Lt. Wallace Tear, together with explanations from Sitting Bull of each image. Tear sent them to Gen. John C. Smith, and they were donated in 1923 to the Bureau of American Ethnology (BAE) by the general's son Robert A. Smith. Writing to General Smith, Lieutenant Tear described how the book came about: "I furnished the book which contains the paintings and from time to time saw him at work on them. These notes were taken down by me after the paintings were completed in Sitting Bull's tipi in the same outlines as given by himself (by an interpreter of course) Bull having the picture before him while giving a description."[78]

Like the Lakota War Book left in the funerary tipi at Little Big Horn, this ledger has been edited by others. It opens with a series of newspaper clippings describing Sitting Bull's death. These are pasted into the flyleaves of the army's blank book. In the latter pages of the book, Gen. John Smith pasted Lieutenant Tear's letter, and the curators of the Bureau of Ethnology have appended to it a letter granting them its use. Because its author was so "notorious" in the popular press, Sitting Bull's War Book soon made it into the pages of the *New York Herald* in a special triple-sheet edition. Calling him "the Napoleon of the Sioux," the *Herald* reported "that nothing can be more interesting than the account this savage warrior has given of himself . . . when everybody is anxious to know anything about him." The reporter then makes a bold claim for his paper's scoop: "[This is] the only extant autobiography of an American Indian ever prepared." The date was July 16, 1876, just a few days after word of the Little Bighorn battle had reached East Coast readers. Castle McLaughlin argues that this reporting, and other articles like it, represents the way "print

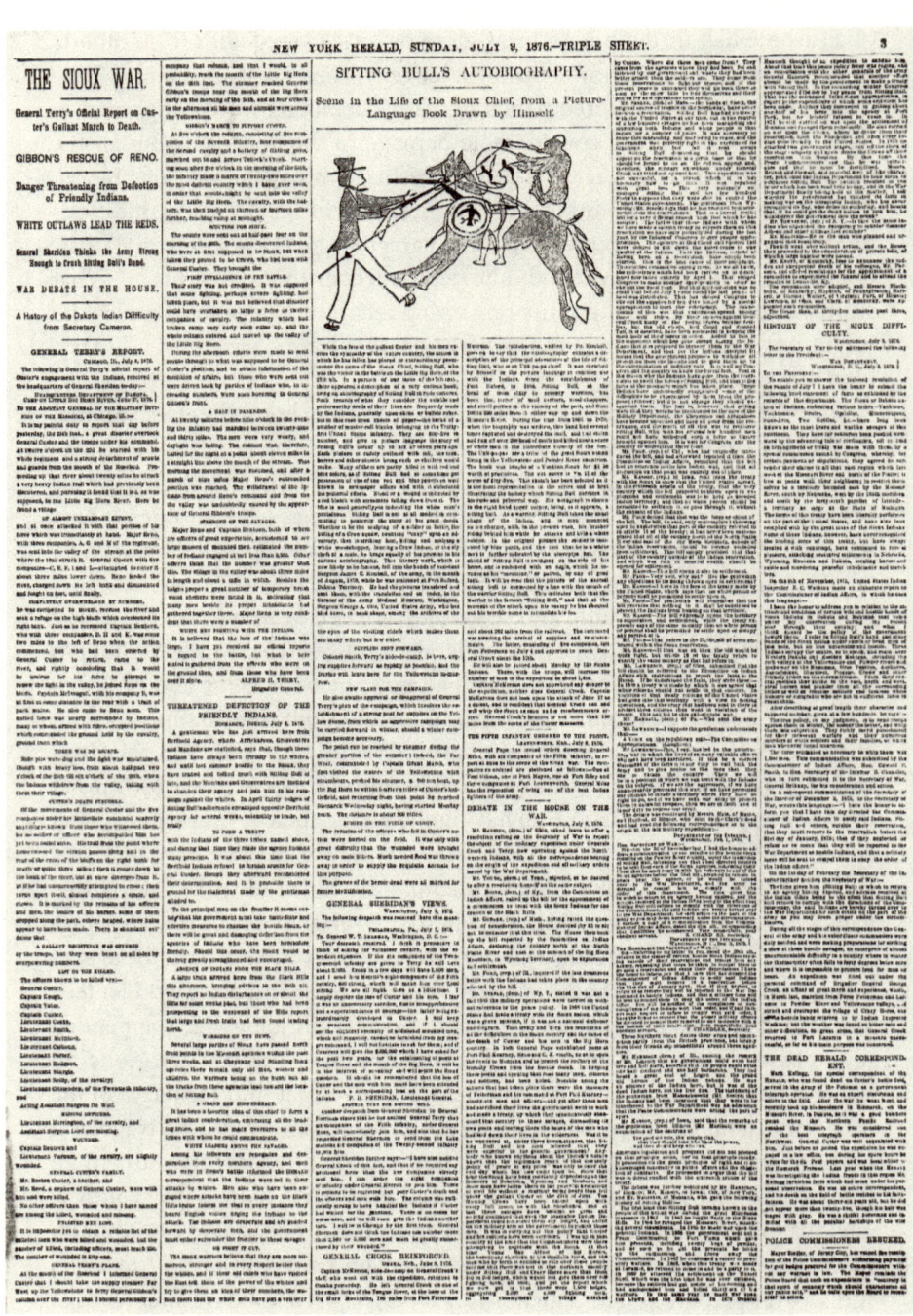

Figure 3.11. A page from "Sitting Bull's Autobiography," as printed in the *New York Herald*, July 9, 1876.

capitalism gave Sitting Bull's enemies a power far greater than of the Plains warriors assembled at Little Bighorn."[79]

As reporter Phocion Howard and his companions surveyed the funerary lodge, they noticed a bag of US mail lying near the body. It had apparently been intercepted by Native warriors in the days before the battle and brought to the village on the Little Big Horn. According to McLaughlin, this demonstrated "the strategic function of intercepting mail during the Indian wars." Sitting Bull was himself reported to have had a European adviser named Frank who helped interpret "quite a lot of manuscript papers" that the spiritual leader accumulated over the period, indicating the growing awareness of the Plains communities of the importance of literacy in their battles with the colonizers.[80]

PIPES AND WINTER COUNTS

In 1931, Oglala Lakota spiritual leader Nicholas Black Elk recited a story that was at the heart of the Lakota way of life and central to the social order of the Oceti Sakowin, the people who came to be known as the Sioux. It is a story of the gift of prayer, of communicating with a world beyond the individual, and of living the right way. In the transcript, Black Elk recalls how White Buffalo Calf Woman appeared to two Lakota scouts, one of whom saw her as corporeal and wanted to possess her. The other saw immediately that she was *wakan* (sacred). The first scout is punished for his obtuseness, reduced to the inevitable outcome of his earthly realm—to worms and bone. The other is honored by being allowed to announce White Buffalo Calf Woman's arrival to his community. She enters the camp singing a song—"In a sacred manner I am walking"—then presents a pipe to the leader of the community. It was like nothing anyone had ever seen, with "a calf carved in one side and . . . twelve eagle feathers tied on with a grass that never breaks." The pipe was still in the possession of the Lakotas when Black Elk told his tale.

At the end of the story, Black Elk lifts his own pipe in prayer, saying, "Grandfather, Great Spirit, lean close to the earth that you may hear the voice I send." He offers the pipe to the four directions, concluding, "This is my prayer, hear me! The voice I have sent is weak, yet with earnestness I have sent it. . . . It is finished *Hetchetu Aloh*! Now, my friend, let us smoke together so that there may be only good between us." As David M. Grant explains, "The pipe is figured as a means to communicate with *Wohpe* (White Buffalo Calf Woman) and to eventually persuade *Wakan Tanka* (Great Spirit), just as prayers are understood in Western religions."[81]

The Lakotas have preserved the story of White Buffalo Calf Woman and her gift of the pipe in oral stories like the one Black Elk recited to Nebraska poet John Neihardt for his book *Black Elk Speaks*. Lakota oral traditions were,

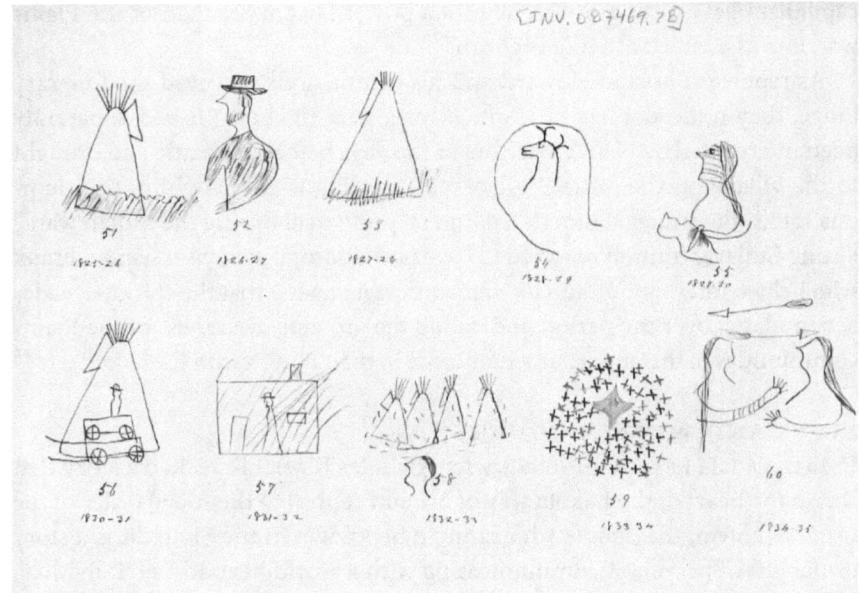

Figure 3.12. American Horse's Winter Count in 1879, showing the year 1833 as a red central star surrounded by a flurry of smaller stars. MS 2372, box 12, folder 7, National Anthropological Archives, Smithsonian Institution, Washington, DC.

however, like those of the Six Nations, deeply rooted in material culture and social practices, like the pipe. The history of the Oceti Sakowin, within which White Buffalo Calf Woman appeared, are called *waniyetu iyawapi* (Winter Counts). Here, the many histories of the bands of the Oceti Sakowin are recorded, often serving as a jumping off point for detailed oral narratives and analyses by tribal members.

Among the many interesting things about this way of taking stock of a year's events is that it is usually made by a designated member of a *tioyspaye*, a Lakota kinship group, and thus often reflects very local concerns. For this reason, not every Lakota Winter Count will record the same image for a given year. But sometimes they do. The most famous case is the Leonid Meteor Shower of 1833–34. Many *waniyetu wowapi* remark on this event. A hand-drawn copy of a Winter Count made by American Horse in 1879 shows the year 1833 as a red central star surrounded by a flurry of smaller stars. Battiste Good's Winter Count depicts that winter as a tipi encircled by stars.

LAKOTA IAPI AND RESERVATION COMMUNITY

By 1881, Sitting Bull was unable to sustain a guerrilla war against the United States, and so on July 20, he and his band surrendered. His surrender had been preceded by those of Red Cloud, Spotted Tail, and American Horse. The twentieth-century historiography of this period of the Oceti Sakowin has, since Robert Utley's foundational *The Last Days of the Sioux Nation*, focused primarily on the Sioux's militancy and characterized it less as a positive assertion of Lakota agency and reaffirmation of tribal identity than as an antiwhite *reaction* to US militarism.[82] This line of argument seems especially fixated on the question of whether the Lakota version of the Ghost Dance in the late 1880s was more militant and white hating than its Arapaho and Cheyenne counterparts. Utley's study also entrenched a narrative of "disappearance," with its first chapter focusing on Wounded Knee and its now-standard account of the Plains Sioux's situation from the 1852 Treaty of Laramie to the 1872 Agreement as a story of a culture's "last days." According to Utley, this period of Lakota history played out as both a war of wills and a war of military might, with the Sioux slowly ceding more and more of their traditional homelands under the pressure of unscrupulous treaty-making and (despite important military victories) overwhelming odds. The beginning of the end, in Utley's view, came with the Treaty of 1868:

> On the face of it, the Treaty of 1868 appeared an abject white Surrender to [Sioux leader] Red Cloud's demand, . . . to abandon the Bozeman Trail, which ran through the Powder River country to the Montana gold fields. But the goal of civilizing the Indians had begun to form in the minds of eastern humanitarians, and the Treaty of 1868 laid the groundwork for that effort. True, the government gave up the Bozeman Trail forts, . . . but the treaty also drew new boundaries around the Sioux homeland. . . . The present borders of South Dakota west of the Missouri River enclosed the Great Sioux Reservation, and although few of the chiefs understood it, they had agreed to settle within this reservation. Many, including Red Cloud himself, set the pattern. Lured by free rations and annuities, they established themselves at the newly built agencies.[83]

Actions like those of Red Cloud and others, so the argument goes, fostered a polarizing factionalism among the Plains Sioux. Disputes between treaty and non-treaty Sioux bands lead directly to the exile of Sitting Bull and his people to Canada in 1877, the assassination of Crazy Horse the same year, and eventually, to Wounded Knee.

Important work by historian Jeffrey Ostler and anthropologist Loretta Fowler has focused on the complexity of the politics surrounding the Ghost Dance in Plains Indian communities. They take a much more Native-centered, holistic approach to a prophetic movement in which the majority of Lakotas actually did not participate. Both Fowler and Ostler challenge the Utley-type narrative, arguing that "the problem with [such] interpretations is that they focus too much on individual Lakota's flaws and intertribal politics," thus neglecting "the broader context [of] ... how US policies set parameters for government officials' decisions and constrained the abilities of Lakotas to act."[84]

For the purposes of the present study, one of the most important aspects of this "broader context" is Siouan-language alphabetic literacy, which can be traced back to the writing practices of the Lakotas' kinsmen, the Dakotas, whose 1862 "uprising" had unveiled a critical role for the written vernacular in its new polity. In order to appreciate how careful attention to Lakota literacy practices can help reorient our understanding of the changes in Lakota society in the years leading up to and after Wounded Knee, we need to explore how individual Lakotas—not just the infamous warriors associated with what Ostler calls "the main axis of factionalism"—non-treaty (militant) versus treaty (agency) leaders—managed this painful transformation of their society. For the social cohort of Lakotas born in the 1840s and 1850s did not split neatly along this "axis" of non-treaty and treaty politics. Instead, they responded to social change and reservation life in mixed ways. Some became Christians and opposed the old ways but demanded books in their Native language. Others advocated the adoption of many European ideas but stopped short of conversion and never gave up the quest to maintain the old Lakota social order. Still others changed their point of view many times, first supporting the Ghost Dance and then rejecting it.

These seemingly contradictory social positions had one thing in common—they all employed the new forms of communication technologies that attended Christian missionization and government bureaucracy. As a geographically divided and marginalized nation, the Lakotas found alphabetic literacy in the 1880s to be a potent means of social formation for tribal members of many different political allegiances, fostering new ways of constituting personhood and community. Significantly, Lakota literacy also took shape within America's burgeoning "postal age," that blend of topography, bureaucracy, and imagined intimacy that David Henkin argues established "the modern posted letter as its own distinctive historical practice" in which "an already powerful state institution [transformed] into a network of popular exchange and sociability."[85] Long before the Ghost Dance appeared at Pine Ridge, the agency had its own post office and letterhead, and personal and official correspondence flowed through the postal system with great regularity.

In much the same way that traditional Lakota social roles intersected with newer Christian and agency status markers, writing followed both traditional and bureaucratic communications circuits. Lakota men and women continued to employ traditional graphic systems like Winter Counts at the

Figure 3.13. Post office masthead of Pine Ridge Agency, 1879. Courtesy of the National Archives and Records Administration, Kansas City, Missouri.

same time as they wrote and dictated alphabetic personal letters and government petitions. At the height of the Ghost Dance crisis, Carlisle-educated Yankton Lakota William Selwyn served as postmaster at Pine Ridge. Among his informal duties was translating English-language letters for community members and forwarding Lakota-language communications to the far-flung camps across the reservation. He was also a government informant. When the Agent of Pine Ridge began to plan for possible military action against the dancers, Selwyn provided him with names.

For previous generations of Lakotas, individual life was sustained by an interlocking set of social groupings. Within the broad category of the Oceti Sakowin, smaller social groups called *tiyospaye* centered the everyday social, political, and ceremonial lives of the people. A circuit of relatives that formed the core of the Lakota social network, *tiyospaye* signifies both the concept of "home" (*ti*, a shortened form of *tipi*), and group or gathering (*ospaye*). So much of the Lakota language is based in what are known as "relative terms," that this level of social organization may be one of the most important in the linguistic and textual dimensions of this society undergoing transformation within the context of American colonialism. It is telling, for example, that the term *"tunkasila"* (grandfather) can be used to refer to either the Great Spirit (*Wakan Tanka*) or the president of the United States. Indian agents might be addressed in letters as *ate* (father) or *mitakola* (my male friend). Politics, religion, and interpersonal relationships were all managed by a vernacular that framed everything as kinship.

At the time the Treaty of 1868 was signed, the Lakotas grouped these *tiyospaye* into seven bands—Oglalas, Hunakpapas, Brules, Minneconjous, Yanktonais, Sans Arcs, and an alliance of two smaller bands, Two Kettles and Sihaspas. During the central ceremony of Plains life, the summertime Sun Dance, these *tiyospaye*, or bands, came together, camping in an enormous circle of lodges, with each band settling in a predetermined location. When asked by Pine Ridge physician and amateur ethnographer James Walker to sketch out such an encampment, George Sword drew a horseshoe shaped gathering whose entryway opened to the east.

Although the military and Indian agents tended to focus on the social category of "Chief" (especially warriors) as the leaders of these bands, the social order of the various *tiyospaye* were enforced by an interlocking group of council leaders, a Chief's Society (led by *wakiconza*), and the *akicita*, a group of "marshals," appointed by band elders to police the encampment and keep order.[86] These men, acting much like justices of the peace in their counterpart Euro-American towns, were chosen from the pools of male age-graded societies that gathered men of like talents and social standing into groups with names like the Big Bellies Society (known for their generosity), and Ska Yuha (White Owner's Society, famous for prowess in warfare). During the reservation period, the *Lakota oyate* was often translated as "nation" by non-Indians, but it also continued to function for many Lakotas as a signifier denoting membership in a linguistic and cultural community that, although it had been physically disrupted by the parceling out of Lakota *tiyospaye* into geographically dispersed agencies and the outlawing of the Sun Dance, still remained connected via vernacular epistolary networks and surreptitious nonagency gatherings. Even though the US government preferred to imagine itself to be dealing with a unified "nation," the Lakotas in fact understood the relationship only in terms of the *tiyospaye*, a circuit of relatives that formed the core of Lakota society.

Over and against these traditional social groupings, new alliances formed around Christian fellowship and Indian agency bureaucracies, creating new amalgamations of Lakota and Euro-Western social spaces. Eastern boarding schools—a collaborative effort between the BIA and Christian philanthropists—had produced one of the most significant new social orders among the Lakotas. In 1879, eighty-six Lakotas from the Spotted Tail and Red Cloud Agencies were enrolled in the first class at the Carlisle Industrial School in Pennsylvania. Later, children from Standing Rock and Pine Ridge Agencies would be routinely "harvested" to fill the rolls at Carlisle or its companion institution, the Hampton Institute in Virginia.[87]

Just as important to Lakota social change in the period, however, is the much less studied network of day schools and on-reservation boarding schools that were scattered across the agencies by the 1880s. In fact, as Lawrence F. Schmekebier noted in his 1927 report on nineteenth-century Indian policy, "Mission schools were the earliest schools used for the education of the Indians, some of them being subsidized by the government and some being maintained solely by their own funds. From about 1870 formal contracts were made with the subsidized mission schools, and they have since been generally known as contract schools." A significant number of young Lakotas attended day schools supported by a unique government/missionary partnership.[88]

This system produced not only a new category of personhood on the reservations but also new jobs and social status for the hundreds of Lakota men and women who were hired as teachers' assistants, cooks, and janitors. Mrs. M. L. DeGrey (listed in Standing Rock Agency records as a "half-breed") reported monthly on the day school at Standing Rock, often expressing frustration that bad weather, an increasingly dispersed student population, and "wild" behavior made it hard to live up to urban philanthropists' expectations. Her reports also illustrate the ways in which the day schools became part of the Lakota social world. Especially telling are her frequent comments that "Chiefs" and families visited the school often, blurring the lines between the *tiyospaye* networks and the civilization project envisioned by the BIA. Research on Pine Ridge day schools has shown that "the reservation's schoolhouses not only buttressed *tiyospaye* ties, they also became valuable community assets that Oglalas used to ameliorate the difficulties of reservation life."[89]

The mission churches attached to these schools engendered new positions of social status. Episcopal converts like George Sword could rise to the position of deacon, and Catholics like Nicholas Black Elk, to the role of itinerant catechist to intertribal communities across the Plains. The Holy Rosary Mission at Pine Ridge established the St. Joseph Society for adult male converts and the St. Mary's Society for women. Both groups were deliberately modeled on older, pre-reservation Lakota sodalities.[90] Vernacular-language publications and Christian newspapers like *Anpao* (*The Daybreak*) and *Iapi Oaye* forged ties within and between such religious groups. Also included were the vernacular constitutions and by-laws of religious clubs like *Dakota Kristian Kośka Okodakiciye woicicaġe woope kin qa woecon woope* (Constitution and By-Laws of the Dakota Young Men's Christian Association; 1890) and *Jesus Htakiniwacinskanpi Okodakiciye, Woope Kin* (Constitution and By-Laws, Society of Christian Endeavor, Constitution and By-Laws; 1890).

Indian agencies themselves served as the locus of a completely different set of social relations, as is suggested by the Lakota term for them, *owakpamni oyanke*, which Ostler translates as "distribution place."[91] This alternative conception of social space and social order suggests the impersonal and dependent contexts that framed the new kinds of identities Lakota men were expected to adopt: farmers, laborers, and teamsters.[92] The difference is particularly stark when it is compared to George Sword's drawing of the old-time camp circles of the *Lakota oyate* and their sacred, protocol-based organization.

Moreover, Ostler observes, "The only significant source of off-reservation income in the 1880s was through Wild West shows."[93] This odd line of work had ironically grown directly out of the agencies' dual roles as trustees of natural resources on Indian land and purveyors of ethnographic resources for scientists and collectors back East. The BIA files from the period are filled with requests for "objects illustrating the habits, customs, peculiarities, and general condition of the various Indian tribes of the U.S., and also . . . relics." Even the Lakota language was viewed as a commodity, and the same correspondent later requested, "in addition to the material objects before enumerated, vocabularies of any tribes." Attached to this circular letter were "proper instructions for recording languages and for ethnological research."[94] For women, this ethnographic capitalism took the form of fashioning tourist items, and Ostler comments only half-jokingly that "if anything didn't move, a Lakota woman would bead it."[95] The bead and quill work that in a previous generation would have signaled family lineages and social status was now treated as a commodity by craftswomen whose families were going hungry.

In this period, the *akicitas* found their role transformed, bureaucratized by the BIA in such a way that they were gathered as an Indian police force in 1878 "to be employed in maintaining order and prohibiting illegal traffic in intoxicating liquor on the several Indian reservations."[96] By 1880, the Pine Ridge Agency police force numbered some twenty-nine privates and two officers. With an average age of thirty-seven, it seems clear that the police force drew heavily from the generational cohort we have been examining. Their pay was low (five dollars per month) and many left the force to find more lucrative work, farming or freight hauling for better wages. But as we will see, the Indian police would play a crucial role in the tribal politics leading up to the murder of Sitting Bull and the massacre at Wounded Knee. These policemen were not merely a "force" but, more importantly, a modified form of the traditional male "societies" that forged new male social groupings during the reservation period. Many of these alliances would be severely tested in the 1880s, when zealous Indian agents and Lakota officers eager to attain status ran afoul of traditional *tiyospaye* power structures.

Perhaps the most vivid thumbnail sketch of how agency life warped Lakota social traditions comes from this admittedly Eurocentric report of a "cattle roundup on an agency in the 1880s":

> The old-fashioned way was for the Indians to assemble at a central supply station on ration day. At a given time the cattle, wild by nature, frightened and desperate by their surroundings, were turned loose to be chased by the Indians, yelling and whooping, and shot down upon the prairie in

Figure 3.14. "Waiting for rations at commisary [sic] P.R. Agency S.D." No. X-31305, Special Collections, Denver Public Library, Denver, Colorado.

imitation of the savage method of buffalo hunting of the early days. When the animal was killed a motley assembly of Indians, ponies, and dogs of all sizes and ages gathered around where it lay. The bucks and sq . . . gorged themselves upon the raw entrails and smoking blood, the hide was taken to the traders. . . . To satisfy a morbid curiosity people used to travel sometimes a long distance to visit the agencies on ration day to witness these savage sights. . . . [But all] of that has been done away.[97]

Wild bison were replaced by domesticated cattle. The time-honored protocols of the hunt—*akicitas* directing the action, wives of the most successful hunters enjoying the choicest cuts, and the reciprocal circulation of food through the social hierarchy of the *tiyospaye*—reduced to a spectacle for tourists. Badly needed sustenance, to be sure, the beef fed the community, but soon it too would be taken away, as government bureaucrats enforced a ban on these kinds of rations and demanded that Native communities receive their meat "on the block" as processed beef products.[98]

As painful as this scene is to recall, it is important to remember that the Lakotas fought hard and often succeeded in making this new environment amenable to *tiyospaye* bonds. Cohort analysis allows us to drill down into the generalized picture of Lakota debasement presented by Indian Commissioner Morgan's account of the cattle roundup and find specific actions taken by individual community members that were intended to keep them firmly tethered to something they still recognized as Lakota. One need only examine the

1880s experiences of Nicholas Black Elk in John Neihardt's *Black Elk Speaks* to appreciate the significance of this cohort-based approach to the relationship between language and social change.

WANAGI WACIPI

The massacre of nearly 200 men, women, and children at Wounded Knee Creek on the Pine Ridge Reservation in December 1890 has been at the center of Euro-American conceptualizations of modern Sioux "nationhood" since at least 1896. That year anthropologist James Mooney (1861–1921) published *The Ghost Dance Religion and the Sioux Outbreak of 1890*, arguing that the precipitating events leading up to the massacre could be traced directly to a revitalizationist religious practice that came to be known as the Ghost Dance.[99] Mooney maintained that this ceremony was "only the latest in a series of Indian religious revivals." Because the Ghost Dance was based on "a hope common to all humanity" (the return of better times, the resurrection of the dead), Mooney felt comfortable prefacing his study of the Lakota ceremony with a detailed chronicle of "the primitive messiah beliefs, and . . . the teachings of the various Indian prophets who [had] preceded" the Ghost Dance in American history. Importantly, Mooney's chronology ties each of these revival movements to "brief sketches of Indian wars belonging to the same periods."[100] Throughout the first half of the twentieth century, Mooney's theory held sway. Through the historiography of the 1960s and 1970s, Native spirituality was often linked with warfare, failed nation building or, as Raymond DeMallie notes, cataloged as merely "an epiphenomenon of social and political unrest."[101] Native revivalism was framed as a passive *response* to imperialism rather than an active interrogation of a community's spiritual and social situation at a given historical point in time.[102]

The principal tenet in Mooney's analysis of the Lakota Ghost Dance is centered on alphabetic literacy: the Ghost Dance "could never have become so widespread, and would probably have died out within a year of its inception, had it not been for the efficient aid it received from the returning pupils of various eastern government schools." Mooney's argument raises the question of how important alphabetic literacy of all kinds was to this watershed event in Lakota history. This is especially true when we view the Ghost Dance as one part of a larger continuum of Lakota social practices whose various logics derived from the turbulent, emergent late-century Lakota *oyate* within which it functioned. In this context, it seems that Mooney got it half right. He thought of literacy as Carlisle literacy, or alphabetic literacy in English. Yet by the time the Ghost Dance arrived on the Plains, Lakota-language alphabetic literacy was widely practiced and, I will argue, this literacy shaped the "modernizing" Lakota Nation (the Oceti Sakowin), where the Ghost Dance was performed.[103]

During his interviews with Neihardt, Black Elk vividly recalled the "famine" that the people suffered during the terrible winter of 1889–90 and the ration restrictions the agency imposed as punishment on the Ghost Dancers for practicing their beliefs.[104] Black Elk decided to witness a Ghost Dance for himself, to see if this was the mode by which he would realize his childhood vision and lead his people:

> I heard that they were dancing below Manderson on Wounded Knee [Creek]. I wanted to find out things, because it was setting strongly in my heart and something seemed to tell me to go . . . so I got on my horse and went to this ghost dance. . . . They had a sacred pole in the center. It was a circle in which they were dancing and I could clearly see this was my sacred hoop. . . . It seemed I could recall my vision in it. The more I thought about it the stronger it got in my mind. . . . I was to be intercessor for my people and yet I was not doing my duty. Perhaps it was this the Messiah [Wovoka] was pointing out and he might have set this to remind me to get to work again.[105]

Thus, the Lakotas continued to dance the special dance Wovoka had envisioned, sang the sacred new songs, and wore the sacred shirts of power. The US Army and local Indian agents became convinced that this revival of Native spirituality was actually an "outbreak" (the term their counterparts in Minnesota had used to describe the Dakota War of 1862). In response, they attacked the dancers. John Neihardt ends *Black Elk Speaks* with the tragedy of Wounded Knee, describing how Black Elk was left in despair. "The sacred tree is dead," Neihardt quotes. The problem is, however, as DeMallie shows in *The Sixth Grandfather*, that Black Elk never said that. The transcript Neihardt's daughter kept of the actual exchange makes no mention of it. Black Elk viewed things differently. Even in the midst of despair, he believed in the power of *Lakota iapi oaye*, the carrying of Lakota talk around the *oyate*. The history of Lakota alphabetic literacy suggests how the Lakotas of Black Elk's generation kept the faith.

One example appears in a Lakota-language letter dated one year before the massacre. Writing from Paris in 1889, Kills Enemy Alone (Isna Toka Kte), a performer in Buffalo Bill's Wild West show, asked his brother-in-law Little Whirlwind (Wamniyomni Cigala) how his family back in Pine Ridge, South Dakota, was doing without him. In addition to asking the whereabouts of his wife and daughter, Kills Enemy Alone engages in small talk within the leaves of a transatlantic epistle, asking after his sister's garden, reporting that he had come to Europe to "make some money," and declaring that he and his fellow Sioux actors were well.[106] It is likely that Kills Enemy Alone and Black Elk crossed paths on the way back to South Dakota, for the 1889 census lists Kills Enemy Alone as "brother-in-law" of a seven-person family living at the reservation.[107]

Within the year, however, either Little Whirlwind or his wife would be dead (exactly who carried the letter that fateful day remains unclear), massacred alongside the other Ghost Dancers at Wounded Knee. We do not have to take the archivist's word for it. Several pieces of circumstantial evidence point to this as being the case. In the letter, Kills Enemy Alone urges his brother-in-law to go to Manderson. Known then as Medicine Root, Manderson was the epicenter of the Ghost Dance that led to the massacre. In addition, Little Whirlwind appears on the roster of Sitting Bull's band when they surrendered in 1881. Sitting Bull's followers were more likely than others to have followed the *wanagi wacipi* practices. It is likely, then, that as the soldiers looted the victims' bodies, they stumbled across the letter from Kills Enemy Alone. Perhaps thinking it would make a good conversation piece, one of them kept it as a souvenir.

The letter resurfaced in the 1960s in the Nebraska State Historical Society archives, where Dr. John Champe had deposited it after having it translated. Stored with it is a letter from Robert Killen of the Nebraska Department of Forestry, explaining how Kills Enemy Alone's letter came to be transcribed. In that note, we feel the full force of what the translation theorist Lawrence Venuti has termed the "assimilative violence" of translation. Dated May 20, 1968, this letter throws into high relief both the complex social horizon of the written Lakota language and the strange afterlife it would have in the twentieth century. In it, Killen regales his correspondent with what he thinks is a comic scene that accompanied the letter's translation. "It seems that this Indian was not too literate," Killen explains, "and it seems he mishandled the dialect he was supposed to be writing in." To get the translation, Killen had to speak to the county attorney, requesting that he release from jail "two drunken Indians . . . to do this interpretation." The translation "must be right," Killen reasons, "only an Indian could write like that. Hope this gives you a chuckle." Yet Killen's failed attempt at humor does illuminate something quite interesting—Lakota men and women could still read and write in their own language in the 1960s. Not only that, they had very culturally specific complaints about the way this letter was written, arguing over whether or not it was "good" Lakota.[108]

This cultural battle over the written vernacular and its role in defining Lakotaness appears to have heated up during the Ghost Dance crisis. Espe-

Figure 3.15. Portrait of Mi-Wa-Kan Yu-Ha-La, called Sword, captain of Native Police and judge of Native Court, 1875 (*left*). George Sword in his uniform as captain of the Pine Ridge Police, 1891 (*right*). BAE GN 03203A, National Anthropological Archives, Smithsonian Institution, Washington, DC.

cially significant in this regard is George Sword (ca. 1847–1910), whose lengthy Lakota-language texts formed part of new discourse of an emergent, "modern" Lakota Nation. In September 1896, Sword narrated part of his life story to Bruce Means, who translated it into English and provided a copy to James Walker. In this interview with Means, Sword describes the several social roles he had occupied up through the Ghost Dance period. "I was *Wicasa Wakan* [Holy Man]," he told Means, having "conducted the Sun Dance." He also bore "scars on his body" showing he had been a dancer. He had been a healer, a member of the Bear Medicine Society. During encampments, he had served as *wakiconze*, the leader of the *akicita*, and had led many war parties in his own right. Having fought battles and having prayed deeply to "the Lakota *Wakan Tanka*," Sword became disillusioned as the Sioux began losing battles to the Americans. On a trip to Washington, DC, in 1877 with the Sioux delegation, he realized the enormity of the Lakotas' disadvantage, viewing houses "that the white people dug in the ground and could not be moved."

It was there that he adopted the surname Sword, "because the leaders of the white people wore swords." He became a member of the Pine Ridge police force during the troubled 1880s and an "informer" against those who practiced the Ghost Dance, reporting to white schoolteachers and the Indian agent the names of those whom he knew to be involved.[109] Although he admitted to not being able to speak English, he did however, "learn to write Lakota . . .

[like] the old Lakota talked in the formal manner." The photographic record vividly illustrates Sword's physical transformation during this period.

Yet, Sword resigned his police commission when "the Oglala ceased to thinking about fighting the white people" (ca. 1891). He was proud to become a "deacon in the [C]hristian church" and promised to be so until his death, but remained wary of the power of his Native language and refused to use the language of the shamans. While retaining his regalia from his shaman days, Sword refused to speak the sacred language that accompanied it, believing that "if a shaman offends his ceremonial outfit it will bring disaster upon him."[110]

Just as Black Elk saw his collaboration with Neihardt as a way to "publish" and complete the Thunder Beings' vision, so too did Sword believe that his work with the amateur ethnographer James Walker and the voluminous Lakota writings Walker eventually produced proffered a return of power to the *Lakota oyate*. Especially revealing in this regard is his description of language change among the younger generation: "I write the Lakota words as I speak them. They are short words. Now the young men write long words, and speak in the same way. They make one long word of many short words."[111] This perhaps reflects Sword's recognition of a phonemic shift indicative of a broader social transformation—certainly his description underscores generational change. Twentieth-century Lakota-language textbooks teach students this change, noting the introduction of things like contractions and slang, the sort of thing Sword may have in mind here.

The archive of the Brigham Young University Library, in fact, contains several of George Sword's notebooks that he kept while he worked as police captain at Pine Ridge. These were simple cardboard bound, lined blanks provided to him by the BIA. In one, it appears he shared his blank book with his daughter Lucy, who was attending a day school on the reservation. The juxtaposition of the monolingual Lakota father's almost calligraphic hand and his unusual use of the space of the page with the schoolgirl's cursive lines that reach all the way to the margins of the notebook suggest some of the subtle changes that were going on in written Lakota, changes that Sword perhaps oversimplified in his interview as resulting from print, but which clearly were underway, even in his own *tiyospaye*.

Yet even though Sword's comment on language change might seem pessimistic, echoing Niehardt's insertion of the words "the sacred tree is dead" into Black Elk's narrative, Sword continued to write. Not only that, but other Lakotas picked up their pens and attempted to carry a Siouan-language alphabetic tradition into the twentieth century.[112] For his part, George Sword kept working with the written vernacular on into the twentieth century. However negatively he may have felt toward the Ghost Dance (and he did), his writ-

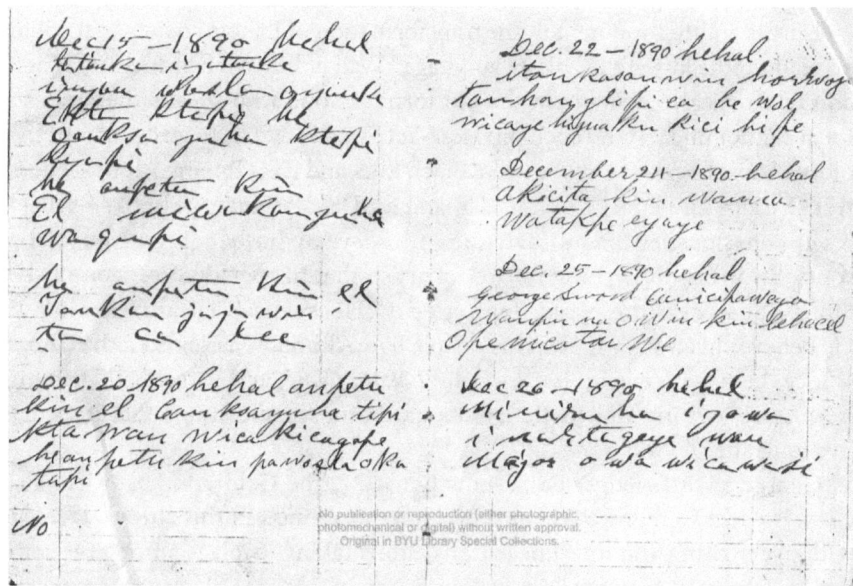

Figure 3.16. Page spread from George Sword and Lucy Sword's diary, 1890. The journal is open to the date December 15, 1890, and records the killing of the Lakota leader Sitting Bull. L. Tom Perry Special Collections, Harold B. Lee Library, Brigham Young University, Provo, Utah.

ing must be considered as consonant with those ceremonies, practices (to quote Diana Taylor) that "have historically been kept discrete, supposedly free-standing, ontological and epistemological discourses," but which in reality are part of what Cherokee scholar Christopher Teuton has characterized as Native American literature's "textual continuum."[113]

When writing out the famous Lakota traditional story of Stone Boy for James Walker in 1896, Sword spent as much effort experimenting with the written vernacular as he did with his tale's accuracy. Walker wrote to Clark Wissler of the Bureau of American Ethnology, "This legend is of interest because Sword usually wrote in the old form of Lakota, while in this legend he attempted to write in the modern form of that language, and mixed these two forms in such a manner as to exemplify the transition of the language." As Walker saw it, Sword at times employed elisions more characteristic of the "new" Lakota language, and "in the modern form in which such phrases have been compounded into words, they have become unchangeable so that other words cannot [sic] be introduced within them without destroying their meaning.... For these reasons it is difficult to finde [sic] one who can translate the writings of Sword. Recognizing this difficulty Sword wrote this legend in a style to aid in translating [sic] his other writings."[114]

Here is another moment in the transformation of Lakota society that could be read as "the last of the Lakota language." Walker himself comments, "When an Oglala speaks formally in the old form . . . one who speaks the modern form cannot understand such phrases." Yet Sword's efforts to write in both the old and new forms of Lakota—like Black Elk's and Kills Enemy Alone's letters from Europe and James Garvey's demand for Dakota-language books—reflect a self-consciousness about saving the *tiyospaye* by husbanding its linguistic roots. Sword is not writing in two forms so that his personal version of the Stone Boy story is preserved "for posterity." He is no salvage anthropologist. He believes his work will help his people live. Although he rejected the Ghost Dance, he never gave up hope on the *Lakota oyate*, and it seems that in his later years, writing alphabetic Lakota gave him some comfort that it would live long after he was gone.

George Sword's ledger book, now housed at the Colorado Historical Society, is—like so many of the texts we have examined in this study—layered with overwriting and interlinear translations taking its place among the several palimpsestic texts we have explored. Yet, in this case, the layers are taken up with largely Dakota on Lakota conversations between Ella Deloria and her predecessor in script. In a published commentary on some of Sword's writings, Deloria emphasized that she did not approve of its "inadequate" orthography and thought of the text primarily as a linguistic resource and a salvaged version of an old ceremony.[115] But as the Lakota scholar and writer Delphine Red Shirt points out, "The narrative's significance . . . [also] lies in its literary content and value." Red Shirt, who is a heritage speaker of Lakota, has written a book that uncovers George Sword's stylistic and narrative structures as evidence of an oral composition mode that predates settler incursions and alphabeticism. Because so much of what Sword wrote is based in his personal experience in Lakota men's medicine societies that passed down important protocols in narrative form, a close reading of Sword's deeper structures reveals that he used a special language that Red Shirt calls a register, "which Hymes defines as 'major speech styles associated with recurrent types of situations.' Thus Sword's way of speaking in these narratives reflects how Lakota oral narratives are composed. George Sword, it could be argued, chose to use this special register, knowing that his Lakota audience had specialized knowledge of this register in the dialect he spoke."[116]

The implications of Red Shirt's research for establishing new understandings of alphabetic literacy in the Oceti Sakowin are significant. As we have seen in the Haudenosaunee examples, Sword's use of an alphabetic orthography actually works to preserve the very oral tradition that the missionaries who developed the spelling system had hoped to eradicate.

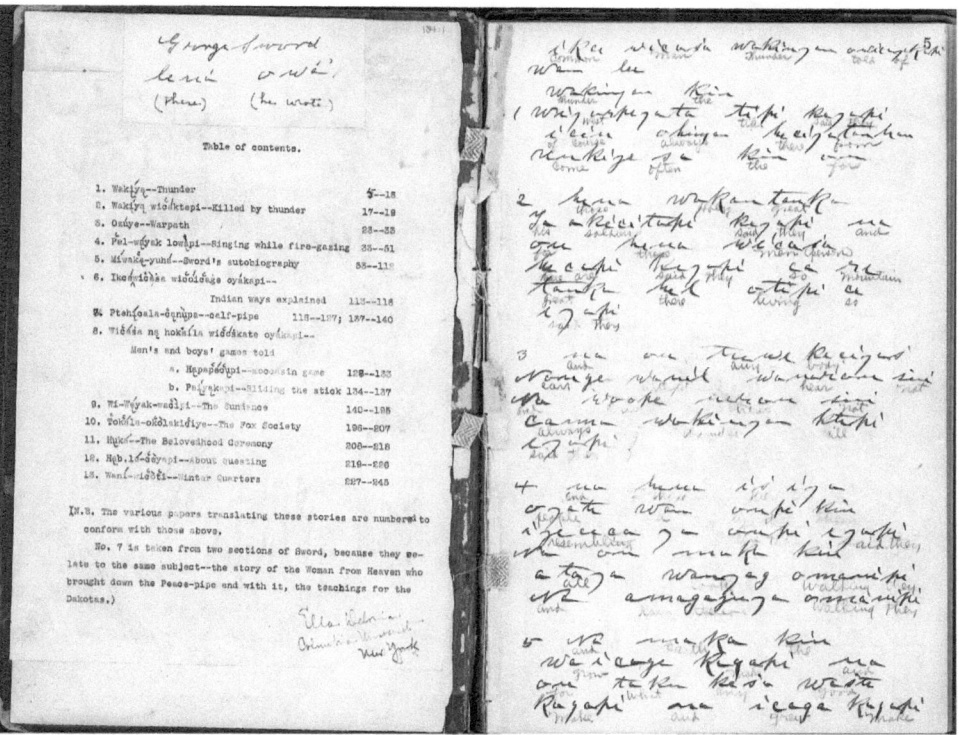

Figure 3.17. George Sword's ledger, n.d. James Walker Papers, Colorado History Center, Denver.

Sword's ledger also inadvertently captures the social exchanges between generations over the nature of the vernacular language and Lakota identity that inhere in such instances of alphabeticism. The young Dakota woman, working in the settler "man's world" of anthropology, producing phonetic transcriptions for Franz Boas, interrogates the *akicita* about his "incorrect" usages. In Red Shirt's own re-encounter with the Sword manuscripts, however, we find a creative mind at work. Its narratives are not the product of the anthropologist's "great memory" recitation, but a set of generative techniques that Red Shirt believes Sword drew from the oral tradition and adapted to writing. This, then, is Sword's great accomplishment. He found a way to write Lakota in a Lakota way. Because of his steadfast refusal to abandon his language in the face of both reservation injustices and the arrival of printed forms of Lakota that he felt did damage to the tradition, Sword has given us the opportunity to say with Nicholas Black Elk, "Mitakola wotanin ieska wowapi wanji lecala iwacu, ua lila ibluskin ye lo Lakota"—Let us rejoice in seeing the Lakota language in writing!

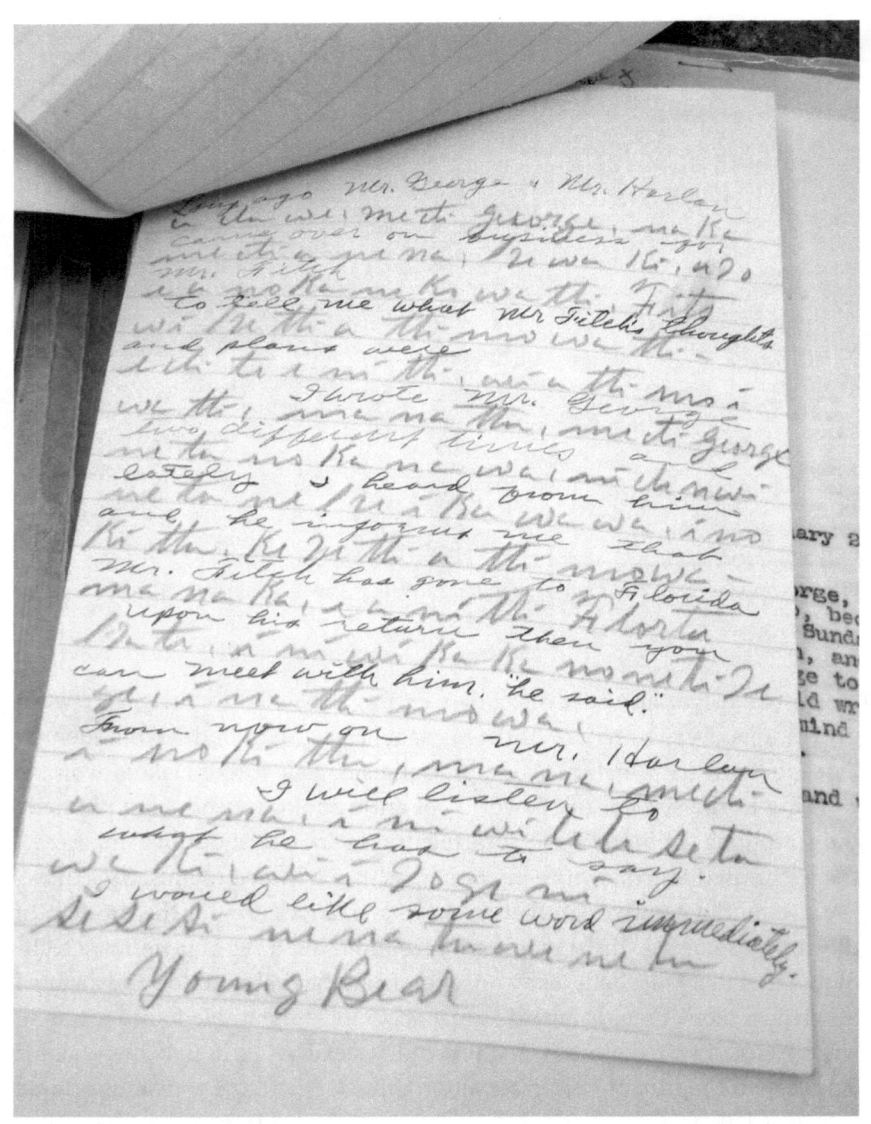

Figure 4.1. Letter of Robert Young Bear to Edgar Harlan, 1934. Edgar R. Harlan Papers, State Historical Society of Iowa, Des Moines.

4 : *Paw-pa-pe-po*
THEY TOLD ME THAT ONE HAD INVENTED AN ALPHABET

> After my father's return to L'Arbre Croche [ca. 1814–15], he became quite an orator, and consequently he was appointed as the head speaker in the council of the Ottawa and Chippewa Indians.... My father was the only man who was friendly to education. When I was a little boy, I remember distinctly his making his own alphabet, which he called "Paw-pa-pe-po." With this he learned how to read and write; and afterwards he taught other Indians to read and write according to his alphabet. He taught no children, but only grown persons. Our wigwam, which was about sixty or seventy feet long, where we lived in the summer time, was like a regular school-house, and they had merry times in it. Many Indians came there to learn his Paw-pa-pe-po, and some of them were very easy to learn, while others found learning extremely difficult.
> —Andrew Blackbird, *History of the Ottawa and Chippewa Indians of Michigan*, 1887

Andrew Blackbird wrote *History of the Ottawa and Chippewa Indians of Michigan* in an effort to fill a gap in the historical record.[1] Perusing white histories of the Great Lakes, Blackbird was dismayed to find "no very correct account of the Ottawa and Chippewa Indians, according to our knowledge of ourselves, past and present."[2] Blackbird was experiencing a phenomenon that historian Michael Witgen and other Native scholars have begun to address—the "long invisibility of the Native New World" in the historiography of the Great Lakes region. Witgen's own study of the area, *An Infinity of Nations*, reveals "the existence of an intact, and unconquered, Indian social world in the heartland of North America." Known to the Indigenous peoples of the region as the Anishinaabewaki, it was "polyglot [and] cosmopolitan," stretching from Lake Erie to the headwaters of the Mississippi.[3] Dominated by riverine and lacustrine ecosystems, it was a hybrid terrestrial and aqueous world whose human populations were interwoven in a skein of villages, watersheds, and alliances knit together by social logics that, in addition to being improvisational and ad hoc, were forever shifting.

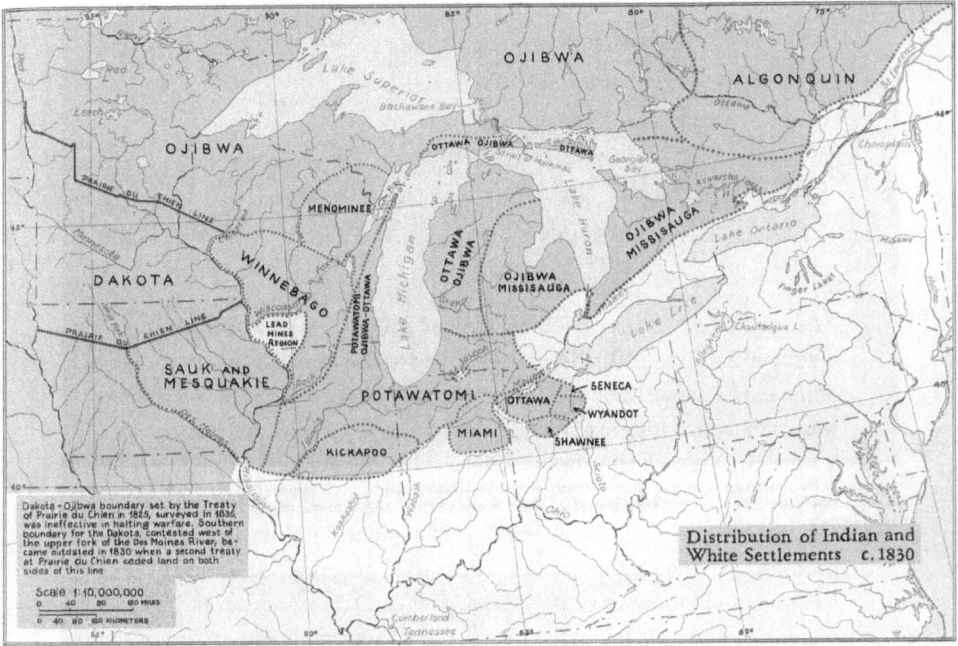

Figure 4.2. The Anishinaabewaki. Map in Hornbeck, *Atlas of Great Lakes History*, 123. Courtesy of University of Oklahoma Press, Norman.

Beyond the mere fact of the presence of "Ottawa and Chippewa Indians" in the Anishinaabewaki—and their corresponding absence in white histories of the region—Blackbird's account of his father's youth and coming of age in the period 1790–1820 highlights the role that writing played in shaping the Odawas' "knowledge of [them]selves" and their right to the lands they had always inhabited. Alongside its seemingly benign recitation of ethnographic "curiosities" (their "mode of traveling," worship, marriages, and the like), Andrew Blackbird's *History of the Ottawa and Chippewa Indians* traces a story of dispossession and reaffirmation that centers on the role of alphabetic literacy, translation, and long-distance communication in reconstituting a nation fragmented by war and federal removal policy.

Andrew Blackbird's father's Odawa name was a reference to a black hawk that was mistranslated as "Blackbird." Born sometime in the 1780s, Macka-de-pe-nessy remembered his father's and grandfather's service in the Revolutionary War; and in his teenage years he worked as a trapper in the fur trade in and around Manitoba, in present-day Canada. It was there that he developed a healthy distrust of Europeans that shadows his son's narration of his adaptation to alphabetic literacy and his role as a translator for Euro-Americans negotiating with the Odawas and Ojibwes. For during Macka-de-pe-nessy's time working as a guide in the fur trade, white people left him to die in the wilderness, sparking a lifelong skepticism about their motives. As Andrew Blackbird writes:

> From this time hence my father lost all confidence in white men, whatever the position or profession of the white man might be, whether a priest, preacher, lawyer, doctor, merchant, or common white man. He told us to beware of them, as they all were after one great object, namely, to grasp the world's wealth. And in order to obtain this, they would lie, steal, rob, or murder, if it need be; therefore he instructed us to beware how the white man would approach us with very smooth tongue, while his heart is full of deceit and far from intending to do us any good. (29)

Disillusioned, Macka-de-pe-nessy left Manitoba and re-entered the Native space of the Anishinaabewaki around his home of L'Arbre Croche in 1800. He found the country aflame with Nativist ideology. The "Shawanee [sic] prophet, Waw-wo-yaw-ge-she-maw," Macka-de-pe-nessy discovered, had "advised the Ottawas and Chippewas to confess their sins and avow their wrongs and go west, and there to worship the Great Spirit according to the old style as their forefathers did, and to abandon everything else which the white man had introduced into the tribes of Indians."[4]

In fact, it was the 1806 cession of land in Indiana by then governor Harrison that drove the Shawnee prophet and his brother, Tecumseh, to establish his Prophetstown community near present-day Lafayette, Indiana, for refugees from the now-divided Anishinaabewaki. As the historian John Reda reports,

> The Prophet and his followers constructed a vibrant and fluid town. At its height, the Indian residents cultivated between one hundred and two hundred acres of corn in order to feed the seasonal migrations of indigenous visitors, in addition to tending a small herd of domesticated cattle despite the Prophet's demand that Indians stop practicing animal husbandry in the Euroamerican fashion. A few lodges were visible near the crops that lined the river, but the center of the town was atop a hill from the river's edge near the meeting house and storage facilities.[5]

The Prophet hoped that all his followers would follow the guidelines "that [had] come immediately from the Great Spirit through [him]." Significantly, he declared that "Indians needed to unite politically and militarily."[6]

It was in this new context of Native dislocation and rival models of Indigenous sovereignty that Macka-de-pe-nessy became a vernacular orator of some repute, weaving together traditional Odawa rhetorical and social practices with literacy education. Thus, Andrew Blackbird remembered his father as "the only man who was friendly to education," whose adoption of European practices involved "making his own alphabet called 'Paw-pa-pe-po.'" While it is clear that the elder Blackbird was using and teaching some form of a vernacular orthography, we are not sure of its form because, as linguist Ives Goddard notes, no vernacular texts have survived from L'Arbre Croche. It is thus most likely that Macka-de-pe-nessy's orthography was a form introduced to the Odawas in 1827 by "the French Roman Catholic missionary Auguste Dejean, who started a school and wrote a catechism and primer in Ottawa using a spelling system like that of other French missionaries working on closely related languages." While there has been persistent speculation that Blackbird's *Paw-pa-pe-po* was an early version of a totally Indigenous scripting system, Goddard reasons that because "Blackbird's own Ottawa writings use a mixture of French-based and English-based spelling systems," it does not "seem to be influenced by the distinctive conventions of the Great Lakes Algonquian Syllabary." That was an alphabet first observed by ethnographers in 1880, with separate letters for consonants and vowels written in syllabic blocks, like the Korean alphabet, and based upon "a European cursive form of the Roman alphabet."[7]

Andrew Blackbird's text, however, contains several significant clues about the social role of this orthography in the L'Arbre Croche community, all of which suggest its communitarian power as a new mode of communication among the Anishinaabewaki. It is interesting, for example, that Blackbird calls his alphabet *Paw-pa-pe-po* and not "the ABCs," for these four syllables make up the conventional first row of consonant-vowel symbols in later syllabic writings by Central Algonquian speakers. It is also significant that the elder Blackbird "taught no children, but only grown persons," suggesting that there was an "age-graded" component to the orthography's use (at least in Macka-de-pe-nessy's mind), and that it may initially have been reserved for communications among elders. In addition, the younger Blackbird recalls that the elders were taught in his family wigwam, indicating that it was reserved to an Odawa-centered social space and not a European-style building such as the later schoolhouses. Finally, even if Goddard is right in saying that Andrew Blackbird applied the orthography's name retroactively in an effort to connect it to other systems like the Great Lakes syllabary, such naming at the very least suggests that he recognized its social function as somehow cognate with later Native-designed orthographies.

For his own children, however, Macka-de-pe-nessy chose a combination of formal literacy and Christian religious training that was becoming almost paradigmatic for generations of Indigenous North American peoples coming of age just after Removal. Like the Luiseño convert Pablo Tac in 1840s California, one of Macka-de-pe-nessy's youngest sons, Pe-taw-on-e-quot, was taken by Catholic missionaries and educated in the faith and its scribal tradition.[8] By 1833, Pe-taw-on-e-quot (known in English as William) was in Rome, a student under the care of the Vatican Propaganda Fide (the Sacred Congregation for Propagation of the Faith), which had been founded in 1622 for the missionization of Indigenous peoples.

Taking after his father, William soon became "a very eloquent and powerful orator and was considered a very promising man by the people of the city of Rome." He also grew suspicious of the Americans' designs on the Anishinaabewaki, and Andrew Blackbird recounts how, when "the proposition arose in this country to buy out the Michigan Indians by the Government of the United States, . . . he wrote to his people at L'Arbre Croche . . . advising them not to sell out nor make any contract with the United States Government, but to hold on until he could return to America."[9] Here, the value of alphabetic literacy for Odawa sovereignty is crystal clear. William's ability to read and write would allow him to make a better "contract" with the government. It also served the critical function of giving the diasporic Odawa community a way to maintain solidarity, in this case, through the power of epistolary connection.

Sadly, Pe-taw-on-e-quot's life was cut short on June 25, 1833, when he was stabbed to death in his rooms at the school. His brother Andrew viewed William's murder as the direct result of his attempts to use literacy on behalf of Ottawa land tenure cases:

> He was slain, it has been said, because it was found out that he was counseling his people on the subject of their lands and their treaties with the Government of the United States. His death deprived the Ottawa and Chippewa Indians of a wise counselor and adviser, one of their own native countrymen; but it seems that it would be impossible for the American people in this Christian land to make such a wicked conspiracy against this poor son of the forest who had become as wise as any of them and a great statesman for his country. Yet it might be possible, for we have learned that we cannot always trust the American people as to their integrity and stability in well doing with us.[10]

Thus, it would seem, literacy education for Odawa men like Pe-taw-on-e-quot grew more dangerous as it became a threat to settler hegemony.

Yet many Central Algonquian speakers and communities braved these dangers. Their roads to vernacular literacy, especially in orthographic forms that met the linguistic and cultural needs of their communities, were full of false starts. While some of these difficulties resulted from settler interference and political differences within tribal communities, others flowed from the nature of the Central Algonquian language itself.

ANISHINAABEMOWIN

The Central Algonquian dialect of Andrew Blackbird and his father is a form of Anishinaabemowin, the ancestral language of several hundred Indigenous communities. In order to render the spoken word in a written form, Blackbird's father would have had to navigate the many layers of European colonial orthographic misunderstanding and intervention to retain the performativity of his Native tongue and to reclaim the history bound up in the language. For, as Anishinaabe poet and linguist Margaret Ann Noodin explains, in Anishinaabemowin, "meaning radiates from a central spoke of action, and diversity of interpretation is important . . . a high value is placed on creating meaning that can be specific to the context and yet open to interpretation."[11] As an agglutinative language, Anishinaabemowin words form "long strings of meaning that can be shifted by speakers to clarify what is happening [to whom]." To understand an Anishinaabe sentence requires that listeners and/or readers "think in an Anishinaabe way, not just think about the Anishinaabeg because when that is possible, readers will find in Anishinaabe literature unceded identities and a way of looking at the world that resists stasis."[12]

Like their Indigenous brethren in the Iroquoia and the Siouan speakers of the lands of the Oceti Sakowin, the speakers of Anishinaabemowin—those from the Odawa, Potawatomi, Kickapoo, Meskwaki, and Ojibwe communities of the Great Lakes where Blackbird resided—had developed several ways of communicating their side of the story when they wished to set the historical record straight or negotiate to keep what was left of their homelands. Algonquian linguist Rand Valentine has outlined the two major historical strands of the orthographic inscription available to speakers:

> Anishinaabe people use two distinct writing systems. In the south, an alphabetic Roman orthography is used. This writing system was invented in the 1950s by Charles Fiero, a missionary, for use in Minnesota. It is often called the "Double Vowel" system, due its use of doubled-vowel letters to represent long vowels, of which there are 4 in Anishinaabemowin. . . . In the north, a distinct system exists, called syllabics, because each letter stands not for an individual consonant or vowel sound, but for a whole syllable. This syllabary was created by a Methodist missionary named James Evans, at the community of Norway House, in northern Manitoba, in the 1830s. Evans based his syllabary on a British shorthand system. In 1841

Figure 4.3. Syllabary book cover. James Evans, *Hymns, Swampy Indians, Their Speech* (Rossville, Manitoba: Rossville Mission Press, 1841.) Courtesy of the Newberry Library, Chicago.

Evans published a hymn book in syllabics, using handmade type, and the syllabary rapidly spread among Cree and Ojibwe people without the aid of missionaries, who were often reluctant to use it, as the newly literate quickly taught the system to others.[13]

Especially interesting is the fact that the Evans syllabary gained a strong ethnic identification for many Indigenous communities in the north, where "the syllabary has been given a mythical origin in some areas, while in other places it is said to originate from traditional Algonquian bead and quillwork patterns. Its distinctiveness from the colonial alphabetic writing system has contributed immensely to its popularity, and fueled much grassroots speculation concerning its indigenous origins."[14] That is not to say that syllabary writing is "easier" for Indigenous communities. Rather, as Valentine suggests, while "syllabics represents one of the most efficient writings systems ever developed," it required fluency to produce, because it "underspecified phonemic contrasts." It makes no distinction, for example, between long vowels and short vowels, something Valentine has characterized as "a crucial distinction in Ojibwe phonology." Yet, over time, this syllabic system and another devised by the Meskwakis of Iowa became important symbols "of cultural sovereignty for many Anishinaabe people."[15] For both the missionary syllabaries circulating in the north, and the more common alphabetic orthographies in the south, Anishinaabe speakers used the term *pa-pe-pi-po*, an onomatopoeia neologism representing the syllabic sounds of their language (those "underspecified phonemic contrasts" that fluent speakers use) rather than arbitrary "letters" of the Roman alphabet.

For settlers who sought to write Anishinaabemowin for the purposes of trade, negotiation, or evangelization, sounds that were commonplace to Central Algonquian ears seemed almost impossible to emulate in the Roman alphabet. For all the settlers who sang the praises of "sonorous majestic Chippeway," there were many more who maintained that "it is a difficult language for a foreigner to acquire."[16] There was also the issue of settlers from different linguistic backgrounds transcribing the sounds they heard in the Roman-alphabet equivalent in their own vernacular orthographies. As the writer of the *Manual of the Ojebway Language* comments: "The Ojebway, not being a written language has been spelt in many different ways, according to the option of the writer. The French adopt their several styles and the English theirs. Thus, for instance, the word muhzenuhegun (book) will be spelt by the French masinaigan." For his part, the author chose to follow the orthography developed by "the Rev. F. A. O'Meara . . . a style of spelling [that] . . . has certainly the advantage of great simplicity, and no person of ordinary talent need have much difficulty in learning to read tolerably after a few weeks' practice."[17] Once again, however, this orthography—like the syllabaries of the north—foundered on the complex syntactic and phonemic patterns that characterize Central Algonquian. Thus, the author of the *Manual* decided to include instructive couplets in English to demonstrate to his European readers how they might "*acquire the flow of the language*, so as to read on smoothly."[18]

If phonemic difficulties, syntactic complexities, and variant European spellings shadowed the implementation of these orthographies, Anishinaabe people of various backgrounds nevertheless embraced them as effective tools in the struggle against colonialism. Over time, they were used to produce tropes of Indigenous self-formation. In a lecture Ojibwe convert Peter Jones delivered to an audience in Leeds, England, he attributed his own awakening to Christianity to a community member's determination to find a way to write: "He had no alphabet by him, and he had no paper, so he thought he would go into the woods and look for something else, and there he found some birch trees, from which he took the bark, and when he came home he got some charcoal, with which he made the letters, and taught the children their ABC."[19] The material culture of this scene is profoundly Ojibwe. The birch bark that serves as "paper" had for many generations been used as a writing surface for medicinal information and ceremonial protocols in the forms of scrolls incised with pictographic signs.

Yet the use of vernacular literacy in Central Algonquian communities was not simply a Christian missionizing endeavor. Scripts would soon take on the role of new social practices that supplemented traditional forms of communication (like pictographic symbols on birch bark) and oral recitation. It is significant that the largest tribal group occupying the Anishinaabewaki during the period leading up to the massive dislocations that Andrew Blackbird recounts was a community uniquely associated with communication in forms of graphic inscription. As Brenda Child notes, "One widely held view about the name Ojibwe is that it relates to the practice of writing down information and sacred songs in drawings and glyphs on birch bark, from the root *ozhibii*. It was the Ojibwe's ceremonial responsibility within the council [of the Three Fires Confederacy (Odawa, Ojibwe, and Potowatomi)] to maintain these birch bark scrolls."[20]

Alan Corbiere's research on his home community at Manotoulin Island has outlined the expansion of alphabetic literacy practices from within already-extant communications protocols. In his research, Corbiere discovered that "chiefs started to expand the domain of Ojibwe literacy from strictly religious purposes to the pursuit of political goals."[21] He writes, "Through all the challenges to their autonomy, to the encroachments on their lands, to the suspicious dealings of their Superintendent, the chiefs responded indignantly and defiantly with petitions written in Ojibwe." Corbiere argues that the significance of using script rather than interpreters suggests it represented a kind of communication autonomy that mirrored the political sovereignty the tribes sought. Users of the orthography included "warriors and headmen," and at Michigiwadinong (present-day M'Chigeengon Manitoulin Island), a new social role opened up for a tribal member of the community, "the Wikwemikong Chiefs' Secretary." Native Anishinabemowin speaker Francis Metosage undertook the job and produced several alphabetic petitions on behalf of the community. It therefore appears that many members of the Anishinaabewaki "used Ojibwe writing to communicate various matters to a diverse audience. The samples further show that a number of Nishnaabeg were literate in Ojibwe; literacy was not confined to the missionaries. Admittedly, missionaries, particularly the Jesuits, played a major role; however, the Nishnaabeg, particularly the chiefs and their sons, were instrumental in this literacy movement."[22]

A closer examination of one alphabetic Central Algonquian document offers us a view into the often subtle, but sovereign, role that such scripts might play in Indigenous communities. The *Life of Ma-ka-tai-me-she-kia-kiak*, perhaps the most famous "Indian" book of the 1830s, is a transcript of the Sauk leader's life as told to the French-Potawatomi interpreter Antoine Le Claire while Black Hawk was imprisoned. Of course, the book is in English, and a century and a half of scholarship have dissected most corners of this work

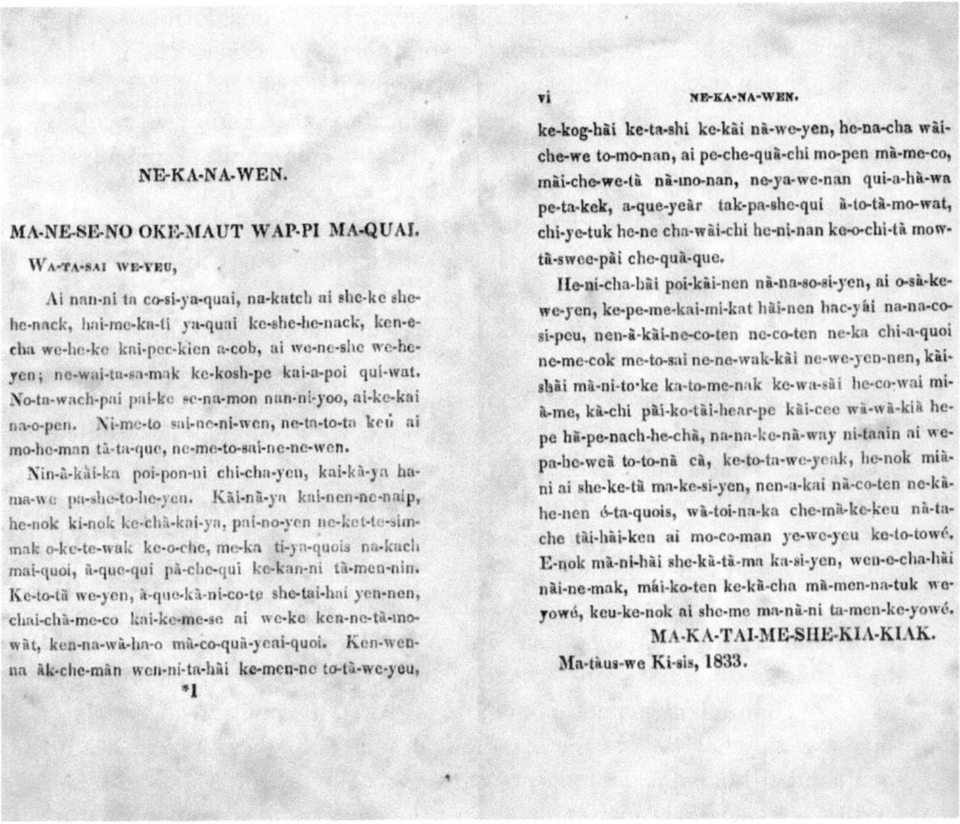

NE-KA-NA-WEN.

MA-NE-SE-NO OKE-MAUT WAP-PI MA-QUAI.

W<small>A-TA-SAI</small> W<small>E-YEU</small>,

Ai nan-ni ta co-si-ya-quai, na-katch ai she-ke she-he-nack, hai-me-ka-ti ya-quai ke-she-he-nack, ken-e-cha we-he-ke kai-pec-kien a-cob, ai we-ne-she we-he-yen; ne-wai-ta-sa-mak ke-kosh-pe kai-a-poi qui-wat. No-ta-wach-pai pai-ke se-na-mon nan-ni-yoo, ai-ke-kai na-o-pen. Ni-me-to sai-ne-ni-wen, ne-ta-to-ta keŭ ai mo-he-man tā-ta-que, ne-me-to-sai-ne-ne-wen.

Nin-à-kài-ka poi-pon-ni chi-cha-yeu, kai-kà-ya ha-ma-we pa-she-to-he-yen. Kāi-nā-ya kai-nen-ne-naip, he-nok ki-nok ke-chà-kai-ya, pai-no-yen ne-ket-te-sin-mak o-ke-te-wak ke-o-che, me-ka ti-ya-quois na-kach mai-quoi, à-que-qui pà-che-qui ke-kan-ni tā-men-nin. Ke-to-tā we-yen, à-que-kà-ni-co-te she-tai-hai yen-nen, chai-chà-me-co kai-ke-me-se ai we-ke ken-ne-tā-mo-wāt, ken-na-wà-ha-o mā-co-quà-yeai-quoi. Ken-wen-na āk-che-màn wen-ni-ta-hài ke-men-ne to-tā-we-yeu,
*1

vi NE-KA-NA-WEN.

ke-kog-hāi ke-ta-shi ke-kāi nā-we-yen, he-na-cha wāi-che-we to-mo-nan, ai pe-che-quā-chi mo-pen mā-me-co, māi-che-we-tā nā-mo-nan, ne-ya-we-nan qui-a-hā-wa pe-ta-kek, a-que-yeăr tak-pa-she-qui à-to-tā-mo-wat, chi-ye-tuk he-ne cha-wāi-chi he-ni-nan ke-o-chi-tā mow-tā-swee-pāi che-quā-que.

He-ni-cha-bāi poi-kāi-nen nā-na-so-si-yen, ai o-sā-ke-we-yen, ke-pe-me-kai-mi-kat hāi-nen hac-yāi na-na-co-si-peu, nen-à-kài-ne-co-ten ne-co-ten ne-ka chi-a-quoi ne-me-cok me-to-sai ne-ne-wak-kāi ne-we-yen-nen, kāi-shāi mā-ni-to·ke ka-to-me-nak ke-wa-sāi he-co-wai mi-ā-me, kā-chi pāi-ko-tāi-hear-pe kāi-cee wā-wā-kiā he-pe hā-pe-nach-he-chā, na-na-ke-nā-way ni-taain ai we-pa-he-weā to-to-nā cā, ke-to-ta-we-yeak, he-nok miā-ni ai she-ke-tā ma-ke-si-yen, nen-a-kai nā-co-ten ne-kā-he-nen ó-ta-quois, wā-toi-na-ka che-mā-ke-keu nā-ta-che tāi-hāi-ken ai mo-co-man ye-we-yeu ke-to-towé. E-nok mā-ni-hāi she-kā-tā-ma ka-si-yen, wen-e-cha-hāi nāi-ne-mak, māi-ko-ten ke-kā-cha mā-men-na-tuk we-yowé, keu-ke-nok ai she-me ma-nā-ni ta-men-ke-yowé.

MA-KA-TAI-ME-SHE-KIA-KIAK.

Ma-tāus-we Ki-sis, 1833.

Figure 4.4. Dedication page spread. From Black Hawk, *Life of Ma-Ka-Tai-Me-She-Kia-Kiak, or Black Hawk.*

for its overly mediated (and sometimes outlandish) portrayal of Native life in the 1830s.[23] One section of the book, however, has only recently received the attention it deserves. That is the so-called dedication to Gen. Henry Atkinson that appears in its opening pages. A Central Algonquian and English-language version of this text appears in sequence, implying that the English rendition is a translation of the original Sauk language text.

The Sauk dialect text is written in Roman type, with hyphens separating the vowel and consonant clusters that make up the essential sounds of Central Algonquian dialects. The linguist Ives Goddard has reported that many Meskwakis he interviewed traced the origins of the Great Lakes syllabary (discussed below) to Le Claire's use of these syllabic transcriptions. Although he found "no evidence of the conventions of the syllabary" in Le Claire's text, it is interesting that the Indigenous community would associate it with a vernacular-language syllabary of their own devising. This suggests, at the very least, that Le Claire's transcript contains something valuable—in both form and content—to modern-day Sauk, Fox, and Meskwaki peoples.[24] The orthography also shows signs of settler colonial conventions. As the linguist Gordon Whittaker notes, "The first thing which catches the eye is the abundance of syllables resembling French spelling: maut with silent t is one example, another is the convention of writing ai for what an English speaker would typically render as ay or a."[25]

Whittaker decided to translate the original Sauk text to see if the English transcript was an accurate translation, or even a translation at all. He discovered that the transcription of syllabic Sauk was in fact not the same text as the English-language dedication published on the subsequent page: "It is clear that this long-ignored bilingual is a coherent, and historically significant, document with much to say about Black Hawk's perspective on war and fate." In fact, Whittaker's new translation reveals "the text as a whole contains grammatical Sauk and is not simply a collection of words strung together for the purpose of legitimizing the edition."[26]

Whittaker's retranslation reveals the sharp political points of Black Hawk's speech. He does not defer to General Atkinson but instead emphasizes their relative equal social stature. Rather than dedicating the text to his captor, Black Hawk employs self-identifying markers of the dignity of his own recitation of events. The Central Algonquian words "'Nekanawîni' 'My (ne-) Words' or 'Nekanawi(w)eni' 'My Speech'" replace "dedication" in the Sauk text. Although the use of the pronoun "my" does not appear to be very significant in the English translation, Lucy Thomason, an expert in the Meskwaki language, has noted in her work on such texts that the community always uses the quotative "ipi" when the discourse is not a personal recollection or experience of its speaker. Thus, Le Claire had heard Black Hawk's insistence on his own legitimacy and authority when he addressed the general. Whittaker's translation in fact shows that Black Hawk's address contained a warning for his captor: "I tell of my life, and in some measure, I tell of *your* life" [italics by Whittaker]. That is, Black Hawk notes, the story is one of "him who was once as proud of himself as you are of yourself today."[27]

The body of the text begins in a gesture of sovereignty much like those described by Andrew Blackbird and Michael Witgen; Black Hawk contends that "justice [has] not [been] done to himself or nation." Sounding very much like Blackbird, he continues, "that is why I am telling you this—telling it accurately, you see, is why I am telling you. However, those who observed these things precisely seem not to have told it accurately. So that is why I am saying this to you. For that reason may you report how accurate it is."[28] Black Hawk remains, however, carefully diplomatic. He uses the Sauk word the missionaries taught for their "God" in a way calculated not to offend Christian readers. This is the "judicious entextualization" principle we have seen at work in so many newly alphabetic Indigenous communities. In short, this brief bit of accurate transcription goes a long way to supporting the view that written literacy had become an important and recognized way for the Sauk and Fox to address a settler colonial world. The transcription and translations are at such variance that the political dimensions of Black Hawk's story are essentially buried in editorial mediation. Given this situation, the Central Algonquians of the Great Lakes would invent a form of writing to remedy their silencing as well as to minimize the great distances removal had inflicted upon their communities.

The life trajectories of Black Hawk and Andrew Blackbird's father and brother are in many ways paradigmatic of the role of literacy in the lives of Central Algonquian speakers whose Great Lakes homelands were increasingly under pressure from settlers. Between 1810 and 1830, the settler population of the Anishinaabewaki increased from 345,000 to some 1.7 million. By the time of the Indian Removal Act (1830), the Indian population of the region was reduced to a mere 72,000.[29] As John Reda reminds us, "A person who was born . . . [here] in the early 1760s [who never relocated] would have lived by the age of sixty under the sovereignty of France, Great Britain, Virginia, the Northwest Territory, Indian Territory, Illinois Territory, and finally, the state of Illinois."[30] Helen Hornbeck Tanner notes, "In the wake of Black Hawk's defeat, the Pottawatomi were forced to cede their remaining lands in Illinois and Wisconsin, and cessions were also obtained from the Winnebago [Ho-Chunk], Menominee, Sauk and Meskwuakie."[31]

Thus, by the latter half of the 1830s, the Removal Act and many land cession treaties had codified the kinds of displacement that Macka-de-pe-nessy had witnessed among the followers of Tecumseh and the situation Black Hawk described regarding his people. Within these displaced and silenced communities, it was clear that "cultural sovereignty"—in the form of the vernacular language and a script entirely "owned" by the Central Algonquian speakers and writers who used it—would be necessary to secure community solidarity. This was especially true because, as Reda notes, the multiethnic communities that resulted from Removal made realizing the "social and political spaces imagined by the various ethnic factions" very difficult to maintain. Continued regional instability also played an important role in the ethnogenesis of Indian and non-Native communities because it forced peoples "to vocalize their ethnic identities as they defended their physical boundaries and material interests."[32] That vocalization, in the Central Algonquian communities we examine here, often took the form of writing.

Given the fluidity of the situation, how are we to understand the techniques that these new and increasingly dispersed intertribal communities employed to maintain their sovereignty? How are land and language connected? And how do diasporic communities maintain cohesion when their homelands and languages are under constant pressure from land cessions, assimilationist educators, and missionaries?

ANISHINAABEWAKI

As we have seen throughout this study, the concept of Native space crucially theorizes the inextricable relationships between land and language, communication and topography, and kinship and community—relationships that the peoples forced out of the Anishinaabewaki had to find new ways to maintain. As we saw in the first case study in this book (chapter 2), the examination of the Haudenosaunee Condolence Ceremony, Lisa Brooks (Wabanaki) mapped the seventeenth- and eighteenth-century information flow within her homelands (the Alnobawogan, Wlogan, Awikhigan), and found a close connection between the new European technologies of alphabetic writing and codex and the landforms and social relationships within which they began to circulate when they reached Native communities. The flow of these precontact communication technologies/systems, of materials like birch bark and wampum, exemplified a new Indigenous mode of reconstructing the "Native body politic" through something she called "a spatialized writing tradition." For Brooks, this new kind of "text," comprising graphic practices, oral recitations, and critically landed venues and routes, demonstrated "that writing was operating as a tool of communication and delineation in Native space, independent of colonial institutions and even in direct opposition to the colonial project."[33]

If we apply Brooks's brilliant analysis of how space and writing came together in her homelands to Witgen's rich description of the Anishinaabewaki, we find striking similarities at the turn of the nineteenth century. Like the Alnobawogan, the dynamism of this Indigenous Great Lakes communications circuit was both geographic and intercultural. Where Brooks reminds us that a profound intermingling of tribal ethnicities was "a prominent feature of Native space" and that communication and its transmission paths were mutually constitutive of meaning, Witgen describes the Anishinaabewaki as a Native space "in which the social logic of condolence rituals, feasts, captive taking, and strategic violence served to redirect power throughout the region to maintain balance and order among Indigenous communities and the European interlopers they encountered."[34] The Europeans whom Witgen describes often found themselves completely at the mercy of political and trade relations that existed before their arrival and that often trumped European efforts to co-opt them. In Witgen's description, the Anishinaabewaki was a place where Native people mattered much more than the newcomers from across the Atlantic.

Like Brooks's Alnobawogan, it was also a place where "political power and social identity... did not take territorial form as a sovereign nation, wherein the body politic exercised supreme authority within a fixed and bordered land base defined by individual property rights." "Among the Anishinaabeg," Witgen writes, "social identity and political autonomy derived from lived relationships forged across a shared and infinitely expandable landscape. Politics and place were relational, and power was multipolar within Anishinaabewaki. Political power manifested itself in a variety of cultural forms, which were adapted to create optimal social relations of production in specific physical locations, environments, and social settings. The multipolar nature of Anishinaabe political power created a fluid and flexible social formation that changed form and function in reaction to cyclical changes linked to political economy and the ritual calendar."[35]

Such spaces were profoundly generative of social and cultural innovation; they were "sites within which," anthropologists Grant Arndt says, "we can investigate the emergent discourses of identity and groupness among Native American[s]... and their relationship with the ideological uses of Indians in [Euro]-American society."[36] The new texts and communication practices that flowed through the Native spaces of the Anishinaabewaki, the Mississippian trade routes and watersheds, and the built environments that housed them—along with the oral traditions that animated their iconography—constitute what Matt Cohen calls a "continuous informational topography."[37] Europeans may have preferred to view the New World as a *vacuum domicilium*, an empty space to be organized by Christianity and rationalism ("reduced" was the word most often used to characterize their colonizing goals); but the "Native spaces" Witgen, Cohen, and Brooks describe were neither empty nor destined to be "reduced." They hummed with voice and song, bristled with all manner of media, and sometimes absorbed alphabetic writing into their constantly adapting communications practices.

A closer look at one Kickapoo community on the Wabash, led by a man named Kenekuk, and slated for removal by the federal government, reveals how script played a constitutive role in community formation when this group relocated to Kansas Territory along with some allied members of diasporic Potawatomi bands from the same region.

THE KICKAPOO PROPHET

Kenekuk, known to settlers as the "Kickapoo Prophet," was born around 1790 near the Wabash River in Indiana. Locals remembered him as an abusive drunk in his youth who left the community just prior to the War of 1812 and who wandered the country without purpose. Sometime during the war, however, Kenekuk had a transformative vision. The Great Spirit reached out to him in his misery and gave him "a piece of His heart, which would instruct the Indians in the ways of peace and love." Kenekuk fashioned a symbolic representation of the Creator's message into narrow ten-inch walnut boards that he inscribed with a private symbol system. These were arranged in a five-character group toward the bottom of the stick, with an eleven-character cluster near the top. The apex of the stick was often carved into a diamond shape, reminiscent of the point of a crown. The rectangular "head" of these staffs also featured an escutcheon on the left side of which was depicted a building with a similar diamond shape on the roof, while the right side featured what earlier ethnographers thought was a row of corn stalks.[38]

In 1815, Kenekuk returned to his people, the Vermillion Band of Kickapoos, who were living along the Wabash and Vermillion Rivers in Indiana and Illinois, and the message of his vision spread. The timing of his return was particularly propitious. It occurred just at the moment when "federal officials, hoping to put their removal plans into motion, sought peace agreements with Potawatomis, Sacs and Foxes, [and] Kickapoos."[39] Kenekuk soon rose to the position of trusted council to Little Duck, an important leader of the Vermillion settlements. By 1819, however, the Americans grew tired of waiting for the Kickapoos' land and went about cajoling the Vermillion group for treaty negotiations. In ill health, Little Duck ceded his authority to Kenekuk, who refused to negotiate even when his kinsmen, the Prairie Kickapoos, agreed to surrender all claims to their Illinois lands. Thus began Kenekuk's role as a leader of an anti-assimilationist church and a vocal negotiator for Kickapoo sovereignty. During this period, George Catlin painted a portrait of Kenekuk when he visited the Kickapoo community in Illinois, just before the community's removal to eastern Kansas. Catlin found his sitter to be a formidable man: "The present chief of this tribe, whose name is Keean-ne-kuk, usually called the Shawnee [sic] Prophet, is a very shrewd and talented man. When he sat for his portrait, he took his attitude as seen in the picture, which was that of prayer."[40] It is interesting that Kenekuk posed so that Catlin could fill in the details of the prayer stick at a later time, suggesting its importance to the public identity he wished to project through the artist's portrait. He is wearing regalia that no doubt points to his identity within the Kickpoo community.

Figure 4.5. George Catlin, *Kenekuk*, ca. 1865. "When he sat for his portrait," Catlin reported, "he took this attitude as seen in the picture, which was that of prayer." From George Catlin, *Souvenir of the North American Indians*, 1852. Courtesy of the Newberry Library, Chicago.

After a decade of escalating pressures on the Vermillion Band's land base, Kenekuk journeyed to St. Louis in 1827 for a meeting with Superintendent of Indian Affairs William Clark about his people's desire to remain in the Indiana-Illinois region. He and twenty followers returned the next year to again confer with Clark. By 1831, the situation along the Vermillion River was becoming intolerable for the Kickapoos, and Kenekuk invited his white neighbors out to his settlement for a last-ditch attempt at negotiation. Through an interpreter, the Prophet advised his audience, "Mind the book he has given for your instruction, attend to its commands, and obey them, and each step you take ... will be easier."[41] By now, Kenekuk had established his credentials as a soldier for Kickapoo sovereignty, with his new religion at the center of it all. Every time the Kickapoos were exploited and their land base decimated, Kenekuk made a religious plea that framed the actions of the Americans as controverting the will of God. Kenekuk eventually founded a church based on the teachings he received in his vision. Every member of the community who wished to join the congregation had to acquire one of Kenekuk's prayer sticks. When outsiders asked about them, the congregants replied that they were "the Bible," and (according to Baptist missionary Isaac McCoy), "No Indian thought of retiring for the night without first consulting his board."[42] When an adherent of the Prophet died, his prayer stick was buried with him.

Some outsiders thought (incorrectly) that the prayer sticks perhaps functioned like Catholic rosary beads. The sticks, however, contain no crosses, no Christ, and no Mary. Instead, they incorporate graphic marks unrelated to Catholicism. A diamond is not a cross, and corn is not a sacramental plant for Christians; but these images did indeed have symbolic valences for the Native Americans who followed the Prophet's teachings. In fact, there are several possible interpretations of these images at the staff's head that would be better suited to the multiethnic Potawatomi-Kickapoo congregation. Perhaps the vegetation represented on the right side of the panel is a wood, and the building on the left, the Kenekuk church. If so, then perhaps the apotheosis of the liturgy alludes to a clearing of Native space (wherever the community finds itself) that the Creator has marked out for them, which will protect them.[43] Most importantly, the prayer sticks appear to have established a reading practice that was unique to this Kickapoo community. A contemporary witness described the stick's use as follows:

> Congregational worship is performed daily and lasts from one to three hours. It consists of a kind of prayer, expressed in broken sentences, often repeated in a monotonous singsong tone, equaling about two measures of a common psalm tune. All in unison engage in this; and in order to preserve harmony in words each holds in his or her hand a small board, about an inch and a half broad and eight or ten inches long, upon which is engraved arbitrary characters, which they follow up with the finger until the prayer is completed.[44]

This depiction of the congregation "reading" clearly shows that the prayer sticks functioned as more than mnemonic devices. Their clusters of symbols organized the cadences of the prayers, functioning much as culturally specific "lines" do in Dell Hymes's important ethnopoetic transcriptions.[45] The sticks help the congregation to "harmonize," that is, to constitute themselves as a community of believers whose oral recitation confirms their membership. By using their fingers to trace up the prayer stick toward its diamond-shaped head, the parishioners enacted a material practice in which reading became devotional.

Further evidence of the activities surrounding the prayer sticks suggests that the liturgy they inscribed served a new kind of anti-assimilationist ideology that voiced Kickapoo sovereignty. Kenekuk's parishioners "steadfastly refused to speak English, and they always performed their traditional music and dancing at religious ceremonies."[46] Like Protestant congregations of earlier centuries, Kenekuk's church separated men and women in the pews, making gender difference manifest in a bifurcated church seating arrangement, split down the middle aisle. But Kenekuk went even further and in a

Figure 4.6. George Catlin, *Ah-tón-we-tuck, Cock Turkey, Repeating His Prayer*, 1830. Smithsonian American Art Museum, Washington, DC. Gift of Mrs. Joseph Harrison Jr.

distinctly vernacular direction. Menstruating women were expressly banned from services, in a gesture that reaffirmed centuries-old traditional practices in Kickapoo communities. Even more scandalous to outsiders, the Kickapoo church regularly featured the flagellation of self-professed sinners. The Prophet's syncretic melding of Catholic and Protestant theology and ritual and Kickapoo traditional social order, however, earned praise from such travelers as the painter George Catlin, who "was singularly struck with the noble efforts of this champion of the mere remnant of a poisoned race, so strenuously laboring to rescue the remainder of his people from the deadly bane ... of drinking whiskey in his tribe."[47]

When the Black Hawk War erupted in 1832, the Kickapoos realized their residence along the banks of the Vermillion River would no longer be tolerated. Thus, early in 1833, Kenekuk and about 400 followers, including more than 100 Potawatomi converts, left Illinois to settle along the west bank of the Missouri River, a few miles north of Fort Leavenworth. After a short time, Kenekuk's congregation had established a prosperous village there. When American traveler John Irving visited Kenekuk's village in 1833, he was greeted by a bucolic scene. The settlement was situated on a "prairie, dotted with wild-flowers. Three of its sides were enclosed by a ridge of hills, at the foot of which meandered a brook with a range of trees along its borders. The fourth side was hemmed in by a thick forest, which extended back to the banks of the Missouri."[48] Irving thought the village, in its retired, rural spot, was virtually "shut out from the world, and looked as if it might have been free from its cares also." Especially since he had no idea that Kenekuk's band had sheltered in that location precisely to regroup as a distinctly Indigenous society, resisting missionization and land-grabbing at every turn.

Once in the town proper, Irving was introduced to the "chief," and to a "tall, bony" man "who was the prophet of the tribe." Irving expressed surprise that the man's "face was full of intelligence," even as "his outward appearance was rather unclerical; for when we entered he was leaning on a long rifle, and appeared to be accoutered for a hunt. He laid aside the gun as we came in, and with the aid of an interpreter commenced a conversation with us." Later, a villager told Irving that his easy access to Kenekuk was unusual, "as he habitually kept aloof from intercourse with whites." Irving further noted that although Kenekuk appeared to have great power in the village, the political leader of the Kickapoos listened to his judgments and there was "no appearance of jealousy or heart-burning between them."[49]

While Kenekuk's followers were prospering, many Prairie Kickapoos succumbed to alcoholism and poverty. Local traders plied the Shawnees, Delawares, and Kickapoos with whiskey in order to facilitate underhanded land deals. "Some freeze to death when drunk," the Indian agent reported in October 1839, while noting that "several drunken Indians have been drowned in the Missouri River this season."[50] By 1839, this divergence of fortunes within the once-allied Potawatomi and Kickapoo communities led some of the Prairie bands to voluntarily relocate to Indian Territory, Texas, or Mexico. Meanwhile, Kenekuk's village continued to prosper. Under his guidance, the community cleared and plowed fields. Soon, their farms produced a surplus of corn, beans, pumpkins, potatoes, beef, and pork, which they sold to traders for a profit. The local Indian agent found them a "lively, fearless, independent persevering people"—words we might use to describe a sovereign society. The thriving condition of the Vermillion people attracted other bands into the Prophet's fold, and the Potawatomi chief Nozhakem, a devout follower of Kenekuk, presented a formal petition to join with Kenekuk's community to the commissioner of Indian Affairs on December 22, 1849.[51]

An observer of Kenekuk's Sunday services in this period reported 300 participants—an astounding number of congregants for any denomination on the frontier.[52] Significantly, Kenekuk preached in the church building the US government had built for Euro-American missionaries, thus usurping US sovereignty and replacing it with Kickapoo and Potawatomi ownership. Kenekuk's popularity, his congregation's "occupation" of a federal building,

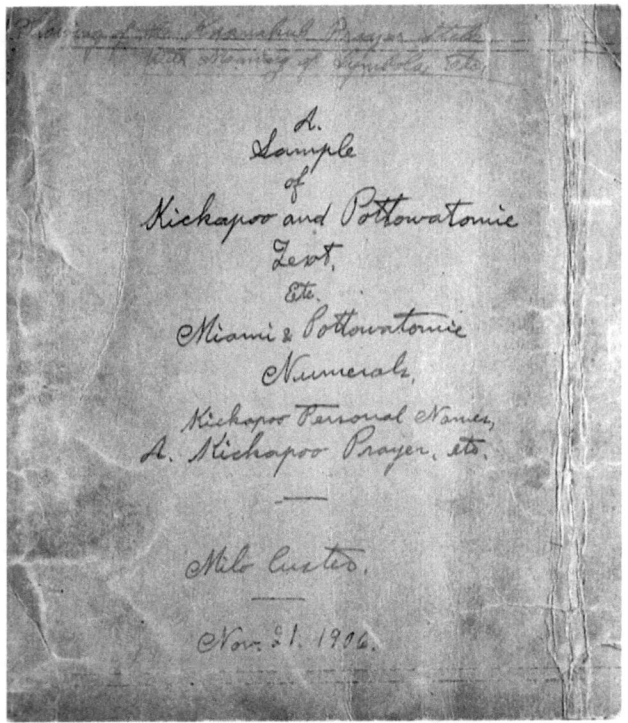

Figure 4.7. Milo Custer, "A Sample of Kickapoo and Pottowatomie Text, Etc. [. . .]," November 21, 1906. From Milo Custer Writings Relating to the Kickapoo Indians, 1906–16, WA MSS S-2351, Yale Collection of Western Americana, Beinecke Rare Book and Manuscript Library, Yale University, New Haven, Connecticut.

and his embrace of certain aspects of capitalism all suggest that more was going on in this Native village than Indian agents or missionaries could fathom. The community continued to innovate its social and religious practices throughout the 1830s and 1840s, inviting in Methodist and Jesuit missionaries, treating them civilly, but rejecting them both in time, suggesting that its sovereignty resided in resiliency and adaptation on Kickapoo terms. The Prophet's religion lasted for at least seventy-five years. Its durability was due, in large part, to the successful transition its later practitioners made into alphabetic literacy. Kenekuk's ministry was first succeeded by Wansuk, a Potawatomi who lived in the intertribal community in Kansas, followed by four disciples who led the congregation until 1907. At some point in the 1850s, Wansuk transcribed the Prophet's teaching into an alphabetic form and wrote it into a manuscript codex. In 1906, the amateur ethnographer and antiquarian Milo Custer made a copy of the sacred Kenekuk liturgy.

When he arrived at Kickapoo Nation in 1906, Custer befriended the pastor of the Kenekuk Church, John Masquequaqua, who agreed to show Custer the manuscript liturgy that had been handed down to him by previous leaders of the church. The text Custer saw was about thirty pages long and "written in

Pottawatomie with English letters." Custer had copied only a few pages when a tribal elder came to Masquequaqua's house to ask that the transcribing be halted. Although Custer interpreted the elder's request as rooted in "superstition," he acquiesced and stopped copying the manuscript. Upon discovering that Custer had been given a prayer stick, the elder sought to retrieve it, offering to allow Custer access to the manuscript liturgy if he returned the sacred object. Custer declined, and what our archive now shows is a text whose meaning was fraught with local, national significance, and which was not freely given to outsiders.[53]

By the time Custer gathered the material from the Kenekuk religious community it was much diminished. The diasporic Kickapoos who had been forced out of the Wabash drainage south into Kansas and Oklahoma had taken on at least three distinctive linguistic approaches to Kickapoo personhood and sovereignty. As we have seen, the group around Kenekuk allied with Potawatomis, developed a separatist church, and scripted a special liturgy that enunciated their new social formation as a response to the Creator's call for a purified form of community. In 1906, when Custer visited, however, they numbered a paltry twenty-five members. Another group, much larger in Custer's view, preferred to revitalize older traditions native to the Kickapoo communities on the Wabash. They followed something Custer refers to as the "dance religion." In fact, Kenekuk's own son abandoned his father's church for this revitalization of Kickapoo traditions.[54] A third community of Kickapoos had left Kansas long before Custer visited the Kenekuk Church. They continued to move south, first to Oklahoma, then to Texas, before finally settling in Nacimiento, Coahuila, Mexico, in 1850. It is this group of diasporic Central Algonquian speakers who offer us a final case study of the surprising role of Central Algonquian literacy practices in diasporic settings after Removal.

THE GREAT LAKES SYLLABARY

Andrew Blackbird's history describes how an alternate form of orthography, centered in Native sovereignty rather than in missionary zeal, and first employed by Odawa community members perhaps as early as 1830, served as a Native-centered approach to alphabeticism that better suited many Central Algonquian speakers in their quest for control over their homelands. At Manitoulin Island, warriors and chiefs mandated an Indigenous scribe to pen petitions to the colonial government from the 1840s forward.[55] For the Kickapoo and Potawatomi followers of Kenekuk, a sacred script of cryptic symbols helped create a shared sense of identity, which only slowly gave way to alphabeticism in the second and third generation of followers. Sometime between 1860 and 1880, however, an even more Native-centered writing system emerged among Central Algonquian language speakers, becoming standard with the Meskwakis of Iowa and Oklahoma, the Kickapoos of Oklahoma and Mexico, and surprisingly—given that they speak a Siouan language quite different from Algonquian—the Ho-Chunks (Winnebagos) of Wisconsin and Nebraska.

This system, now formally called *pa-pe-pi-po* by its Meskwaki innovators, came to be known in the anthropological literature as the Great Lakes Algonquian syllabics. But, as linguist Ives Goddard explains, "It is a syllabary of a very particular kind. It has nothing to do with the Cree syllabary devised by James Evans. It is rather an adaptation of the roman alphabet in which consonant and vowel letters are written together syllable by syllable. Very similar and obviously closely related writing systems are used by the Sauk, Kickapoo, and Potawatomi."[56] This was a written script, not used for print, and its punctuation practices were sparse, employing only a word divider, which "variously appears as a dot, a small line, or an (x) or (+)."[57] It was, in fact, somewhat akin to a cipher, and more than one ethnographer found that its "decryption"—even by a Native speaker—could sometimes be very difficult. As the linguist Lucy Thomason notes, "The traditional Meskwaki syllabary is easy to write but challenging to read." When they do receive a written text, Thomason reports, "even native speakers of Meskwaki have to do some puzzle-solving when they read Meskwaki."[58]

Alice Fletcher, the ethnographer who first witnessed the syllabary's use in the 1880s, reported, "In the winter of 1883–84, while I was with that Winnebago tribe which resides in Nebraska, a party of Indians arrived to make a visit. They numbered fifteen[,] were in old-time Indian costume, and seemed bent on old-time pleasures. There were feasts and dances, Indian gayety. I met the visitors on several occasions, and many of them spent considerable time with me, talking over many subjects. Among other matters, they told me that one had invented an alphabet, and that many of the Indians use it to write their native language."[59]

Allie Busby, who had been among missionaries with the Meskwakis in the 1880s, recalled the script's social significance to the tribal members who visited the Ho-Chunks in 1880:

> The Language of the Sac and Fox tribe consists of small words, or syllables only, in this differing from that of any others. . . . The syllables comprising the language of this tribe are twelve in number; these have different changes, four in each order. They are spelt as nearly as possible as the pronunciation goes, the English letters, however, are made slightly different. The letter i is always sounded e, and e a. . . . With these words, or

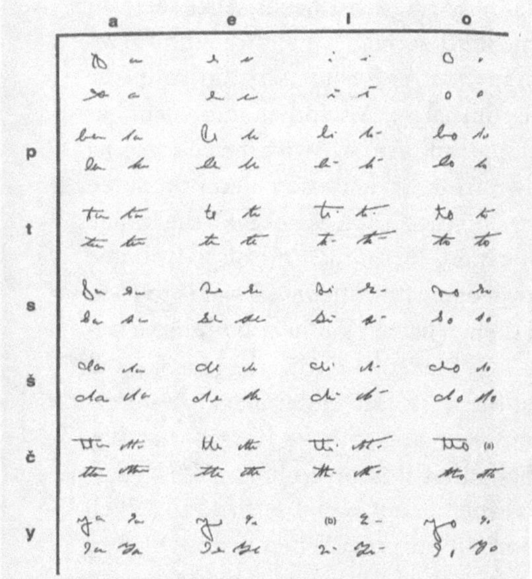

Figure 1. The basic matrix of the Mesquakie syllabary illustrated from manuscripts by four writers. Clockwise from top left in each cell: Alfred Kiyana, Jim Peters, Charley H. Chuck, Sakihtanohkweha. *Handbook of North American Indians*, v. 17: *Languages* (Karen Ackoff, from MSS in the National Anthropological Archives.)

Figure 1 (cont.). Notes: (a) No example found. (b) Kiyana does not write (yi), using (ye) instead. (c) (kwo) occurs in syllabary matrices but is rare or absent in words; one example is known from Kiyana (perhaps a spelling error), but there are none from the other writers.

Figure 4.8. The Fox (Mesquakie) syllabary (basic matrix). Figure 10 in Goddard and Sturtevant, *Languages*, 170–71.

rather these syllables when formed into words, the Indians carry on a large correspondence with friends in Indian Territory, and elsewhere. Even the smaller children understand the art of writing, according to this system, and nearly all, old and young, understand how to read and write in their own language."[60]

What Busby describes here is a set of social practices that combine methods of sustaining intergenerational community ("even the smaller children understand") with an ability to communicate with relations over large distances. When the ethnobotanist Huron Smith visited the Meskwakis of Iowa in 1923, he noted, "The Meskwaki have written their language for two decades and possibly longer in corresponding with absent members of the tribe, and during our field work, we used their syllabary since the syllables could be readily understood by them."[61]

The *pa-pe-pi-po* works by employing cursive Roman letters to stand in for consonant pairs. As shown in figure 4.9, the left-hand margin denotes the rows of consonant sounds, which are then paired with the vowel sounds arrayed across the top of the chart. Because this chart compares the real-world handwriting of four different Meskwaki writers, it reveals the idiosyncrasies of the scribal form.

But the syllabary served more than simply pragmatic needs. Alice Fletcher suggested that its origins involved some kind of religious and/or cultural revival. The Algonquian speaker who taught it to her in 1884 did so in the context of an outpouring of religious enthusiasm: "My Indian informant has all the zeal of a new convert and talks long and earnestly with me concerning the religious beliefs that had come down from his ancestors, and he assured me that were the pure codes of morality enforced, such as he cited, the Indian would rise to be far superior to the white man."[62] Huron Smith also attributed his exploration of ethnobotanical knowledge within the Meskwakis to their supposed cultural "conservatism" and their syllabary's ability to preserve tradition: "It was at the suggestion of Dr. S. A. Barrett and Mr. Alanson Skinner (deceased) of the Public Museum, that the work was undertaken ... among the Meskwaki Indians, because ... many ethnologists have averred that they are more primitive in their customs than other Wisconsin Indians."[63]

Like Busby, Smith observed several interesting social settings in which the syllabary served an especially important purpose. When he interviewed the medicine man John McIntosh (Kepeosatok), he discovered the Meskwaki healer had kept "note-books of medicinal formulae that he had written in Indian words, explained what each plant was and its use, and showed the most of them in the field. The present bulletin, then, according to his wish, is his contribution to posterity."[64] This usage mirrors the way that the Cherokee syllabary functioned in that society.[65] From Smith's limited point of view, McIntosh was unique in a society that had "quit the medicine lodge" that propagated the botanical knowledge the medicine man was now collecting, and his adoption of the syllabary was thus reflective of his generation's "regret" at abandoning that lodge. McIntosh's notebooks therefore served a multipurpose role in his community. They were not only a practical encyclopedia of medicinal formulas but also a way of maintaining intergenerational continuity of culture, for "individual knowledge was ... handed down from father to son among those families that still practiced the teachings of the medicine lodge."[66] The syllabary enabled this passing on of information in an otherwise dispersed society.

Other evidence from the historical record suggests that the syllabary's power also resided in its ability to sustain the oral practices of the language. More than one commentator has noted that it demanded a special set of reading practices that may have actually encouraged orality rather than suppressing it:

> Readers [of the syllabary must] develop certain strategies. Typically they read over to themselves unfamiliar words or segments of a text, sounding

them out syllable by syllable with long vowels and plain consonants. If some words or parts of words are recognized, these may be pronounced correctly. This technique sometimes results in reading pronunciations that mix correct and incorrect renderings of different parts of a word. Because readers are used to encountering some variation in the shapes of words and do not automatically substitute their own pronunciations, their reading pronunciation may be a compromise between how they would say a word and how they see it written. Also, to aid the enquiring linguist, speakers may use spelling pronunciations, with all long vowels, when repeating words. Such pronunciations are also learned by children in language classes in school, drawing critical comments.[67]

Thus, the power of the syllabary also resides in the way it forces its recipient to re-perform an oral recitation, sounding out syllables, trying out the missing long or short vowels, until the meaning is worked out. As the Meskwaki syllabary letter that serves as the visual epigraph to this chapter demonstrates, letters like this enabled Young Bear (who spoke no English) at the Meskwaki Settlement to communicate with Edgar Ruby Harlen, curator of the State Historical, Memorial, and Art Department of Iowa, located in Des Moines. In this case, Harlan relied on Jonas Poweshiek, a tribal member who worked for him, to recite the letter's message.[68]

When the Ho-Chunk collaborator Sam Blowsnake wrote vernacular-language stories in the syllabary for the linguist Amelia Susman, she noticed the writing system "sometimes caused noticeable delay in Blowsnake's reading back of his own transcriptions, and very often his first interpretation was the wrong one."[69] Her observation is noteworthy because it demonstrates that the syllabary was not a superior technology to either the ethnographers' phonetic transcriptions of the Ho-Chunk language in the Roman alphabet or the English-language alphabetic translations—at least where speed and ease of intelligibility were concerned. This suggests that the syllabary is an example of something archaeologists call "a maladaptive attribute," a cultural practice that has been selected and put into use by a large number of members of a community, even though that practice appears to be technologically insufficient to the task. People will employ a technology like the syllabary, even if it is inefficient, if that technology becomes politically "potent."[70]

Thus, it would seem that for the period from its "invention," down through at least the 1930s, the Meskwaki syllabary script demonstrated great efficacy on several important levels necessary to the preservation of Meskwaki sovereignty. As ephemeral texts intended as the most efficient means of maintaining kin and community over the long distances forced on the people by

Removal, the script facilitated "popular exchange and sociability" through the state-sponsored networks of the postal system.[71]

Letters in script also served a more political function, as is the case in the series between Young Bear and Edgar Ruby Harlen now archived at the Historical Society of Iowa. Eric Zimmer argues, in fact, that these letters played a role in the way in which "the Red Earth People buttressed their struggles to regain political control in the 1920s, and later, to survive the deprivations of the Great Depression."[72] Finally, the script—described time after time by ethnographers and linguists as "difficult" or "inefficient"—seemed to exhibit all the properties of a "maladaptive attribute" in a material practice. In the case of the syllabary, the difficulties in translating the written text into an intelligible speech act (that might then be transcribed in English) may have encouraged the continued oral and aural protocols that were under pressure of disappearance due to settler assimilation programs.

Yet it is also true that the syllabary appears to have inaugurated the growth of Meskwaki language written literature. Between 1911 and 1938, the ethnographer Truman Michelson supplied the Meskwaki community near Tama, Iowa, with thousands of pages of ruled paper so that they could write traditional stories out for him in the syllabary. This is one of the largest written Central Algonquian language "libraries" in North America. A community member named Bill Leaf, who was a storyteller, filled more than 1,200 pages with syllabary narratives. Another Meskwaki storyteller, Alfred Kiyana, filled more than 10,000. Within this corpus of written Meskwaki texts, Michelson noted the presence of a newer style of narrative. Goddard calls this the "deliberate style" and contrasts it with the casual usages found in syllabary letters and postcards.[73]

Among the many interesting texts the Meskwakis penned for Michelson in the syllabary is one he published under the title of *Autobiography of a Fox Woman* (1918). This text originated in a syllabic script transcription of an unidentified local woman's oral recitation of her life story to Henry Lincoln, a Meskwaki community member. He was assisted by his wife. In their 1995 study of Native women's autobiography, Gretchen Bataille and Kathleen Sands describe the *Autobiography of a Fox Woman* as

> the story of one woman growing up in this culture which, despite the intrusions of the outside, yet today maintains many of the traditions of the past. Her life story focuses on her tribal education and integration into the ways of her people, what she was expected to know in order to take her place within that society. She tells of "growing up"—making dolls, planting, weaving belts, and learning the many necessary tasks which would

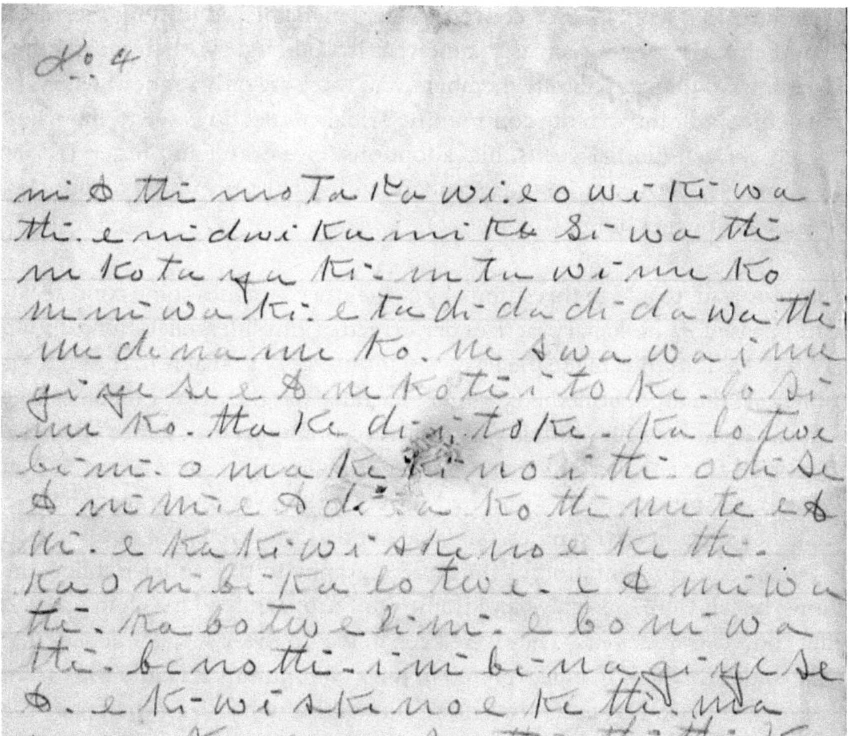

Figure 4.9. Mr. Bill Leaf's handwriting. UAN: NMNH-2697_04, National Anthropological Archives, Smithsonian Institution, Washington, DC.

be hers as a woman. Her concern is personal—her education, marriage, and children. She is seen as a somewhat isolated figure; the important relationships are with family members, and there are only vague allusions to friends and others in the community. Tribal connections seem important only for ceremonial needs, like adoptions, giveaways, and funerals. Her strength is derived from the extended family, first her mother and uncles, later her own children.[74]

It is important to add to this summary of the story's themes some contextualization based in the social practices performed by this intergenerational group of Meskwakis as they made the Fox woman's life story available to the ethnographer. As the unidentified Fox woman narrated her life to the Lincolns, note that she included only "things which seemed of importance to her." Because she hailed from an earlier generation than the Lincolns, she was not herself well versed in the syllabary and had to rely on the younger transcribers to relate her story in terms understandable to other Meskwakis. What is erased in Michelson's presentation of the autobiography to the settler public—the things he felt were too "naïve and frank" for European readers—had no such effect on the transcribers. They were keen to record those social practices that were under threat of being forgotten in their community. It would thus seem that for the period from its "invention" down through at least the 1930s, the Meskwaki syllabary script demonstrated great efficacy on several important levels necessary to the preservation of Meskwaki sovereignty.

THE CASE OF SAM BLOWSNAKE

We conclude this study of the Great Lakes syllabary by examining how removal and assimilation efforts drove the adoption of new forms of communication and community-building by the Ho-Chunk Nation, known to settlers as the Winnebagos. The Ho-Chunks (often translated as The People of the Big Voice), are a Siouan people whose homeland at the beginning of the nineteenth century spanned the southern half of the present-day state of Wisconsin and reached well into Illinois. Like the other communities examined in this book, the Ho-Chunks experienced withering geographic dislocation and cultural depredation between the 1820s and 1860s. After the Black Hawk War of 1832, the Ho-Chunks were removed over several decades to locations across the trans-Mississippi prairie. The Winnebago Tribe of Nebraska explains what happened next on their official website: "The Tribe was moved from what is now northeast Iowa, to Minnesota to South Dakota, and finally to their current location in Nebraska where the Winnebago Indian Reservation was established by treaties of 1865 and 1874. Following this displacement to the treeless plains of South Dakota, a nocturnal gravitation occurred during which many of the dispossessed Winnebagos, under cover of darkness, traveled down the Missouri River to rejoin remnants of their tribe in Nebraska."[75] During the move to South Dakota, "a quarter of the tribe died on the journey in 1863." Some members of the Ho-Chunk Nation resisted these removals and stayed in their Wisconsin homelands.[76]

The Meskwakis visited the Winnebago Reservation in Nebraska sometime around 1884 and shared the *pa-pe-pi-po* with their Ho-Chunk hosts. Alice Fletcher noted its quick adoption by the Ho-Chunks, and in 1888 "inquired concerning this alphabet, and found that the people generally were quite well aware of its existence, and they invariably told me that they had gained it from the Sauk." Fletcher contacted a local Ho-Chunk community member "who upon his visit to the Sauk in 1884 or 1885 first acquired the alphabet, [and] soon discovered its adaptability to the writing of the Winnebago language, and he at once put it to that use. He taught others of his tribe, and the knowledge spread rapidly among the Winnebagos of Nebraska, and also to that part of the tribe living in Wisconsin, so that at the present time the principal correspondence of the tribe takes place by means of these characters."[77]

Their Algonquian-speaking tutors had developed the Great Lakes syllabary for conveniently inscribing their language in letters and other documents, but for the Ho-Chunks to use their system, it was necessary to make wholesale changes to the way it was organized. Willard Walker explains that the "discrepancies between the Winnebago and Fox sound systems forced the Winnebagos to [adapt] . . . a Fox orthography that was, and still remains, essentially phonemic and converted it into a morphophonemic system which represented 36 phonemes with 18 letters and a number of spelling conventions based on an ordered set of 16 context restricted rules."[78]

This is very significant. As Ellen Cushman's study of the Sequoyan writing system demonstrates, morphophonemic syllabaries tend to contain "instrumental and interpretive logics" that are quite different from alphabetical systems, and they tend to be very closely related to a society's unique orientation to the world around them. Rather than being arbitrary (like alphabets), syllabary signs are often treated as embodying "a direct, tangible connection to meaning." In Cherokee, for example, "speakers work to find the meaning in the words, rather than simply the sound of the syllable," thus suggesting that "each glyph potentially represents sound and meaning together" and is an extension of specific Indigenous epistemological practices.[79] Even though the Ho-Chuck system relies on alphabetic figures for its glyphs, it seems that it, like the Cherokee syllabary, embodied deeply felt cultural practices that went far beyond mere translation. In fact, "encoding spoken Winnebago into written form involves, not only a set of letters, but a set of spelling conventions also."[80]

In 1908, the ethnographer Paul Radin journeyed to the Nebraska Winnebago Reservation, and over the next four years collected materials that would make up his greatest literary achievement, *The Winnebago Tribe* (1923). Radin had specifically sought out the Nebraska Ho-Chunk community because of their reputation for being "fairly conservative." He was preoccupied with "discovering what the real Indian is like." There he met a family named the Blowsnakes that proved especially interesting in this regard. Two of the young men "were quite well known in the tribe ... [and] had lived the most exciting of lives." Soon Sam, the younger of the two, captured Radin's imagination. "Having heard vaguely of the adventures and tribulations of [Sam], ... which seemed to bear all the marks of a true rake's progress," Radin decided that getting Sam to tell his own story would "throw more light on the real Indian than any of the more elaborate things I had collected in the usual external fashion which is the pride of scientific procedure among ethnologists."[81] After a series of false starts, he convinced Sam to transcribe the events of his life in the Ho-Chunk vernacular. The resulting text, written in an American Chief notepad, employed the *pa-pe-pi-po* as its vernacular-language script.

What Sam Blowsnake produced, however, was much more than an ethnographic autobiography, or even an auto-ethnography (to use Mary Louise Pratt's term). As he plied the pencil and paper Radin had given him, Blowsnake appears to have used the notepad as a mediating technology by which to work out some personal and community struggles concerning his difficult relationship with his father's traditionalism, his own immersion in the new Peyote ceremonies that took hold on his reservation in the 1890s, and the larger issues of acculturation and assimilation that a written life story engenders. In Blowsnake's case, the syllabary allowed him to explore feelings of sibling rivalry and his awkward relationship with his father within the safety of the Ho-Chunk vernacular, coded by the syllabary to resist the prying eyes of the general public. In this way, Blowsnake thematized his personal problems in a complex storytelling event whose praxis centered on using the episodes and language of time-immemorial story cycles to navigate his way through his own immediate problems.

When Blowsnake tells several folk tales about Coyote, for example, he digresses into the origin of his clan, the Thunderbird. The clan could trace its beginnings to the heroic actions of the mythic figure known as Red Horn, and as Blowsnake began to relate the hero's story, it took on parallels with his own life. His Thunderbird clan traces its origins to the descent to earth of four brothers, Kunuga (Red Horn), Henuga, Hagaga, and Nagiga. These are

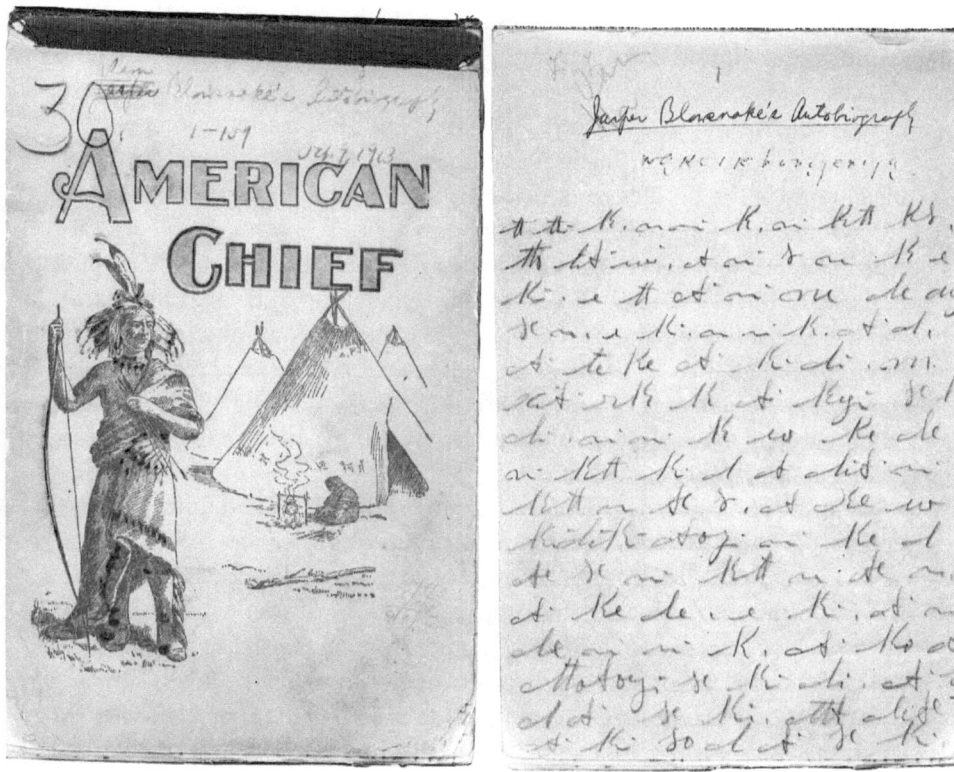

Figure 4.10. Sam Blowsnake's manuscript "Autobiography." The inscription at the top of the page "Jasper Blowsnake's Autobiography" has always puzzled scholars, who believe it is simply an error on Radin's part. Paul Radin Papers, American Philosophical Society Library and Museum, Philadelphia, Pennsylvania.

the names given to Red Horn and his brothers in the fuller Red Horn story cycle. As Blowsnake narrates Red Horn's important role in the foundation of his clan, he relates obvious parallels between Red Horn's awkward relations with his brothers and those between himself and his brother, Jasper.

The autobiography also helped Sam Blowsnake navigate his own struggles with the traditions of his father's generation. In his narrative, his father attempts to remedy his son's lack of faith by setting him and his brother out on a vision quest in a specially built lodge away from the village. Every day, he arrives to tell his sons a traditional story of Ho-Chunk historical figures who attained greatness through ceremony, attempting to inspire them to achieve similar life-changing visions. With each passing day, Sam becomes more disenchanted and finds his father's stories more oppressive the longer they fail to attain the desired effect. Jasper obtains a vision, and Sam is left to lie about the revelation he never has. Despite his father's and fellow lodge-members' efforts to initiate him into this rite, however, Blowsnake feels that it is all sham and goes through the motions of the ceremony simply to "boast of its greatness in the presence of women, in order to make a good impression upon them."[82]

Grant Arndt's study of twentieth-century Ho-Chunk ceremonialism offers insight into why Sam Blowsnake used his written autobiography in this way: "Blowsnake was born when the traditional way of life of his people was already largely impossible to realize in daily practice, and yet his autobiography documents the fact that the ideals of behavior and the values organizing traditional social life remained vital in the Ho-Chunk community." Sam seems proud of his father and his father's own adherence to traditional practices, but they do not hold the same value for him. Thus, in Arndt's view, "Blowsnake's autobiography is clearly plotted as an account of his attempt to resolve the contradictions of his situation."[83]

Over the course of the rest of the narrative, Blowsnake succumbs to alcoholism, performs in a Wild West show, commits a murder, and serves time in prison. Only when he joins the Peyote meetings, a new religion based on the ritual consumption of peyote from the reservations of southwestern Indian Territory that drew upon earlier ceremonies from northern Mexico and traditional theologies from the southern Plains cultures, does he finally feel authentic. Its spirituality is real to him, much more genuine than his father's traditions. At the end of his autobiography, Blowsnake offers its moral: "After I had eaten a good deal of peyote, I learned the following from it; that all I have done in the past had been evil. This was plainly revealed to me. What I thought was holy, and by thus thinking was lost, that I now know was false. It is false, this giving of the pagan feasts, of holding the Winnebago things holy, such as the Medicine Dance and all other customs."[84]

Yet his rejection of tradition was perhaps less of an abandonment of Ho-Chunk identity than he realized. Other tribal members who underwent similar conversions continued to integrate the old with the new. One convert "recalled that he had inherited power from the Thunderbirds as a member of that clan. Even after he ate peyote, he admitted that he still believed in the Thunderbirds and their power."[85] Although Radin went looking for "real Indians" whose "conservative" values reflected time-immemorial tradition, what he found was a community who were engaging in a myriad of creative practices by which they hoped to remain Ho-Chunk in a colonial world that treated them as undifferentiated, marginal "Indians."

Arndt points out that Blowsnake's role as Radin's "informant" during a time of increasing tensions between traditionalists and practitioners of the peyote way provides an important context for his autobiography. For both the ethnographer and the members of the peyote meetings, there was much to be gained by eliciting traditional stories and ceremonies from the "conservatives." Arndt describes how "Radin and the leader of the Peyote movement" collaborated to convince traditionalists "to show that they had truly rejected the . . . traditional religions such as the Medicine Lodge," by allowing Radin to "record traditional teachings before they were lost."[86]

Sam Blowsnake's syllabary autobiography is itself an extension of his community's origin story, one that focuses on the establishment of his father's Medicine Dance. More importantly, it is an origin story that the younger Blowsnake has put to a very particular use in a very specific historical context, long after his father's death. It is, therefore, something much more material and social than simply a disembodied "text." It is, rather, a "text artifact," a material culture object whose creation entails a complex give and take between individual agency and social constraints codified in "tradition."[87]

To draw out this practice-centered understanding of the Blowsnake narrative, we must explore its "entextualization," that "process of rendering a given instance of discourse . . . detachable from its local context." If the oral traditions upon which the Ho-Chunks ground their origins, migrations, and ceremonials are *discourse* ("the unremarked and un-repeated flow of utterances in which most human activities are bathed"), then works like Blowsnake's autobiography are text-artifacts—"created when . . . discourse [is] made available for repetition or re-creation in other contexts."[88] Because oral traditions are indeed verbal and transitory, dying in the air soon after they are spoken, their transmission through time is often treated as simple "memorization," and their cadences and textures, as little more than mnemonic devices. Yet human societies actually employ the discourse of oral tradition strategically, immersing it in the historic moment by entextualizing it for purposes immediately relevant to the community. Every time the Medicine Dance songs were sung and the ceremonies performed, the Ho-Chunks entextualized the oral traditions that underwrote them, changing them as social and historical circumstances required.

The first step in unpacking the entextualization of Blowsnake's autobiography is to define what kind of social act it entails. Because "texts are used to do things" and are "one of the things people do," we need to figure out what was done by Blowsnake writing his autobiography. At its simplest, Blowsnake's text is a transactional artifact. Radin paid Blowsnake for his time and effort. But the work of a text like this does not stop at simple *doing*. In such a text-object, discourse has been entextualized so that it rises above discourse to become noteworthy, set apart from everyday speech and fixed in a written form-object. Radin asked for an autobiography, and Blowsnake provided one; but the particulars contained within its pages bear the marks of having been selected by the author for singling out and rendering memorable. In addition to "fixing" discourse in the more stable form of writing, Blowsnake's narrative provides "commentaries upon, and interpretations of, social facts." It is not only "part of social reality but . . . also take[s] up an attitude to social reality . . . a part of the apparatus by which human communities take stock of their own creations."[89] In the autobiography, Blowsnake observes the Ho-Chunk society of his youth with some detachment, at times a nonbeliever, at others a wry ironist.

Viewed from within its role as an origin story, Sam Blowsnake's text represents a continuation of the Ho-Chunk storytelling tradition. Every clan has an oral traditionalist who is responsible for safeguarding a section of the community's storytelling corpus, which the Ho-Chunks organized into four primary genres: origin stories, trickster tales, mythologies, and legends. There is no special category for autobiography, although certain elders shared their visions and powers with others in the form of stories that recounted whence they derived them. As the son of an important member of the Thunderbird Clan, Blowsnake can reasonably be considered as taking on the traditional role of oral traditionalist within that social group. But Blowsnake's life story is also a hybrid form of Ho-Chunk storytelling. In it, he subsumes several genres—origin, myth, legend, history—at the same time folding the events of his own historical period into it as well. All the narrative details, both "modern" and "ancient," are "told from the Winnebago tribal point of view," a technique Ho-Chunk oral traditionalist Linda Tuiwai Smith explains as "how the tribal people express themselves in the modern world, while still using their own history, culture, and traditions."[90]

Its material form, the handwritten syllabary, represents a further innovation in this tradition. When Blowsnake sat down to write his life story at Radin's behest in a series of cheap American Chief notebooks, he chose to employ a material practice that was itself marked as uniquely Ho-Chunk and perhaps created in conscious opposition to English-language literacy practices that missionaries and the federal government had forced upon Native communities in the final decade of the nineteenth century. Sam seems proud of his father and his father's own adherence to traditional practices, but they do not hold the same value for him. Thus, in Arndt's view, "Blowsnake's autobiography is clearly plotted as an account of his attempt to resolve the contradictions of his situation."[91]

Anthropologists categorize the practices Radin encountered on the Nebraska Winnebago Reservation as forms of "articulation," "a non-reductive way to think about cultural transformation and the apparent coming and going of 'traditional forms.'" "In articulation theory," James Clifford explains, "the whole question of authenticity is secondary, and the process of social and cultural persistence is political all the way back. It is assumed that cultural forms will always be made, unmade, and remade." By employing the term "articulation" to describe Sam Blowsnake's social and cultural choices, we may better appreciate him as a political being, actively engaged in his community's "processes of consensus, exclusion, alliance, and antagonism that are inherent in the transformative life of all societies."

Blowsnake's invocation of Red Horn is, counterintuitively perhaps, part of a repertoire of material practices that represent "the full range of indigenous ways to be 'modern' . . . patterns of visiting and return, of desire and nostalgia, of lived connections across distances and differences."[92] In the midst of rejecting his father's way, Blowsnake was recording and extending it on behalf of a belief system he felt to be more applicable to his generation of Ho-Chunk people. Rather than being the static "real Indian" Radin sought, Sam Blowsnake emerges in his written autobiography as a man of his time and of his Native nation.[93] The tacit politics of writing in a syllabary form of the vernacular must in turn therefore be linked to the overt politics of Sam Blowsnake's life story in order to understand its totality as practice.

CONCLUSION

When Andrew Blackbird reminisced about his father's literacy practices in 1888, versions of the *Paw-pe-pi-po* that Macka-de-pe-nessy had used and taught a generation earlier had become potent communications media throughout the displaced bands of the Potawatomi, Kickapoo, Meskwaki, Sauk and Fox, and Ho-Chunk Nations. With its syllabic rendition of the central sounds of the Central Algonquian dialects, it performed a kind of mnemonic celebration of what an Ojibwe elder has called the language's "totality of communication in several dimensions of reality." The syllabary embodied Central Algonquian's ability to match sound and semantics in phrases that demonstrated "the ever-expanding concentric circles of associations created in sound" for those to whom the language was perhaps the last anchor to their homelands.[94] Once linked to a common landscape in the Southern Great Lakes, these dialects now floated in a diasporic circuit that flowed farther and farther south—from present-day Illinois to Northern Mexico—as settler incursion continuously drove communities to seek their sovereignty elsewhere.

If their geographic locations were no longer the same, however, their agglutinative discourse remained, both as spoken in the lived everyday of those who were still conversant in the language, and in the writing and translating of *pa-pe-pi-po* texts. Whether using the syllabary or an alphabetic script, the Indigenous writers who plied the recognized rhetoric of their languages in the two-dimensional space of a paper letter or a ruled notebook maintained a set of protocols that placed "a high value . . . on creating meaning that can be specific to the context and yet open to interpretation."[95] Theirs were dialects whose written forms filled the page with "long strings of meaning" that settlers found hard to interpret. Most often, these syntactic chains contained a myriad of subtleties—a syllable or two might indicate hearsay, others might suggest whether the subject of the message was animate or inanimate, and addressees could be "hailed" as near or far, with us or against us. Black Hawk employed such techniques when he underscored how much of the "autobiography" transcribed by Antoine Le Claire was something he had himself experienced, and when he clarified through his vernacular's intricacies what he really felt toward his captors and their religion.

For Kenekuk, the Kickapoo Prophet, a supernatural script given by the Creator worked to maintain the sovereignty of a mixed dialect community of Kickapoos and Potowatomis in an embodied set of liturgical practices whose power resided in resiliency and adaptation to the historical forces of removal and settler missionization on Indigenous terms. When they later transcribed the symbols into alphabetic text, subsequent generations of congregants of Kenekuk's church treated this script as sacred, such that when an outsider like Milo Custer sought to transcribe it, elders stepped in to prohibit its use. To the Meskwakis in Iowa, it was a necessary medium of communication between those who had purchased a piece of land in Iowa to serve as their "settlement" (not a reservation) and those of their community who scattered across Kansas and Oklahoma.

By 1888, these Meskwaki scribes were sharing their literacy practices with diasporic Ho-Chunks who seemed—as Alice Fletcher put it, "eager to learn." That is because for those Ho-Chunks, now dispersed across Wisconsin, Nebraska, and South Dakota, "the native language syllabary the Ho-Chunk developed and refined from the late nineteenth to the mid-twentieth centuries was important. It provided families and friends with a way to communicate and maintain ties between Nebraska and Wisconsin through years of forced separation, persistent poverty, and cultural suppression. It contributed to the Ho-Chunk tribe's survival as a people."[96]

The writing of Great Lakes syllabary texts, like those in alphabetic scripts penned by the Haudenosaunees and members of the Oceti Sakowin, again demonstrate that script functions as much more than a mnemonic device, or the "salvage" mode of archiving tradition in the history of Indigenous communications practices. Writing in a vernacular script engenders a new set of social practices that often prove to be greater than the sum of their parts, offering Native communities innovative communications pathways between generations and within the contemporary moment of their inscription.

Coda

THE SOVEREIGN REALITY OF PHONEMES

Throughout this book, we have examined how Indigenous communities, when faced with developing written versions of their languages, often encountered an effect the linguist Edward Sapir called "the psychological reality of phonemes." In a 1934 essay of that title, Sapir argued that a phoneme (the smallest phonetic unit in a language that is capable of conveying a distinction in meaning) could not be "sufficiently defined in articulatory or acoustic terms but needs to be fitted into the total system of sound relations peculiar to the language." "To reduce speech to a simple physical process," as John Pickering and John Wesley Powell had done, was not enough. "In the physical world," Sapir reasoned, "the naïve speaker and hearer actualize and are sensitive to sounds, but what they feel themselves to be pronouncing and hearing are phonemes." That is, the lived world of a language was much more than the sum of its constituent phonetic parts. More importantly, phonemes played a crucial role in shaping language into socially "functional and aesthetically determinate shapes." There could be no artistry nor orature derived from texts written in strictly phonetic orthographies.[1]

Sapir discovered this important fact by listening to Native collaborators who worked alongside him to produce written forms of their communities' languages. He learned the lesson the hard way. When he tried to teach the standard orthographies to Native students, he found it "exceedingly difficult, if not impossible, to teach a native to take account of purely mechanical phonetic variations which have no phonemic reality for him." As a result, his Native teachers had to show him another way. With his Paiute consultant Tony Tillohash, for example, Sapir practiced saying the Paiute word for mother over and over again until he could reproduce the correct vowel length with his own vocal apparatus and write down its transcription accordingly. Sapir realized that "Tony was not 'hearing' in terms of the actual sounds"; he was "feeling" the language the way Paiute people from his community had felt it for generations. Sapir's epiphany crystalized on Vancouver Island where he worked with Alec Thomas, a member of Teseshet Nation. Calling Thomas "the most successful American Indian pupil I have had in practical phonetics,"

Sapir praised the young man's innovative approach to transcription. With Thomas's help, Sapir created an orthography that he deemed "phonologic in spirit throughout." It was "largely from a study of [Thomas's] texts" that Sapir finally "learned to estimate at its true value the psychological difference between a sound and a phoneme."[2]

Indigenous orthographies encode not just information but also the aural and performative regimes that obtain for spoken language and graphic images in their home communities. In this way, Native peoples worked to protect their vernacular languages from the reification imposed by inscription and print. They did so by reinvesting translation and transcription with what one anthropologist has called the "neglected sonic dimensions of social experience." More and more ethnographers, and even some literary historians, have begun to explore "the subject-creating dimensions of listening: an active and socialized process—one in which 'literacies of listening' are inculcated."[3] This book, in its own small way, has sought to invest the history of alphabetic and syllabary literacy practices in Native North America with these "literacies of listening" and their accompanying social and material practices. Thus, I close with a brief consideration of how these vernacular literacies have arrived in the twentieth and twenty-first centuries as critical elements of contemporary Native American fiction and poetry.

In an interview with the Canadian Broadcasting Company, Indigenous language educator Belinda Daniels of the Sturgeon Lake First Nations in Canada observed, "In order for a nation to exist, the Nehiyawak [Sturgeon Lake First Nations], for example, require five elements: land, culture, governance, people and a language."[4] A Native community's pursuit of language revitalization is intertwined with the other four elements of cultural survival Daniels cites—language embodies culture, enunciates governance, knits people together. Language is more than a medium of expression for these writers; it is a practice; it creates the sense of home. As a cultural technique, it unites kinship groups across time, mobilizes time-honored ceremonial and storytelling practices in new ways to meet new political obstacles, and in many cases is viewed as an organic outgrowth of an Indigenous homeland, grounding the speaker, writer, and listener in what the ethnographer Keith Basso has called "the wisdom of places."[5]

In the twentieth and twenty-first centuries, Indigenous writers, in both their native languages and English, have sought to realize the psychological and social realities of their own languages and to find ways to harness English to their own purposes. In *House Made of Dawn*, the novel that I used to provide our initial tableau for the uneasy relationship between the scripted word and Indigenous communities, N. Scott Momaday sought to use the vernacular language of his protagonist, a veteran from the Walatowa Pueblo, to clear a space for the scripted words of his own story so that they might function more like the oral recitations of traditional storytelling and thereby escape the stultifying fixity of print. *Dypaloh*, the story begins. It is a conventional expression used by Pueblo storytellers to begin, to set aside the discourse of everyday life for a place in which the storyteller may weave together words so as to construct a world. The novel ends with *Qtsedaba*, it is done. The story space is closed and language must return to its quotidian usage. These bracketing phrases work to clear, to cleanse, to open a space for discourse. They are the clearing in the woods where the Condolence Ceremony may begin. They are Black Elk's tipi and arbor, and Standing Bear's flaming rainbow tipi cover. They are Kenekuk's prayer sticks, and Sam Blowsnake's American Chief notebook. Without them, the North American Native writer is stranded in the either/or world of the printed word, their utterances hemmed in by associations with assimilation and violence. Especially if they write in English.

The Okanagan poet Jeanette Armstrong offers a clear-eyed articulation of the dilemma faced by the contemporary Indigenous intellectual. Armstrong is of the "opinion that Okanagan, my original language, constitutes the most significant influence on my writing in English." In addition to the "landed" nature of Indigenous languages that lie behind a Native writer's English literary works, Armstrong notes a profound difference in the way that nouns and images are understood and employed in Okanagan. In Okanagan, many "things" are more a verb than a noun, and when Armstrong employs this understanding to her English-language works, she "attempt[s] to construct a similar sense of movement and rhythm through sound patterns."[6] Her poem "Winds" exemplifies these practices:

Winds	moving			clouds
past		earth		sky
are		one		moves
around	me	silent		colors
drifting	sometimes	present		dark
with	soft		white	
			flakes	touching
life		rich	lacework	unknown
	hands		twined	with care
a place	forever	still	tracing	quietly
a line	stretched	to a	horizon	
fading			with time	and gently
ending		breath		

The influence of the Okanagan language on Armstrong's poetry goes beyond the morphological and syntactic elements. The way English is spoken on the Okanagan Reserve is considered a kind of dialect of the English language that, in its various forms, is known in Indian Country as "Rez English." Like Armstrong's poetic lines in English, "Okanagan Rez English has a structured quality semantically and syntactically closer to the way the Okanagan language is arranged," and Armstrong argues that "Rez English from any part of the country, if examined, will display the sound and syntax pattern of the area." She explains how this might work in the following example: "Trevor walked often to the spring to think and to be alone. Rez English would be more comfortable with a structure like this: Trevor's always walking to the spring for thinking and being alone. The Rez style creates a semantic difference that allows for a fluid movement between past, present, and future."[7] In both her Rez English usage and her ethnopoetic approximations of Okanagan verbal arts structures, Armstrong feels her "writing in English is a continual battle against the rigidity in English."

In a very different landscape and language located on the southern border of the United States, we find similar techniques in the Tohono O'odham Nation and the poetry of tribal member and linguist Ofelia Zepeda. Two of Zepeda's poetry collections, *Ocean Power* and *Jewed Jewed 'i-Hoi*, are compilations of bilingual O'odham/English verse. Many of Zepeda's poems "originated in the O'odham language," and when she offers an English counterpart, she cautions the reader that "they are not translations of the O'odham into English." She explains in the introduction to *Jewed Jewed 'i-Hoi*: "Written O'odham is a relatively new phenomenon" and employs an orthography "developed in the middle of the twentieth century by Albert Alvarez and Kenneth Hale." Sanctioned by the O'odham Nation, "It is the writing system most commonly used for classroom teaching. Literacy in the O'odham language is accessible only to young people in schools that offer O'odham language classes, and to adults who make the choice of becoming literate" (7–8). Thus, Zepeda's O'odham language poems stand in a unique relation to the verbal traditions that lie behind them. A case in point is her use of traditional songs to bring the rain to her desert homeland as a jumping off point for these two versions of "Cloud Song":

Ce: daghim 'o 'ab wu: sañhim.
To:tahim 'o 'ab wu: sañhim.
Cuckuhim 'o 'ab him.
Wepeghim 'o 'abai him.

Greenly they emerge.
In colors of blue they emerge.
Whitely they emerge.
In colors of black they are coming.
Reddening they are right here.[8]

As in Armstrong's verse, the O'odham language exerts a special morphological influence on its English counterpart. The repetitions of word ending auxiliaries common in O'odham to emphasize what is the "experiential" nature of nouns in the vernacular must be abandoned in the English version. Adverbial phrases shape the lines of the second version, adding a fifth to the four in O'odham. It is a choice that sacrifices the medial caesura/half-line of the O'odham song, but one that Zepeda feels is necessary to capture the movement, what Armstrong called "the experiential" nature of traditional verbal art.

A similar situation applies to writers of prose and hybrid forms of creative writing. Take, for example, *Black Eagle Child*, Ray A. Young Bear's autobiographical novel largely written in verse-like short lines.[9] Young Bear, a member of the Meskwaki and Sauk Nations of the Mississippi, describes the work as "a creative emulation," one that he believes is both a continuation of traditional storytelling, "word collecting," and vision and healing practices, as well as a "divergence," and a necessary transformation pressed on him by the "dynamic trends" of twentieth-century language use (both vernacular and English) by the "bilingual/bicultural worlds [he] lives in." Like Zepeda and Armstrong, Young Bear is wary of relying on mere translation to ground the aesthetic of Indigenous literature. That is because, for him, "the poetic forms I have adopted and adapted (from English, a second language) have little significance in the tribal realm."[10] The tribal writer's work, in Young Bear's mind, is a profoundly ambivalent one. In it, the artist must steer a precarious course between speaking that which is never to be spoken to outsiders, while collating the story worlds of his community into something viable for the current situation of the People of the Red Earth (Meskwakis).

Moreover, Young Bear sees the hegemonic nature of the English language at the heart of many of his community's social problems, which he fictionalizes in the novel. To subvert this kind of English-language usage, Young Bear allows his narrator to satirize the acronym-laden language of the US government and the Bureau of Indian Affairs. Speaking of his fellow tribal members as "separated from each other by infinite miles," the novel's protagonist comments,

> . . . while we all recognized the lineage abbreviations
> Got out of hand, we all resided in the same
> Hellhole. Provided no one made waves—be it
> And EBNO, and EBNAR (Enrolled But Not A Resident),
> BRYPU (Blood Related Yet Paternally Unclaimed),
> UBENOB (Unrelated By Either Name Or Blood),
> EBMIW (Enrolled But Mother Is White),
> And so forth . . .[11]

But by far the most common approach Young Bear uses to battle the linguistic hegemony of outsiders is code-switching from Meskwaki to English. Early in the novel, as protagonist Edgar Bearchild and his best friend Ted Facepaint race around the community with two other Indian friends from different nations, they toggle back and forth between Meskwaki *pa-pe-pi-po* and English:

> Ted Turned on the single headlight and wipers
> And pretended to strain for a look.
> "*A sa mi win a ni.* That's too much."
> "I know," I said, breaking into English
> For the benefit of the Ontarios.
> I was going to translate what I had just said,
> But Ted sensed my plans and cut me off.
> "*E ye bi me a tti mow a nit e bi ke me ko*
> *A ski ki wa sqwe se a wi ta bi ma ta.*"
> Before you say anything, the girl you
> Are sitting with is quite young.

Ted and Edgar's bilingual banter exemplifies the kind of linguistic play that Keith Basso defined as "code-switching" in Native verbal performances: "language alternations . . . [that] may be strategically employed as an instrument of metacommunication . . . an indirect form of social commentary."[12] It is a doubling as well, since the way Young Bear inscribes the Meskwaki language harks back to his ancestor's use of the *pa-pe-pi-po* in letters to Edgar Harlan, to the way that the syllabary had played (and continues to play) a vital role in language revitalization in the community.

Most recently, Nimiipuu (Nez Perce) writer Beth Piatote's multigenre collection, *The Beadworkers* employs the vernacular script of her Plateau community to make visible the "vanishing Indian" of settler colonial mythology, and to make *real* her Plateau homelands and its people in the face of debasing abstractions like "savage" and euphemisms like "removal." In "Feast II,"

The Sovereign Reality of Phonemes   225

Piatote explores this central feature of Indigenous writing when she recounts the true story of the Sinxit, a Plateau Native community the government of Canada declared extinct:

> A few years ago one of the unextinct Sinixt men killed an elk in his homelands. Then he called the game officials in Canada and turned himself in. They took the bait. When the province pressed charges against him for taking big game without a license, he pleaded not guilty. He cited his aboriginal rights to hunt in his own territory. And now that case is in court, and Canada will have to look at that man, standing in the middle of the room, and all his people around him, and Canada will have to admit that the Sinixt are not extinct.[13]

Here, several of the political elements that characterize Indigenous writing in North America come together. The settler discourse of willful misrecognition has rendered the Sinixt community invisible. But how to dismantle the rhetoric of erasure that has stolen their homelands and declared that they do not exist? The answer: use the rhetorical power of palimpsest. Let the reality of continued Indigenous traditions and Indigenous community cohesion "show through" the puppet trial of the settler court. In other parts of the book, however, Piatote draws on the vernacular language of her community to make present the linguistic and epistemic reality of the homelands of Plateau peoples.

The Beadworkers opens with a triptych that mirrors the Nimipuu creation story. Its first word, *kú.s*, the vernacular word for water, is the essence of the Nez Perce homeland. Over the course of its three "movements," Piatote's opening "Feasts" assembles the Nez Perce homeland in a lyrical catalog of its constitutive elements: *kú.s, nasó?x, wewúkiye, ?imes, lit'á.n, qémes, qá.ws, tims, cemí.tx* (water, salmon, service berries) without ever directly translating them. Instead, in each of the movements these vernacular elements of the homeland find meaning in lyrical contexts that do not define them but rather invoke them. *Kú.s* emerges as "the first taste of life," and then as the medium that bears the Nez Perce narrator, like "the entire ocean of words," back home. The other constituent parts of the homeland come into focus in similar fashion—*tims*, the Service Berries of the Plateau surface from the narrator's memory as she and her mother prepare them for canning; Coyote scatters all the remaining edible and medicinal plants, saying, "Here the Indian people will find them, and they will be happy."[14] Piatote thus crafts her collection so that "the words ... appear as themselves ... maintaining as much of the linguistic information as possible." For Piatote, "The process of language revitalization is a kind of restoration work, and is not only parallel to land restoration but of a piece with it." "I am proud of my language," she says, "and want it to take up space, to be seen and heard. It's important work to do."

Piatote traces her use of a scripted form of Nimiipuut, the language of the Nez Perce, to her education in a language revitalization program whose historical roots can be traced to orthographies generated by Catholic and Protestant missionaries as well as to "organic orthographies of folks who could/can speak and simply wrote/write things phoenetically." Like so many of the Indigenous orthographies explored in *Inscribing Sovereignties*, however, the scripts embody painful histories, for the territorial government employed them "to publish a set of 'laws' that laid out cruel punishments such as public flogging and hanging, to Nez Percé people for things like stealing cattle and fornication." Piatote notes that "because these laws were published in the language, their cruelty cuts especially deep. . . . What I think is important is to look at the language through its multiple texts and contexts and to be able to read all of the orthographies, and see the pulse and grammar of the language no matter how it is being used or recorded."[15]

For that reason, her use of a particular orthography signals a political stance toward the historical events recorded in their inscription. Although that choice is no longer much of an issue in the community, this was not always the case. "Going back to competing missions between the Catholics and the Presbyterians and the bitter factionalization that emerged during the fraudulent signing of the 1868 treaty and the Nez Perce War in 1877," Piatote comments, "deep, deep divisions between families [were] mapped onto writing systems. One's orthography was an expression of identity and lineage—you would be staking yourself with your family (and which side you were on) with every letter." Thankfully, she notes, "most people have gotten over the Orthography Wars in our community. Something that helped was the establishment of the Nez Perce Listserv by Phil Cash in the early 2000s. Someone wrote in that it didn't matter what orthography we used, we just had to work together on the language."

The work of Indigenous writers like Beth Piatote, Ray A. Young Bear, and Ofelia Zepeda demand reading strategies that recognize (in fact, insist on) the linguistic contexts for the poets' and storytellers' choices. Such an approach will enhance our understanding not only of each individual text but also of the larger context for all Native American literature as part of an ongoing and long-standing effort to express in print and alphabetic type the various verbal arts traditions of the more than 500 nations that reside in the United States today. The nations featured in this book are just a few examples. Even for writers who did not grow up as bilingual speakers, there remains a constant awareness of the vernacular-language performative traditions that still exist in many communities. For Indigenous writers of all backgrounds, it is "the pulse and grammar of the language" that animates their literary works, whether they are written in English or in the vernacular scripts of their respective communities.

ACKNOWLEDGMENTS

No book is the work of one individual, and this study of Indigenous orthographies, ten years in the making, is certainly no exception. My spouse of more than thirty years, Teresa Lopes, has supported me throughout the process and has read every word of the original manuscript, offering important suggestions that I have incorporated along the way. I have also received the support of many institutions and individuals without whom this book would not have been published. Research for this project was supported by a John Simon Guggenheim Memorial Fellowship in 2013, and by short-term fellowships from the American Philosophical Society, the Huntington Library, and the Newberry Library. At the American Philosophical Society, I was lucky enough to have worked with Brian Carpenter of the Indigenous Program. At the Newberry Library, Will Hansen, the Roger and Julie Baskes Vice President for Collections and Library Services, kindly answered all my questions and pointed me in the direction of sources in the library that I did not know about. A series of directors of the McNickle Center for the American Indian at the Newberry Library routinely aided me in my research and made my work available to their many outreach and education programs. I was blessed to have worked with Brian Hosmer, Scott Manning Stevens, Patricia Maroquin Norby, and Rose Miron in this capacity. I could not have researched the Lakota language and history that I drew upon for use in this book without the invaluable help of Craig Howe and the Center for Indigenous Research and Native Studies at Pine Ridge Reservation. Margaret Anne Noodin and Mike Zimmerman similarly helped me with Central Algonquian language materials, as did Professor Alan Corbiere of York University. Around the country, younger scholars in the fields of Indigenous studies and early American literature inspired me to do my best work, and I would like to recognize just a few of them here: Caroline Wigginton, Lisa Brooks, Hilary Wyss, Kelly Wisecup, Cristina Stancius, Drew Lopenzina, Dan Radus, and Amy Gore. At the University of Iowa, my longtime colleagues in Native American and Indigenous studies—Jacki Rand, Stephen Warren, Erica Prussing, and the late Michelene Pesantubbee—provided me a community of scholars and friends who taught me more than I can say about the study of Native history.

NOTES

Abbreviations
ABCFM-TR   American Board of Commissioners for Foreign Missions, Transcripts of letters from missionaries among the Indians of Minnesota, Dakota, and Oregon, 1830–78, Newberry Library, Chicago, IL
APS   American Philosophical Society Library and Museum, Philadelphia, PA
CHS   Colorado Historical Society, Denver, CO

Prelude
1. From William Bradford's manuscript "Of Plimoth Plantation," written between 1630 and 1651.
2. US Bureau of Indian Affairs, *Correspondence on the Subject of Teaching the Vernacular*, 20.

Introduction
1. A "Road Man" is an itinerant preacher of the Peyote religion.
2. Momaday, *House Made of Dawn*, 96–97.
3. Momaday, *House Made of Dawn*, 96–97.
4. Momaday, *House Made of Dawn*, 98.
5. See Hugh R. Mackintosh's discussion of the word *logos* in his book *The Doctrine of the Person of Jesus Christ*, 115–18.
6. The quote is Genesis 11:1, "And the whole earth was of one lip."
7. Thomas Williamson to Davis Greene, 1837, ABCFM-TR; Stephen R. Riggs to David Greene, October 1838, Stephen R. Riggs and Family Papers, 1837–1958, Minnesota Historical Society, St. Paul; Riggs, preface to *Grammar and History of the Dakota Language*, ii.
8. Wilson, *Essay on Bible Translation*, 9.
9. Storrs, *Conversion of the World*, 5.
10. It is useful to note that Momaday employs Tanoan language conventions at the beginning and end of his novel in order to mark out the story as akin to the "traditional" oral performative space similarly marked out by storytellers. Thus, all the events and narration within the book are figured as taking place, undergoing utterance in a sacred venue.
11. Daniels and Bright, *World's Writing Systems*, 577.
12. Daniels and Bright, *World's Writing Systems*, 578.
13. Lepsius, *Standard Alphabet*, 27.
14. Winford, *Introduction to Contact Linguistics*, 10–11, 34.
15. Müller, *Proposals for a Missionary Alphabet*, 1.
16. The idea of settler colonialism as a structure is based on Patrick Wolfe's often-quoted formulation in "Settler Colonialism and the Elimination of the Native," 387–409. Throughout this book, we will explore how discourses surrounding language ideologies participate in the structural maintenance of settler society through the disciplining of Indigenous languages. For a response that suggests how we might articulate the Indigenous structures at play in the settler colonial model, see Kauanui, "A Structure, Not an Event." On the presence of these language ideologies in the missionization of the Maya peoples, see also Hanks, *Converting Words*.

17. Kelsey, *Reading the Wampum*, xii.
18. Mithun, *Languages of Native North America*, 1.
19. Mithun, *Languages of Native North America*, 34.
20. Howse, *Grammar of the Cree Language*, 11; Rand, *Short Statement of Facts*, 112; McGuffey and Menaul, *Laguna Indian Translation*, 17.
21. Armstrong, "Land Speaking," 177.
22. Foster, "Language and Cultural History," 99. Foster explains, "the reconstruction of natural history terms provides a strong basis for inferring the location of a linguistic homeland."
23. Armstrong, "Land Speaking," 177.
24. Lyons, "There's No Translation for It," 130.
25. Basso, *Wisdom Sits in Places*, 7, 108.
26. Mithun, *Languages of Native North America*, 39. Early systems typically involved conventionalized symbols, though they were not usually associated with specific sounds.
27. Rand, *Short Statement of Facts*, 24.
28. Mithun, *Languages of Native North America*, 36.
29. In Lakota, the word for writing and books is *wowapi*, derived from the verb *owa*, to paint.
30. This discourse of "peoples without letters" could produce some startling paradoxes, as when John Wilson commented in *A Grammar of the Mpongwe Language*: "How an uncultivated people, like those of the Gaboon, could have come in possession of a language so beautiful and so philosophical in all of its arrangements is a question which cannot be easily answered" (viii).
31. Herrin, *Kenekuk*, 24.
32. Round, *Removeable Type*, 254.
33. Bonnell, *Translation of the Sioux*.
34. R. Williams, *Key into the Language of America*.
35. Lepsius, *Standard Alphabet*, 289.
36. Müller, *Proposals for a Missionary Alphabet*, 2, 26, 29.
37. Venuti, "Introduction," 171.
38. Venuti, "Introduction," 171.
39. Sebba, *Spelling and Society*, 83.
40. Barber, *Anthropology of Texts*, 71.
41. Cohen and Glover, *Colonial Mediascapes*, 4.
42. Gitelman, *Always Already New*, 7.
43. Pauketat, "Practice and History," 88.
44. Piquette and Whitehouse, *Writing as Material Practice*, 5.
45. Elkins, *Domain of Images*, 4.
46. Elkins, *Domain of Images*, 83.
47. See Walker and Sarbaugh, "Cherokee Syllabary," on the proof of Sequoyah's single-handed production of the symbol system.
48. Round, *Removable Type*, 127.
49. Bender, *Signs of Cherokee Culture*, 36.
50. Cushman, *Cherokee Syllabary*, 5; Round, *Removeable Type*, 126.
51. Cushman, *Cherokee Syllabary*, 5. Scott Lyons describes this "oral/literate binary" at the center of Native Americans' struggle for rhetorical sovereignty as "a scheme which seems to be based on Western stereotypes of the other." Lyons, "There's No Translation for It," 459.
52. Cushman, *Cherokee Syllabary*, 58, 59, 13.

53. Lyons, "There's No Translation for It," 449.
54. Lyons, "There's No Translation for It," 459.
55. Lyons, "There's No Translation for It," 457.
56. Warrior, *Tribal Secrets*, 101, 117. Warrior defines "intellectual trade routes" in *The People and the Word*.
57. McDougall and Nordstrom, "Ma ka Hana ka 'Ike," 99.
58. Gone, "'As if Reviewing His Life,'" 75–76.
59. Osorio, *Remembering Our Intimacies*, 89.
60. Teuton, *Deep Waters*, xix.
61. Cruikshank, *Social Life of Stories*, 41.
62. Kapchan, "Learning to Listen," 67.
63. Samuels et al., "Soundscapes," 15–66, 332–33. Veit Erlmann's introduction to a collection of essays on the subject profitably asks a simple question: "What of the Ethnographic Ear?" Like Samuels and his coauthors, Erlmann argues that studying the "sonic economies" of different societies allows us to understand more fully the continuum of semiotic messaging across the artificial divide we have created between seeing and hearing in different ethnographic contexts. Thus Erlmann's collection explores "how listening has come to play a role in the way people in modernizing societies around the globe deal with themselves as subjects in embodied sensory and especially auditory ways. Hearing and associated sonic practices, instead of being sequestered in their own domain . . . are seen to have worked in complicity with the panopticon, perspectivism, and commodity aesthetics, and all the other key visual practices of the modern era we know so much about." Erlmann, *Hearing Cultures*, 5. Most importantly for our study, Erlmann's collection emphasizes aural cultural studies as a way of "overcoming the hegemony of textual analogies" (3) and for "the need for the cultural and historical contextualization of auditory perception." The key contextualizations we offer in this book are those related to how the written and spoken work together in the formation of Indigenous orthographies.
64. Mooney, *Calendar History*, 238.
65. Mooney, *Calendar History*, 238.
66. Palmer, *Telling Stories the Kiowa Way*, 63ff.
67. Mooney, *Calendar History*, 239.
68. Samuels, "Truth and Stories," 62.
69. General Howard, as quoted in Samuels, "Truth and Stories," 62.
70. Nevins, *Lessons from Fort Apache*, 97.
71. Although Samuels has questioned the validity of indexing cultural continuity through language, his most recent work does not "dispense with the idea of indexical grounding." It instead "trace[s] out the complex ways in which contemporary cultural expressions are grounded," focusing on "the moral authority of tradition on the reservation" and "the continuity of feeling" that continues to link Apache language users to each other, regardless of other political differences they might have. Samuels, *Putting a Song on Top of It*, 8, 10–11.
72. Watt, *Don't Let the Sun Step Over You*, 50.
73. Watt, *Don't Let the Sun Step Over You*, 50.
74. Contact linguists call this effect diglossia. It occurs when "two related language varieties are employed in complementary distribution across different situations. In diglossic communities, one of the varieties, designated H(igh) language, is employed in more official, public domains such as government, education . . . while the other, designated the L(ow) language, is used in more private and informal domains."

Notes to Chapter 1

(Winford, *Contact Linguistics*, 112). Among the Western Apache at San Carlos, the missionaries codified a printed form of Apache language writing that was meant to stand as the H(igh) version of Apache, but extra-educational and ministerial social practices freely employed the Apache language in ways that militated against this form becoming the "standard" for speaking Apache.

75. Samuels notes of Britton Goode, "As a tribal council member from Seven Mile Wash in the 1950s, he was instrumental in the introduction of indoor toilets to homes on the reservation. He was an inveterate linguist, interpreter, and historian. Always attuned to the nuances of language, Goode worked with the Summer Institute of Linguistics on the Western Apache adaptation of the New Testament, and in this capacity, he enjoyed a close working relationship with the linguist Faith Hill." Samuels, *Putting a Song on Top of It*, 13.

76. Samuels, "Bible Translation and Medicine Man Talk," 538.

77. See also Silas John Edwards Papers, 12–21, in Harry Hoijer Collection, APS.

78. Basso, "A Western Apache Writing System," 20. Italics added.

79. "Texts—San Carlos Apache. Informant—Lewis Russell. Taken August 1933." David Mandelbaum Papers, MSS 497.3.H68, San Carlos Apache Texts, box 7, Harry Hoijer Collection, APS.

80. Samuels, "Bible Translation," 532.

81. Basso, "A Western Apache Writing System," 22.

82. Samuel Worcester, as quoted in American Philosophical Society, *Report of the Committee Appointed by the American Philosophical Society to Assist the Commission on Amended Orthography*, 1.

83. On the "Great Divide," see Lyons, "There's No Translation for It," 459; and Cohen and Glover, *Colonial Mediascapes*, 4ff.

84. Bauman, as quoted in Palmer, *Telling Stories the Kiowa Way*.

85. V. Deloria, *We Talk, You Listen*, 12.

86. Clifford, "Indigenous Articulations," 478.

87. Clifford, "Indigenous Articulations," 481.

88. Basso, *Wisdom Sits in Places*, 75.

89. V. Deloria, *We Talk, You Listen*, 13.

Chapter 1

1. Worcester, as quoted in American Philosophical Society, "Report of the Committee," 1.

2. Sebba, "Phonology Meets Ideology," 19–47.

3. Cassedy, *Figures of Speech*, 39. Cassedy's stimulating study of the transatlantic orthographic innovations and controversies for English in the transition from the eighteenth to the nineteenth centuries is illuminating for its recovery of long-forgotten orthographic experiments that shaped the way Americans understood spelling and its relationship to membership in a community.

4. Meriwether Lewis, "August 11, 1806," Journals of the Lewis and Clark Expedition, https://lewisandclarkjournals.unl.edu/item/lc.jrn.1806-08-11.

5. Davis, Houck, and Upton, "'Sett Out Verry Eairly Wensdy,'" 137–48.

6. In reimagining the role of orality in the emergent American public sphere of the nineteenth century, Sandra Gustafson asks, "What if oratory and not print was the defining genre of political modernity?" Gustafson, "American Literature," 471.

7. Priestly, *Course of Lectures*, 22; Asher Wright, *Elements of the English Languages*, 2nd ed., Rome, NY, 1842, Rare Books, Huntington Library, San Marino, CA.

8. Sorby, *Schoolroom Poets*, xvii, xxix.

9. Pratt, "The Advantages of Mingling Indians with Whites," 265.

10. Crain, *Story of A*, 4, 56.

11. See Le Jeune, *WAWA Shorthand Instructor*; Scott-Browne, *Scott-Browne's Text-Book*; and Kimball, *First Lessons in Tachigrafy*.

12. B. Foster, *Foster's System of Penmanship*, iii.

13. Kneeland, *Brief Sketch*, 3.

14. Smalley, *American Phonetic Dictionary*, v.

15. ABCFM, *Constitution, Laws and Regulation*, 2; *Phonetic Journal for 1853*, 2, APS.

16. See John S. Pulsipher, *Phonal Depot*, Orwigsburg, PA, 1848, APS: "In presenting a new specimen of the English language clothed in a new dress to your generous consideration . . . to simplify the orthography of the language by using a new set of characters; each character to have one invariable sound, and to adapt the orthography of all words to the sound as they are pronounced in good common parlance" (3).

17. According to Cherokee scholar Chris Teuton, the syllabary characters alluded to a graphic form that had been outlawed in the distant past because of its implication with witchcraft. Teuton, *Deep Waters*, 3.

18. See Walker and Sarbaugh, "Early History of the Cherokee Syllabary," on the proof of Sequoyah's single-handed production of the symbol system.

19. See Round, *Removable Type*, 148–49.

20. Perdue, *Cherokee Editor*, 12.

21. [Worcester], "Description of the Cherokee Alphabet," 181–84.

22. Watt, *Mormon Passage of George D. Watt*, 22.

23. A letter of Christopher Columbus, [between 1816 and 1899?], Incunabula Collection, Library of Congress, Washington, DC.

24. Murray, "Vocabularies," 595–96, 611–13. Murray has observed that missionary vocabularies' structural layout ("two columns of words on opposite sides of the page, separated by white space or punctuation") implies an essentially "metaphorical conception of translation in which languages may be switched but never mingled." Their strange, abstract rendering of conversations out of context, as "non-narrative, non-situated" dialogs, provide their readers "with the illusion of direct access to moments of history while rendering the vernacular of indigenous peoples something akin to the material artifacts displayed from an archaeological dig."

25. See Round, *By Nature and by Custom Cursed*, 216.

26. Wolfe, "Settler Colonialism," 387–409.

27. Tocqueville, *Democracy in America*, 29.

28. Sleeper-Smith, *Why You Can't Teach United States History*, 270.

29. Sleeper-Smith, *Why You Can't Teach United States History*, 271.

30. As O'Brien argues, "[New England] took the lead in this genre, and [a] writer there produced an enormous body of literature there in the nineteenth century. New Englanders dominated this culture of print, obsessed over its self-fashioned providential history, and defined itself as the cradle of the nation and seat of cultural power. Part and parcel of this self-fashioning is the genre of local history writing that became crucial in defining Indians out of existence." O'Brien, *Firsting and Lasting*, xii.

31. Gunn, *Ethnology and Empire*, x, 175.

32. Wolfe, "Land, Labor, and Difference," 866–905.

33. Dixon, *Personal Narrative*.

34. Rand, *Short Statement of Facts*, 24.

35. Atwater, *Writings*, 61.

36. Huhndorf, *Mapping the Americas*, 44.
37. US Department of the Treasury, *Report of the Secretary of the Treasury, on the Subject of Public Roads and Canals*.
38. Howe, *What Hath God Wrought*, 3.
39. Harvey, *Native Tongues*, 219.
40. Harvey, *Native Tongues*, 223.
41. Harvey, *Native Tongues*, 219.
42. Howe, *What Hath God Wrought*, 33.
43. D. Vine, *God Is Red*, 138. "A Broadside from Buffalo, NY," 1872, Printed Ephemera Collection, portfolio 134, folder 13, Library of Congress, Washington, DC.
44. Casey, *Two Years on the Farm*.
45. See Siegert, *Relays*.
46. Murray, "Vocabularies," 611, 616.
47. Rivett, *Unscripted America*, 237.
48. Du Ponceau, as quoted in Swiggers, "Philologists Meet Algonquin," 348. For an example of Du Ponceau's recommendations put into practice, see Naphegyi, *Album of Language*.
49. Pickering, *Essay on a Uniform Orthography*, 5, 7, 2, 3. Sean Harvey notes that Pickering's orthography became a missionary standard because "it promised a useful combination of relative precision with the familiarity and accessibility of the roman alphabet . . . within a decade, the American Board mandated that its missionaries use it." Harvey, *Native Tongues*, 9.
50. Pickering, *Essay on a Uniform Orthography*, 2–3, 5, 33.
51. Trumbull, *Best Method*, 3, 25.
52. Trumbull, *Best Method*, 4, 5, 6.
53. Trumbull, *Best Method*, 10, 13.
54. Powell, *Introduction*, 2.
55. Powell, *Introduction*, 2, 3.
56. Powell, *Introduction*, 3.
57. Powell, *Introduction*, 17.
58. Amory and Hall, *History of the Book*, 1:7, 12, 28.
59. T. Wilson, *Essay towards an Instruction of the Indians*, v, ix.
60. T. Wilson, *Essay towards an Instruction of the Indians*, ii–iii.
61. J. Brooks, "Six Hymns by Samson Occom," 94–95.
62. Warrior, *People and the Word*, 181.
63. White, *Middle Ground*, xxvi.
64. Calloway, *Pen and Ink Witchcraft*, 2, 5.
65. Amory and Hall, *History of the Book*, 1:512.
66. Calloway, *Pen and Ink Witchcraft*, 40–42.
67. Lyons, *X Marks*, 189, 25.
68. Calloway, *Pen and Ink Witchcraft*, 7.
69. Carl Van Doren, as quoted in L. Brooks, *Common Pot*, 229.
70. See Hampton, *Fictions of Embassy*.
71. Jefferson, *Notes on the State of Virginia*, 66.
72. Eastman, "Indian Censures the White Man," 556, 563.
73. ABCFM, *Constitution, Laws and Regulation*.
74. Ringwalt, *American Encyclopaedia of Printing*, 62.
75. Thornton, *Handwriting in America*.
76. Wyss, *English Letters and Indian Literacies*, 157.

77. Wyss, *English Letters and Indian Literacies*, 15, 183.
78. Wisecup, "Practicing Sovereignty."
79. See Frankel, *States of Inquiry*.
80. Gitelman, *Paper Knowledge*, 35.
81. Schools modeled on the plan soon opened in Philadelphia, New Haven, Pittsburgh, and Washington City (later Washington, DC), and the plan was employed from the founding of the New York City public school system in 1806.
82. Rayman, "Joseph Lancaster's Monitorial System," 402.
83. See Wyss, *English Letters and Indian Literacies*, note 32.
84. Rayman, "Joseph Lancaster's Monitorial System," 404.
85. Kaestle, *Pillars of the Republic*, 95.
86. Goodbird, *Goodbird the Indian*, 48.
87. Kaestle, *Pillars of the Republic*, 64.
88. Kaestle, *Pillars of the Republic*, 69, 71, 91–92.
89. Gallaudet, *Sermon*, 8.
90. Noah Porter voiced a similar point of view concerning literacy and books when he opened his text with the attention-getting example: "Were a South Sea islander to be suddenly taken up from his savage home and set down in one of the great cities of Europe,—among the many strange objects which he would see, one of the most incomprehensible would be the *public library*. The mystery of the library to the savage would be the books in it." Porter, *Books and Reading*, 18.
91. Margaret Ann Noodin, personal correspondence with the author, March, 2013.
92. J. Carr, S. Carr, and Schultz, *Archives of Instruction*, 129.
93. J. Carr, S. Carr, and Schultz, *Archives of Instruction*, 146, 81.
94. J. Carr, S. Carr, and Schultz, *Archives of Instruction*, 122.
95. J. Carr, S. Carr, and Schultz, *Archives of Instruction*, 143.
96. La Flesche, *Middle Five*, xv, xviii.
97. La Flesche, *Middle Five*, xvii, xix, xx.
98. La Flesche, *Middle Five*, 14.
99. La Flesche, *Middle Five*, 20.
100. La Flesche, *Middle Five*, 65–66. Even though La Flesche seeks to give the boys agency in his depiction of literacy education, he titles this chapter "Fraudulent Holidays" to suggest how the Indian students' "freedom" (they can play outside if they read aloud) is severely circumscribed by settler educational institutions. For an insightful discussion of how such poetry recitations served American settler social and cultural needs, see Sorby, *Schoolroom Poets*.
101. La Flesche, *Middle Five*, 151.
102. J. Carr, S. Carr, and Schultz, *Archives of Instruction*, 92.
103. See a transcript of the 1868 report, US Indian Peace Commission, *Annual Report*, 26–50.
104. The secondary literature on the Indian boarding schools is enormous. See especially, B. Johnson, *Indian School Days*; Lomawaima, *They Called It Prairie Light*; Mauro, *Art of Americanization*. For BIA publications directing teachers in literacy instruction, see US Bureau of Indian Affairs, *Course of Study for the Indian Schools*; US Office of Indian Affairs, *Easy Reading Lessons*; and *Teaching Indian Pupils to Speak English*.
105. Reuben, "Nez Perce Indians," 363.
106. Peabody, "Sarah Winnemucca's Practical Solution," 7.
107. Peabody, "Sarah Winnemucca's Practical Solution," 3, 17, 110–11.

Chapter 2

1. Gibson, *Concerning the League*, 139. Gibson's text recounts the actions of Tekanawita, the prophet known as the Peacemaker. According to the official history of the Haudenosaunee Confederacy, Tekanawita "was sent by the Creator to spread the *Kariwiio* or good mind. With the help of Hiawatha (also known as Aiionwatha or Hayehwatha), the Peacemaker taught the laws of peace to the Haudenosaunee people. Traveling from community to community they both succeeded in persuading the Chiefs of each nation to join in the Great League of Peace and founded the only government with a direct connection to the Creator." Haudenosaunee Confederacy, "Confederacy's Creation," accessed February 16, 2024, www.haudenosauneeconfederacy.com/confederacys-creation/.
2. Gibson, *Concerning the League*, 329–30.
3. Simpson, *Mohawk Interruptus*, 15.
4. Woodbury, *Onondaga/English Dictionary*, 126.
5. Richter, *Ordeal of the Longhouse*, 32.
6. Richter, *Ordeal of the Longhouse*, 48–49, 49.
7. Hale, *Iroquois Book of Rites*, 63; Tooker, "League of the Iroquois," 438.
8. Richter, *Ordeal of the Longhouse*, 41–42.
9. Aupaumut, "Narrative," 87; Abler, *Chainbreaker*, 52.
10. Hale, *Iroquois Book of Rites*, 63.
11. Gibson, *Concerning the League*, 347.
12. On the limitations of viewing wampum as a mnemonic device, see Monture, *We Share Our Matters*, 14.
13. Occom, *Collected Writings*, 102, 263.
14. Kelsey, *Reading the Wampum*, xii.
15. Monture, *We Share Our Matters*, 214.
16. Marge Bruchac, March, 2019, personal communication with the author. Cuoq defines these terms on the same page of his dictionary as: *Kahionha* = "rivière, fleuve"; *Kaionni* = "collier diplomatique, collier de porcelaine, de wampum."
17. Alfred, *Peace, Power, and Righteousness*, xii.
18. Simpson, *Mohawk Interruptus*, 15.
19. L. Smith, *Decolonizing Methodologies*.
20. Simpson, *Mohawk Interruptus*, 189, 109.
21. Simpson, *Mohawk Interruptus*, 109.
22. L. Brooks, *Common Pot*, 8–12.
23. L. Brooks, *Common Pot*, 43. Audra Simpson has criticized Brooks's formulation, inasmuch as it seems to downplay the inherent dynamism of Iroquoia. See Simpson, *Mohawk Interruptus*, 203n15.
24. For an image and discussion of this aspect of Aupaumut's embassy, see Round, *Removable Type*, 106–9.
25. Hale, *Iroquois Book of Rites*, 39.
26. See Walker, "Native Writing Systems," 158ff., for a summary description of how writing was used in Haudenosaunee and other communities.
27. S. Stevens, "Path of the King James Version of the Bible," 10.
28. Wright, *Go' wana gwa'... A Spelling Book in the Seneca Language*, 8.
29. Cuoq, *Lexique de la langue iroquoise*, 203. My translation.
30. Rivett, *Unscripting America*, 7.
31. S. Stevens, "Path of the King James Version of the Bible," 7, comments as follows:

Once the Society for the Propagation of the Gospel in Foreign Parts, or SPG as it is commonly known, was established in 1701 as the officially sanctioned missionary organization of the Church, we begin to see clearly the union of British imperial policy with that of the church. From its very instantiation, the SPG was alert to the strategic importance of Christian converts among Britain's aboriginal allies. The unofficial motto of the Society might have justly been characterized as "fur, flag, and faith." This trinity of trade, national expansion, and evangelizing was long in coming when we compare Spanish and French efforts in the same arenas.

32. Merrell, *Into the American Woods*, 191–93, 219–20. See also Calloway, *Pen and Ink Witchcraft*, 38–41.
33. Hale, *Iroquois Book of Rites*, 43.
34. The location probably had spiritual meaning. See MacLeitch, *Imperial Entanglements*, 73.
35. Richter, *Ordeal of the Longhouse*, 257.
36. Weiser, *Johan Friederich Weisers Buch*, 29.
37. Preston, *Texture of Contact*, 73, 18–19, 78, 158, 288.
38. Daniel Claus came to America in 1749 and journeyed the next year to the Mohawk River Valley, where he engaged in the study of the Iroquois language. After acquiring proficiency in its use, he was often employed as an interpreter. He took part in the Lake George campaign, sometimes serving as a scout; and in 1776 he obtained a captain's commission. The following year he married Sir William Johnson's eldest daughter, Nancy. For a number of years he was deputy agent of Indian affairs in Canada. His handwritten memoir appears in the Claus Family Papers, C-1484, Manuscript Division, Public Archives of Canada, Ottawa, ON.
39. Preston, *Texture of Contact*, 167.
40. MacLeitch, *Imperial Entanglements*, 73.
41. MacLeitch, *Imperial Entanglements*, 85.
42. Johnson, *Papers*, 2:69. See Johnson's use of the Condolence Ceremony, 79–80.
43. David Preston believes that "one of the issues was the disposition of the remaining Indian land" and that local Mohawks refused to sell more land to settlers. Another was that the mixed group of Native peoples living there at the time—Tuscaroras and Delawares and Oneidas—presented an unusual social group to knit together, even with the power of the Condolence Rite. He argues that "David was killed by American forces right at the start of the war, late '76 or early '77." Preston, *Texture of Contact*, 194.
44. M. Foster, *From the Earth to Beyond the Sky*, lix.
45. Lydecker, *Faithful Mohawks*, 37. In a subsequent letter, Andrews mentions having sent back to England a manuscript of the Church Catechism in Mohawk, and he asks that a few horn books in "Indian" be printed.
46. Pascoe, *Two Hundred Years of the S.P.G.*, 140.
47. Norton, *Journal of Major John Norton*, 264.
48. Robert Langan to Daniel Claus, January 13, 1785, Claus Family Papers, C-1478, Manuscript Division, Public Archives of Canada, Ottawa, ON.
49. John Deserontyon to Daniel Claus, May 8, 1780, Claus Family Papers, C-1478, Manuscript Division, Public Archives of Canada, Ottawa, ON.
50. Tooker, "League of the Iroquois," 426. Colin Calloway (*American Revolution in Indian Country*, 153), writes:

> The problem of finding new homes for the Indian Loyalists proved ... difficult. Brant sought land for his refugees and expected the British government to honor its promises. The Senecas offered the Mohawks land in the Genesee Valley, but the Mohawks [did not wish] to return to the United States. The British proposed a grant of lands on the Bay of Quinté, ... but the Senecas felt increasingly vulnerable ... and objected to the Mohawks "seeking an asylum so great a distance from our Abodes." Brant then asked for six miles of land on either side of the length of the Grand River in Ontario. Haldimand, acknowledging that the war and peace had cost the Iroquois their homelands, agreed to Brant's request. ... John Deserontyon and his people accepted a 92,000-acre tract of lands at the Bay of Quinté and became known as the Tyendinaga Mohawk. Brant later accused Deserontyon of fomenting divisions within the nation.

51. Daniel Claus to Frederick Haldimand, December 15, 1783, Claus Family Papers, C-1478.
52. Lachine Community to Daniel Claus, January 8, 1784, Claus Family Papers, C-1478.
53. Hewitt, "Introduction," 89.
54. Hewitt, "Introduction," 89.
55. Audra Simpson makes a similar observation about Hewitt's treatment of the people who live at Kahnawake: [Hewitt] termed them "'mission Indians' or 'praying Indians' those who were, according to Hewitt, 'confused about their culture.'" Simpson, *Mohawk Interruptus*, 94.
56. Daniel Claus to Robert Mathews, August 1784, Claus Family Papers, C-1478.
57. John Deserontyon to Daniel Claus, August 23, 1783. Claus Family Papers, C-1478.
58. Deserontyon, *Mohawk Form of Ritual*, 96.
59. Hewitt, "Introduction," 93–94.
60. Parker, *Parker on the Iroquois*, 2.
61. Parker, *Code of Handsome Lake*, 15.
62. Parker, *Code of Handsome Lake*, 9.
63. Parker, *Life of General Ely S. Parker*, 296.
64. Oberg, *Peacemakers*, 163, 138.
65. Shimony, *Conservatism among the Iroquois*, 192.
66. Parker, *Code of Handsome Lake*, 7.
67. Parker, *Code of Handsome Lake*, 6.
68. Mt. Pleasant, "After the Whirlwind," 143.
69. Mt. Pleasant, "After the Whirlwind," 173–74.
70. Mt. Pleasant, "After the Whirlwind," 14.
71. Abler, "Protestant Missionaries and Native Culture," 29.
72. Fenton and Wright, "Seneca Indians," 308.
73. Fenton and Wright, "Seneca Indians," 316.
74. See, for example, John Jacket, Udo J. Keppler, and William Nelson Fenton, "Words to the Ganoda Chant of the 'Little Water Society' Niga niga ah / [between 1849 and 1870] / Written by John Jacket, direct descendant of Red Jacket," 1849, MS 443, Edward A. Ayer Manuscript Collection, Newberry Library, Chicago, IL.
75. Parker, *Code of Handsome Lake*, 6.
76. Parker, *Code of Handsome Lake*, 6.
77. Parker, *Code of Handsome Lake*, 3.
78. Parker, *Code of Handsome Lake*, 6.

79. Wallace lists several abridged or shortened versions: an Allegany Seneca version recorded by the Christian Benjamin Williams, probably from Governor Blacksnake, Handsome Lake's nephew and apostle, ca. 1846; a Seneca version of Jimmy Johnson, as recorded in several drafts by Ely Parker for Lewis Henry Morgan, at Tonawanda, October 1848. Wallace, *Death and Rebirth*, 341n2. Wallace also reports the existence of "at least three untranslated versions of the Code filed with the BAE," an untranslated text from the New York Onondaga at the Syracuse University Library, copies of which are held by APS and BAE (Bureau of American Ethnology), a Grand River Onondaga text, BAE MS 449, dated c. 1889; a Grand River Mohawk text from Seth Newhouse, BAE MS 3489, dated c. 1880; and one more New York Onondaga text BAE MS 2585, dated c. 1908.

80. Beauchamp, *Civil, Religious, and Mourning Councils*, 352.

81. Hymes argues that "persons growing up in the community in question acquire a grasp of the structures and functions of the genre, such that they are able to judge instances as appropriate or inappropriate not only in terms of overt formal features ('surface structure') but also in terms of underlying relations ('deep structure')." Hymes, *In Vain*, 276. In the case of the manuscripts written to accompany the Code of Handsome Lake and the Condolence Ceremony, it seems that the repetition of vocables and other patterns that Euro-American editors and ethnographers did not find worthy of copying in print editions of these works were in fact critical to the Indigenous performers and auditors who used them, recognizing that alphabeticism did not change the genre in any fundamental way when these vocables and other patterns were correctly inscribed.

82. All quotations from Chainbreaker are from Thomas Abler's 2005 edition of *Chainbreaker*, except those in which manuscript practice are at issue. These manuscript examples are taken from Benjamin Williams, "Life of Governour Blacksnake" (16-F-107-219), Joseph Brandt Papers, Lyman C. Draper Manuscripts, Wisconsin Historical Society, Madison. The page numbers I use to describe Williams's scribal practice thus refer to the hand-lettered pagination Draper provided for the narrative. Draper did not begin his pagination of the "Life" on page one, but rather numbers it cumulatively, as part of the larger collection he titles, the Joesph Brant Papers.

83. Abler, *Chainbreaker*, 8.

84. Abler, *Chainbreaker*, 17.

85. Abler, *Chainbreaker*, 227–28.

86. Parker, *Code of Handsome Lake*, 6.

87. B. Williams, "Life of Governour Blacksnake," 203–15.

88. B. Williams, "Life of Governour Blacksnake," 203–15.

89. Abler, *Chainbreaker*, 10–11.

90. Monture, *We Share Our Matters*, 17.

91. Fenton, "Seth Newhouse's Traditional History and Constitution of the Iroquois Confederacy," 145.

92. Monture, *We Share Our Matters*, 69.

93. Seth Newhouse, preface, 1, Cosmology of De-Ka-na-wi-da's Government of the Iroquois Confederacy, 1885, MSS 970.3.IR6, Seth Newhouse, 1842–1921, APS.

94. Monture, *We Share Our Matters*, 70.

95. Monture, *We Share Our Matters*, 71.

96. Simpson, *Mohawk Interruptus*, 222n36.

97. Campisi and Hauptman, "Talking Back," 444.

98. Campisi and Hauptman, "Talking Back," 444.

99. "Recollections of the WPA Oneida Language and Folklore Project, 1938–1941," 230–31, box 63, Floyd Glen Lounsbury Papers, ca. 1935–98, MS Coll. 95, APS.

100. "Recollections," 232.

101. Because the French had first drafted their alphabet for Mohawk learners, the first alphabet Oneidas used was imperfect, and did not recognize the fundamental fact that Oneida does not use the [r] sound. Thus, in early Oneida writing, the r is used for an l. Similarly, it employed <t> to represent both [d] and [t], different sounds in the Haudenosaunee languages. Despite its limitations, this system was in place for two hundred years.

Chapter 3

1. DeMallie, *Sixth Grandfather*, 8.
2. DeMallie, *Sixth Grandfather*, 5.
3. DeMallie, *Sixth Grandfather*, 7.
4. In 1931, Black Elk recalled his motives for joining the Wild West show. See DeMallie, *Sixth Grandfather*, 245:

> I wanted to see the great water, the great world and the ways of the white men; this is why I wanted to go. So far I looked back on the past and recalled the peoples' ways. They had a way of living, but it was not the way we had been living. I got disgusted with the wrong road that my people were doing now and I was trying to get them to go back on the good road, but it seemed as though I couldn't induce them, so I made up my mind I was going away from them to see the white man's ways. If the white man's ways were better, why I would like to see my people live that way.

5. DeMallie, *Sixth Grandfather*, 10.
6. The translation is by DeMallie, *Sixth Grandfather*, 8.
7. DeMallie, "Black Elk in the Twenty-First Century," 596.
8. While it is true that Alfred Riggs would publish a primer with *Wicoie* in the title, Lakota usage of the word *iapi* always refers to "talk"—that is, social parlance. See Riggs, *Wicoie Wowapi kin*.
9. DeMallie, *Sixth Grandfather*, 11.
10. See Parks and DeMallie, "Plains Indian Native Literatures," xx.
11. DeMallie, *Sixth Grandfather*, 29, 32.
12. DeMallie, *Sixth Grandfather*, 30.
13. US Congress, *U.S. Statutes at Large*, 328.
14. Pexa, *Translated Nation*, 6.
15. Arndt, "No Middle Ground," 27. Unlike Richard White's famous formulation of the pays d'en haut as a "middle ground . . . a spatial metaphor, [conflating] the process of expedient and creative misunderstanding and . . . actual space" (White, *Middle Ground*, 10), these reconceptualizations of colonial American space are topographically more expansive, traversing the Great Lakes–Plains boundary White's study refused to cross (P. Deloria, "What Is the Middle Ground," 21). Just as important, they are more chronologically expansive, moving past White's end-date for the "middle ground" of the pays d'en haut to consider the way Native peoples continued to draw sustenance from these Native spaces long after the infrastructures of European colonialism had snuffed out the creative give and take, or "purposeful misunderstandings" that enabled negotiation and improvisation. They are also more Native-centered, emphasizing the "ground" of encounter more than White's work, defining it more concretely, rooted to specific landforms, histories, and cultural practices that predate encounter with Europeans. For many such historians, the

"ground" of encounter was always already invested with Indigenous meaning, culture, and built environments.

16. Child, *Holding Our World Together*, xviii.

17. See Sleeper-Smith, "Women, Kin, and Catholicism." On Native numerical superiority and other advantages, see Witgen, *Infinity of Nations*, 5–6.

18. Most of the missionaries were under thirty years of age, educated in Protestant theological seminaries like Andover, Lane, Western, and Union. "The majority of ABCFM missionaries came from New England, New York, and the old Northwest, especially Ohio, Indian and Illinois . . . it was headquartered in Boston, grew out of New England Congregationalism, and drew its members from revivals that influenced the northern sections of the country . . . and 1845 Board report called slavery a debased system." Clemmons, *Conflicted Mission*, 25.

19. Pond, "Narrative of Samuel Pond."

20. Pond, "Narrative of Samuel Pond," 17, 20.

21. See Pond, "Narrative of Samuel Pond," 22–23:

> Maj [Lawrence] Taliaferro was then in Pennsylvania but a sub agent, named [Horatio] Grooms, permitted us to occupy a vacant room in one of the agency houses, but not rent free, and from him we received no encouragement. We had not been there long before Maj Bliss sent his orderly requiring us to appear before him and give an account of ourselves. I of course obeyed the mandate, and he told me it was his duty to exclude from the Indian Country all who were not authorized to be here. . . . These little things may seem now hardly worth relating, but whether we were to stay here or be driven away depended on the result of that interview with the Major. We were in fact . . . the missionaries of the [American] Board [of Commissioners for Foreign Missions] did not come here without authority from the Secretary of war. Major [Joseph] Plympton, who succeeded Maj. Bliss in command, received orders to remove all persons from this region who were not authorized to be here, but we were not molested. From the time of my first interview with M[a]jor Bliss both he and Mrs Bliss were our true friends, and when I returned from Kaposia they invited me to reside in their family, and instruct their son, a boy eight or ten years old, but I had other work to do.

22. By 1842, the ABCFM had begun to mandate the use of maps during sermons as a way for their donors to visualize "the Evangelical condition of the World," charting "every country on the globe destitute of protestant Christianity, with a surface dark as India ink could make it." ABCFM, *On the Use of Missionary Maps*, 10.

23. Nord, as quoted in *Conflicted Mission*, 19.

24. Riggs, *Grammar and Dictionary of the Dakota Language*, xix.

25. Clemmons, *Conflicted Mission*, 57.

26. Nystuen and Lindeman, *Excavation of Fort Renville*, 23. The spatial dynamic of this first missionary outpost to the Dakotas was telling. Whereas Renville's home was a twenty-seven by twenty-two-foot chinked log structure, divided by partitions into three rooms, Williamson's was a forty-two by twenty single room, where he lived with his wife for a year while a mission home was built for him outside the Renville compound.

27. Frémont, *Memoirs of My Life*, 36; Riggs, "Dakota Portraits," 536.

28. Hodge, *Handbook of American Indians*, 1:711; Pond, "Narrative of Samuel Pond," 321. Riggs comments, "It must be admitted that the Tokadantee was regarded as quite a family institution; and it was cherished and nourished with quite as much pride by the female, as by the male, part of the family." Riggs, "Dakota Portraits," 536.

29. Clemmons comments, "the ABCFM's strict requirements for conversion and continued church membership made it extremely difficult for Dakotas to become, and remain, church members. Additionally, those few Dakotas who joined the church refused to play a subservient role; rather they demanded to have a voice in church policy and membership." *Conflicted Mission*, 67.

30. Thomas Smith Williamson to David Green, August 14, 1837, ABCFM-TR.

31. Mithun, *Languages of Native North America*, 238.

32. White Hat, *Reading and Writing*, 3.

33. White Hat, *Reading and Writing*, 1.

34. White Hat, *Reading and Writing*, 7, 11.

35. Riggs, *Ta-koo Wah-kan*, 162–63.

36. Riggs, *Mary and I*, 54, 59, 162–63.

37. Riggs, *Ta-koo Wah-kan*, 16.

38. Riggs, "Dakota Portraits," 538.

39. Pond, "Narrative of Samuel Pond," 85.

40. Huggins, diary entry, May 27, 1839, 35, Alexander G. Huggins and Family Papers, 1833–1976, Minnesota Historical Society, St. Paul, MN.

41. Pond, "Narrative of Samuel Pond," 277, 279.

42. Nystuen and Lindeman, *Excavation of Fort Renville*, 31, 23. The researcher at the site concluded, "the artifacts recovered at Fort Renville are typical of the 1826 to 1846 period. . . . As Renville was trading with the Indians, native artifacts were anticipated within the stockade. Those recovered exemplify early and mid-nineteenth-century Dakota Indians" (36).

43. In their early letters to ABCFM overseers, the missionaries often claimed that alphabetic literacy was desired more as a response to imposed distances of the now disjointed Minnesota territory of the Dakotas, who were separated by many miles into small enclaves of land after the Prairie du Chien treaty. Writing in 1850, Riggs commented, "At present the Dakotas are both too near together and too far apart to be operated on effectively. They are too near together as they live in villages; and too far apart, in most instances as regards the villages themselves. There are many evils resulting from their gregarious habits. Idleness is encouraged. A great deal too much time is spent in feasting, dancing and gaming of all kinds. Besides, where there is a village of any considerable size, their planting grounds must necessarily be limited." "Outlines of a Plan for Civilizing the Dakotas," June 1850, ABCFM-TR.

44. Thomas Smith Williamson to David Greene, January 24, 1843, MSS 141, no. 40, ABCFM-TR.

45. Stephen Riggs to ABCFM, September 27, 1839, ABCFM-TR.

46. Eagle Help (Wamdiyokiye) to Thomas Smith Williamson, [before August, 1837], MSS 141, no. 40, ABCFM.

47. Stephen Riggs to David Greene, August 23, 1842, ABCFM-TR.

48. Thomas Smith Williamson to David Green, February 8, 1842, MSS 141, no. 70, ABCFM-TR. "In the first part Wakantonka [sic] the name for God is written as two words in the latter part as one. I wish it be printed as one throughout. . . . I have translated Genesis direct from the Hebrew consulting on the difficult passages not only the English and French, but the Greek of the 70 and Vulgate Latin versions."

49. Riggs, *Tah-koo Wah-kan*, 161–63, 410; Stephen Riggs to David Greene, October 1838, ABCFM-TR.

50. Pond, "Narrative of Samuel Pond," 279.

51. See Fitzgerald, Kuwada, and Round, "Pilgrims in Print"; Bunyan, *Cante teca*.

52. Stephen Riggs to James M. Gordon, May 5, 1858, MSS 244, no. 359, ABCFM-TR.
53. Pond, "Narrative of Samuel Pond," 280.
54. See Clemmons, *Conflicted Mission*, 123.
55. Red Shirt, *George Sword's Warrior Narratives*, 275n6.
56. Stephen Riggs to S. B. Treat, January 21, 1863, ABCFM-TR.
57. Thomas Smith Williamson to S. B. Treat, December 1862, MSS 310, no. 226, ABCFM-TR.
58. Riggs and Howard, *Sunset to Sunset*, 126.
59. Riggs, *Tah-koo Wah-kan*, 342.
60. Riggs, *Tah-koo Wah-kan*, 343.
61. John Peacock, as quoted in Canku and Simon, *Dakota Prisoner of War Letters*, xix.
62. John Peacock, as quoted in Canku and Simon, *Dakota Prisoner of War Letters*, xxvi.
63. Canku and Simon, *Dakota Prisoner of War Letters*, 54.
64. Canku and Simon, *Dakota Prisoner of War Letters*, 55, 59.
65. Canku and Simon, *Dakota Prisoner of War Letters*, 105.
66. Pexa, *Translated Nation*, 11.
67. Anderson, *Through Dakota Eyes*, 264.
68. Riggs, *Tah-koo Wah-kan*, 491.
69. Ostler, *Plains Sioux*, 54.
70. Catholics "achieved exclusive rights over Grand River (Standing Rock), establishing a mission in 1876; Episcopalians got Red Cloud (Pine Ridge and Rosebud), and Cheyenne River, the Congregationalists in 1872." Ostler, *Plains Sioux*, 57.
71. Ostler, *Plains Sioux*, 123, 125. Godfrey was from Colorado and a personal friend of Henry Teller, the secretary of interior.
72. Ostler, *Plains Sioux*, 174.
73. Reilly, *Bound to Have Blood*, 42–43.
74. Reilly, *Bound to Have Blood*, 40.
75. McLaughlin, *Lakota War Book*.
76. Letter of September 21, 1889, from "Frank" and eyewitness to "Joe," Little Fingernail Book Collection, MSS 1006, CHS.
77. Letter of September 21, 1889.
78. McLaughlin, *Lakota War Book*, 12.
79. McLaughlin, *Lakota War Book*, 12.
80. McLaughlin, *Lakota War Book*, 67–68.
81. "The *chanupa* (pipe) is understood as an object through which one can communicate with nonhuman spirits or forces. It is not merely a sacramental device, as is, say, a Christian chalice. It is through the pipe that *Woh'pe* can 'hear . . . prayers' and an instrument to 'send your voices' to greater powers through the loading of prayers into the bowl and the release of the smoke into the air." In this context, *Woh'pe* refers to White Buffalo Calf Woman, a figure of great cultural importance to the Lakota. It was she who gave them the sacred pipe (the *chanupa*). Grant, "Writing 'Wakan,'" 67. Grant terms the pipe a "rhetorical object" and thus a form of media.
82. Utley, in *Last Days of the Sioux Nation*, acknowledges the legitimacy of DeMallie's withering critique of such approaches. DeMallie had singled out Utley's work as part of a body of historiography that wrongly "implies that there was some fundamental similarity between the native religions of the Paiutes and the Lakotas," thus underestimating "the significance of the vast cultural differences between these two tribes." DeMallie was also critical of the way such interpretations "treat the ghost dance

as an isolated phenomenon, as though it were divorced from the rest of Lakota culture. The ghost dance needs to be seen as part of the integral, ongoing whole of Lakota culture and its suppression as part of the historical process of religious persecution led by Indian agents and missionaries against the Lakotas living on the Great Sioux Reservation." DeMallie, "Lakota Ghost Dance," 403.

83. Utley, *Last Days of the Sioux Nation*, 40–41.

84. Ostler, *Plains Sioux*, 86. See also 191, 237. In *Wives and Husbands*, Fowler outlines how social cohort analysis of Plains tribal communities (across gender and both traditional and newly implemented social roles) helps us understand such communities' political responses to colonialism as much more nuanced than Utley's original narrative would suggest.

85. Henkin, *Postal Age*, 42.

86. Walker, "Native Writing Systems," 38.

87. The scholarship on Indian boarding schools is very extensive. See, for example, Adams, *Education for Extinction*. These dislocations were slowly terminated in some areas by "acts passed in 1894 and 1895 [that] prohibit[ed] Indian children being sent to a school not in the state in which they reside without the written consent of the parent, guardian, or next of kin." Schmeckebier, *Office of Indian Affairs*, 71.

88. "In 1860 the first reservation boarding school was opened on the Yakima Reservation, in Washington, . . . Indian pupils were first sent to the public schools in 1890, but only during the last twenty years have these schools been utilized to a large extent. The missionary schools, known as 'contract' schools, reached their greatest extent in the fiscal year 1892, when over $600,000, or more than one-fourth of the total appropriation for education, was expended in this way." Beginning in 1896 the sum expended for contract schools was gradually decreased. Schmeckebier, *Office of Indian Affairs*, 57.

89. "'Traditionalists,' on the other hand, tended to be cultural conservatives wary of sending their children away to be immersed in a foreign culture. Some tried to keep their children out of school altogether, but most preferred day schools," Andrews, "Turning the Tables on Assimilation," 428. DeGrey is listed on the January 15, 1876, report of employees as one of the "half-breed Indians." Series 179: School Reports, August 1, 1882 to May, 29 1936, Records of the Bureau of Indian Affairs, RG 75, National Archives and Records Administration, Kansas City, MO.

90. See DeMallie, *Sixth Grandfather*, 15.

91. Ostler, *Plains Sioux*, 54.

92. Quoted in Schmeckebier, *Office of Indian Affairs*, 252, Indian Commissioner Morgan wrote,

> The ration system is the corollary of the reservation system. To confine a people upon reservations where the natural conditions are such that agriculture is more or less a failure and all other means of making a livelihood limited and uncertain, it follows inevitably that they must be fed wholly or in part from outside sources or drop out of existence. This is the situation of some of the Indian tribes today. It was not always so. Originally and until a comparatively recent period the red man was self-supporting. Leading somewhat of a nomadic life, he roamed with unrestricted freedom over the country in pursuit of game, which was plentiful, or located upon those spots fitted by nature to make his primitive agriculture productive. All this is changed.

93. Ostler, *Plains Sioux*, 144.

94. Circular, January 1875, series 2, Bureau of Indian Affairs, RG 75, National Archives and Records Administration, Kansas City, MO.

95. Ostler, *Plains Sioux*, 146.

96. An 1875 BIA circular asks, "Would the organization of an armed Indian Police, under proper restrictions and discipline, for the enforcement of order, arrest of criminals, and the prevention of incursions of evil-disposed persons on your reservation, prove safe and advisable; and to what extent would such an organization supercede the necessity of a military force?" Series 2, Records of the Bureau of Indian Affairs, RG 75, National Archives and Records Administration, Kansas City, MO.

97. Schmeckebier, *Office of Indian Affairs*, 113.

98. Indian Commissioner Morgan, as quoted in Ostler, *Plains Sioux*, 131.

99. The Lakota Ghost Dance (in Lakota, *wanagi wacipi*—literally, "spirit dance") was a round dance derived from dances performed by Paiute communities in response to visions of a holy man named Wavoka. Both men and women joined hands and danced around a sacred tree, singing newly composed songs until they literally fell down into a trance. Later, they reported seeing dead relatives living in a flourishing world with plentiful buffalo. Some form of this dance was imported by Cheyenne, Arapaho, and Kiowa who had visited the Paiute prophet and returned to their home communities with instructions on how to proceed. Each tribal group took a somewhat different approach to the ceremony. DeMallie, in *Sixth Grandfather*, notes "the extreme importance that the Lakotas of 1890 placed on the dance, as well as the extent to which its suppression has served in later years as a symbol of white oppression [suggests that] . . . for the Lakotas the dance was a symbol of religion, a ritual means to spiritual and physical betterment. Even Lakota nonbelievers accepted the religious motivation of the ghost dance" (391ff).

100. Mooney, *Ghost Dance*, 654.

101. DeMallie, *Sixth Grandfather*, 12. The best descriptions of earlier prophetic movements appear in Dowd, *Spirited Resistance*, and Saunt, *New Order of Things*.

102. Ostler, *Plains Sioux*, 262, characterizes the Ghost Dance thus: "a movement that constituted an ideological, and in many ways, direct challenge to US authority." Thomas Overholt's groundbreaking 1974 study of the Ghost Dance points out that "the act of prophecy is not static, but dynamic" and that "its dynamism is usually ignored in discussions of how events at Wounded Knee developed." Overholt was especially interested in the way that the supernatural and the historical intersect and reinforce each other in such movements: "The prophetic process is defined as one of reciprocal interaction and adjustment between a minimum of three distinct actors or groups: the supernatural, the prophet, and the people to whom the prophet's message is addressed. This interaction takes place within a concrete historical-cultural situation, which is reflected both in the prophet's message and his auditors' evaluation of it." The fact that a minority of Lakota participated in the Ghost Dance seems to confirm Overholt's belief that prospective participants "in coming to their decision . . . will in effect test the cultural 'competence' of that message by deciding whether or not it is in continuity with the broad cultural tradition and congruous with the current socio-political situation." Overholt, "The Ghost Dance of 1890," 58.

103. "In all states the illiteracy rate for all Indians is materially greater than the rate for all classes of the rural population." Schmeckebier, *Office of Indian Affairs*, 200.

104. Ostler describes the government's "20 to 25% reduction in [agency] beef rations" in 1890. Ostler, *Plains Sioux*, 238. He remarks that "the winter of 1889–1890 was especially hard. There was not enough to eat and diseases like influenza and whooping cough claimed many lives" (239).

105. DeMallie, *Sixth Grandfather*, 258.

106. "Isna Toka Kte to Wamniyomni Cigala," 1889, Nebraska State Historical Society, Kills Enemy Alone, RG 4946. The accompanying translation of the letter is as follows:

> Little Whirlwind, brother-in-law, I will tell you something which I wanted to tell you before I left. I want to tell things that came to my mind. I wanted to tell you to move to Medicine Root, but I did not tell you about it and I want you to think it over and tell me, brother-in-law, as I am here overseas and tell me if you are going to move over there. I knew you said you were going on a trip before I left and I do not tell you to move soon but after you return from your trip. From now until fall is when I want you to move and live over there. I know you have heard all I want to tell you and there is nothing more to tell you.

107. Bureau of Indian Affairs, Pine Ridge Census Records, 1889, microfilm, Newberry Library, Chicago, IL.

108. Killen's letter is part of the collection Kills Enemy Alone at the Nebraska Historical Society.

109. See D. F. Royer, Letter and List, 1890, MS 3176, Edward E. Ayer Manuscript Collection, Newberry Library, Chicago, IL. The documents are a November 22, 1890, letter to Royer from John M. Sweeney, a teacher at the No. 8 Day School on the middle branch of Medicine Creek at what was known as Little Wound's Camp, regarding the practice of the Ghost Dance in the Medicine Root district; and a list of Pine Ridge Ghost Dance participants arranged by location and band, prepared by Indian police captain George Sword.

110. James Walker to Clark Wissler, February 10, 1910, James R. Walker Collection, MS 653, CHS.

111. "Change of the Lakota Language," folder 129-2, James R. Walker Collection, MS 653, CHS.

112. Most famous among them was Ella Deloria, a Standing Rock Sioux linguist who worked with Franz Boas and wrote an unpublished novel. Gertrude Bonin (Zitakála Šá), although most famous for her English-language stories, received or wrote as-yet untranslated Dakota letters. During my research at the Nebraska Historical Society, I encountered several pocket diaries and letters written in Lakota by James Red Cloud, grandson of the famous leader in the 1940s and 1950s.

113. Taylor, *Archive and Repertoire*.

114. James Walker to Clark Wissler, February 20, 1910. James R. Walker Collection, MS 653, CHS.

115. Ella Deloria, as quoted in Red Shirt, *George Sword's Warrior Narratives*, 11.

116. Red Shirt, *George Sword's Warrior Narratives*, 159.

Chapter 4

1. Blackbird, *History of the Ottawa and Chippewa Indians*. When Andrew Blackbird refers to his father's writing system for Central Algonquian as *Paw-pa-pe-po*, he is employing a common vernacular term for the orthography that is based in a hyphenated spelling out of the central vowel/consonant sounds of the language. The Great Lakes syllabic system is based in the Roman alphabet, but uses Roman-spelled consonant and vowel clusters to sound out Algonquian words on the page, but it does so with little regard for vowel length and other linguistic properties unique to that family of languages. Thus it is somewhat like a shorthand system, demanding fluency among its readers, as well as a practice of "decoding" that would not have been necessary in spoken

exchanges within Central Algonquian. Present-day Mesquaki community members in Iowa use the term *pa-pe-pi-po* to describe the version of the syllabary now in use at the settlement. For the Ho-Chunk (Winnebago) adapters of the Algonquian system, it has become known as *ba-be-bi-bo*, reflecting the different consonant/vowel clusters that are salient in their Siouan language. Thus, throughout this chapter, readers will encounter these variant spellings depending on the tribal contexts of their use.

2. Blackbird, *History of the Ottawa and Chippewa Indians*, 7.
3. Witgen, *Infinity of Nations*, 3.
4. Blackbird, *History of the Ottawa and Chippewa Indians*, 29.
5. Reda, *From Furs to Farms*, 146.
6. Reda, *From Furs to Farms*, 65–66.
7. Goddard, "Writing and Reading Mesquakie (Fox)," 117.
8. See Round, *Removable Type*, 1–4, for a discussion of Pablo Tac's similar experiences with the Vatican Propaganda.
9. Blackbird, *History of the Ottawa and Chippewa Indians*, 7.
10. Blackbird, *History of the Ottawa and Chippewa Indians*, 42.
11. Noodin, *Bawaajimo*, 10.
12. Noodin, *Bawaajimo*, xx.
13. Rand Valentine, "Ojibwe and Cree Syllabic Writing," n.d., unpublished manuscript, 3.
14. Valentine, "Ojibwe and Cree Syllabic Writing," 9, explains:

> All four of these distinct syllables are written with the same character. This means that one must be fluent in the language in order to properly decode the meanings of messages written in syllabics, because the distinctions that are neutralized are very important, being essentially equivalent to the English contrasts between p/b, d/t and g/k, as well as the vowel distinctions in heed versus hid, and mate versus met, among others. The next thing to notice is that the symbols are systematically organized according to two basic parameters: their shapes, which provides their consonantal values (or none, in the case of vowel-only symbols); and their orientation, which provides their vowel values. For example, simple vowels are represented with a triangle. The determination of vowel quality (as a, e, i, or o), however, is according to the orientation of the triangle. This is what the last column of characters in the syllabic chart is designed for, to represent consonant sounds that come at the end of a syllable. These characters are appropriately called finals.

15. Valentine, "Ojibwe and Cree Syllabic Writing," 12.
16. Quoted in McNally, *Ojibwe Singers*, 59.
17. Wilson, *Ojebway Language*, 12.
18. Wilson, *Ojebway Language*, 13.
19. Jones, *Sermons and Speeches*, 24.
20. Child, *Holding Our World Together*, xvi. "The root word '*ozhibii'ige*' meaning 'to write' has four variants all related to the shaping of lines, marks, meanings and traces of presence." Noodin, *Bawaajimo*, 6.
21. Corbiere, "Exploring Historical Literacy," 57–80.
22. Corbiere, "Exploring Historical Literacy," 57–80.
23. See Round, *Removable Type*, 160–65.
24. Goddard, "Writing and Reading Meskwaki (Fox)," 126.
25. Whittaker, "Words of Black Hawk," 514.
26. Whittaker, "Words of Black Hawk," 514.

250   Notes to Chapter 4

27. Whittaker, "Words of Black Hawk," 516.
28. Whittaker, "Words of Black Hawk," 514.
29. Tanner, *Atlas of Great Lakes Indian Territory*, 96.
30. Reda, *From Furs to Farms*, 146.
31. Tanner, *Atlas of Great Lakes Indian Territory*, 159.
32. Reda, *From Furs to Farms*.
33. L. Brooks, *Common Pot*, 8–12, 43.
34. Witgen, *Infinity of Nations*, x; L. Brooks, *Common Pot*, 27.
35. Witgen, *Infinity of Nations*, 356.
36. Arndt, "No Middle Ground," 27.
37. Cohen, *Networked Wilderness*, 28.
38. Herring, *Kenekuk*, chap. 1.
39. Herring, *Kenekuk*, chap. 5.
40. Catlin, *North American Indians*, 93.
41. Hubbard, "Kickapoo Sermon," 479. It is also significant that Kenekuk distinguishes between non-Indian orthodoxy and that of his own congregation through invocation of the European codex, "He has not instructed them [the Kickapoos] by books."
42. McCoy, *History of the Baptist Indian Missions*.
43. In Custer, "Kannekuk or Keeanakuk," 54, the literal translation of an alphabetic rendering of the liturgical prayer on the prayer sticks explains,

> Our Father, when he worked,
> When he made the world right here
> Where we are now, [and] again made us.

That is, the Creator made a place and a people to be his children when he became lonely in the world. Perhaps this was interpreted by the diasporic congregants as a way of arriving at their own "promised land." Many Indigenous pictographic representations of land and town include very similar markings of stands of trees, similar to those here identified in the literature as corn. The National Museum of Natural History houses a prayer stick under the heading "Prayer Stick," National Museum of Natural History, E178369-0.

44. Berryman asserted that Isaac McCoy had made a "great mistake" in implying that the Indian leader knew little theology. Berryman, "A Circuit-Rider's Frontier Experiences," 50.

45. Hymes describes a Chinook text as exhibiting "grammatico-repetition" as its organizing structure, calling this technique "measure." He contrasts "measure" with the repetitions of a Shakespearean sonnet, which are metrical by virtue of their "phonic numerical regularity." Hymes, *In Vain I Tried to Tell You*, 178. For our purposes, it is important to appreciate the "measure" at work in these prayer sticks and how it differs from that of Christian liturgical practice, just as the Chinook orature differs from that of William Shakespeare. Judging from McCoy's description, the prayer stick did indeed set in motion a kind of "phonic numerical regularity" (he compares each line to "two measures of common psalm tune"), but—as McCoy also notes—the overall rhythm is "broken." Also, the sticks themselves seem to epitomize what Hymes calls the semiotic (as opposed to the phonic) nature of orature, where the stick's shapes and their carved symbols "characterize" the structure of the liturgy "with regard to some unit" that is not readily apparent to listeners (like McCoy) whose experience lies outside the culture performing the recitation and rite. For example, while many scholars have noted that

the sticks contain fifteen symbols, thus likening them to the Rosary, the sequences of the symbols are not even (like the beads) and thus the "stanzas" would not be the same.

46. Herring, *Kenekuk*, chap. 9.
47. Catlin, *North American Indians*, 94.
48. Irving, *Indian Sketches*, 44.
49. Irving, *Indian Sketches*, 47–48.
50. Quoted in Herring, *Kenekuk*, chap. 6.
51. Herring, *Kenekuk*, chap. 6.
52. "A Kickapoo Sermon," 473.
53. "A Visit to the Kickapoos in 1906," Milo Custer Writings Relating to the Kickapoo Indians, 1906–16, WA MSS S-2351, Beinecke Rare Book and Manuscript Library, Yale University, New Haven, CT.
54. Custer, "Kannekuk or Keeanakuk: The Kickapoo Prophet," 53.
55. Andrew Blackbird claims his father created the syllabary sometime before his death in 1861. Blackbird, *History of the Ottawa and Chippewa Indians*, 31.
56. Willard Walker, as quoted in Goddard, "Writing and Reading Mesquakie (Fox)," 118.
57. Goddard, "Writing and Reading Mesquakie (Fox)," 120.
58. Thomason, "On Editing Bill Leaf's Meskwaki Text," 316.
59. Fletcher, "Phonetic Alphabet," 299.
60. Busby, *Two Summers among the Musquakies*, 160.
61. Smith, "Ethnobotany of the Meskwaki Indians," 182.
62. Fletcher, "Phonetic Alphabet," 334.
63. Smith, "Ethnobotany of the Meskwaki Indians," 180. See also William Jones's assessment, written sometime around 1900: "Then there is their language, which, being in some respects the most archaic of the Algonquian tongues, is of great importance to the Algonquian philologist. But the major point of interest lies in the fact that they have earned the distinction, along with their kindred the Mexican Kickapoo, of being ranked among the most conservative of all Indians." Jones, *Ethnography of the Fox Indians*, 1. Jones was himself a Meskwaki from the Oklahoma reservation.
64. Smith, "Ethnobotany of the Meskwaki Indians," 181.
65. See Round, *Removeable Type*, 148.
66. Round, *Removeable Type*, 149.
67. Goddard, "Writing and Reading Meskwaki (Fox)," 28–29. See also Susman, "Accentual System of Winnebago," on Ho-Chunk usage; Walker, "Native Writing Systems"; and Cushman, *Cherokee Syllabary*.
68. Zimmer, "Red Earth Nation," 180.
69. Susman, as quoted in Walker, "Winnebago Syllabary," 409.
70. Pauketat, "America's First Pastime," 81–82.
71. Henkin, *Postal Age*, 42.
72. Zimmer, "Red Earth Nation," 177–83. On ethnographic refusal, see the letter on page 180.
73. Goddard, "Writing and Reading Meskwaki (Fox)," 131.
74. Bataille and Sands, *America Indian Women*.
75. Winnebago Tribe of Nebraska, "Tribal History," accessed December 17, 2023, https://winnebagotribe.com/tribal-history/.
76. Wisconsin Historical Society, "Ho-Chunk Nation: A Brief Introduction," accessed December 17, 2023, www.wisconsinhistory.org/Records/Article/CS4377.
77. Fletcher, "Phonetic Alphabet," 299.

78. Walker, "Winnebago Syllabary," 397.
79. Cushman, *Cherokee Syllabary*.
80. Walker, "Winnebago Syllabary," 404.
81. Blowsnake, *Crashing Thunder*, xxii.
82. Blowsnake, *Crashing Thunder*, 117.
83. Arndt, "No Middle Ground," 165.
84. Blowsnake, *Crashing Thunder*, 202.
85. Thus, Arndt argues, "Peyotism was a creative cultural form through which Ho-Chunk individuals could work on their relationship to the new world order. It also created the conditions under which its members could come to understand their traditional way of life as a culture." Arndt, "No Middle Ground," 27.
86. Arndt, "Indigenous Autobiography en Abyme," 42.
87. Ricoeur, "Model of the Text," 529.
88. Barber, *Anthropology of Texts*, 22.
89. Barber, *Anthropology of Texts*, 3, 4.
90. L. Smith, *Decolonizing Methodologies*, 6.
91. Arndt, "No Middle Ground," 165.
92. Clifford, "Indigenous Articulations," 478, 481, 467.
93. As was the custom of the ethnography of his day, Radin's notes and published interlinear translations of Blowsnake's work always uses the linguist's alphabetic phonetic rendering of the syllabary text.
94. McNally, *Ojibwe Singers*, 187.
95. Noodin, *Bawaajimo*, 10.
96. Danker, "Ba-be-bi-bo-ra," 101.

Coda
1. Sapir, "Psychological Reality," 46–47.
2. Sapir, "Psychological Reality," 48–49.
3. Kapchan, "Learning to Listen."
4. "Belinda Daniels," CBC News Interactives, accessed December 17, 2023, www.cbc.ca/news2/interactives/i-am-indigenous-2017/daniels.html.
5. See Keith Basso's classic study of Western Apache place-names and stories, *Wisdom Sits in Places*.
6. Armstrong, "Land Speaking," 190, 192.
7. Armstrong, "Land Speaking," 190.
8. For a brief description of O'odham syntax and grammar, see Zepeda, *Papago Grammar*.
9. The Library of Congress Subject Headings under which this book is catalogued in libraries call it a "biography" and "ethnography."
10. Young Bear, *Black Eagle Child*, afterword, 254, 253.
11. Young Bear, *Black Eagle Child*, 98.
12. Basso, *Portraits*, 8–9.
13. Piatote, *Beadworkers*, 7.
14. Piatote, *Beadworkers*, 3–4, 11.
15. Beth Piatote, interview with the author, August 2022.

BIBLIOGRAPHY

Manuscript and Archival Collections
Chicago, IL
    Newberry Library
        American Board of Commissioners for Foreign Missions, Transcripts of letters from missionaries among the Indians of Minnesota, Dakota, and Oregon, 1830–78
        Edward E. Ayer Manuscript Collection
Denver, CO
    Colorado Historical Society
        James R. Walker Collection, MS 653
        Little Fingernail Book Collection, MSS 1006
Kansas City, MO
    National Archives and Records Administration
        Records of the Bureau of Indian Affairs, RG 75
Lincoln, NE
    Nebraska State Historical Society
        Kills Enemy Alone, RG 4946.AM
Madison, WI
    Wisconsin Historical Society
        Lyman C. Draper Manuscripts
            Joseph Brant Papers (1710–1879)
New Haven, CT
    Beinecke Rare Book and Manuscript Library, Yale University
        Milo Custer Writings Relating to the Kickapoo Indians, 1906–16, WA MSS S-2351
Ottawa, ON
    Public Archives of Canada, Manuscript Division
        Claus Family Papers
        Indian Records, RG 10, series 2, 1956
Philadelphia, PA
    American Philosophical Society Library and Museum
        Floyd Glen Lounsbury Papers, ca. 1935–98, MS Coll. 95
        Harry Hoijer Collection
            Silas John Edwards Papers
            David Mandelbaum Papers, San Carlos Apache Texts, box 7, MSS 497.3.H68
        Ely Samuel Parker Papers MSS 497.3.P223
    Historical Society of Pennsylvania
        Indian Papers, MS 310
Provo, UT
    Brigham Young University Library
        L. Tom Perry Special Collections
            George Sword and Lucy Sword, diary 1890
San Marino, CA
    Huntington Library
        Rare Books

St. Paul, MN
    Minnesota Historical Society
        Alexander G. Huggins and Family Papers, 1833–1976
        Stephen R. Riggs and Family Papers, 1837–1958
Washington, DC
    National Archives and Records Administration
        Andrew Jackson, "President Andrew Jackson's Message to Congress 'On Indian Removal,'" December 6, 1830, Records of the US Senate, RG 46
    Library of Congress
        Incunabula Collection

Published Sources

Abbot, Clifford, and Loretta Metoxen. "Oneida Language Preservation." *Wisconsin Magazine of History* 96, no. 1 (Autumn 2012): 2–15.

Abler, Thomas, ed. *Chainbreaker: The Revolutionary War Memoirs of Governor Blacksnake as told to Benjamin Williams*. Lincoln: University of Nebraska Press, 2005.

———. "Protestant Missionaries and Native Culture: Parallel Careers of Asher Wright and Silas Rand." *American Indian Quarterly* 16, no. 1 (Winter 1992): 25–37.

Adams, David Wallace. *Education for Extinction: American Indians and the Boarding School Experience, 1875–1928*. Lawrence: University Press of Kansas, 1995.

Alfred, Taiaiake. *Peace, Power, and Righteousness: An Indigenous Manifesto*. Toronto, ON: Oxford University Press, 1999.

American Board of Commissioners for Foreign Missions (ABCFM). *Constitution, Laws and Regulation of ABCFM*. Boston: Crocker and Brewster, 1835.

———. On the Use of Missionary Maps at the Monthly Concert. Boston: Crocker and Brewster, 1842.

American Philosophical Society. "Report of the Committee Appointed (January 6, 1888) by the American Philosophical Society to Assist the Commission on Amended Orthografy, Created by Virtue of a Resolution of the Legislature of Pennsylvania." *Proceedings of the American Philosophical Society* 26, no. 129 (1889): 306–29.

Amory, Hugh, and David D. Hall, eds. *The Colonial Book in the Atlantic World*. Vol. 1 of *A History of the Book in America*, edited by David D. Hall. Chapel Hill: University of North Carolina Press, 2009.

Anderson, Gary Clayton, and Alan R. Woolworth, eds. *Through Dakota Eyes: Narrative Accounts of the Dakota Indian War of 1862*. St. Paul: Minnesota Historical Society, 1988.

Anderson, Rufus. *Memoir of Catharine Brown*. Philadelphia: American Sunday School Union, 1831.

Andrews, Thomas G. "Turning the Tables on Assimilation: Oglala Lakotas and the Pine Ridge Day Schools, 1889–1920s." *Western Historical Quarterly* 33, no. 4 (2002): 407–30.

Apess, William. *On Our Own Ground: The Complete Writings of William Apess, a Pequot*. Edited by Barry O'Connell. Amherst: University of Massachusetts Press, 1992.

———. *A Son of the Forest: The Experience of William Apes, a Native of the Forest*. New York: published by the author, 1831.

Armstrong, Jeanette. "Land Speaking." In *Speaking for Generations: Native Writers on Writing*, edited by Simon Ortiz. Tucson: University of Arizona Press, 1998.

Arndt, Grant. "Indigenous Autobiography en Abyme: Indigenous Reflections on Representational Agency in the Case of Crashing Thunder." *Ethnohistory* 59, no. 1 (2012): 27–49.

——. "No Middle Ground: Ho-Chunk Powwows and the Production of Social Space in Native Wisconsin." PhD diss., University of Chicago, 2004.
Atwater, Caleb. *Writings of Caleb Atwater*. Published by the author; printed by Scott and Wright, 1833.
Aupaumut, Hendrick. *A Narrative of an Embassy to the Western Indians, from the Original Manuscript of Hendrick Aupaumut*. [1791]. Memoirs of the Historical Society of Pennsylvania, Vol. 2, Pt. 1, 61–131. Philadelphia: M'Carty and Davis, 1827.
Babcock Jr., Willoughby M., and S. R. Riggs. "Dakota Portraits." *Minnesota History Bulletin* 2, no. 8 (November 1918): 481–568.
Barber, Karin. *The Anthropology of Texts, Persons and Publics: Oral and Written Culture in Africa and Beyond*. Cambridge: Cambridge University Press, 2007.
Bartlett, Samuel. *Historical Sketch of the Missions of the American Board among the North American Indians*. Boston: The Board, 1876.
Basso, Keith. *The Cibecue Apache*. New York: Holt, Rinehart and Winston, 1970.
——. *Portraits of the Whiteman Linguistic Play and Cultural Symbols among the Western Apache*. Cambridge: Cambridge University Press, 1979.
——. *Wisdom Sits in Places: Landscape and Language among the Western Apache*. Albuquerque: University of New Mexico Press, 1996.
Basso, Keith, and Ned Anderson, "A Western Apache Writing System: The Symbols of Silas John." *Science* 180, no. 4090 (1973): 1013–22.
Bataille, Gretchen M., and Kathleen Mullen Sands. *American Indian Women: Telling Their Lives*. Lincoln: University of Nebraska Press, 1987.
Beauchamp, William. *Civil, Religious, and Mourning Councils*. New York: New York State Education Department, 1907.
——. *The Iroquois Trail, or Footprints of the Six Nations in Customs, Tradition, and History in Which Are Included David Cusick's Sketches of the Ancient History of the Six Nations*. Fayetteville, NY: H. C. Beauchamp, Recorder Office, 1892.
Bender, Margaret. *Signs of Cherokee Culture: Sequoyah's Syllabary in Eastern Cherokee Life*. Chapel Hill: University of North Carolina Press, 2002.
Berg, Richard. "Archaeological Remains of Two Mid-Nineteenth Century Dakota Homes Associated with the Riggs/Hazelwood Mission Site." *Minnesota Archaeologist* 65 (2006): 129–74.
Berryman, Jerome C. "A Circuit-Rider's Frontier Experiences." *Collections of the Kansas State Historical Society* 16 (1923–25): 177–226.
Blackbird, Andrew J. *History of the Ottawa and Chippewa Indians of Michigan*. Ypsilanti: Ypsilantian Job Printing House, 1887.
Black Elk, and John Gneisenau Neihart. *Black Elk Speaks: Being the Life Story of a Holy Man of the Ogalala Sioux / as Told to John G. Neihardt (Flaming Rainbow). Illustrated by Standing Bear*. New York: Morrow, 1932.
Black Hawk. *Life of Ma-ka-tai-me-she-kia-kiak, or Black Hawk: An Autobiography*. Edited by J. B. Patterson. Boston, 1834.
Blowsnake, Sam. *Crashing Thunder: The Autobiography of an American Indian*. Lincoln: University of Nebraska Press, 1983.
Boas, Franz, and Ella Cara Deloria. *Dakota Grammar*. Washington, DC: Government Printing Office, 1941.
Bonnell, O. H. *Translation of the Sioux: Figures, Money, Definitions, Words, Sentences*. Chamberlain, Dakota Territory: Democrat Print, 1880.
Boscana, Geronimo. *Chinigchinich (Chi-nich-nich): A Revised and Annotated Version of Alfred Robinson's Translation of Father Geronimo Boscana's Historical Account of the*

Belief, Usages, Customs and Extravagencies [sic] *of the Indians of This Mission of San Juan Capistrano*. Santa Ana, CA: Fine Arts Press, 1933.

Bowes, John P. *Exiles and Pioneers: Eastern Indians in the Trans-Mississippi West*. Cambridge: Cambridge University Press, 2007.

Brooks, Joanna. "Six Hymns by Samson Occom." *Early American Literature* 38, no. 1 (2009): 67–87.

———. "This Indian World: An Introduction to the Writings of Samson Occom." In *The Collected Writings of Samson Occom*, edited by Joanna Brooks, 3–43. New York: Oxford University Press, 2006.

Brooks, Lisa Tanya. *The Common Pot: The Recovery of Native Space in the Northeast*. Minneapolis: University of Minnesota Press, 2008.

Buechel, Eugene. *A Grammar of Lakota: The Language of the Teton Sioux Indians*. Buffalo Grove, IL: John S. Swift Company, 1939.

Bunyan, John. *Cante teca: The Pilgrim's Progress*. Translated into the Dakota Language by Stephen R. Riggs. New York: American Tract Society, 1858.

Burlington and Missouri River Railroad Co. *Millions of Acres. Iowa and Nebraska. Land for Sale on 10 Years Credit by Burlington and Missouri River R.R. Co. [. . .]*. Buffalo, NY: Commercial Advertiser Printing House, 1872.

Busby, Alice. *Two Summers among the Musquakies: Relating to the Early History of the Sac and Fox Tribe [. . .]*. Vinton, IA: Herald Book and Job Rooms, 1886.

Calloway, Collin G. *American Revolution in Indian Country: Crisis and Diversity in Native American Communities*. Cambridge: Cambridge University Press, 1996.

———. *Pen and Ink Witchcraft: Treaties and Treaty Making in American Indian History*. New York: Oxford University Press, 2013.

Campbell, William W. *Annals of Tryon County: or, Border Warfare of New York, during the Revolution*. New York: Baker and Schribner, 1849.

Campisi, Jack, and Laurence M. Hauptman. "Talking Back: The Oneida Language and Folklore Project, 1938–1941." *Proceedings of the American Philosophical Society* 125, no. 6 (December 1981): 441–48.

Canku, Clifford, and Michael Simon. *The Dakota Prisoner of War Letters*. St. Paul: Minnesota Historical Society Press, 2012.

Carpenter, Roger M. *The Renewed, the Destroyed, and the Remade: The Three Thought Worlds of the Huron and the Iroquois, 1609–1650*. East Lansing: Michigan State University Press, 2004.

Carr, Jean Furgeson, Stephen L. Carr, and Lucille M. Schultz. *Archives of Instruction: Nineteenth-Century Rhetorics, Readers, and Composition Books in the United States*. Carbondale: Southern Illinois University Press, 2005.

Casey, Charles. *Two Years on the Farm of Uncle Sam*. London: Richard Bentley, 1852.

Casper, Scott E., Jeffrey D. Grovers, Steven W. Nissenbaum, Michael P. Winship, and David D. Hall, eds. *The Industrial Book, 1840–1880*. Vol. 3 of *A History of the Book in America*, edited by David D. Hall. Chapel Hill: University of North Carolina Press. Kindle.

Cassedy, Tim. *Figures of Speech: Six Histories of Language and Identity in the Age of Revolutions*. Iowa City: University of Iowa Press, 2018.

Catlin, George. *North American Indians: Being Letters and Notes of the Manners, Customs and Conditions, 1839–1832*. Edinburgh: John Grant, 1903.

Chainbreaker [Gov. Blacksnake]. *Chainbreaker: The Revolutionary War Memoirs of Governor Blacksnake as told to Benjamin Williams*. Edited by Thomas S. Abler. Lincoln: University of Nebraska Press, 1989.

Child, Brenda J. *Holding Our World Together: Ojibwe Women and the Survival of Community*. New York: Viking, 2012.
Church of England. *Portions of the Book of Common Prayer, Psalms, and Hymns, and the First Epistle General of John, in Cree*. London: Church Missionary House, 1856.
Clemmons, Linda M. *Conflicted Mission: Faith, Disputes, and Deception on the Dakota Frontier*. St. Paul: Minnesota Historical Society Press, 2014.
Clifford, James. "Indigenous Articulations." *Contemporary Pacific* 13, no. 2 (2001): 467–90.
Cohen, Matt. *The Networked Wilderness: Communicating in Early New England*. Minneapolis: University of Minnesota Press, 2010.
Cohen, Matt, and Jeffrey Glover, eds. *Colonial Mediascapes: Sensory Worlds of the Early Americas*. Lincoln: University of Nebraska Press, 2014.
Copway, George. *The Life, History, and Travels of Ka-ge-ga-gah-bowh*. Edited by Lavonne Brown Ruoff and Donald B. Smith. Lincoln: University of Nebraska Press, 1997.
Corbiere, Alan. "Exploring Historical Literacy on Manitoulin Island." In *Papers of the Thirty-Fourth Algonquian Conference*, edited by H. C. Wolfart, 57–80. Winnipeg: University of Manitoba, 2003.
Crain, Patricia. *The Story of A: The Alphabetization of America from* The New England Primer *to* The Scarlet Letter. Stanford, CA: Stanford University Press, 2000.
Cruikshank, Julie. *The Social Life of Stories: Narrative and Knowledge in the Yukon Territory*. Lincoln: University of Nebraska Press, 2000.
Cuoq, J. A. *Lexique de la langue iroquoise par M. l'abbé Cuoq, prêtre de St-Sulpice : étude bibliographique*. Montréal: J. Chapleau et Fils, 1882.
Cushman, Ellen. *The Cherokee Syllabary: Writing the People's Perseverance*. Norman: University of Oklahoma Press, 2011.
Cusick, David. *David Cusick's Sketches of Ancient History of the Six Nations*. Lockport, NY: Cooley and Lothrop Printers, 1827.
Custer, Milo. "Kannekuk or Keeanakuk: The Kickapoo Prophet." *Journal of the Illinois State Historical Society* 11, no. 1 (April 1918): 50.
Dahlstrom, Amy. "Highlighting Rhetorical Structure through Syntactic Analysis: An Illustrated Meskwaki Text by Alfred Kiyana." In *New Voices for Old Words: Algonquian Oral Literature*, edited by David J. Costa, 118–34. Lincoln: University of Nebraska Press, 2015.
Daniels, Peter, and William Bright, eds. *The World's Writing Systems*. New York: Oxford University Press, 1996.
Danker, Kathleen. "Ba-be-bi-bo-ra: Refinement of the Ho-Chunk Syllabary in the Nineteenth and Twentieth Centuries." In *Advances in the Study of Siouan Languages and Linguistics*, edited by Catherine Rudin and Bryan J. Gordon, 83–103. Berlin: Language Science Press, 2016.
Darnton, Robert. "What Is the History of Books?" In *The Book History Reader*, edited by Alistair McCleery and David Finkelstein, 2–96. London: Routledge, 2002.
Davis, Lawrence M., Charles L. Houck, and Clive Upton. "'Sett Out Verry Eairly Wensdy': The Spelling and Grammar in the Lewis and Clark Journals." *American Speech* 75, no. 2 (2000): 137–48.
Deloria, Philip J. "Historiography." In *A Companion to American Indian History*, edited by Philip J. Deloria and Neal Salisbury, 6–24. London: Blackwell, 2002.
———. "What Is the Middle Ground, Anyway?" *William and Mary Quarterly* 63, no. 1 (January 2006): 15–22.
Deloria, Vine. *Custer Died for Your Sins*. Toronto, ON: Macmillan, 1969.
———. *God Is Red: A Native View of Religion*. Golden, CO: Fulcrum, 1972.

———. *We Talk, You Listen: New Tribes, New Turf*. Lincoln: University of Nebraska Press, 2007.

DeMallie, Raymond J., ed. "Black Elk in the Twenty-First Century." *Ethnohistory* 53, no. 3 (Summer 2006): 595–601.

———. "The Lakota Ghost Dance: An Ethnohistorical Account." *Pacific Historical Review* 51, no. 4 (1982): 385–405.

———. *The Sixth Grandfather: Black Elk's Teachings Given to John G. Neihardt*. Lincoln: University of Nebraska Press, 1984.

Deserontyon, John, ed. *A Mohawk Form of Ritual of Condolence, 1782*. Translated and with an introduction by J. N. B. Hewitt. New York: Museum of the American Indian, Heye Foundation, 1928.

Dixon, James. *Personal Narrative of a Tour through Part of the United States*. New York: Lane and Scott, 1849.

Dowd, Gregory Evans. *A Spirited Resistance: The North American Indian Struggle for Unity, 1745–1815*. Baltimore, MD: Johns Hopkins University Press, 1992.

Du Ponceau, Pierre. "Report of the Corresponding Secretary to the Committee." *Transactions of the Historical and Literary Committee of the American Philosophical Society*, Vol. 1, Pt. 1. Philadelphia, 1819.

Eastman, Carolyn. "The Indian Censures the White Man: 'Indian Eloquence' and American Reading Audiences in the Early Republic." *William and Mary Quarterly* 65, no. 3 (July 2008): 535–64.

Elkins, James. *The Domain of Images*. Ithaca, NY: Cornell University Press, 2001.

Emerson, Benjamin Dudley. *The National Spelling-Book and Pronouncing Tutor [. . .]*. Boston: Richardson and Lord, 1828.

Erdrich, Louise. *Books and Islands in Ojibwe Country*. Washington, DC: National Geographic, 2003.

Erlmann, Veit, ed. *Hearing Cultures: Essays on Sound, Listening and Modernity*. London: Routledge, 2004.

Fenton William N. "Seth Newhouse's Traditional History and Constitution of the Iroquois Confederacy." *Proceedings of the American Philosophical Society* 93, no. 2 (May 1949): 141–58.

Fenton, William N., and Asher Wright. "Seneca Indians by Asher Wright (1859)." *Ethnohistory* 4, no. 3 (1957): 302–21.

Fitzgerald, Stephanie, Bryan Kuwada, and Phillip H. Round. "Pilgrims in Print: Indigenous Readers Encounter John Bunyan." *Commonplace: The Journal of Early American Life* 15, no. 4 (Summer 2015). https://commonplace.online/article/pilgrims-in-print-indigenous-readers-encounter-john-bunyan/.

Fletcher, Alice. "The Phonetic Alphabet of the Winnebago Indians." In *Proceedings of the American Association for the Advancement of Science*, edited by Frederick W. Putnam, 354–567. Salem: n.p., 1889.

Folsom, David. "Prospectus for the Choctaw Intelligencer." *Indian Advocate*, November 1848, 1.

Foster, Benjamin Franklin. *Foster's System of Penmanship: Or the Art of Rapid Writing Illustrated and Explained [. . .]*. N.p.: H. Perkins, 1836.

Foster, Michael K. *From the Earth to Beyond the Sky: An Ethnographic Approach to Four Longhouse Iroquois Speech Events*. Ottawa, ON: National Museums of Canada, 1974.

———. "Language and Cultural History of North America." In *Languages*, edited by Ives Goddard and William C. Sturtevant, 64–116. Vol. 17 of *Handbook of North American*

Indians, edited by William C. Sturtevant. Washington, DC: Smithsonian Institution, 1996.
Fowler, Loretta. *Wives and Husbands: Gender and Age in Southern Arapaho History*. Norman: University of Oklahoma Press, 2010.
Frankel, Oz. *States of Inquiry: Social Investigations and Print Culture in Nineteenth-Century Britain and the United States*. Baltimore, MD: Johns Hopkins University Press, 2006.
Frémont, John C. *Memoirs of My Life*. Chicago: Belford, Clarke, 1887. https://archive.org/details/memoirsofmylifeoofr.
Gallaudet, Thomas. *Gallaudet's Picture Defining and Reading Book: Also, New Testament Stories, in the Ojibua Language*. Boston: American Board of Commissioners for Foreign Missions, 1835.
———. *Sermon, On the Duties and Advantages of Affording Instruction to the Deaf and Dumb [. . .]*. Concord, NH: Isaac Hill, 1824.
Gibson, John Arthur. *Concerning the League: The Iroquois League Tradition as Dictated in Onondaga by John Arthur Gibson*. Winnipeg: Algonquian and Iroquoian Linguistics, 1992.
Gilmore, William. *Reading Becomes a Necessity of Life: Material and Cultural Life in Rural New England, 1780–1835*. Knoxville: University of Tennessee Press, 1992.
Gitelman, Lisa. *Always Already New: Media, History, and the Data of Culture*. Cambridge, MA: Massachusetts Institute of Technology Press, 2007.
———. *Paper Knowledge: Toward a Media History of Documents*. Durham, NC: Duke University Press, 2014.
Goddard, Ives. "Writing and Reading Meskwaki (Fox)." In *Papers of the Twenty-Seventh Algonquian Conference*, edited by David H. Pentland, 117–34. Winnipeg: University of Manitoba Press, 1996.
Goddard, Ives, and Sturtevant, William C., eds. *Languages*. Vol. 17 of *Handbook of North American Indians*, edited by William C. Sturtevant. Washington, DC: Smithsonian Institution, 1996.
Gone, Joseph. "'As if Reviewing His Life': Bull Lodge's Narrative and the Mediation of Self-Representation." *American Indian Culture and Research Journal* 30, no. 1 (2006): 67–86.
Goodbird, Edward. *Goodbird the Indian, His Story*. New York: Fleming H. Revell, 1914.
Grant, David M. "Writing 'Wakan': The Lakota Pipe as Rhetorical Object." *College Composition and Communication* 69, no. 1 (September 2017): 61–86.
Greene, Candace S. *Silver Horn: Master Illustrator of the Kiowas*. Norman: University of Oklahoma Press, 2001.
Gunn, Robert Lawrence. *Ethnology and Empire: Languages, Literature, and the Making of the North American Borderlands*. New York: New York University Press, 2015.
Gustafson, Sandra M. "American Literature and the Public Sphere." *American Literary History* 20, no. 3 (2008): 465–78.
Hale, Horatio. *The Iroquois Book of Rites*. Toronto, ON: University of Toronto Press, 1963.
Hampton, Timothy. *Fictions of Embassy: Literature and Diplomacy in Early Modern Europe*. Ithaca, NY: Cornell University Press, 2011.
Hanks, William F. *Converting Words: Maya in the Age of the Cross*. Berkeley: University of California Press, 2010.
Harkin, Michael, ed. *Reassessing Revitalization Movements: Perspectives from North America and the Pacific Islands*. Lincoln: University of Nebraska Press, 2004.

Harvey, Sean P. *Native Tongues: Colonialism and Race from Encounter to the Reservation.* Cambridge, MA: Harvard University Press, 2015.

Henkin, David. *The Postal Age: The Emergence of Modern Communications in Nineteenth-Century America.* Chicago: University of Chicago Press, 2007.

Herring, Joseph B. *Kenekuk: The Kickapoo Prophet.* Lawrence: University Press of Kansas, 1988.

Hewitt, J. N. B. "Introduction." In *A Mohawk Form of Ritual of Condolence, 1782,* by John Deserontyon. Translated and with an introduction by J. N. B. Hewitt. Edited. New York: Museum of the American Indian, Heye Foundation, 1928.

Hodge, Frederick Webb. *Handbook of American Indians north of Mexico, Part I. Bureau of American Ethnology: Miscellaneous Publications.* Washington, DC: Government Printing Office, 1907.

Hopkins, Sarah Winnemucca. *Life among the Paiutes: Their Wrongs and Claims.* 1883. Reno: University of Nevada Press, 1994.

Howe, D. W. *What Hath God Wrought: The Transformation of America, 1814–1848.* New York: Oxford University Press, 2009.

Howse, Joseph. *A Grammar of the Cree Language, with Which Is Combined an Analysis of the Chippeway Dialect.* London: J. G. F. and J. Rivington, 1844.

Hubbard, Gurdon S. "A Kickapoo Sermon." *Illinois Monthly Magazine* 1 (October 1831): 472–76.

Huhndorf, Shari. *Mapping the Americas: The Transnational Politics of Contemporary Native Culture.* Ithaca, NY: Cornell University Press, 2009.

Hymes, Dell. *In Vain I Tried to Tell You: Essays in Native American Ethnopoetics.* Lincoln: University of Nebraska Press, 2004.

Irvin, Samuel, and William Hamilton. *Original Hymns in the Ioway Language.* Iowa Territory: Ioway and Sac Mission Press, 1843.

Irving, John Treat, *Indian Sketches, Taken during an Expedition to the Pawnee and Other Tribes of American Indians.* London: J. Murray, 1835.

Jackson, Donald, ed. *Black Hawk: An Autobiography.* Urbana: University of Illinois Press, 1965.

Jacobs, Peter. *Journal of the Reverend Peter Jacobs, Indian Wesleyan Missionary.* Boston: G. C. Rand, 1853.

The Jesuit Relations and Allied Documents: Travels and Explorations of the Jesuit Missionaries in North America (1610–1791). With an introduction by Reuben Gold Thwaites. Selected and edited by Edna Kenton. New York: Albert and Charles Boni, 1925.

Johnson, Basil. *Indian School Days.* Norman: University of Oklahoma Press, 1988.

Johnson, Elias. *Legends, Traditions and Laws of the Iroquois or Six Nations and History of the Tuscarora Indians.* Lockport, NY: Union Printing, 1881.

Johnson, Joseph. *To Do Good to My Indian Brethren: The Writings of Joseph Johnson, 1751–1776.* Edited by Laura J. Murray. Amherst: University of Massachusetts Press, 1998.

Johnson, William. *The Papers of Sir William Johnson.* Prepared for publication by the Division of Archives and History, James Sullivan, PhD., Vol. 2. Albany: University of the State of New York, 1921.

Jones, Peter. *The Sermons and Speeches of the Rev. Peter Jones, alias Kah-ke-wa-quon-a-by [. . .].* Leeds, UK: H. Spink, 1831.

Jones, William. *An Algonquin Syllabary.* New York: n.p., 1906.

———. *Ethnography of the Fox Indians.* Edited by Margaret Welpley Fisher. Washington, DC: Government Printing Office, 1939.

Judkins, Russell A., ed. *Iroquois Studies: A Guide to Documentary and Ethnographic Resources from Western New York and the Genesee Valley*. Genesco, NY: Department of Anthropology, State University of New York and Genesco Foundation, 1987.

Justice, Daniel Heath. *Our Fire Survives the Storm: A Cherokee Literary History*. Minneapolis: University of Minnesota Press, 2006.

Kaestle, Carl. *Literacy in the United States: Readers and Reading since 1880*. New Haven, CT: Yale University Press, 1991.

——. *Pillars of the Republic: Common Schools and American Society, 1780–1860*. New York: Macmillan, 1981.

Kapchan, Deborah. "Learning to Listen: The Sound of Sufism in France." *World of Music* 51, no. 2 (2009): 65–89.

Kauanui, J. Kēhaulani. "'A Structure, Not an Event': Settler Colonialism and Enduring Indigeneity." *Lateral* 5, no. 1 (2016). DOI:10.25158/L5.1.7.

Kelsay, Isabel Thompson. *Joseph Brant, 1743–1807, Man of Two Worlds*. Syracuse, NY: Syracuse University Press, 1984.

Kelsey, Penelope Myrtle. *Reading the Wampum: Essays on Hodinöhsö:ni' Visual Code and Epistemological Recovery*. Syracuse, NY: Syracuse University Press, 2014.

Kerstetter, Todd. "Spin Doctors at Santee: Missionaries and the Dakota-Language Reporting of the Ghost Dance and Wounded Knee." *Western Historical Quarterly* 28, no. 1 (Spring 1997): 45–67.

Kimball, Duran. *First Lessons in Tachigrafy, a System of Brief and Wrapid Writing [. . .]*. New York, 1879.

Kneeland, Abner. *Brief Sketch of a New System of Orthography*. Walpole, NH: Nichols and Hale, 1807.

LaFlesche, Francis. *The Middle Five: Indian Schoolboys of the Omaha Tribe*. 1900. Lincoln: University of Nebraska Press, 1978.

Le Jeune, Jean Marie Raphael. *The WAWA Shorthand Instructor, or, The Duployan Stenography*. Kamloops, BC: 1896.

Lepsius, Karl R. *Standard Alphabet for Reducing Unwritten Languages and Foreign Graphic Systems [. . .]*. 2nd ed. London: W. Hertz, 1863.

Littlefield, Daniel, and James Parins, eds. *American Indian and Alaska Native Newspapers and Periodicals*. Westport, CT: Greenwood Press, 1984.

Lomawaima, K. Tsiana. *They Called It Prairie Light: The Story of Chilocco Indian School*. Lincoln: University of Nebraska Press, 1995.

Luckenbach, Abraham. *Forty-Six Select Scripture Narratives from the Old Testament. Embellished with Engravings, for the Use of Indian Youths*. New York: Daniel Fanshaw, 1848.

Lydecker, John Wolfe. *The Faithful Mohawks*. Cambridge: Cambridge University Press, 1938.

Lyons, Scott. "There's No Translation for It: The Rhetorical Sovereignty of Indigenous Languages." In *Cross-Language Relations in Composition*, edited by Bruce Horner, Min-Zhan Lu, and Paul Kei Matsuda, 127–41. Carbondale: Southern Illinois University Press, 2010.

——. "What Do American Indians Want from Writing?" *College Composition and Communication* 51, no. 3 (February 2000): 447–68.

——. *X-Marks: Native Signatures of Assent*. Minneapolis: University of Minnesota Press, 2010.

Mackintosh, Hugh R. *The Doctrine of the Person of Jesus Christ*. 1912. Reprint, New York: Charles Scribner's Sons, 1942.

Maclean, John. "Concurring Opinion." Worcester v. Georgia. 31 US 515 (1832).
MacLeitch, Gail D. *Imperial Entanglements: Iroquois Change and Persistence on the Frontiers of Empire*. Philadelphia: University of Pennsylvania Press, 2011.
Mallery, Garrick. *Picture-Writing of the American Indians*. Washington, DC: N.p., 1894.
Marshall, John. "Majority Opinion." Cherokee Nation v. State of Georgia. 30 US 1 (1831).
Mauro, Hayes Peter. *The Art of Americanization at the Carlisle Indian School*. Albuquerque: University of New Mexico Press, 2011.
McCoy, Isaac. *History of Baptist Indian Missions*. Washington, DC: W. M. Morrison; New York: H. and S. Raynor, 1840.
McDougall, Brandy Nālani, and Georganne Nordstrom. "Ma ka Hana ka 'Ike (In the Work Is the Knowledge): Kaona as Rhetorical Action." *College Composition and Communication* 63, no. 1 (September 2011): 98–121.
McGuffey, William Holmes, and John Menaul. *Laguna Indian Translation of McGufeyf's[!] New First Eclectic Reader / Translated and Printed by John Menaul*. Laguna, NM: printed by the author, 1882.
McKenzie, D. F. *Bibliography and the Sociology of Texts*. New York: Cambridge University Press, 1999.
McLaughlin, Castle. *A Lakota War Book from the Little Bighorn: The Pictographic "Autobiography of Half Moon."* Cambridge, MA: Peabody Museum Press, 2013.
McMurtrie, Douglas. *Jotham Meeker: Pioneer Printer of Kansas*. Chicago: Eyncourt Press, 1930.
———. "Pioneer Printing of Kansas, 1855–1850." *Kansas Historical Quarterly* 1, no. 1 (November 1931): 3–16.
———. "The Shawnee Sun: The First Indian-Language Periodical Published in the United States." *Kansas Historical Quarterly* 2, no. 4 (November 1933): 338–42.
McNally, Michael. *Ojibwe Singers: Hymns, Grief, and a Native Culture in Motion*. St. Paul: Minnesota Historical Society, 2009.
Merrell, James. *Into the American Woods: Negotiators on the Pennsylvania Frontier*. New York: W. W. Norton, 1999.
Michelson, Truman, ed. *The Autobiography of a Fox Woman*. Washington, DC: Government Printing Office, 1918.
Minnich, Harvey C. *William Holmes McGuffey and His Readers*. New York: American Book Company, 1936.
Mithun, Marianne. *The Languages of Native North America*. Cambridge: Cambridge University Press, 1999.
Monture, Rick. *We Share Our Matters: Two Centuries of Writing and Resistance at the Six Nations of the Grand River*. Winnipeg: University of Manitoba Press, 2014.
Momaday, N. Scott. *House Made of Dawn*. 1968. New York: Harper and Row, 1989.
Mooney, James. *Calendar History of the Kiowa Indians*. Washington, DC: Government Printing Office, 1898.
———. *The Ghost-Dance Religion and the Sioux Outbreak of 1890*. Lincoln: University of Nebraska Press, 1991.
———. *The Swimmer Manuscript: Cherokee Sacred Formulas and Medicinal Prescriptions*. Washington, DC: Government Printing Office, 1932.
Mt. Pleasant, Alyssa. "After the Whirlwind: Maintaining a Haudenosaunee Place at Buffalo Creek, 1780–1825." PhD diss., Cornell University, 2007.
Müller, Max. *Proposals for a Missionary Alphabet; Submitted to the Alphabetical Conferences held at the residence of Chevalier Bunsen in January 1854*. London: A. and G. A. Spottiswoode, 1854.

Murray, Laura J. "Vocabularies of Native American Languages: A Literary and Historical Approach to an Elusive Genre." *American Quarterly* 53, no. 4 (2001): 590–623.

Naphegyi, Gábor. *The Album of Language: Illustrated by the Lord's Prayer in One Hundred Languages [. . .]*. Philadelphia: J. B. Lippincott, 1869.

Nevins, M. Eleanor. *Lessons from Fort Apache: Beyond Language Endangerment and Maintenance*. Chichester: John Wiley and Sons, 2013.

Noodin, Margaret. *Bawaajimo: A Dialect of Dreams in Anishinaabe Language and Literature*. East Lansing: Michigan State University Press, 2014.

Nord, David Paul. *Faith in Reading: Religious Publishing and the Birth of Mass Media in America*. New York: Oxford University Press, 2004.

Norton, John. *The Journal of Major John Norton, 1816*. Edited by Carl F. Klinck. Toronto, ON: Champlain Society, 1970.

Nystuen, David W., and Carla G. Lindeman. *The Excavation of Fort Renville: An Archaeological Report*. St. Paul: Minnesota Historical Society, 1969.

Oberg, Michael Leroy. *Peacemakers: The Iroquois, the United States, and the Treaty of Canandaigua, 1794*. Oxford: Oxford University Press, 2016.

O'Brien, Jeanie. *Firsting and Lasting: Writing Indians Out of Existence in New England*. Minneapolis: University of Minnesota Press, 2010.

Occom, Samson. *A Choice Collection of Hymns and Spiritual Songs [. . .]*. New London, CT: Timothy Green, 1774.

———. *The Collected Writings of Samson Occom, Mohegan*. Edited by Joanna Brooks. New York: Oxford University Press, 2006.

O'Meara, Frederick. *Report of a Mission to the Ottawwahs and Ojibwas, on Lake Huron*. London: Society for the Propagation of the Gospel, 1846.

Osorio, Jamaica. *Remembering Our Intimacies: Moʻolelo, Aloha ʻĀina, and Ea*. Minneapolis: Minnesota University Press, 2021.

Ostler, Jeff. *The Plains Sioux and U.S. Colonialism: From Lewis and Clark to Wounded Knee*. Cambridge: Cambridge University Press, 2004.

Overholt, Thomas. "The Ghost Dance of 1890 and the Nature of the Prophetic Process." *Ethnohistory* 21, no. 1 (Winter 1974): 37–63.

Palmer, Gus. *Telling Stories the Kiowa Way*. Tucson: University of Arizona Press, 2003.

Parker, Arthur Caswell. *The Code of Handsome Lake, the Seneca Prophet*. Albany: University of the State of New York, 1912.

———. *The Life of General Ely S. Parker, Last Grand Sachem of the Iroquois and General Grant's Military Secretary*. Buffalo, NY: Buffalo Historical Society, 1919.

———. *Parker on the Iroquois: Iroquois Uses of Maize and Other Food Plants; the Code of Handsome Lake, the Seneca Prophet; the Constitution of Five Nation*. Syracuse, NY: Syracuse University Press, 1981.

Parker, Arthur Caswell, and Seth Newhouse. *The Constitution of the Five Nations*. Albany: University of the State of New York, 1916.

Parks, Douglas R., and Raymond J. DeMallie. "Plains Indian Native Literatures." *boundary 2* 19, no. 3 (Autumn 1992): 105–47.

Pascoe, Charles Frederick. *Two Hundred Years of the S.P.G.: An Historical Account of the Society for the Propagation of the Gospel in Foreign Part, 1701–1900*. London: Society's Office, 1901.

Pauketat, Timothy R. "America's First Pastime." *Archaeology* 62, no. 5 (2009): 20–25.

———. "Practice and History in Archaeology: An Emerging Paradigm." *Anthropological Theory* 1, no. 1 (2001): 73–98.

Peabody, Elizabeth Palmer. *Sarah Winnemucca's Practical Solution of the Indian Problem: A Letter to Dr. Lyman Abbot of the "Christian Union."* Cambridge, MA: J. Wilson and Son, 1886.

Perdue, Theda, ed. *Cherokee Editor: The Writings of Elias Boudinot.* Athens: University of Georgia Press, 1983.

Pexa, Christopher. *Translated Nation: Rewriting the Dakhóta Oyáte.* Minneapolis: University of Minnesota Press, 2020.

Piatote, Beth. *The Beadworkers: Stories.* Berkeley: Counterpoint, 2019.

Pickering, John. *An Essay on a Uniform Orthography for the Indian Languages of North America, as Published in the Memoirs of the American Academy of Arts and Sciences.* Cambridge, MA: University Press, Hilliard and Metcalf, 1820.

Piquette, Kathryn E., and Ruth D. Whitehouse. *Writing as Material Practice: Substance, Surface, and Medium.* London: Ubiquity Press, 2013.

Pond, Samuel. "The Narrative of Samuel Pond." In Theodore C. Blegen, "Two Missionaries in the Sioux Country: The Narrative of Samuel W. Pond." *Minnesota History* 21, no. 3 (1940): 272–83.

Porter, Noah. *Books and Reading, or What Books Shall I Read, and How Shall I Read Them?* New York: Scribner, 1870.

Powell, John Wesley. *Introduction to the Study of Indian Languages: With Words, Phrases and Sentences to be Collected.* Washington, DC: Government Printing Office, 1880.

Pratt, Mary Louise. *Imperial Eyes: Travel Writing and Transculturation.* London: Routledge, 1992.

Pratt, Richard H. "The Advantages of Mingling Indians with Whites." In *Americanizing the American Indians: Writings by the "Friends of the Indian" 1880–1900*, compiled by Francis Paul Prucha, 260–71. Cambridge, MA: Harvard University Press, 1973.

Preston, David L. *The Texture of Contact: European and Indian Settler Communities on the Frontiers of Iroquoia.* Lincoln: University of Nebraska Press, 2009.

Priestly, Joseph. *A Course of Lectures on the Theory of Language, and Universal Grammar.* Warrington: W. Eyres, 1762.

Radin, Paul. *The Winnebago Tribe.* Lincoln: University of Nebraska Press, 1990.

Rand, Silas. *A Short Statement of Facts Relating to the History . . . of the MicMac Tribe of Indians.* Halifax, NS: Times Howes and Sons, 1850.

Rayman, Ronald. "Joseph Lancaster's Monotorial System of Instruction and American Indian Education." *History of Education Quarterly* 21, no. 4 (Winter 1981): 295–409.

Reda, John. *From Furs to Farms: The Transformation of the Mississippi Valley, 1762–1825.* Ithaca, NY: Cornell University Press, 2016.

Red Shirt, Delphine. *George Sword's Warrior Narratives: Compositional Processes in Lakota Oral Tradition.* Lincoln: University of Nebraska Press, 2016.

Reilly, Hugh. *Bound to Have Blood: Frontier Newspapers and the Plains Indian Wars.* Lincoln: University of Nebraska Press, 2011.

Renville, Joseph, James Constantine Pilling, Stephen Return Riggs, Alfred Longley Riggs, Gideon Hollister Pond, Samuel William Pond, and Thomas Smith Williamson. *Dakota dowanpi kin = Hymns in the Dakota or Sioux language / composed by Mr. J. Renville and sons, and the missionaries of the A.B.C.F.M.* Boston: Crocker and Brewster, 1842.

Reuben, James. "The Nez Perce Indians." *Chronicles of Oklahoma* 12, no. 3 (September 1934): 363.

Ribbans, F. Bolingbroke. *Essay on the Utility, Origin, and Progress of Writing.* London: Longman, Orme, Brown, Green, and Longmans, 1840.

Richmond, Legh. *The Dairy [Man's Daughter]: An Authen[tic] Narr[ative]: In Five Parts*. London: J. Evans and Son, 1816.
Richter, Daniel K. *The Ordeal of the Longhouse: The Peoples and the Iroquois League in the Era of European Colonization*. Williamsburg, VA: Institute of Early American History and Culture; Chapel Hill: University of North Carolina Press, 1992.
Ricoeur, Paul. "The Model of the Text: Meaningful Action Considered as a Text." *Social Research* 38, no. 3 (1971): 529–62.
Riggs, Alfred L. *Wicoie Wowapi kin / The Word Book*. New York: American Tract Society, 1877.
Riggs, Stephen R. *Dakota ABC WOWAPI KIN*. Chicago: Penn and Ottaway Steam Printers, 1866.
———. "Dakota Portraits." *Minnesota History Bulletin* 2, no. 8 (November 1918): 481–568.
———. *Grammar and Dictionary of the Dakota Language*. Washington, DC: Smithsonian Institution, 1852.
———. *Grammar and History of the Dakota Language. Collected by the Members of the Dakota Mission. Ed. By Rev. S.R. Riggs [. . .] under the Patronage of the Historical Society of Minnesota*. Washington, DC: Smithsonian Institution, 1852.
———. *Mary and I: Forty Years with the Sioux*. Chicago: W. G. Holmes, 1880.
———. *Tah-koo Wah-kan: Or, The Gospel among the Dakotas*. Boston: Cong. Sabbath School and Publishing Society, 1869.
———. *Wayawa Tokaheya. Model First Reader*. Chicago: Geo. Sherwood and Co., 1873.
Riggs, Stephen R., and Gideon Pond. *The Dakota First Reading Book*. Cincinnati, OH: Kendall and Henry, 1839.
Riggs, Thomas Lawrence, and Margaret Kellogg Howard. *Sunset to Sunset: A Lifetime with My Brothers, the Dakotas / Thomas Lawrence Riggs, as Told to Margaret Kellogg Howard ; with a New Introduction by Paula M. Nelson*. Pierre: South Dakota State Historical Society Press, 1997.
Ringwalt, J. Luther, ed. *American Encyclopaedia of Printing*. Philadelphia: J. B. Lippincott, 1871.
Rivett, Sarah. *Unscripted America: Indigenous Languages and the Origins of a Literary Nation*. New York: Oxford University Press, 2017.
Round, Phillip H. *By Nature and by Custom Cursed: Transatlantic Civil Discourse and New England Cultural Production, 1620–1660*. Hanover, NH: University Press of New England, 1999.
———. *Removable Type: Histories of the Book in Indian Country*. Chapel Hill: University of North Carolina Press. 2010.
Samuels, David W. "Bible Translation and Medicine Man Talk: Missionaries, Indexicality, and the 'Language Expert' on the San Carlos Apache Reservation." *Language in Society* 35, no. 4 (2006): 529–57.
———. "Ethnopoetics and Ideologies of Poetic Truth." *Journal of Folklore Research* 5, no. 1–3 (2013): 251–83.
———. *Putting a Song on Top of It: Expression and Identity on the San Carlos Apache Reservation*. Tucson: University of Arizona Press, 2004.
———. "Truth and Stories." *Linguistic Anthropology* 26, no. 1 (May 2016): 62–80.
Samuels, David W., Louise Meintjes, Ana Maria Ochoa, and Thomas Porcello. "Soundscapes: Toward a Sounded Anthropology." *Annual Review of Anthropology* 39, no. 1 (2010): 329–45.

Sapir, Edward. "The Psychological Reality of Phonemes." In *Selected Writings of Edward Sapir in Language, Culture, and Personality*, edited by David J. Mandelbaum, 46–60. Berkeley: University of California Press, 1988.

Saunt, Claudio. *A New Order of Things: Property, Power, and the Transformation of the Creek Indians, 1733–1816*. Cambridge: Cambridge University Press, 1999.

Schmeckebier, Laurence F. *The Office of Indian Affairs: Its History*. Baltimore, MD: Johns Hopkins University Press, 1927.

Schmidt, David L., and Murdena Marshall, eds. and trans. *Mi' Kmaq Hieroglyphic Prayers: Readings in North America's First Indigenous Script*. Halifax, NS: Nimbus, 1995.

Schoolcraft, Jane Johnston. *The Sound the Stars Make Rushing through the Sky: The Writings of Jane Johnston Schoolcraft*. Edited and with an introduction by Robert Dale Parker. Philadelphia: University of Pennsylvania Press, 2007.

Scott-Browne, D. L. *Scott-Browne's Text-Book of Phonography*. New York: printed by the author, 1885.

Sebba, Mark. "'Phonology Meets Ideology': The Meaning of Orthographic Practices in British Creole." *Language Problems and Language Planning* 22, no. 1 (1998): 19–47.

———. *Spelling and Society: The Culture and Politics of Orthography around the World*. Cambridge: Cambridge University Press, 2007.

Severance, Frank H., ed. *Narratives of Early Mission Work on the Niagara Frontier and Buffalo Creek*. Buffalo, NY: Buffalo Historical Society, 1906.

Shimony, Annemarie. *Conservatism among the Iroquois at the Six Nations Reserve*. Syracuse, NY: Syracuse University Press, 1994.

Siegert, Bernard. *Relays: Literature as an Epoch of the Postal System*. Stanford, CA: Stanford University Press, 1999.

Sigsby, William. *Life and Adventures of Timothy Murphy, the Benefactor of Schoharie*. Schoharie, NY: W. H. Fallup, 1839. Reprint, Tarrytown, NY: W. Abbatt, 1926.

Simpson, Audra. *Mohawk Interruptus: Political Life across the Borders of Settler States*. Durham, NC: Duke University Press, 2014.

Sivertsen, Barbara. *Turtles, Wolves, and Bears: A Mohawk Family History*. Bowie, MD: Heritage Books, 1996.

Sleeper-Smith, Susan. *Why You Can't Teach United States History without American Indians*. Chapel Hill: University of North Carolina Press, 2015.

———. "Women, Kin, and Catholicism: New Perspectives on the Fur Trade." *Ethnohistory* 47, no. 2 (2000): 423–52.

Smalley, Daniel S. *American Phonetic Dictionary of the English Language*. Cincinnati, OH: Longley Bros., 1855.

Smith, David Lee. *Folklore of the Winnebago Tribe*. Norman: Oklahoma University Press, 1997.

Smith, Donald B. "Kahgegagahbowh." In *Life, Letters, and Speeches*, by George Copway, 1–22. Lincoln: University of Nebraska Press, 1997.

———. *Sacred Feathers: The Reverend Peter Jones (Kahkewaquonaby) and the Mississauga Indians*. Lincoln: University of Nebraska Press, 1987.

Smith, Huron. "Ethnobotany of the Meskwaki Indians." *Bulletin of the Public Museum of the City of Milwaukee* 4 (1928): 175–326.

Smith, Linda Tuiwai. *Decolonizing Methodologies: Research and Indigenous Peoples*. London: Bloomsbury Academic, 2021.

Sorby, Angela. *Schoolroom Poets: Childhood, Performance, and the Place of American Poetry, 1865–1917*. Durham, NH: University of New Hampshire Press, 2005.

Sterling, Matthew Williams. "Three Pictographic Autobiographies of Sitting Bull (with 46 Plates)." *Smithsonian Miscellaneous Collections* 97, no. 5 (1938): 1–57.
Stevens, Laura. *The Poor Indians: British Missionaries, Native Americans, and Colonial Sensibility*. Philadelphia: University of Pennsylvania Press, 2004.
Stevens, Scott Manning. "The Path of the King James Version of the Bible in Iroquoia." *Prose Studies* 34, no. 1 (2012): 5–17.
Storrs, Richard S. *The Conversion of the World*. Boston: Perkins and Marvin, 1840.
St. Paul's Evangelical Lutheran Church. *Records of St. Paul's Evangelical Lutheran Church in the Town of Schoharie, Schoharie County, N.Y.* New York, 1916.
Susman, Amelia. "The Accentual System of Winnebago." PhD diss., Columbia University, 1943.
Swiggers, Pierre. "Philologists Meet Algonquian: Du Ponceau and Pickering on Eliot's Grammar." In *Papers of the Twenty-Second Algonquian Conference*, edited by William Cowan, 346–58. Ottawa: Carleton University, 1991.
Tanner, Helen Hornbeck, ed. *Atlas of Great Lakes Indian History*. Cartography by Miklos Pinther. Norman: University of Oklahoma Press, 1987.
Taylor, Diana. *Archive and Repertoire: Performing Cultural Memory in the Americas*. Durham, NC: Duke University Press, 2003.
Teuton, Christopher B. *Deep Waters: The Textual Continuum in American Indian Literature*. Lincoln: University of Nebraska Press, 2010.
Thomason, Lucy. "On Editing Bill Leaf's Meskwaki Text." In *New Voices for Old Words: Algonquian Oral Literature*, edited by David J. Costa, 315–49. Lincoln: University of Nebraska Press, 2015.
Thornton, Tamara Plakins. *Handwriting in America: A Cultural History*. New Haven, CT: Yale University Press, 1996.
Tigerman, Kathleen. *Wisconsin Indian Literature: Anthology of Native Voices*. Madison: University of Wisconsin Press, 2007.
Timberlake, Henry. *The Memoirs of Lt. Henry Timberlake: The Story of a Soldier, Adventurer, and Emissary to the Cherokees, 1756–1765*. Edited by Duane H. King. Cherokee, NC: Museum of the Cherokee Indian Press, 2007.
Tocqueville, Alexis de. *Democracy in America*. Edited by Harvey C. Mansfield and Delba Winthrop. 1840. Reprint, Chicago: University of Chicago Press, 2002.
Tooker, Elisabeth. "The League of the Iroquois: Its History, Politics, and Ritual." In *Northeast*, edited by Bruce G. Trigger and William C. Sturtevant, 418–41. Vol. 15 of *Handbook of North American Indians*, edited by William C. Sturtevant. Washington, DC: Smithsonian Institution, 1978.
Trumbull, John. *On the Best Method of Studying the American Languages*. Hartford, 1871.
US Bureau of Indian Affairs. *Correspondence on the Subject of Teaching the Vernacular in Indian Schools: 1887–'88*. Washington, DC: Government Printing Office, 1888.
US Bureau of Indian Affairs. *Course of Study for the Indian Schools of the United States: Industrial and Literary*. Washington, DC: Government Printing Office, 1901.
———. *Indian Census Rolls, 1885–1940*. Washington, DC: National Archives, 1965.
US Congress. *U.S. Statutes at Large, Volume 7. Treaties Between the United States and the Indian Tribes (1789–1845)*. Library of Congress. www.loc.gov/item/llsl-v7/.
US Department of the Treasury. *Report of the Secretary of the Treasury, on the Subject of Public Roads and Canals: Made in Pursuance of a Resolution of Senate, of March 2, 1807*. Washington, DC: R. C. Weightman, 1808.
US Indian Peace Commission. *Annual Report of the Commissioner of Indian Affairs for the Year 1868*. Washington, DC: Government Printing Office, 1868.

US Office of Indian Affairs. *Easy Reading Lessons for Indian Schools.* Washington, DC: Government Printing Office, 1875.

———. *Teaching Indian Pupils to Speak English: Primary Methods and Outlines [. . .].* Washington, DC: Government Printing Office, 1904.

Utley, Robert M. *The Last Days of the Sioux Nation.* 1963; New Haven, CT: Yale University Press, 2004.

Venuti, Lawrence. "Introduction." *Critical Inquiry* 27, no. 2 (Winter 2001): 169–73.

Vibert, Elizabeth. "'The Natives Were Strong to Live': Reinterpreting Early Nineteenth-Century Prophetic Movements." *Ethnohistory* 42, no. 2 (Spring 1995): 197–229.

Walker, Willard B. "Native Writing Systems." In *Languages,* edited by Ives Goddard and William C. Sturtevant, 158–86. Vol. 17 of *Handbook of North American Indians,* edited by William C. Sturtevant. Washington, DC: Smithsonian Institution, 1996.

———. "The Winnebago Syllabary and the Generative Model." *Anthropological Linguistics* 16, no. 8 (1974): 393–414.

Walker, Willard B., and James Sarbaugh. "The Early History of the Cherokee Syllabary." *Ethnohistory* 40, no. 1 (Winter 1993): 70–94.

Wallace, Anthony F. C. *The Death and Rebirth of the Seneca.* New York: Vintage, 1972.

Warkentin, Germaine. "In Search of 'The Word of the Other': Aboriginal Sign Systems and the History of the Book in Canada." *Book History* 2, no. 1 (1999): 1–27.

Warren, William W. *History of the Ojibway People.* 1885. St. Paul: Minnesota Historical Society Press, 1984.

Warrior, Robert. *The People and the Word: Reading Native Nonfiction.* Minneapolis: University of Minnesota Press, 2005.

———. *Tribal Secrets: Recovering American Indian Intellectual Traditions.* Minneapolis: University of Minnesota Press, 1995.

Watt, Eva Tulene. *Don't Let the Sun Step over You: A White Mountain Apache Family Life, 1860–1975.* Tucson: University of Arizona Press, 2004.

Watt, Ronald G. *Mormon Passage of George D. Watt: First British Convert, Scribe for Zion.* Logan: Utah State University Press, 1954.

Watts, Isaac. *The Second Set of Catechisms and Prayers, or Some Help to the Children, and Their Knowledge of the Scriptures, From Seven to Twelve Years of Age.* London: C. E. Knight, Williams and Smith, et al., 1806.

Webb, J. Russell. *Model First Reader.* Chicago, 1873.

Weiser, Conrad. *Johan Friederich Weisers Buch: Containing the Autobiography of John Conrad Weiser (1696–1760).* Edited by Frederick S. Weiser. Hanover, PA: John Conrad Weiser Family Association, 1976.

White, Richard. *The Middle Ground: Indians, Empires, and Republics in the Great Lakes Region, 1650–1815.* New York: Cambridge University Press, 1991.

White Hat, Alfred, Sr. *Reading and Writing the Lakota Language.* Provo: University of Utah Press, 1999.

Whittaker, Gordon. "The Words of Black Hawk: Restoring a Long-Ignored Bilingual." In *New Voices for Old Words: Algonquian Oral Literatures,* edited by David J. Costa, 490–538. Lincoln: University of Nebraska Press, 2015.

Wigginton, Caroline. *Indigenuity: Native Craftwork and the Art of American Literatures.* Chapel Hill: University of North Carolina Press, 2022.

Willard, Samuel. *Secondary Lessons; Or, The Improved Reader.* N.p., 1827.

Williams, Roger. *A Key into the Language of America [. . .].* London: Gregory Dexter, 1643.

Williamson, Thomas. *Wiconi owihanke wannin tanin kin*. Boston: Crocker and Brewster, 1837.
Wilson, Edward Francis. *The Ojebway Language: A Manual for Missionaries and Others Employed among the Ojebway Indians. In Three Parts: Part I. The Grammar. Part II. Dialogue and Exercises. Part III. The Dictionary. / By the Rev. Edward F. Wilson*. London: Society for Promoting Christian Knowledge, 1874.
Wilson, George. *An Essay on Bible Translation*. Wooster, OH: D. N. Sprague, 1851.
Wilson, John L. *A Grammar of the Mpongwe Language: With Vocabularies*. New York, 1847.
Wilson, Thomas. *An Essay towards an Instruction for the Indians*. London: J. Osborn, W. Thorn, 1740.
Winford, Donald. *An Introduction to Contact Linguistics*. London: Wiley-Blackwell, 2003.
Wisecup, Kelly. *Assembled for Use: Indigenous Compilation and the Archives of Early Native American Literatures*. New Haven, CT: Yale University Press, 2021.
———. "Practicing Sovereignty: Colonial Temporalities, Cherokee Justice, and the 'Socrates' Writings of John Ridge." *NAIS: Native American and Indigenous Studies* 4, no. 1 (Spring 2017): 30–60.
Witgen, Michael. *An Infinity of Nations: How the Native New World Shaped Early North America*. Philadelphia: University of Pennsylvania Press, 2012.
Wolfe, Patrick. "Land, Labor, and Difference: Elementary Structures of Race." *American Historical Review* 106, no. 3 (June 2001): 866–905.
———. "Settler Colonialism and the Elimination of the Native." *Journal of Genocide Research* 8, no. 4 (December 2006): 387–409.
Wood, William, and Alden T. Vaughan. *New England's Prospect*. Amherst: University of Massachusetts Press, 1993.
Woodbury, Hanni. *Onondaga/English Dictionary*. Toronto, ON: University of Toronto Press, 2003.
[Worcester, Samuel A.] "Description of the Cherokee Alphabet." *American Annals of Education* 2 (April 1832): 181–84.
Wright, Asher, ed. *Go' wana gwa' ih sat' hah yon de'-yas da gwah; A Spelling Book in the Seneca Language: With English Definitions*. Buffalo Creek, NY: Seneca Mission House, 1842.
Wyss, Hilary E. *English Letters and Indian Literacies: Reading, Writing, and New England Missionary Schools, 1750–1830*. Philadelphia: University of Pennsylvania Press, 2012.
Young Bear, Ray A. *Black Eagle Child: The Facepaint Narratives*. New York: Grove Press, 1996.
Zepeda, Ofelia. *Jewed 'i-Hoi : O'odham c milga:n s-ke:g ha'icu cegĭtodag = Earth Movements: A Collection of Poems in O'odham and English*. Tucson, AZ: Kore Press, 1997.
———. *Ocean Power: Poems from the Desert*. Tucson: University of Arizona Press, 1995.
———. *A Papago Grammar*. Tucson: University of Arizona Press, 1983.
Zimmer, Eric. "Red Earth Nation: Environment and Sovereignty in Modern Meskwaki History." PhD diss., University of Iowa, 2016.

INDEX

Page numbers in italics refer to illustrations.

ABCFM. *See* American Board of Commissioners for Foreign Missions (ABCFM)
Allegany Reservation, 119
American Board of Commissioners for Foreign Missions (ABCFM), 45, 65, 141–44, 149–52, 243n18, 243n22, 244n29
American Encyclopaedia of Printing (Ringwalt), 51, *52*
American Horse (Lakota), 166–67; Winter Count, *166*, 166
American Spelling Book (Webster), 40
American Sunday School Union Press, 74
American Tract Society, 19, 65
Anishinaabemowin (language), 6, 188, 190. *See also* Central Algonquian
Anishinaabe people. *See* Ojibwe Nation
Anishinaabewaki (Ojibwe homeland), 6, 183–87, *184*, 191, 194–96
antiwhite sentiments, 167
Apaches, 9; language of, 233n71, 233n74; and New Testament translation, *xiv*, 30, 234n75; and sovereignty, 25–33
Apess, William (Pequot), 74; *A Son of the Forest*, 74
Archiquette, John (Oneida), 127–28; journal of, *129*
Armstrong, Jeanette (Onondaga), 8–9, 221–23; "Winds," 221
assimilative violence, as concept, 14
Atwater, Caleb, 51
Aupaumut, Hendrick (Mahican), 87, 92, 108, 110, 119
awikhiganak. *See* birch back writings

ba-be-bi-bo. *See pa-pe-pi-po*
Basso, Keith, 9, 31, 33, 35, 220, 224
birch bark writings, 6–7, 91, 190, 191, 195; Mi'kmaq characters in, *11*
Blackbird, Andrew (Odawa), 184–88, 191, 193, 217; and father, 183–84, 194, 217, 248n1; *History of the Ottawa and Chippewa Indians of Michigan*, 183
Black Elk, Nicholas (Lakota), 131–38, 151, 165, 171–75, 178, 181

Black Hawk (Sauk and Fox), 191, 193–94, 218; *Life of Ma-Ka-Tai-Me-She-Kia-Kiak*, 191–92, *192*
Black Hawk War, 200, 210
blank books, 66, 67, 69, 163, 178
blood quantum, 79
Blowsnake, Sam (Ho-Chunk), 207, 210; "Autobiography," 212–17, *213*
boarding schools: abuse of Indigenous children in, 27, 30, 78; alphabetic literacy and, 27; English-only education in, 26, 137; Native identity and, 170–71; on-reservation, 170. *See also* common schools; *and names of individual schools*
Book of Common Prayer (Mohawk), 95, *95*, 97, 102
Bradford, William (printer), 95
Brainerd Mission School, 70
Brant, Joseph (Mohawk), 22, 97, 100, 102–3, 109
Brown David (Cherokee), 22, 45
Brown, Catharine (Cherokee), 22, 74
Buffalo Bill's Wild West show, 131–32, 134, 175
buffalo robes, 6
Bureau of Indian Affairs (BIA), 60, 78, 157–58, 170–72, 178, 223

Carlisle Industrial School for Indians, 27, 169, 170, 174
Cash, Phil (Nez Perce), 226
Catlin, George, 148, 197–98, 200; *Kenekuk*, *198*; *Ah-tón-we-Tuck*, *200*
Cayuga Nation, 84, 109
Central Algonquian (language), 9, 80, 186, 188, 190, 191, 193–94, 203–4, 208, 217
Chainbreaker. *See* Governor Blacksnake (Chainbreaker; Seneca)
Cherokee Nation, 18–19, 43, 45, 63, 66, 67, 70
Cherokee syllabary, 18–20, *20*, 45, 47, 59, 74, 206, 211
Christianity: conversion to, of Indigenous people, 2, 27, 43, 50–51, 61, 70, 74,

Christianity (*continued*)
141–43, 157–58, 244n29; Indigenous resistance to, 28, 30, 33, 45, 96–97, 109, 113–14, 134, 150, 152, 153, 168, 186–87, 190–91; and literacy missionary work, 4, 17, 65, 93, 128, 146, 170–71; Native identity erasure through, 3, 29, 48, 56, 151, 196, 214
Civil War, 41, 58, 66, 71, 78, 127
Clark, William, 40, 198
Claus, Daniel, 99, 102–8
Cold Springs Reservation, 115
colonial narratives. *See* settler colonial discourses
common schools, 41, 80; as sites of Indigenous resistance, 74–76, 79, 187; as tools of Indigenous erasure, 42, 51, 66, 70–74, 79, 80; as movement, 60, 73
communications revolution, x, 35, 43, 52, 73, 161
Condolence Ceremony, 36, 80, 89, 100, 195, 221; alphabetic writing and, 90–92, 98, 100, 103, 106, 108, 119–23, 125; and Code of Handsome Lake, 109–10, 112, 116–17, 241n81; as history, 108; and intertribal negotiations, 87, 107; origin of, 83–87; use of wampum in, 100, 103
"Constitution of Minnesota in the Dakota Language, The," 151
contact linguistics, 5, 233n74
copybook, 66; of John Ridge, 67
Cornwall Mission School, 22, 66, 67
Cuoq, J., 89, 96, 238n16
Cusick, David (Tuscarora), 122–23
Custer, George Armstrong, 159; death announcement of, 160
Custer, Milo, 202–3, 218; "A Sample of Kickapoo and Pottowatomie Text," 202

Dakota Tawoonspe / Dakota Lessons (Riggs), 149
Dakota War, 150, 175
David of Schoharie (Mohawk), 98–100, 113, 121
Deganawidah. *See* Tekanawita
"Deganawidah Epic," 118
Deloria, Ella (Lakota), 145, 180
Deloria, Vine (Lakota), 34–35, 56

DeMallie, Raymond J., 132, 134, 136, 174, 175, 245n82, 247n99
Deseret Alphabet, 45–47; *Deseret Primer,* 46
Deserontyon, John (Mohawk), 100–109, 113, 119, 121, 126; letter from, to Daniel Claus, 104; "Roghya Gonghsera," 100, *101*
Dictionary of Indian Tongues, 39
diplomacy, 61–63, 65, 87, 92, 97, 106
Du Ponceau, Pierre, 54, 57

Edwards, Silas John (Apache), 28–33; script of, *32*
entextualization, 15, 22, 194, 215
Equiano, Olaudah, 61
Evans, James, 188; *Hymns, Swampy Indians, Their Speech, 189;* syllabary, 188–89, 204

"Flame's History," 130
Fletcher, Alice, 204, 206, 211, 218
Fort Apache Reservation, 25–27
Fort Belknap Reservation, 22
Fort Snelling, 141–43, 152–53

Gaiatonsera (Williams), 128
Gai'wiio', 84, 87, 92, 109–10, 112–13, 116
Gallatin, Albert, 52, 54
Gallaudet, Thomas, 71, 73, 150; *Gallaudet's Picture Defining and Reading Book,* 72
Gallaudet's Picture Defining and Reading Book (Gallaudet), 71, *72*
general council meeting, announcement of, *116*
General Specimen Book of the Dickison Type Foundry, The, 53
Ghost Dance, 167–69, 174–78, 245n82
Gibson, John Arthur (Seneca), 83–85, 87, 126
Gone, Joe (Gros Ventre), 22, 28
Goode, Britton (Apache), 28–30
Good Message. *See* Gai'wiio'
Governor Blacksnake (Chainbreaker; Seneca), 119–23, 241n79
graphesis, 20, 90
graphogenesis, 4, 18–19, 33, 89–91
Great Divide theories, 19, 33, 234n83
Great Sioux Reservation, 132, 167, 246n82

Half Moon, drawing of Sioux chief by, *162*
Hampton Institute in Virginia, 170
Handsome Lake (Seneca), 109–17, 121; and the Good Message, 109–10, 112–13, 116
Harjo, Hillis (Muskogee), 12
Haudenosaunee peoples, 6, 20, 33, 83–97, 102–3, 108, 110, 113–14, 117, 122–23, 125–28, 180, 195; and alphabetic script, 90–95; and confederacy, 84, 88, 89, 93, 97, 238n1; and Longhouse, 6, 84–86, 90, 96, 106, 110, 112, 121–23
Hazelwood Republic (Dakota), 143, 151
Henry Two-Guns announcement, *116*
Hewitt, J. N. B. (Tuscarora), 105–7
Hiawatha, 83–87, 110; wampum belt of, *82*. See also Condolence Ceremony; wampum
hide painting, 6, 10, 16, 80
Ho-Chunk Nation (Winnebago), 157, 194, 204, 210–16
Homestead Act, 157–58
Hopkins, Robert (Dakota), 155; letter from, to Stephen Riggs, *155*
Huggins, Alexander, 141, 147
Hymes, Dell, 117, 180, 241n81, 250n45

Iapi Oaye (newspaper), 132, 134, 136, 151, 157, 171, 175; title page of, *135*
Indian Act (1867), 122–23, 125
Indian Country, ix, 3, 4, 34, 73, 97, 148, 161, 222; and Peace Commission of 1968, 78, 158; literacy in, 18–19, 22, 42, 45, 60, 63, 67, 73, 90–91, 139; settler infrastructure in, 27, 114
Indian Removal Act (1830), 55, 80, 194
Indigenous graphic practices: birch bark writings, 6–7, 91, 190, 191, 195; buffalo robes, 6; hide painting, 6, 10, 16, 80; tipi covers, 6, 137. See also wampum
intellectual sovereignty, 21, 79
Iroquois peoples. See Haudenosaunee peoples
Isna Toka Kte (Lakota), 175

Jefferson, Thomas, 40, 52, 57, 65
Jones, Peter (Ojibwe), 190

Kanaka Maoli print culture, 21–22
Kenekuk (Kickapoo Prophet), 10, 197–203

Kickapoo Nation, 10, 80, 188, 196–202; and Christianity, 200; and *pa-pe-pi-po*, 204, 217; and sovereignty, 203
Kiowa Nation, 1–4, 14, 24–25, 69, 161; and storytelling, 24

LaFlesche, Francis (Omaha), 74, 79; *The Middle Five*, 74
Lancastrian system (education), 73
land surrender, by Chippewas, *64*
language ideologies, 18, 38; landedness of, 9, 232n22; of settlers, 3, 36, 155
LeClaire, Antoine, 191, 193, 218
ledger books, 80, 122, 159–63, 180–81. *See also* War Books
Lepsius, Karl Richard, 13
Lewis, Merriweather, 40–41, 57
literacy, 91; as allegedly superior to orality, 4, 42, 50–51, 71, 74, 93, 180; and diplomacy, 26, 97; and Indigenous graphic practices, 90; and missionization, 3, 10, 51, 93, 147; and Native identity, 26–30, 33, 36, 76, 79, 80, 96, 101, 134; and orality, 15, 18–19, 33; and US citizenship, 22, 41–42, 50, 74, 78. *See also* boarding schools; common schools; diplomacy; Indigenous graphic practices; missionization; Native identity; oral tradition; US citizenship
Longhouse, 6, 84–86, 90, 96, 106, 110, 112, 121–23
Lounsbury, Floyd, 126–28

Macka-de-pe-nessy. See Blackbird, Andrew: father
Manifest Destiny, 49, 50, 56
maps: Anishinaabewaki, *184*; Dakota Territory, *133*; Map of Ho-De-No-Sau-Nee-Ga, *85*; Map of the Indian Tribes of North America, *55*; native languages, *8*; present-day Minnesota, *140*
McGuffey Readers, 73, 76, 80
McLuhan, Marshall, 35
media, as concept, 15–17
Memoir of Catharine Brown, 74
Meskwaki Nation: Fox (Meskwaki) syllabary, *205*; Mr. Bill Leaf's handwriting, *209*. See *pa-pe-pi-po*
Michelson, Truman, 208

274 Index

Mi'kmaq Nation, 7, 10, 50–51; and bark book writings, 11
missionization, 31, 48, 96, 187; Indigenous resistance to, 22, 168, 200–201; and literacy, 3, 10, 50–51, 93, 147; as a tool of colonialism, 56, 142–44
Mission School for Native children, 114
Mitchell's School Geography, 75
Mi-Wa-Kan Yu-Ha-La. *See* Sword, George (Lakota)
Mohawk Institute Residential School, 123
Mohawk Nation, 62, 83–84, 86, 88–89, 99, 103, 105–6, 109, 126; and language, 7, 89, 92–93, 98, 102, *104*, 107–8, 123; and literacy, 97, 100, 103, 127
Momaday, N. Scott, 1–3, 24, 220
Moor's Charity School, 22
mouth maps, 12–14, *12*; "Qee'esh Mouthmap," *13*
Mt. Pleasant, Alyssa (Tuscarora), 114
Müller, Max, 5, 14, 38

Native body politic, as concept, 91, 195
Native identity, 21, 23, 26, 27, 35, 45, 74, 77, 167, 214; and identity politics, 23; and literacy, 75, 181, 203, 226; role of land in, 139, 196
Native languages, distribution of, 8
Native space, 62, 91, 139, 185, 195, 199
Neihardt, John, 136–37, 165, 175, 178
Newhouse, Seth (Mohawk), 118, 122–23, 125–26; preface to "Cosmology," *124*; "Deganawidah Epic," *118*
New Philology, 54
Nez Perce Nation (Nimiipuu), 78, 224–26

Occom, Samson, 22, 61–62, 87–88
Oceti Sakowin, 20, 33, 131–32, 137–39, 141, 144; and languages, 146, 154, 157, 165–67, 169, 175, 180, 188, 217
Odawa Nation, 184–88, 191, 203
Ojibwe Nation, 9, 20, 49, 71, 73, 139, 141, 188–89, 217; and birch bark writings, 6–7, 190–91. *See also* Anishinaabemowin; Anishinaabewaki
Oneida Nation, 62, 84, 87; writing system of, 126–28
Onondaga Nation, 84–85, 109, 121, 123

oral tradition, 21, 23, 25, 63, 119, 165–66, 196, 215–16
Orhoengene. See *Book of Common Prayer*
orthography, 5–6, 9–10, 38, 43, 45, 60, 71, 90, 92–93, 96–97, 113, 134, 136, 139, 142, 188; role of, in Indigenous sovereignty, 26, 190–91, 203; study of, 54, 58; as supporting Indigenous languages, 23, 127–28, 145, 180, 186, 211, 220, 222, 226; as system of oppression, 15, 71, 142, 145–49, 153, 158, 193

Paiute Nations, 79, 219, 247n99
pa-pe-pi-po, 36, 189, 204–5, 211–12, 217, 224
Paw-pe-pi-po. See *pa-pe-pi-po*
Parker, A. (Seneca), 109–10, 113, 116–17, 121
Park Hill Mission Press, 74
Peacemaker. *See* Tekanawita
Peace Policy of 1867, 157–59
Phonal Depot (Pulsipher), 43, *44*
Piatote, Beth (Nez Perce), 225–26
Pickering, John, 58–59, 146, 219
Picquet, François, prayer book of, 94
Pine Ridge Agency, 169, 170, 172, *173*; post office masthead, *169*
Pine Ridge police force, 177, *177*, 178
Pine Ridge Reservation, 28, 136, 171, 174, 229
place-names, as markers of historical events, 9
Pond, Samuel, 141, 147–48, 150, 152
Pond Gideon, 141, 146
Potawatomi Nation, 188, 191, 196, 199–204, 217
Powell, John Wesley, 59–60, 67, 219
Pratt, Richard Henry, 27, 42, 60
prayer book, 10, 62, *94*, 157
precontact modes of inscribing: birch bark writings, 6–7, 91, 190, 191, 195; buffalo robes, 6; hide painting, 6, 10, 16, 80; tipi covers, 6, 137. *See also* wampum
printing presses, 45, 51, 56, 114; Asher Wright, 114–15; American Sunday School Union Press, 74; Park Hill Mission Press, 74; William Bradford, 95
print statism, 67, 69
Pulsipher, John S., 43; *Phonal Depot*, 43, *44*

Rand, Silas, 7, 10, 50
ration card, 158; from Rosebud Reservation, 69
Red Cloud (Lakota), 28, 158, 167, 170
Red Horn (mythological figure), 212–13, 217
Renville, Joseph, 141–44, 146–48, 150
residential schools. *See* boarding schools
Reuben, James (Nez Perce), 78–80
Revolutionary War, 102, 109, 121, 126, 184
Rez English, 154, 222
rhetorical sovereignty, 20–21
Ridge, John, 22, 66–67
Riggs, Stephen R., 3, 73, 141–44, 146–55, 157–58; *Dakota Tawoonspe / Dakota Lessons*, 149
rigorous paraphrase, 23, 37
Ringwalt, Luther J., 52; *American Encyclopaedia of Printing*, 51, 52
"Roghya Gonghsera" (Deserontyon), 100, *101*

San Carlos Reservation, 25–29
Sapir, Edward, 9, 219–20
Schoharie Village, 98–101, 108, 113, 115, 121
Sebba, Mark, 38
Seneca Nation, 84, 93, 109–10, 113–17, 119, 121
Sequoyah (Cherokee), 18–19
settler colonial discourses: and Indigenous literacy, 3, 14, 193; Indigenous resistance to, 89; of Native dispossession and erasure, 14, 21–22, 48, 50, 54, 65–66, 77, 142–43, 225; trope of "vanishing Indian" in, 48, 63, 142, 224. *See also* Manifest Destiny; missionization; settler colonialism
settler colonialism, 48–49, 56, 60, 78, 92, 125, 139, 142, 146, 231n16; and *people without letters*, 3, 36, 50–52, 232n30
Seven Council Fires of the Great Sioux Nation. *See* Oceti Sakowin
Silas John Edwards script, 32
Sitting Bull (Lakota), 163, 165–67, 172, 179; "Sitting Bull's Autobiography," *164*
Smith, Huron, 205–6, 216
Southern New England Algonquian (language), 12, 48, 58, 59
sovereignty, 19, 20; of Kickapoo, 199, 201; US, 202, 203, 207, 210, 217, 218; and literacy, 43, 45; Longhouse and, 89, 90, 122, 146, 156, 185, 187, 189, 191, 193–95, 197, 198; and Mormons, 67, 74, 79, 80; as political sovereignty, 34, 36; various forms of, 84–85; and writing, defined, 21, 22, 23, 25, 26, 28, 33
Standing Bear (Lakota), 137–38; "Flaming Rainbow," *138*
Sword, George (Lakota), 170–71, 177–81, *177*; and ledger, 180, *180*; and Lucy Sword diary, *179*

Tecumseh (Shawnee), 185, 194
Tekanawita, 83–86, 110, 126, 238n1
Thomas, Alec (Tseshaht), 120
Tillohash, Tony (Paiute), 119
tipi covers, 6, 137
Tiyospaye, 138, 156, 169–73, 178, 180
Tohono O'odham Nation, 222–23
translation: aurality and inscription, 4, 7–8, 24, 29, 34–35, 41, 59, 73, 75, 220, 233n63; as colonial violence, 14, 154, 176, 221; of Dakota/Lakota, 73, 136–37, 144, 146–47, 153–54, 156; of Iroquois, 95, 97, 109, 116, 123; of Ojibwes, 71, 189; and rigorous paraphrase, 23, 37; of Sauk and Fox, 193; as theory, 14–15
Treaty of Canandaigua, 110, *111*
Trumbull, J. Hammond, 58–60
Tuscarora Nation, 84, 105

US citizenship: and literacy, 22, 41–42, 47, 50, 60; and Native identity, 22, 42, 151

visual culture, 17, 51, 88

wampum, 6, 10, 36, 38, 84–93, 98, 106–8, 113, 129, 195; replica of, *82*; role of, in Condolence Ceremony, 87, 90–91, 100, 106, 117; role of, in Indigenous sovereignty, 84, 125–26; strings of requickening, 88. *See also* Condolence Ceremony
wanagi wacipi, 167–69, 174–78, 245n82
waniyetu wowapi. *See* Winter Counts
War Books, 161, 163
Webster, Noah, 40; *American Spelling Book*, 40

Western Apache New Testament, xiv, 234n75, 30
Wheelock, Eleazar, 62, 102
Wheelock's Indian School, 62, 102
White Hat, Albert (Lakota), 145–46
Williams, Benjamin (Seneca), 119–21
Williams, Eleazar (Oneida), 127; *Gaiatonsera*, 128
Williams, Roger, 12
Williamson, Thomas, 2, 141, 143–44, 146–50, 152
Wilson, Thomas (Bishop), 62
Winnebago Reservation, 210–12, 216
Winnemucca, Sarah (Paiute), 79
Winter Counts, 6, *130*, 137, *166*, 166, 168–69

Worcester, Samuel, 19, 38, 45, 50
word lists, 54, 57–58; blank, *68*
Works Progress Administration (WPA), 22, 126, 127
Wright, Asher, 93, 113–15
writing sovereignty, 19

Youngbear, Ray (Meskwaki), 223–24, 226
Young Bear, Robert (Meskwaki), 207–8; letter from, to Edgar Harlan, *182*
Yupik language, 7, 9

Zepeda, Ofelia (Tohono O'odham), 222–23, 226; "Cloud Song," 222–23

www.ingramcontent.com/pod-product-compliance
Lightning Source LLC
Chambersburg PA
CBHW030529230426
43665CB00010B/813